LITERARY STRUCTURES

Edited by John Gardner

Homer's *Iliad*

THE SHIELD OF MEMORY

Kenneth John Atchity

Foreword by John Gardner

Southern Illinois University Press
Carbondale and Edwardsville

Feffer & Simons, Inc.
London and Amsterdam

Library of Congress Cataloging in Publication Data

Atchity, Kenneth John.
  Homer's Iliad.

  (Literary structures)
  Bibliography: p.
  Includes index.
  1. Homerus.   Ilias.   I. Title.
PA4037.A725   883'.01   77–17065
ISBN 0–8093–0809–6

TO LOWRY

οὕνεκ᾽ ἐπητής ἐσσι καὶ ἀγχίνοος καὶ ἐχέφρων

Contents

Foreword

During the past quarter century the study of classical literature, and of Homer in particular, has gone through something like a revolution. Part of the reason for the new look at Homer was something called "the Homeric question"—really a cluster of questions, all of them more or less wrongheaded but important nonetheless: did Homer compose orally, making up his poetry on the spot, brachiating from formula to formula ("swift-footed Achilles," "Hektor of the shining helm"), or did he use writing and achieve his majestic effects by means of revision, like an ordinary mortal? Was there ever a "Homer" in fact, or were the *Iliad* and the *Odyssey* high-class folktales, shaped, expanded, modified through a long process of folk or court tradition? What makes such questions seem wrongheaded is of course the beauty and intellectual density of the poetry. The Yugoslavian oral poets whose practice set off "the Homeric question" were interesting people and occasionally achieved rather interesting effects, but even the most sympathetic critic must admit that their work is feeble, almost silly beside Homer's. Homer, we know, was free to write, instead of compose orally, if he wanted to. We have no evidence that he was, as tradition claims, blind, like his own fictitious bard Demodokos, in the *Odyssey*; and even if he was blind, he could easily get someone else to write his words down and read them back to him, as did John Milton. More important, common sense would argue, it was at about Homer's time that writing came back into general use. The rediscovered tool made someone like Homer practically inevitable. Before Homer, heroic lays were apparently all short, usually about the length of a book or two of the *Iliad*. With the ability to look back, read one's work over carefully and thoughtfully, came the ability to weave in symbols—the connected bow symbolism that runs through the *Iliad*, the emblems of art Professor Atchity points out, and so forth. When one works out in full detail, as Professor Atchity does here, the imagistic, dramatic, and philosophical structure of the *Iliad*, it becomes difficult to believe that the poem is anything but a work achieved by the process of writing and revising.

To say that a thing is difficult to believe is of course not any sort of proof. Scholars for some reason devoted to the notion that Homer composed on his feet, like a Yugoslavian bard or the traditional black American minister, point out Homer's fondness for traditional formulae (though they cannot seem to agree among themselves about which formulae are traditional), and they ask, shaking their fingers at us, "Why would Homer use formulae if he was writing with a pen and had no need for them?" That is easily answered: poets before Homer—oral poets—had used formulae; he was imitating their methods, merely for tone, or out of love and respect, much as modern ministers occasionally say, for love of their tradition, "Brothers and sisters we are gathered this day." But this too is merely a plausible answer, not a proof.

The more one works at the Homeric question the more annoying it gets, but for all that, the raising of the question has been wonderfully beneficial. Though some scholars have made the question a stumbling block, refusing to listen to even the most reasonable and obvious readings of Homer's verse on the grounds that no man composing on his feet—and certainly no tradition of oral composers—could possibly be so subtle, the best of our scholars have responded to the question by looking more closely than anyone ever did before (at least in print) at the structure and texture of Homer's poetry. Finally, of course, it makes no difference whether Homer composed on his feet or at his desk, or whether Homer was one man or twenty—though we all have our opinions and may incline to think contrary opinions rank foolishness. The only important Homer question is: How do the *Iliad* and the *Odyssey* work? How tight are the poems? how beautiful? how profound?

As if "the Homeric question" had never been raised, Professor Atchity raises these more important questions about the *Iliad*, then answers them. (He is presently at work on another book which will do the same for the *Odyssey*.) He proves what we all suspected all along, that the poem is a brilliantly organized work, philosophically profound, perhaps the noblest work of art produced in the entire tradition of Western Civilization. His method is close analysis, tracing particular images and themes throughout the poem so that the general reader, not just the Homer specialist, can return to the poem and experience it more richly. I know of no better introduction to this splendid poem. In fact, I know of no other book as good.

Kenneth Atchity is an associate professor of comparative literature at Occidental College. He has written and lectured on subjects ranging from Homer to Wallace Stevens, wrote the libretto for a sinfonia cantata, *In Praise of Love*, produced at Lincoln Center in New York, has published numerous poems, a collection of essays on Spenser, a collection coedited with Giose Rimanelli, on Italian literature, and is presently editor of *CQ, contemporary quarterly: poetry and art*.

John Gardner
New York, 1977

Acknowledgments

This study of the *Iliad* originated in my first reading of the poem under the direction of R. J. Schork, and in experiments in metaphysical criticism guided by Wilfrid D. Desan, at Georgetown College. I owe much to their inspiration and encouragement. I'm also grateful to the late Adam Parry, Joseph A. Russo, Paolo Vivante, and especially to Cedric and Anne Whitman for practical and technical criticism at various stages of writing. I appreciate the advice and moral support of Thomas G. Bergin, A. B. Giamatti, and Thomas Greene. I learned much from discussions with Elizabeth Barber, Shirley Bean, Steven E. Greenebaum, C. Scott Littleton, Michael Nagler, and Robert S. Ryf; and am indebted, in various ways, to my students and apprentices in the last five years, Robin Epstein, Dana Gerhardt, Barbara Heinzen, Mark Hunter, Caroline Hwang, John B. Lima, Doug Lohmar, Bonnie Moore, Sara Saxe, Sharon Scull, Catherine Tinker, and especially Bennett Munsey. My colleagues Jean Wyatt and Lewis Owen helped generously in the process of revision, a process brought to focus by John Gardner and by my wife, Bonnie Fraser. But criticism is always a personal responsibility, which I accept with delight, in the hope my interpretation of Homer's *Iliad* will send the reader promptly back to the poem, where we all belong.

To pay my critical dues to those whose readings have sent me back to the poem, while at the same time avoiding the distraction of numerous footnotes, I have discussed Homeric criticism in an annotated bibliography at the end of the book. (Within the book, direct quotations are followed by page numbers, which refer to the work[s] cited in the essay.) For the same reason, I have placed in an appendix speculations about the social hierarchy of Homer's poem; and in the bibliography references to the Homeric Question—whether there was one Homer or many, when he/she or they lived, how he/she/they composed the *Iliad* and/or the *Odyssey*. Literary critics have too long been frightened away from the *Iliad* by classical philologists. The point is that it was written. We have the epic before us, and it's time again for us to recognize, as the Greeks themselves did, that Homer's poem is a truly coherent artistic masterpiece, unsurpassed in its genre. Like Achilles before his divine shield, we are struck first by the marvel of the whole, which is much greater than the sum of its parts (as Dante told *his* reader).

Acknowledgments

I appreciate the financial support this work has received: a Faculty Summer Grant from Occidental College, along with generous funds for research and clerical expenses; the John Addison Porter Prize from the Kingsley-Amis Trust of Yale University (1971); and a National Endowment for the Humanities Summer Stipend (1972). It is a pleasure to thank Richmond Lattimore for the superb translation that first made Homer accessible to the English-reading generalist in this century. All quotations of the poem are from the Lattimore translation, by permission of Professor Lattimore and the University of Chicago Press.

Finally I wish to thank my friend and adviser at Yale, Lowry Nelson, Jr., whose wisdom and confidence have been a consistent inspiration to this reading of Homer's *Iliad*.

K. J. A.

Los Angeles
January 16, 1977

Introduction

The central image of Homer's great epic story of the wrath of Achilles is the invulnerable shield made for the poem's hero at the Olympian forge of Hephaistos. The magnificent artifact takes shape before our eyes, as the narrator lets us watch with him over the smith-god's shoulder. We watch in order to learn. Hephaistos tells Thetis before he begins his orderly creation that, although it will not save her son from death, the shield will be a wonder to behold, as unforgettable as it will be elaborated all around. When Thetis returns to earth bearing the splendid shield, the eyes of the Myrmidons are dazzled and they can't look upon its surface. But Homer has allowed us to behold the divine masterpiece as it is being born—even before Achilles himself looks upon it, admires, and accepts it—because it is a symbol of the poem itself, its mnemonic technique, purpose, and function. As our ears adjust to the vision depicted on the great shield, we begin gradually to recognize—as Achilles does immediately and intuitively—Zeus' and the poet's thematic plan: the establishment of order. This is the central theme whose final sublime resolution is achieved when Achilles bears his great shield into battle. So we see that what Hephaistos does as we watch through the narrator's eyes, Homer does as we listen or read. The artist creates the world, through and to his own vision of order.

Achilles' shield contains the whole cosmos known to Homeric man—of the inanimate stars and waters, and of all life and time and space and action. Forged into the very substance of this supreme tool of warfare is a detailed vision that transcends all momentary circumstances, all individual fates, and reveals humanity in its continuing, essential character. In the process of its making, the ideal and real become one dynamic continuum. We understand, with the Achilles who no longer shuns death, that the shield gives him access to an immortality that is purely human: though he, like all who share human nature, can't escape mortality in time, he will have an orderly place forever in the minds of men to come who will hear how he carried this shield into battle to restore the honor of his dear friend and of the Argive nation. Excavations and reconstructions will never give us more than we have now of Homer's masterful shield. Anything more than the words would be too weak.

For Achilles' shield has survived, much more certainly than what Schliemann thought was Agamemnon's death mask or Nestor's golden cup. We have the shield in the only medium sufficient to preserve it—in Homer's words, as the ancient Greeks remembered and recorded them. Hephaistos' artistry, because it is Homer's, remains untarnished as only a memory can be. And as we maintain that breathtakingly clear vision in our memory, it directly affects how we view ourselves and our actions, instilling in our minds the very order that fashioned it. That was the historical function of the poet in an oral culture. And Homer's poem is the last great expression of the traditional cohesive force of memory. The ability to communicate such a transcendent orderly perspective is extraordinary, divinely inspired. For this reason the poet from earliest times was associated with the priest, the prophet, the seer, the magus, the medicine man, the leader of the *choros*—and is called the "first legislator." Through the poet's memorial record, society awards the orderly individual with immortality—the perpetuation of his name and deeds in the memory of men to come. If a hero acts in a proper orderly fashion during life—one in keeping with Zeus' governing principle—his name will serve as an incentive toward orderly action on the part of those to whom it is recalled by some future singer. And the knowledge that this will happen, based upon the memory that it has happened to others in the past, becomes a force of great benefit to society. When Achilles finally goes into battle he protects all the Argives who follow him, behind the shield made by Hephaistos—and protects us, who follow his actions in Homer's verbal shield shaped by the Muses, daughters of Zeus and Memory.

The *Iliad* is the shield of memory because it reveals, like the surface of Achilles' shield, the structure of the universe. Out of chaotic divine forces Zeus personally creates order by his Olympian law; Hephaistos creates an image of that order; Achilles (with increasing insight) sees and imitates the order of the shield; and we are to imitate Achilles. We see that poetry, as Homer conceives of and practices it, is the ordering agent in human affairs, a form of worship as well as a sign of man's awareness of divine order. From a detachment that is virtually Olympian—because the Muses possess the poet with a vision of past, present, and future, and of both sides of the conflict in all their complications—Homer presents the happy results of orderly human action and the disastrous consequences of disorderly behavior. All mortals and immortals within the Iliadic world are polarized by these cosmic opposites: order and disorder. Each character is defined in terms of his link with one or the other. The great shield is a magnificent emblem of poetic order from which ideal human society issues. Its perfect correlative is the final character of Achilles, in which all opposites are held in stable tension.

The world of the *Iliad* is hierarchical: that is, it ascends vertically in value from the lowest level of horizontal relations through other analogous levels to the highest, the most comprehensive, where quality becomes indistinguishable from quantity. The value, defining which is highest or lowest, depends upon the system, and the social system of the Homeric world is in an uneasy state of equilibrium because it is constructed from two opposing hierarchies. In the "heroic" hierarchy, the highest value is the individual, for whose sake confederations are formed by oath; in the "familial" hierarchy, the highest is the city for whose sake the individual exists (see Appendix 1). Homer's vision, as emblemized in the great shield, projects a new poetically synthesized hierarchy in which individual and the widest community are perfectly balanced, their necessary reciprocity recognized, the tension between them made a constructive force, one serving the other. For the new poetic hierarchy borrows the emotional strength of the familial system (the love that binds individual to individual and individual to family) and the pragmatic force of the heroic system (the honor that holds individual to tribe and individual to extended tribe or confederation).

This book is a reexamination of the *Iliad*, focusing on images of artifacts, such as the great shield, which serve as signposts in the vast but coherent landscape that shapes character, action, and symbolism into a clear expression of Homer's instructive theme. That theme is the relationship between order and disorder, on all levels, from the most personal to the most widely social, from the human to the divine. Specifically the poem is a statement of the consequences to order when disorder is inserted at any level of the hierarchical cosmos as Homer conceives of it, and the restoration of order through the obliteration of the disorderly intrusion. Order, once interrupted, can only be returned through the destruction of disorder: that is the lesson of the *Iliad*. The epic ends with a vision of order reestablished and simultaneously raised to a higher level of potential stability, through the expanding force of love. Achilles' personal love for Patroklos becomes, at the end of the story, the pattern for the international love between him and the old king of Troy; and the epic ends, not with the death of Achilles or even of Troy or Priam, but with a ritual that promises the continuity of human order—made possible by Achilles' loving gesture: the return of Hektor's body. That gesture is embodied in the robes he gives back with the body, robes that had once been objects of disorder but are now orderly.

⤙ 1 ⤚

From Object to Order

The *Iliad* is a treasure-house of beautiful objects of art—swords, cups, robes, bows, beds, shields. The poem's most beautiful symbols are, first of all, perfectly useful objects. No object has purely decorative value. The epic poet's delight in naming things is always accompanied, in Homer, by the process which simultaneously relates them to the larger setting. One function of the artifact, of course, is to express its user's identity: that is, the artifact shows his skill in particular kinds of action, so that Aias, for example, comes to be identified by the towering shield behind which he himself stands firm as a tower—or Hektor by his flashing helm which serves as a beacon to the charging Trojans. In this way, Aphrodite's girdle, Athene's aegis and helmet, and Apollo's bow and lyre are images that make it easy to remember their users' various roles in the epic scheme.

Directly related to this immediate function is the role the artifact plays in the structure and composition of the poem. Consider the simile used to describe Menelaos' wound in Book 4:

> and straightway from the cut there gushed a cloud of dark blood.
>   As when some Maionian woman or Karian with purple
> colours ivory, to make it a cheek piece for horses;
> it lies away in an inner room, and many a rider
> longs to have it, but it is laid up to be a king's treasure,
> two things, to be the beauty of the horse, the pride of the horseman:
> so, Menelaos, your shapely thighs were stained with the colour
> of blood, and your legs also and the ankles beneath them.
>
> (4.140–47)

Specifically set aside for its beautiful craftsmanship, the cheekpiece is both a treasured object and a useful one; and even its usefulness goes beyond purely pragmatic function: it is inspirational, a source of pride. In much the same way, the elaborate simile is both functional—it describes Menelaos' wound—and beautifully significant in itself; yet its intrinsic beauty serves to heighten our appreciation of the singularity of

1

this wound. As the poet's direct address also emphasizes (4.146), Menelaos is not just anybody. He is a king, and brother to the king of kings. This fact, marked by Agamemnon's extraordinary solicitousness, reaches outward symbolically to remind us of the cause of war. Even from this example—somewhat special since the cheekpiece appears within a simile—we can see the way in which artifacts function as mnemonic devices (or structural reminders). Within a poetic presentation (oral delivery) that depends upon the memory of the audience, the artifacts and the contexts surrounding them focus the major theme and motifs of the epic so that those motifs are brought instantly to mind whenever an element of a particular imagistic pattern recurs. Homer's poetry is, in this mnemonic sense at least, profusely symbolic.

The organizing effect of artifact-images is seen more clearly in the case of Agamemnon's sceptre. The recurrence in Books 1 and 2 of either Agamemnon or of the sceptre (in Odysseus' hands when he beats Thersites with it, for example) is enough to recall the sceptre's divine and genealogical origins described in the key context of Agamemnon's attempt to deceive his army (2.100–141). The reminder of this full-scale treatment of the sceptre makes us immediately appreciate the irony that it is Odysseus who wields it effectively, and Achilles who respects it, not Agamemnon. The deception scene, then, is the key sceptre-image whose careful fashioning unlocks the pattern implicit in all other contexts throughout the *Iliad* in which sceptres appear. In this way Homer, while bringing full attention to the foreground of events, never allows us to lose sight of the background. The ideal reader (like the singer's audience) cannot be absentminded. If we compare the two staffs, that of Agamemnon and the one Achilles dashes to the ground, we do so because the poem demands that we do so.

The widely symbolic role played by the artifacts can be seen by considering two important exchanges of gifts. In the exchange between Aias and Hektor the warriors themselves state the symbolic nature of the gifts. Hektor proposes that they terminate their duel because of the approaching night, rejoicing in each other's valor—as their two peoples will rejoice in their glorious chivalry.

> 'Come then, let us give each other glorious presents,
> so that any of the Achaians or Trojans may say of us:
> "These two fought each other in heart-consuming hate, then
> joined with each other in close friendship, before they were parted." '
>   So he spoke, and bringing a sword with nails of silver
> gave it to him, together with the sheath and the well-cut sword belt,
> and Aias gave a war belt coloured shining with purple.
>   (7.299–305)

Here the artifacts' mnemonic role within the Iliadic world is analogous to the way in which the poet's images affect our memory. The sword to the Achaians, the belt to the Trojans, will be a sign of remembrance—calling to mind, in whatever age they are seen (or in which they are memorialized in song), the heroic moment of this battlefield meeting between Aias and Hektor. In a corresponding way the artifact-image, visualized clearly for us by the poet, calls to mind whenever it recurs the motifs with which it has been associated. This particular exchange proves that an individual in one of the warring camps is able, on a purely human level, to associate himself with an individual in the other. Suspended from practical function, reserved as honored gifts, the sword and belt find new symbolic roles in the continuity of memory. Within the poem's world, the artifact becomes potentially dynamic; something may come of it in the future. With regard to Homer's poem, the two artifacts have been made dynamic; for this juxtaposition of "heart-consuming hate" (7.301) and "close friendship" (7.302) points forward to the meeting of Priam and Achilles.

Much more complex is the famous exchange in Book 6. Recognizing, in Glaukos' genealogical recitation, their grandparents' mutual bond,

> Diomedes of the great war cry was gladdened.
> He drove his spear deep into the prospering earth, and in winning
> words of friendliness he spoke to the shepherd of the people:
> 'See now, you are my guest friend from far in the time of our fathers.
> Brilliant Oineus once was host to Bellerophontes
> the blameless, in his halls, and twenty days he detained him,
> and these two gave to each other fine gifts in token of friendship.
> Oineus gave his guest a war belt bright with the red dye,
> Bellerophontes a golden and double-handled drinking-cup,
> a thing I left behind in my house when I came on my journey. . . .
> 'Therefore I am your friend and host in the heart of Argos;
> you are mine in Lykia, when I come to your country.
> Let us avoid each other's spears, even in the close fighting.
> There are plenty of Trojans and famed companions in battle for me
> to kill, whom the god sends me, or those I run down with my swift feet,
> many Achaians for you to slaughter, if you can do it.
> But let us exchange our armour, so that these others may know how we
> claim to be guests and friends from the days of our fathers.'
> So they spoke, and both springing down from behind their horses
> gripped each other's hands and exchanged the promise of friendship;
> but Zeus the son of Kronos stole away the wits of Glaukos
> who exchanged with Diomedes the son of Tydeus armour
> of gold for bronze, for nine oxen's worth the worth of a hundred.

(6.212–21, 224–36)

The mnemonic function of the artifacts, implied in the exchange between Aias and Hektor, is made explicit in this double exchange—between Oineus and Bellerophontes, Glaukos and Diomedes. As in the case of Hektor and Aias, here the "war belt bright with the red dye" of Oineus and the "golden and double-handled drinking-cup" of Bellerophontes were removed from the realm of purely practical action to become tokens of remembrance. The two exchanges are so far parallel. But in this one, the dynamic potential of the artifacts' mnemonic function has been fully realized. The physical presence of Bellerophontes' cup in the household of Diomedes has reincarnated a friendship (one marked by high-hearted impracticality, as the poet's interjection happily suggests, 6.234–36) which existed long ago between their ancestors. An essential pattern of orderly behavior is reinvested with concrete form, translated from history to present actuality. Moreover Diomedes' assertion that this new exchange will have its own mnemonic effect someday brings the symbolism to a beautiful cyclical close, reaffirming a faith in the continuity of memory—and, through it, of orderly human institutions—that is shared alike by characters, poet, and audience.

We learn a great deal about Iliadic social values from this scene, as well as something about the thematic concerns of the poet who created that world. Of greatest consequence is the indication that the guest-friend relationship is considered as sacrosanct as the familial-political bond. How deep the relationship between guest and friend can be is clear in the cases of Achilles and Patroklos or of Peleus and Phoinix. How pervasive it is can be appreciated when we remember that Homer's poem begins and ends by portraying a guest-host relationship, the one radically unfriendly, the other radiantly friendly. Achilles' acceptance of Priam's ransom (Book 24) is set opposite Agamemnon's inhospitable treatment of the suppliant Chryses (Book 1). Finally the guest-friend relationship lies at the center of the poem's motivational framework: Paris' blatant disrespect for his guest-host relationship with Menelaos—his stealing of Menelaos' wife—caused the war; it is the crime paid for ultimately by the destruction of Troy. The overriding social importance of the bond, therefore, is apparent. An entire people must pay for its infraction by a single individual.

In the world portrayed in the epic, guest-friend loyalty is associated with genealogical ties. The link between the familial and the guest-friend bonds is that the individual in the Iliadic world must be defined socially. The expatriate's separation from his natural social coordinates—the lines of political and family relations that intersect in him so uniquely as to define his characteristic fate—is a precarious condition that demands hospitality. And the host must welcome the stranger into the protection of his household precisely before his guest has identified himself socially. The taboo, imposed under the auspices of Zeus himself (the protector of guests), is based upon a faith in reciprocity. By duly respecting the stranger, the host insures—within the cosmic perspective of Zeus' hierarchical government—that he himself would receive such treatment should he find himself in a similar position. The guest is granted a "substitute" social or familial definition so that he may function effectively despite separation from his original one. The religion of Olympian Zeus supports the guest-friend bond as a universal human ethic that transcends political and even national boundaries.

This association between familial and guest-friend bonds is demonstrated in the exchange between Glaukos and Diomedes. The outcome of their confrontation, so different from what it might have been, testifies to the association; for the exchange magnificently disproves Glaukos' often-misinterpreted remarks, moving though they are, about the irrelevance of his genealogy to the fighting at hand. Fearing that he might be face to face with a god, Diomedes is properly (after his disorderly rampage in Book 5) circumspect in asking Glaukos, "Who among mortal men are you?" (6.123). Glaukos' disparaging reply, suspiciously enough, is inconsistent both in itself and in light of Homer's general emphasis on the importance of family background.

> Then in turn the shining son of Hippolochos answered:
> 'High-hearted son of Tydeus, why ask of my generation?
> As is the generation of leaves, so is that of humanity.
> The wind scatters the leaves on the ground, but the live timber
> burgeons with leaves again in the season of spring returning.
> So one generation of men will grow while another
> dies. Yet if you wish to learn all this and be certain
> of my genealogy: there are plenty of men who know it.'
>
> (6.144–51)

Glaukos' contemplative metaphor of the ephemeral nature of the individual is rare in the Iliadic world, characteristic of the kind of beauty (shared by Achilles, Helen, and Paris) that kills. Yet we are far from Wallace Stevens' statement that "Death is the mother of beauty." The leaf simile is beautiful, but Glaukos misinterprets it badly as implying a total lack of continuity among the generations of men. When he abruptly turns, with surprisingly little transitional logic, to recite his social identification in the fullest terms, we understand that our suspicion and surprise are responses to the poem's magnificent irony. If Glaukos had hesitated, he would have died.

Instead, his recitation strikingly presents the societal consciousness of

the *Iliad* and its belief in the endurance of mankind despite the transience of individuals. It is, of course, the warrior's awareness of continuity that gives him motivation; Glaukos is ready to sacrifice himself for
the survival of the Trojan community. Insofar as such a sacrifice is the
individual's duty, the warrior is practically indistinguishable from his
companions-in-arms. Diomedes recognizes this when he says, " 'There
are plenty of Trojans and famed companions in battle for me / to kill' "
(6.227–28). But Glaukos has been spared because he remembers his
family history. The truce between them is brought about by Diomedes'
memory of ancestral friendship and hospitality. Glaukos' lengthy narrative, as it associates him with a social hierarchy, also defines him as a
noteworthy individual among the Trojans (6.151). And when "heart-
consuming hate" has been transformed into "close friendship," an
Achaian shares that recognition. So the exchange, in which the essential
humanity of each man is revealed to the other (and to us), is, as E. T.
Owen says, "a promise, the suggestion of a hope, stored in the mind,
waiting for fulfillment" (p. 59). The scene posits and at the same time
proves the existence of a universal humanity, characterized by the
reverence for fatherhood and all that is implied by genealogy, which
places the Trojan War in perspective. Like the individuals that may be
referred to by Glaukos' leaf-simile, nations too will pass away; man,
however, will prevail.

Cedric Whitman comments that, "in the epic tradition generally, arms
had a high significance; they were part of the whole warrior, and to lose
them, even in death, was to lose not an adjunct, but a part of the heroic
personality" (p. 203). So the poet speaks of the clash of the armies as
"shield on shield, helmet on helmet, man against man" (13.131). Stripped
of his armor the individual is alone, without social significance.
This is the meaning of Sarpedon's words of encouragement to
Glaukos:" '. . . you yourself also must fight for me with the bronze
spear. / For I shall be a thing of shame and a reproach said of you /
afterwards, all your days forever, if the Achians / strip my armour here
where I fell by the ships assembled' " (16.497–500). In Sarpedon's mind,
it is a social responsibility as well as a personal one, to protect this last
vestige of individuality, the armor—for society's sake, as well as for
Sarpedon's (16.495–96). Unless Glaukos and the Lykians preserve Sarpedon's honor in death they cannot retain their own (16.501). We have not
been convinced, up to now, that Troy cannot protect her own. Although
Glaukos and Hektor rally to defend Sarpedon's body, Zeus must intervene to insure its honorable escape from Achaian hands (16.666 ff.); but
Sarpedon's armor is carried away to the Achaian ships (16.665).

This fascination with armor is marked throughout the *Iliad*. At one point, Homer describes how, in the midst of a furious encounter, the two opposing sides indistinguishably "fought their battle with sharp hatchets and axes, with great / swords and with leaf-headed pikes, and many magnificent / swords were scattered along the ground, black-thonged, heavy-hilted, / sometimes dropping from the hands, some glancing from shoulders / of men as they fought, so the ground ran black with blood" (15.711–15). In another place, it is as if we are hearing the dry inflections of an objective museum cataloguer: "Many fine pieces of armour littered the ground on both sides of the ditch, as the Danaans fled" (17.760–61). And the implied metonymy is more poignant for its reference to men "on both sides of the ditch."

A more telling illustration of the poet's association of armor with social identity is his reference to the Lokrians. Their leader, Aias son of Oïleus, does indeed stand bravely with Telamonian Aias in defense of the ships, "as two wine-coloured oxen" (13.703), and

> Now with the son of Telamon many people and brave ones
> followed as companions, and took over the great shield from him
> whenever the sweat and the weariness came over his body.
> But no Lokrians went with the great-hearted son of Oïleus.
> The heart was not in them to endure close-standing combat,
> for they did not have the brazen helmets crested with horse-hair,
> they did not have the strong-circled shields and the ash spears,
> but rather these had followed to Ilion with all their confidence
> in their bows and slings strong-twisted of wool; and with these
> they shot their close volleys and broke the Trojan battalions.
> So now these others fought in front in elaborate war gear
> against the Trojans and Hektor the brazen-helmeted, and the Lokrians
> unseen volleyed from beyind, so the Trojans remembered
> nothing of the joy of battle, since the shafts struck them to confusion.
> (13.709–22)

By a kind of associative logic Homer excludes the Lokrians from the category of "brave people" (13.709, 712). Their lack of heroic armor is causally related to their background position, ὄπιθεν ópithen ("unseen," or "from behind"—13.721). Fighting in the national ranks is not characteristic of them (13.713), and they seem less than fully assimilated into the Achaian alliance. Behind the confederate ranks they stand as an individualistic tribe protected by society—whose contribution to the common cause, although it is considerable, is out of the ordinary because it depends upon that social protection. They are therefore set in contrast with the heroic individual who can stand firmly upon his personal ability to protect society. Individual heroes, too, depend upon the community's support, even here, where the natural reciprocity of them and society is clearly marked (13.710–11). But Homer's vision characteristically focuses on contexts that emphasize the importance of the individual. And so, although it is "many people" of the Achaians (13.709) who fight against the Trojans (13.720), most clearly visualized are the two Aiases (13.701–8) standing against Hektor (13.720). In this sense, the identification of the Lokrians with their lack of armor has wide-ranging implications. They are symbolically defined as an extraordinary entity in the hierarchical world.

Homer also relates the functional effectiveness of armor to its artistic excellence. Wounded by Pandaros, Menelaos quiets his panicked brother, saying: " 'The sharp arrow is not stuck in a mortal place, but the shining / war belt turned it aside from its course, and the flap beneath it / with my guard of armour that bronze-smiths wrought carefully.' " (4.185–87). As Machaon removes the armor to tend the wound the description is repeated (4.215–16). The emphasis on the smiths' conscientious artistry, recalling the elaboration of the cheekpiece and its artisan (4.141–45), heightens our appreciation of Menelaos' special stature among the Achaians. As a royal twin he has readily available the craftsmen and fine materials which have just been identified with his lifeblood. The armor in this context, like the cheekpiece, is what Eric Havelock calls a "unit of vision." The two artifact-images are related by the mnemonic process Whitman terms "creative association," both by the poet and by his audience. The consistent association between technical excellence and practical effectiveness will become poignantly ironic in the case of the central artifact, Achilles' shield; for Hephaistos clearly says that it will not keep Thetis' son from death, although it will be a wonder to behold (18.464–67).

Rebuffed by Agamemnon, Chryses prays to Apollo "of the silver bow" (1.37) for assistance. When Apollo soon after appears (1.45), the detailed description of the artifact underlines its symbolic and thematic function.

> So he spoke in prayer, and Phoibos Apollo heard him,
> and strode down along the pinnacles of Olympos, angered
> in his heart, carrying across his shoulders the bow and the hooded
> quiver; and the shafts clashed on the shoulders of the god walking,
> angrily. He came as night comes down and knelt then
> apart and opposite the ships and let go an arrow.
> Terrible was the clash that rose from the bow of silver.
> First he went after the mules and the circling hounds, then let go
> a tearing arrow against the men themselves and struck them.
> The corpse fires burned everywhere and did not stop burning.
>
> (1.43–52)

Here the bow's artistic quality is matched perfectly by its function. The bow concretely identifies, in the memory of the audience, Apollo's power to make the Achaians pay for Agamemnon's slight to his priest. The arrows issuing from it punish the warriors for their communal transgression; at the same time they remind us that Agamemnon, belittling the power of his sceptre (1.28), badly miscalculated Chryses and his divine sponsor. The artifact's symbolic function is unmistakable: a single arrow causes all those funeral pyres (1.51). The development of the bow image, from Chryses' prayer (1.37) to Apollo's dreadful response (1.43–52), immediately recalls the opening lines of the epic, with their reference to slain heroes and dogs (1.3–5). The "pains thousand fold" (1.2) for the Achaians have already begun—and even before the Trojans are introduced. The rapidity with which Homer inserts us into the middle of violent action is breathtaking.

A different treatment of the same artifact, the bow, emphasizes its background as well as its effect. In Book 4, following the abortive duel of Menelaos and Paris, Pandaros, at the instigation of a divine council, is persuaded by Athene (disguised as Lykaon) to break the truce:

> So spoke Athene, and persuaded the fool's heart in him.
> Straightway he unwrapped his bow, of the polished horn from
> a running wild goat he himself had shot in the chest once,
> lying in wait for the goat in a covert as it stepped down
> from the rock, and hit it in the chest so it sprawled on the boulders.
> The horns that grew from the goat's head were sixteen palms' length.
> A bowyer working on the horns then bound them together,
> smoothing them to a fair surface, and put on a golden string hook.
> Pandaros strung his bow and put it in position, bracing it
> against the ground, and his brave friends held their shields in front of him
> for fear the warlike sons of the Achaians might rise up and rush him
> before he had struck warlike Menelaos, the son of Atreus.
> He stripped away the lid of the quiver and took out an arrow
> feathered, and never shot before, transmitter of dark pain.
> Swiftly he arranged the bitter arrow along the bowstring,
> and made his prayer to Apollo the light-born, the glorious archer,
> that he would accomplish a grand sacrifice of lambs first born
> when he came home again to the city of sacred Zeleia.
> He drew, holding at once the grooves and the ox-hide bowstring
> and brought the string against his nipple, iron to the bowstave.
> But when he had pulled the great weapon till it made a circle,
> the bow groaned, and the string sang high, and the arrow, sharp-pointed,
> leapt away, furious, to fly through the throng before it.

(4.104–26)

This bow-image fits its position in Homer's narrative perfectly; the detailed description of the artifact's history dramatizes its vital role in the unfolding story. As Book 3 ends, Menelaos is left in unchallenged control of the field; Paris is safely in the arms of Helen. Agamemnon declares to the Trojans that his brother is clearly the victor and the terms of the solemnly arranged truce should by all rights be honored: Helen should be returned, the war should come to an end (3.456–61). The ignominious deed of Pandaros is Homer's solution to the technical problem of how to continue his poem when by its own logic it should end here.

The deed originates in the Olympian council which opens Book 4. Even here Homer delays the eventuality of continuation in order to further heighten our appreciation of the magnitude of Pandaros' crime. The words of Zeus make it clear that the truce might indeed end the war. Troy might indeed have been preserved for its people (4.14–19). Yet Hera's barbaric thirst for vengeance will be satisfied, and Zeus makes a terrible bargain with his wife (who often represents unreasoning willpower): to exchange Troy's destruction for that of whatever city of hers he might choose to annihilate at some future time (4.34–50). The bargain—and the nature of the gods' role in mortal affairs (Hera's cannibalistic tendencies recall the vulture-gods of the Gilgamesh epic, 4.34–35)—is made to appear all the more terrible when Zeus declares that Troy was to him the dearest of all human cities (4.39–50).

But having acceded to Hera's demands Zeus sees to it that the responsibility for renewing the strife will rest on the Trojan side by taking her advice and sending Athene—who represents cunning here more than reason—down among the waiting warriors. The disastrous effect of Athene's descent is made all the more poignant by being presented in the same context of equality which was emphasized at the beginning of the duel when Homer showed the parallel armings of Menelaos and of Paris (3.326–29). The two armies watch her descent from Olympos with like amazement; each side recognizes it as ominous, though neither army knows how the omen should be interpreted. This general equality between the two camps is strikingly presented as Athene lands in that middle ground between them.

> in such likeness Pallas Athene swept flashing earthward
> and plunged between the two hosts; and amazement seized the beholders,
> Trojans, breakers of horses, and strong-greaved Achaians.
> And thus they would speak to each other, each looking at the man next him:
> 'Surely again there will be evil war and terrible
> fighting, or else now friendship is being set between both sides

by Zeus, who is appointed lord of the wars of mortals.'
Thus would murmur any man, Achaian or Trojan.

(4.78–85)

The use of the iterative form εἴπεσκεν *eipesken* ("would speak"—4.81, 85) emphasizes the common quality of the men's reaction to the goddess' appearance. The common formulaic line 80 also occurs in 3.343 to describe the two armies' similar reaction to the appearance of Paris and Menelaos. The same half-line is used to describe the equal amazement of the beholders in each army (4.79 = 3.342). That this balance is all too soon to be shattered by Pandaros' arrow makes the reiteration of it here particularly effective, a formal close to a unit of action. In these same brief lines Homer reveals that his men themselves know what we have just learned in the council scene: that the gods are agents in human affairs (4.84). This ambiguity of responsibility is part of the inherent fatality of the poem's world and does not mitigate the personal guilt of Pandaros. Movement toward order proceeds simultaneously on both the human and the divine level (Nestor, among men, tries to move toward order; Zeus, with Hephaistos' technical assistance, bullies the unruly gods toward his Olympian order). Disorder occurs when one level interferes, and is allowed to interfere, with the other. Sometimes, as with Pandaros here, an individual human disorder must be initiated in order to restore universal order among men; but that does not make the disorder less fatal or less reprehensible to its agent (Pandaros) and his whole community. Troy must live out to its disastrous end the initial disorderly action of Paris, and Pandaros' deed puts Ilium back on the wrong track.

So Pandaros allows himself to be deceived by Athene about the nature of the deed he will shortly perform. He doesn't see through her disguise in the way other men sometimes recognize the gods (Helen, for example, recognizes the aged wool-dresser as Aphrodite in 3.395 ff.). In a very real sense, Pandaros allows Athene, as the cunning force of Zeus' orderly will, to possess him; but it is important to note that the possession is a conscious compliance, not forced by the god. The responsibility is mutual; Athene appeals to Pandaros' baser motives and he, in turn, gives them full play. That is why Homer calls him a fool (4.104): Pandaros is not only doing the wrong thing; he's also doing it for the wrong reasons. The cunning goddess appeals both to his desire for glory and to his wish to receive the gratitude of his people (4.95), combining a personal with a social argument. She makes him think that he will be acting for the common good and even implies—by telling him to pray to Apollo " 'the glorious archer' " (4.101), identifying his deed with the wise and just bowman of the gods—that he *can* act effectively at this crucial point, because his own personal prowess is divinely supported. Flattery has gotten her everywhere.

For with the wounding of Menelaos, Pandaros has virtually brought down the roof upon the Trojans—and given the poem new impetus. His self-deception is now all too evident. Though Pandaros was flattered into action by being called wise (4.93) and by being mockingly identified with Apollo (a god of wisdom, art, and order), the narrator's evaluation is proved the accurate one: it is a "fool's heart" (4.104) which, by breaking the sacred truce, makes Pandaros a "new Paris" whose perfidy is the direct cause of Troy's ruin. Apollo, we recall, first appears in the *Iliad* as the bringer of death, associated with Zeus' orderly purpose; only in this ironic sense is Pandaros identified with the divine bowman. We remember that Paris, too, is a bowman. By reference to the preceding narrative the bow scene here heightens our awareness of the disastrous effectiveness of Pandaros' deed. And by reference to what follows the association of the bow with Troy's destruction is crystal clear—the wounding of Menelaos revitalizes Agamemnon's (and therefore the army's) determination. At the same time it convinces Agamemnon that the victory of his cause is ordained by the gods.

> 'So, the Trojans have struck you down and trampled on the oaths sworn.
> Still the oaths and the blood of the lambs shall not be called vain,
> the unmixed wine poured and the right hands we trusted.
> If the Olympian at once has not finished this matter,
> late will he bring it to pass, and they must pay a great penalty,
> with their own heads, and with their women, and with their children.
> For I know this thing well in my heart, and my mind knows it.
> There will come a day when sacred Ilion shall perish,
> and Priam, and the people of Priam of the strong ash spear,
> and Zeus son of Kronos who sits on high, the sky-dwelling,
> himself shall shake the gloom of his aegis over all of them
> in anger for this deception. All this shall not go unaccomplished.'
> (4.157–68)

Juxtaposing this passage with the bow's description proves the thematic function of the artifact-image. We see that the bow's less than deadly effect precludes the one possibility of Troy's preservation—Menelaos' death (4.169 ff.). Because Agamemnon's brother's life has been spared, Troy will not be. The Argive king recognizes that Zeus' favorable attitude toward Troy must now be reversed through the Olympian's role as protector of sacred oaths. The divine machinery is now rolling, irreversibly, toward Ilium's doom.

Homer presents the bow's action in a remarkably elaborate manner that makes us pause to appreciate the exact moment in the narrative when the machinery starts to move. The poet emphasizes the action by meticulously detailing the process of the bow's stringing (4.112), its positioning (4.112–13), readying the arrow (4.116–17), its arming (4.118), drawing back the string (4.122–24), and releasing the arrow (4.125). Not enough that each step is so precisely noted, a particular step is even analyzed to display its component parts (4.122–24). Homer's attention to the firing process prepares us to appreciate the bow's thematic significance. Slowing down the action in this cinematic manner also associates the scene here visualized most effectively with what has gone before. For it is the bow's *potential* that Homer wants to impress on us. Until the arrow has been released, the truce might have allowed Troy to survive. At the same time we recall that the bow may shatter human equilibrium; Pandaros' invocation to Apollo associates his own arrow with the one which brought such havoc upon the Achaians in Book 1. The "bitter arrow" (4.118) is concrete and universal at once—like Apollo's (1.52). Though it was "never shot before" it is, also like Apollo's, a "transmitter of dark pain" (4.117)—the fatality of its objective nature allied with the fatality of Pandaros' foolhardy but characteristic decision. Against the peaceful potential of the truce stands the irrevocable consequence of the bow's activation: destruction for the people of Troy.

The irremediable nature of the bow's influence, then, makes it singularly significant as an image. The artifact appears in the poem as a thematic necessity. In contrast with this "static" quality of the bow is the dynamic way in which Homer has identified the artifact with Pandaros: a tension has developed between the particular and the general. As the arrow issues from the bow, its fury extends the self-deceiving furor of Pandaros to all men (4.126). Yet it also makes concrete the "blind force" which Rachel Bespaloff would elevate to the dominating theme of the *Iliad*. The poet prepares us for this motif when he describes Pandaros' ambush of the wild goat (4.105). The ambush is related here to Pandaros' attack on Menelaos, Pandaros' hiding place in the covert to his secure position behind the shields of his brave friends (4.113–14). This is Pandaros' particular technique for confronting the everyday occasions of life, his characteristic behavior. Homer identifies Pandaros with the bow by showing us how the Trojan himself furnished the very materials from which the artifact was fashioned. It is clearly Pandaros, not only Athene, who is responsible—from the very beginning. In this way, Homer ties fate to character.

But if the bow is static with regard to its *effect*, its objective visualization is accomplished by dynamic means. We see the bow first as it is being made just as later we see it being used. It is never treated as an object for detached appreciation; it cannot be extricated from its original

involvement with Pandaros, the situation at hand, and the war itself.
Homer's emphasis here on the process of the bow's creation, meticulously artistic as we see it to have been, suggests that the bow was
destined to play this fatal role. So it is not surprising that the symbolic
function of Pandaros' bow radiates outward to encompass all the great
themes of the poem. This is perhaps evident already but is worth spelling
out. The bow is symbolically significant, on one level, because it is
directed against Menelaos, suggesting a parallel between Pandaros and
Paris; but its context also has wider connotations, revealing the reciprocal relationship between the individual and society that stands as one
of the great motifs of the poem. What the community, individuals acting
in concert, accomplished (the truce) is destroyed by a single man pursuing personal interests. This tension between the common interest—of
both armies—and the individual who has made peace impossible shows
brilliantly in "everyman's prayer" before the duel. The prayer refers to
Paris and Menelaos, but is just as applicable to Pandaros: "Thus would
murmur any man, Achaian or Trojan; / 'Father Zeus, watching over us
from Ida, most high, most honoured, / whichever man has made what
has happened happen to both sides, / grant that he be killed and go
down to the house of Hades' " (3.319–22). The prayer ends with a moving
suggestion of how the duel might bring peace to all the warriors: " 'Let
the friendship and the sworn faith be true for the rest of us' " (3.323).
This is not Homer's comment on the injustice of the Iliadic world. Instead
it eloquently marks the fact that these men, in their overwhelming desire
to end the fighting and return to domestic concerns, have forgotten
momentarily the way things are in that world. They speak of the way
things should be. Finally it is not only the truce which is destroyed by
Pandaros but also the hierarchical stability of Troy itself which motivated
and made possible the truce. Agamemnon's speech (4.157–68) makes it
clear that it will take all the Trojans to pay for one man's crime. Symbolic
action on a wide plane is implied in the bow scene.

The tension between the general and the particular appears in the fact
that it was the protection of his companions that made Pandaros' arming
of the bow secure (4.113–15). The extraordinary nature of his individuality is like that of the Lokrians who are bowmen too. Perhaps it is simply
the fact that the bow must be restrung, demanding a temporary respite
from the oncoming enemy, before it can take an active part once more. At
any rate the implication of these lines is that the responsibility for
breaking the truce rests not only with Pandaros, not only with the gods,
but also with the Trojans as a group. For their tactical support of
Pandaros provides the necessary occasion for actualizing his bow's
potential. The bow and arrow, visualized in isolation, is a useful image

of this social-personal reciprocity common to heroic poetry and uncommonly emphatic in the *Iliad*: "He drew, holding at once the grooves and the ox-hide bowstring, / and brought the string against his nipple, iron to the bowstave. / But when he had pulled the great [bow] till it made a circle, / the bow groaned, and the string sang high, and the arrow, sharp-pointed, / leapt away, furious, to fly through the throng before it" (4.122–26). As in the case of shield and spear, the abstract relationship is that of the circle to the straight line (radius) that generates it, of potentiality to actualization. For the fully-drawn bow—the artifact's circular condition—is potentially effective only because the community has supported Pandaros' action (protecting him with their shields while he arms his weapon just as the circular walls protect the city itself). The individual bowman is able to act only through a communal arrangement. That is clear also when Aias' shield allows Teukros to rearm his bow in Book 8. Not surprisingly, the motivations suggested by Athene, gratitude and glory, are both social ones.

But the arrow is the actualization of the bow's potential, just as the individual alone is the effective agent in human life. He alone can act. One may draw an empty bow, so to speak, but that would be absurdly ineffectual; just as propelling the arrow without the bow would be ridiculous—making the missile impotent. Moreover when the arrow leaves one circle (the bow) to pierce another (the opponent's shield), we understand that it is the individual who is the point of contact between two societies at war. In the present situation, we recall how close Iliadic men came to peace through the orderly contact of the two individuals, Menelaos and Paris, most responsible for their societies' conflict. But that orderly one-to-one confrontation ended with Aphrodite's disorderly intervention (as the force of blind passion); now, as a result, every Trojan individual must pay the price. And Pandaros' arrow is the individual vector which connects the two social circles, Troy and Argos, in their last contact. For one circle must inevitably destroy the other, since their initial contact (Paris abusing Menelaos' hospitality and abducting his queen) was breaking the rules of the game. Later we will see Homer reemphasizing that in the individual resides the common humanity that will allow Priam and Achilles (like Glaukos and Diomedes or Aias and Hektor) to communicate with each other through their sharing of universal human emotions. They do so precisely as individuals; for "Troy" and "Argos" cannot communicate with each other as social entities. Peace is made, if at all, only man to man; whereas kings—insofar as they are representatives of their embattled communities—must be at odds. As in chess, kings are the only individuals who cannot touch each other—Agamemnon and Priam never meet. And Priam meets

Achilles only when the Trojan king specifically puts aside his national identity, his royal status. Achilles, in turn, will put aside his Argive identity to greet Priam simply as a host, man to man. This mutual abdication of social identity as the basis for their friendship in Book 24 is necessary because Pandaros' arrow has doomed their two societies to fight to the death of one.

Tension between the individual and the group is not presented only by symbolic means in the *Iliad*. Nearly line by line, the reciprocity between the two expresses itself in word, thought, deed, or image. A summary of the events in Book 1 becomes a survey of individual-communal tensions. The effect of one man's wrath on all his people is the singer's opening motif (1.1–2). Apollo's anger at one king brings pestilence on all the people (1.9–10) because the god's priest invoked all the people through their leaders (1.15–16). The interlocking necessity that connects the fate of each person and his society is never absent from the poem: Although all the Achaians want Chryses' request to be honored, it is sufficient that Agamemnon doesn't (1.23–24); one man can call the army to assembly (1.54); Kalchas, the seer, speaks with "kind intention toward all" (a formulaic reminder of the poem's social consciousness, 1.73); but even the seer fears the king, because all obey him (1.78–79); the king's singularity equals the combined individualities of all his subjects (1.90–91); Kalchas says all the people must pay for one god's anger against one man (the king, 1.97–98); Agamemnon himself recognizes the social damage that could result from his selfishness (1.117–19); Achilles says Agamemnon's greed is unequaled among *all* men (1.122) and he promises that all the Achaians will show their gratitude to Agamemnon if the king relents (1.127–29); Agamemnon recognizes that his own personal prize should come from the community (1.135); Achilles questions *any* individual's ability to obey a king like Agamemnon (1.150) and points out that all the Achaians came to Troy only for Agamemnon's sake (1.157–58), making it all the worse that Agamemnon is taking the prize they all gave to him (1.161–62). At this point Achilles threatens to secede from the confederation, speaking on behalf of all the Myrmidons (1.180–82). Achilles speaks of the individual man's duty to all the gods as, sheathing his angry sword, he obeys one god, Athene (1.217); Zeus' house is identified with all the gods (1.222), so that we see the individual-social connection exists among divinities as well as among humans. Achilles says that Agamemnon's alleged singularity has never been proved in public (1.225–30) and that he will make all the Achaians recognize his singular prowess by going away (1.240–44). From the moment he stands up, Nestor's description and speech are entirely dominated by the individual-community motif (1.250–72), as we will see

later. Agamemnon points out that Achilles is as excessively individualistic as he is (1.286–87); strife between these two key individuals breaks up
the harmonious assembly (1.305); the Achaians carry out a ritual cleans-
ing at their leader's command (1.313); in contrast to their obedient
busyness, Agamemnon is still intent upon his selfish anger (1.318) and
threatens to come with a troop to take Briseis from Achilles by force
(1.324–25). Achilles asks all to witness that Agamemnon's selfishness is
what has provoked his own alienation from the community (1.338–44)
and goes to sit alone "apart from his companions" (1.349). When Thetis
comes to see what troubles her son, Achilles recapitulates the social
distribution of spoils to each according to his due (1.368) and tells her of
Chyrses' mission (1.374–79); then he calls on Thetis' singular relationship with Zeus in order to claim for himself a society with the gods in lieu
of the human society that won't give him due honor (1.393–400). We
learn that all the Olympians are frightened by one giant (1.406). Then
Achilles states his request, asking Thetis to make the Trojans victorious
" 'so that thus they [Achaians] may all have profit of their own king, /
that Atreus' son wide-ruling Agamemnon may recognize / his madness, that he did no honour to the best of the Achaians' " (1.410–12).
Thetis agrees to his request, telling her son to keep to himself while she
goes (1.421–22). Meanwhile Odysseus tells Chryses his delegation has
come to " 'propitiate / the lord who has heaped unhappiness and tears
on the Argives' " (1.445). Chryses asks Apollo to cease his wrath (1.455–
56). Harmony between the community of men and the angry god is
restored, and marked by harmony among the men themselves (their
hymn, 1.472); Apollo sends a favorable wind to all (1.479). Homer turns
back to the camp to underline the unnaturalness of Achilles' alienation
(1.490), while, on Olympos, Thetis tells Zeus her individual relationship
with him should make him exalt Achilles' individual honor above all the
Achaians because he is the shortest-lived of all mortals (1.504–10); if he
refuses, Thetis thinks she will be "the most dishonoured of all gods"
(1.516). Zeus, the supreme individual, is worried about another single
god, Hera, who is "forever among the immortals / . . . at me" (1.520).
Even when it comes to gods, Homer seems unable to speak of individuals without simultaneous reference to the group(s) to which they belong.
And Zeus' oath is a public sign, not a private decision (1.525). All the
gods rise as he enters, "not one had courage / to keep his place" (1.533–
35). Hera thinks Zeus' oath to exalt Achilles over the other Achaians is
unfair (1.559) but Zeus silences her with the reminder that he is stronger
than them all put together (1.566–67). Hephaistos rises to intercede
between them, as Nestor had between the two squabbling human
leaders, because he knows that their argument affects all the gods

(1.570–71); he stresses how disastrous a quarrel would be for all of them (1.574)—the feast would be disrupted. Even his story, illustrating Zeus' singular power, ends with an almost superfluous reference to another group, the Sintians, who treated an individual well (1.594). And Hephaistos brings them together with wine for each one (1.597) and communal laughter directed at him (1.599–600). Then Homer summarizes the scene with the formulaic line: "they feasted, nor was anyone's hunger denied a fair portion" (1.602), which reminds us of the human feast on Tenedos at the completion of the successful return of Chryseis (1.468). Finally Apollo's individual singing is set against the harmonious antiphony of the Muses' (1.603–4), and "they went away each one to sleep in his home" which Hephaistos, the singular unifying agent, built for each one (1.606), a beautiful closing image of the variety in unity that characterizes Zeus' ideal of Olympian order.

The correspondence we have seen here between the human feast on Tenedos and the divine feast on Olympos is an early indication of another motif, already hinted at in the discussion of shared responsibility between Pandaros and Athene: the constant association of men and gods, both orderly and disorderly in its motivations, occurrences, and consequences. The review of Book 1 has already suggested the parallels in action and emotion on the human and divine level that extend through the narration from the beginning. A concentrated look at one particular passage, the astounding close of Book 8, makes the motif even clearer:

> And they set free their sweating horses from under the harness
> and tethered them by the reins, each one by his own chariot.
> They led forth also out of the city oxen and fat sheep
> in all speed, and conveyed out also the kindly sweet wine,
> with food out of their houses, and heaped many piles of firewood.
> They accomplished likewise full sacrifices before the immortals,
> and the winds wafted the savour aloft from the plain to the heavens
> in its fragrance; and yet the blessed gods took no part of it.
> They would not; so hateful to them was sacred Ilion,
> and Priam, and the city of Priam of the strong ash spear.
>   So with hearts made high these sat night-long by the outworks
> of battle, and their watchfires blazed numerous about them.
> As when in the sky the stars about the moon's shining
> are seen in all their glory, when the air has fallen to stillness,
> and all the high places of the hills are clear, and the shoulders out-jutting
> and the deep ravines, as endless bright air spills from the heavens
> and all the stars are seen, to make glad the heart of the shepherd;
> such in their numbers blazed the watchfires the Trojans were burning
> between the waters of Xanthos and the ships, before Ilion.
> A thousand fires were burning there in the plain, and beside each
> one sat fifty men in the flare of the blazing firelight.

And standing each beside his chariot, champing white barley
and oats, the horses waited for the dawn to mount to her high place.
(8.543–65)

The superb drama of this vision of the Trojan camp is achieved through artful construction. At the same time that the structural pattern of the passage emphasizes continuity between men and gods in the Iliadic world it also suggests something of the poem's aesthetic. The description opens with the human details of the scene in proper order (8.543–47); and when the narrator turns to the gods, he does so from a human perspective: the sacrifice may have a divine object but its origin and agency are human and natural (8.548–49). Connecting the two realms of being, the wind plays a communicative role similar to that of the singer in heroic society, or of Nestor who tells the present generation of the deeds of their ancestors, or of Hephaistos who reminds the gods of events from their immortal past. But because Paris' crime and, more recently, Pandaros' perfidy have made Troy essentially disorderly (note the paradox in the otherwise common epithet, "sacred Ilion," 8.551), the wind is ineffective. It belongs to the image pattern which includes Paris' lyre, scorned by Hektor, and Hekabe's offering of robes, rejected by the statue of Athene. In itself the sacrificial fragrance is sweet; the gods will not accept it because of its origins (8.550–52).

The poet's description so far shows the way things are when the universe is at odds with itself because of human disorder. Now he turns to suggest the way things should be. The narrator depicts the men below at their numerous campfires (8.553–54). The extended simile (8.557–64), like others in which Homer's hand can be seen clearly in the fictional world, compares these mortal fires to the stars shining gloriously about the moon. The simile is a remarkable example of the way in which Homer's art achieves its didactic purpose through the function of memory. We see how the familiar mnemonic device of hysteron proteron is used to tacitly justify an analytical comparison of the two parts of the description (8.542–51 and 552–65): the first part begins with the horses and food, the second ends with food and the horses. The development is cyclic; but it is simultaneously progressive, since the horses are now eating the food prepared for them before. The passage also presents a cyclic progression of aesthetic elements. First the poet gives us history, logos, the facts of the situation (8.542–54); and he returns to this emphasis at the end (8.572–75). So the circumference directs our attention to the focal center. In the center is the simile (8.555–61), which provides the philosophical perspective, or mythos, relating these past events to the continuum of human life, but particularly to the present. For the shepherd exists in no specific time, but in eternity—tangential to the fictional past as well as to the audience's present. Yet this center, once revealed, defines the circumference even more clearly than before.

A schematization, based on Aristotle's statement that history presents things as they *are* or *were* while poetry (more philosophically) presents things as they *might be* or *should be*, clarifies the paradoxical structure. In the first part of the scene, things as they *were* are presented. The description begins on earth (8.542–47) and proceeds with the wind, to heaven (8.548–50). Movement in the opposite direction, however, is prohibited because of the disorderliness of Troy. It is the narrator's intrusive explanation which returns us to earth (8.551–54). This particular moment in human history in this particular place (the Trojan camp) is not ideal. In the second part of the passage, things as they *should be* are implied by the focal shift from earth (8.553–54) to heaven (8.555 ff.) and back to earth again (8.560–61). Communication between time and eternity, between the limited and the infinite aspects of man's nature, is perfectly reciprocal. As if to emphasize the continuity of the cyclic progression, the movement continues from earth (8.564) again to heaven (8.565). The implication of the last line, moreover, is that the dawn awaited by the dutiful horses will yet again affect earthly events.

But the movement in the second part is also from the fictional past, a specific point in history (8.543–44), to the continuous dimension of time represented by the unchanging aspect of the heavens (8.555–58)—which includes, by implication, the present as well (8.559). The shepherd is analogous both to the orderly hero and to the audience. Like the hero, he is gladdened by his vision of order. Like the audience, he is made joyful by this story even though its present scene is tragic because the poet has allowed us to comprehend the whole. That is what the image of the shepherd does for Homer's reader.

Now consider the intricacies of movement within the simile, the symbolic action defining the essential significance of this fictional action. The image begins with the heavens (8.555), but immediately refers to the earthly vista from which they are seen (8.556). Next it indicates the air which is the medium bringing the two realms into contact (8.556) as it makes not only the heavens but also the earth clear to the observer (8.557).

From earth the description returns to heaven which is now defined as the source of the communicating air that has such effect upon the shepherd (8.558–59). The brightness of the air (8.558) suggests the clarity of Homer's vision which produces clear vision in the audience. Like the air (whose influence it describes), like song itself (which it suggests imagistically), this line in which the shepherd appears also moves from heaven to earth (8.559). Here, then, is a summary of the simile's movement:

heaven
earth-air, the mediator between earth and heaven, here defined
    as being immanent on earth
earth
earth-air, the mediator whose heavenly origin is here
present-heaven
heaven (through the air, now fully defined as both transcendent and
    immanent)-earth (where it affects man)

The simile becomes a minor exegesis of the Iliadic aesthetic. Like the invocation to the catalogue of ships in Book 2, the simile here begins with an emphasis upon the divine source of poetry but concludes by focusing on the transitory human reality affected by that transcendence.

It is also significant that the description closes with the image of the horses (see Appendix 2). They are neutral in the present conflict, neither gods nor men. Like Achilles' steeds these Trojan horses—although even more appropriately because they are anonymous—embody the cosmic spirit of order shaping the poem. Despite the ominous nature of the coming dawn, they go about their business—which is, like all eating in the *Iliad*, a both serious and joyful affirmation of the continuity of life—with equanimity and no desire to avoid the confrontations of the morrow. However their confidence comes from ignorance, whereas that of Homer issues from his full knowledge of man's eternal nature.

Moreover the descriptive narration that frames the simile provides a contrapuntal movement that heightens the overall sense of universality evoked by the entire passage. For whereas the simile moves from heaven to earth, the framing description moves from earth—with the Trojans making camp (8.542 ff.)—to heaven (8.565). This opposing movement is characteristic of the Iliadic aesthetic, with its constant balance of antitheses, its consistent insistence on the circularity of experience—whether spatial or temporal—that never leaves us with a linear, periodic impression. And so this examination of the passage in Book 8 suggests how intricately enmeshed in the texture of the *Iliad* is Homer's awareness of the continuity between the cosmic and the mundane, between the perpetual and the temporary, among the three dimensions of human time (past, present, future), between the collective nature of man and its heroic individual manifestations. From the inspiration of the Muse of Memory Homer derives the artistic vision by which logos and mythos, history and philosophy, things as they were and things as they should be, are synthesized to reveal the cyclic continuum of human experience. In the human circle, as in this passage, Homer presents the focus and the circumference as somehow beautifully and mysteriously interchangeable.

⤳ 2 ⤫

Helen and Her Galaxy: 1

The Mysterious Heroine

Helen of Troy is the archetypal enigmatic woman in Western litera-ture. The mystery of her character has fascinated the imagination more deeply and more consistently than even that of Eve—about whom, by comparison with Helen, we know very little. Perhaps it is because we know so much about Helen that her character seems so intriguing. The plethora of legends associated with her name has made it a symbol of the inherent limitations of human knowledge; knowing so much about her becomes even more perplexing than not knowing enough. We unwrap one mystery only to find another. The mythic Helen is paradox incarnate, uniting in the unfathomable center of her being a host of elemental opposites, including life and death. In the heart of Homer's *Iliad*, it is Helen's beat that answers Achilles'. Unlike other Homeric women—Briseis, for example, who has no history outside the poem, and no real name within it (we know her only by her patronymic)—Helen was a familiar figure to Homer's audience before they heard his version of her. It may have been partly because she enjoyed so diverse a prehistory as a saga heroine that Homer felt constrained to treat Helen so delicately, with such reserve. Like Achilles, she remains peculiarly apart from the other characters in the epic; and the *Iliad* complements his glorious, ideal shield, made by the god, with her austerely realistic weaving in Book 3.

The legends that envelop Helen's identity in mysterious shadow suggest the challenge Homer faced when he came to fashion her into the texture of his poem. As an enchantress displaying a demonic command of drugs and magic, Helen has been connected with the Sirens. Accord-ing to one tradition, Achilles wanted to meet Helen in Hades—and Thetis worked with Aphrodite to bring them together. Aphrodite, goddess of desire, sex, marriage, and birth, is Helen's divine patron. But Helen's uncanny aloofness from the precarious condition of other mor-tals relates her equally to the antithetical goddess, Artemis, known for her purity and austerity.

22

This conflict of divine associations is less surprising considering that Helen's very birth is diversely reported in Greek lore. As the daughter of Zeus and Nemesis, Helen was regarded as purely immortal. Yet it is puzzling that her equally immortal twin brothers, Kastor and Polydeukes, managed to die. Helen's own immortal status is also qualified by the fact that Nemesis, the unnatural daughter of Night (Erebus), was listed by Hesiod as the sister of Doom, Death, Age, Strife, and the three Fates. Such a genealogy, then, has mortal as well as immortal— chthonic (or underworldly) as well as ethereal—implications. The gods from whom Helen has sprung are those strangely primitive forces who, while themselves eternal, control the transience of man. Helen's remote and paradoxical origins are similarly suggested by an alternative legend that makes her the daughter of Okeanos and Tethys, the archaic deities who are somehow nearest to the heart of all things (belonging to the pre-Olympian, Uranian pantheon). Helen's immortality has been portrayed traditionally as a mixed blessing, at once sinister and beneficial. Her celestial appearance as ball lightning (St. Helen's fire) was regarded by mariners as an omen, whether of good or evil; Helen has even been considered a moon goddess, in another association with Artemis. Yet even though she is the niece of Death, Helen was known for her longevity and ageless beauty. Cyrus Gordon sees in her a parallel to Sarah, the daughter of El, who bore a child at the age of ninety.

On the other hand, we find a vague legend that Helen was entirely mortal, daughter of Leda and Tyndareus (in this account, she is Klytaimestra's sister, making the Argive-Trojan story even more incestuously complicated). It may be in relation to this birth story that we get the tradition that she attained immortality only after her earthly death. The most widespread legend, however, is the one used by W. B. Yeats ("Leda and the Swan") which made Helen a proper heroine (half-god, half-human), as the child of Zeus and Leda (in one version hatched, with Klytaimestra, from the same egg). Yet in this account, too, her nature is equivocal; for the human facet of her character is strangely qualified by Zeus' erotic epiphany to Leda in bestial form. As simultaneously less and more than human, Helen is associated with the animal kingdom. This manifestation of her curious identity is itself not without contradiction, since Helen is elsewhere connected with the vegetable realm. The most arcane and intriguing remnants of Helen folklore reveal her deification as a vegetation goddess. Isocrates, Pausanias, and Theocritus speak of sacred trees dedicated to her (there were arboreal cults among the Dorians). Minoan civilization knew Helen as a vegetation goddess who was raped annually by the god of wealth. The fertility ritual implied by this religious metaphor suggests that from earliest times Helen's chthonic character was thought to enhance her role as a marriage goddess.

In Sparta, one of many places where Helen was worshipped in connection with marriage, the wedding ritual insisted upon her being abducted and ravished, providing a divine model for the marriage rite. Helen's affinity with Hera in the *Iliad*, with respect to their wifely roles and their association with Aphrodite's girdle of love, gains significance from the fact that Hera was worshipped as a marriage goddess at Samos. The motif of ceremonial abduction and rape is also found in the stories of Kore-Persephone (ravished by Pluto), Ariadne (ravished by Theseus), and the Ugaritic epic of Kret. Although the abduction motif was widespread among the Indo-Europeans, there seem to have been two consistent elements in the various Helen stories—in which she is sometimes thought to have been taken by Hermes to Egypt, to Sidon or Troy by Paris-Alexandros (sometimes with Aineias), to Deceleia by Theseus or by the Apharetidae, or to Mount Parnon by a nameless robber: Helen is always restored by twins (for example, the Dioscouri—her brothers—themselves or the "twin" Atreidae, Menelaos and Agamemnon). And, because the image of the goddess had to be returned to the temple after the ceremonial abduction had been reenacted, Helen was connected with an εἴδολον *eídolon* ("phantom")—like her in appearance, but not really she. It was as such a phantom that Helen was worshipped by her Egyptian cult. Legends of her immortality may have been initiated by this ghostly appearance in connection with the marriage ritual. Menelaos is granted perpetual life only because of his marriage to her; he and Helen were both worshipped as gods in the temple at Therapnae.

How many of these diverse legends were known to Homer, no one can say. Some of them, at least, must have influenced him. But a comparison of the Iliadic Helen with her counterpart in the *Odyssey* strongly suggests that the composer of the *Iliad* put Helen's traditional ambiguity to good account—making her a living symbol of the total confusion of normal social order that comes with war. The characterization of Helen in one epic may differ in some details from that in the other, but what is most striking is the consistency between the two portraits—a consistency that comes down, essentially, to the calculated portrayal of Helen's inconsistency. It is worth pausing for a close look at the two epic heroines—Helen in peace time and Helen in war. In *Odyssey* Book 4 we see Helen associated with creativity, but not actually creating—as if that part of her life were over. As we will see, in the *Iliad* (and it is equally true in the *Odyssey*, and later epics like the *Argonautica* and the *Aeneid*) creativity is connected with mortality, the individual's need to create an artifact that outlasts him—a need directly parallel to the hero's need to overcome death and to influence the future by heroic acts. The two needs, artistic and active, are complementary. When we meet her in the *Odyssey*, Helen has no need to create for herself, as she had in the *Iliad* when her life was precarious and her identity uncertain. In the *Odyssey* her immortality as Menelaos' queen is insured. Having no longer to worry about her own status the Helen of the *Odyssey* turns her energies outward, for the benefit of others. And she is mightily capable of benefiting human beings. As she was in the *Iliad*, here, too, Helen is the knower of names, the discerner of identity. Although the others have not done so, Helen immediately recognizes Telemachos; she is as much like Proteus in this respect as Menelaos is, although the comparison is not made by the poet (*Odyssey* 4.400 ff.). For she sees through appearances to the underlying truth, a matter of defining essential identities. What is different from the *Iliad* here is that Helen's knowledge is realized in action. Her outgoing energy is not only interpretative but also effective—as when she drugs the visitors' and courtiers' wine to erase for the moment ineradicable sorrow. These drugs are Egyptian (*Odyssey* 4.219–34). As she suspends the effect of reality's pressure on Telemachos, Helen displays a kind of demonic power. Her enchantment provides the anguished boy with hope and determination—in short, with a perspective from which he may now more purposefully confront the demands of his situation.

As Helen's first appearance in the *Odyssey* concludes, so her second entrance into the narrative begins as we see her by the side of Menelaos in their royal bed. It is generally true in both Homeric epics that the bedding-down of man and woman symbolizes domestic harmony—as it does in *Iliad* 1, 3, 14, 23, and 24. But unlike the beddings-down of the *Iliad* this one gives evidence of no sinister element, no qualification from appearing to be forced. We take the visual unit at face value, remembering only the atypical nature of the spouses involved.

When the royal couple enters their treasure room to select gifts for Telemachos the poet clearly means to emphasize Helen's peculiarity. He distinguishes meticulously the way in which each gift is selected and carried out of the chamber. Menelaos himself takes a "two-handled cup" (*Odyssey*, 15.102). Megapenthes, at his father's bidding, takes a "mixing bowl of silver" (*Odyssey*, 15.103–4).

But Helen's choice is her own, and specifically appropriate to her (as the other gifts are not explicitly made appropriate to Menelaos and Megapenthes): "but Helen went to stand by the storing boxes, / where there were elaborately wrought robes. She herself had made them. / And Helen, shining among women, lifted out one of them, / that which was the loveliest in design and the largest / and shone like a star. It lay beneath the others" (*Odyssey*, 15.104–8). The gown is singularly appropriate not only because Helen is associated consistently with glorious robes in general (both in the *Odyssey* and in the *Iliad*), but also because she herself had woven it. The way the robe works imagistically in the poem imitates directly the way in which it works mnemonically in the fictional world, as we learn from her presentation speech to Telemachos: " 'I too give you this gift, dear child: something to remember / from Helen's hands, for your wife to wear at the lovely occasion / of your marriage. Until that time let it lie away in your palace, / in your dear mother's keeping; and I hope you come back rejoicing / to your own strong-founded house and to the land of your fathers' " (*Odyssey*, 15.125–29). Anyone familiar with the *Iliad*, whether he be listener or reader or singer, cannot help recalling the robe Helen wove in Book 3 of that epic. Helen's robe in the *Odyssey*, like the exchange of gifts between the ancestors of Glaukos and Diomedes, is a potential symbolic force made actual. The mnemonic function of Telemachos' new robe connects the past with the future by associating Helen's creativity with the entire spectrum of social order: conjugal, parental, political or national (the island), and the royal hall in which the political and the domestic concerns come together. Helen's symbolic involvement with the social structure of human life is embodied in the robe she bestows on Telemachos.

Just as in Book 4 of the *Odyssey* the poet stopped short of presenting Helen in the process of creation (although all the materials for weaving were at hand), here too, in *Odyssey* 15, we see that her creativity is a thing of the past. Her relationship with the created product is defined by its ability to serve the interests of others; she is the transmitter rather than the creator of the artifact. The emphasis in the *Odyssey* is on Helen's "real life" action rather than upon her "artistic" action. Her presence is medicinal (the drugs), inspirational (the tale), sponsorial (the robe). It is fitting that the last we see of Helen in the *Odyssey* is yet another instance of her conversion of knowledge into action. We see her finally as the interpreter of hidden meaning (the omen), just as we see her first as the recognizer of Telemachos' identity.

In the *Iliad*, because of Aphrodite's manipulation, Helen is incapable of either self-serving action or of effective outgoing acts. She can help the Trojans no more than she can help herself. Her causal deed, the elopement with Paris, is merely a "given" in the poem; and responsibility for it is itself ambiguous owing to the agency of the goddess. In the *Iliad* Helen is suspended from events, but very differently from the way she is in the *Odyssey*; for here her final status has yet to be determined. She must await the outcome of the war. We do not know whether her creativity will have fruition; what is important is that it has potential.

What is sustained in the characterization of Helen in each poem is the mystery of her existence, her paradoxical inconsistency. That paradox permeates and determines all contexts in which the Spartan queen appears in the *Iliad*. The ambiguity associated with her is apparent in the range of discrepancy revealed in the various judgments made upon her by men and gods. The two Olympian parties are polarized by reference to their attitudes toward Helen, and among human beings evaluation of Helen is even more divided. She has set at odds not only Argos and Troy, but also factions within each nation. There are Achaians as well as Trojans for and against Helen.

Nestor, encouraging Agamemnon to rally the demoralized Danaans, recalls the omen of victory sent by Zeus when the fleet was leaving Aulis, and concludes, " 'Therefore let no man be urgent to take the way homeward / until after he has lain in bed with the wife of a Trojan / to avenge Helen's longing to escape and her lamentations' " (2.354–56). Because a royal Argive couch has been deprived of its wife and queen a Trojan wife must sleep with every Achaian. The disruption of Troy must occur at the very spring of its domestic and political stability, just as the sexual roots of Danaan well-being have been cut. To prevent the recurrence of such a threat, the temporary disordering of Argos must issue in the permanent destruction of Troy. The sexual assimilation, that is, must involve two entire peoples, to be conclusive. In the minds of Iliadic men, Helen's very name implies the social—personal and communal— significance of the conjugal bed.

For Agamemnon, too, Helen's name evokes the spectre of disorder. To the king, her importance to the Argives goes beyond the fact that she is Menelaos' wife. Even if his brother were to die it would still be a thing of reproach for Agamemnon to leave Helen to the Trojans (4.171 ff.). Yet the familial motivation obviously must support political interests; for the Achaians will not be willing to continue the war after the death of the jilted husband (4.172). As far as they as individuals are concerned, only the reestablishment of the Spartan household provides a worthwhile incentive for risking their particular households. When that reestablishment is no longer possible, owing to the death of Menelaos, each man will direct his loyalty first to the well-being of his own family, despite the national dishonor such a redirection would mean. Consequently, to Agamemnon, the death of Menelaos would result in nothing less than the destruction of Argos as an effective social entity. Zeus knows that only Helen's return to her proper husband can save Troy as a fitting abode for men (4.19).

References to Helen among the Trojans, too, show a diversity of attitude. The argument in the Trojan assembly following the burial truce in Book 7 is a telling contrast to the harmony signified by the exchange of gifts between Hektor and Aias. Antenor feels that only by returning Helen will the Trojans compensate for dishonoring their pledges and insure continued well-being for the city (7.350–53). But Priam supports Paris' refusal. Helen has polarized the factions within Troy; we learn elsewhere that Antimachos opposes her return because Paris has paid him "beyond all others" (11.123). Cooperation, therefore, is maintained only tenuously. Helen is the malign presence in the body politic. Every time she is mentioned she is associated with the disorder, both political and sexual, which forms the major thematic pattern of the poem.

Yet through all of this Homer himself observes her mystery without fail and refrains from judging Helen in any definitive way. The poet presents Helen's self-recriminations without comment. He must remain silent. The purpose of his poem is didactic wonder.

Instead of judging, Homer enhances Helen's image by drawing attention to its enigmatic character by every means he knows. He suggests the aura of mystery about Helen by emphasizing the emotional value of her regular association with riches, her remarkable self-consciousness, her connection with gods and goddesses, intimations of immortality revealed in her references to song, her conscious awareness of the communal implications of individual acts and, above all, her singular beauty. As Bespaloff has written, Helen's beauty "isolates and elevates . . . with the inexorability of force or fate, . . . transcending all contingencies" (pp. 66–67).

The full symbolic significance of Helen's weaving can be appreciated only in light of the galaxy of characters with whom she is associated throughout the poem. Certain crucial figures are related to Helen and to one another through the creative association of the images of particular artifacts: loom, bed, house, robe, and the special case of "song." It may be a useful generalization to call this image-galaxy surrounding Helen that of disorder; and the poem's second image-galaxy, surrounding Hephaistos, the galaxy of order. Each of them defined by the ambiguity of Helen herself, the characters of Paris, Aphrodite, Priam, Hektor, and Andromache, can be said to exist within the galaxy of disorder. But the fact that Hektor is juxtaposed with Achilles, Paris with Menelaos, Priam with Agamemnon, and so on, indicates how the two galaxies are connected like mirror-images (since the tragic irony is that Hektor is consistently more orderly than Achilles, or Priam than Agamemnon), so that together they express the poem's major theme. The confluence of the two galaxies of characters and artifacts is dictated by that theme, which is the relationship between order and disorder illustrated in the conflict between two social systems. Helen has a peculiar intergalactic status. The central star of one galaxy has been abducted and given a crucial position in the other; as a result, the entire cosmos is in disarray.

The most thoughtful exposition of Helen's part in the war comes, appropriately, from Achilles. While Menelaos himself never declares his personal feelings for his wife, we are given an insight into what such feelings might be when Achilles describes his own emotional attachment to Briseis:

> 'Yet why must the Argives fight with the Trojans?
> And why was it the son of Atreus assembled and led here
> these people? Was it not for the sake of lovely-haired Helen?
> Are the sons of Atreus alone among mortal men the ones
> who love their wives? Since any who is a good man, and careful,
> loves her who is his own and cares for her, even as I now
> loved this one from my heart, though it was my spear that won her.'
>
> (9.337–43)

The interpenetration of the two thematic galaxies is evident in Achilles' statement. Agamemnon is revealed as parallel with Paris, Briseis with Helen, the sons of Atreus with Troy. The wrath is a microcosm of the war itself specifically by reference to marriage. For the present disorder of the Achaian army was caused by Agamemnon's abduction of Briseis, even as the general discord among men—the war—was initiated by Paris and Helen.

Artifact-images relate Helen to the major figures of her galaxy. That galaxy is defined primarily by a poignant ambiguity of emotions and attitudes which, in keeping with the mystery of Helen herself, reveals each of its stars (Paris, Priam, Hektor, Andromache) to be searching for order in a context of action that has been disordered irreversibly. The poetic beauty of these figures, then, is distinctively related to that of Helen.

The Bed of Paris

Of the four arming scenes in the *Iliad*, that involving Paris is most undistinguished—the one usually described as most evidently formulaic, traditional, and typical. His "fair greaves" are "linked with silver fastenings" (3.330–31), but are certainly no more particularly personalized than is his "sword with the nails of silver" (3.334), his "great shield, huge and heavy" (3.335), his "well-fashioned helmet with the horse-hair crest" (3.336–37), or his "strong-shafted spear"—even though the spear was "fitted to his hand's grip" (3.338). As his helmet is undistinguished, at least in appearance, from Hektor's, so we are told that Alexandros dons the corselet "of Lykaon his brother since this fitted him also" (3.333). The conventionality of the narration suggests, if anything, only the typicality of Paris' armor, and the one significant departure from the traditional arming pattern—the mention of Lykaon's corselet—does not deny, but instead supports the typicality. When the action to which his arming leads is considered, the single particularized line proves the thematic significance of the arming description. Homer proceeds from Paris' arming directly to the duel, dismissing Menelaos' arming with a curt, "In the same way warlike Menelaos put on his armour" (3.339).

As the duel progresses we notice that the armor of the two men is indeed treated identically. First Paris' spear strikes Menelaos' "perfectly symmetrical shield" (3.347); then it is Menelaos' which strikes Paris' "perfectly symmetrical shield" (3.356). Throughout their confrontation Homer emphasizes the equality of these two warriors—an unmistakably symbolic equality, since the very action before us has for its essential cause the fact that each man is the husband of Helen, and each therefore an indirect cause of the war. In a sense, then, their duel is a microcosm of the Trojan-Achaian conflict itself. Just as Homer pits the two heroes equally against each other in this passage, he makes us aware of the wider import of their match by showing us the corresponding and equal reactions of the two opposing armies: "Now when these two were armed on either side of the battle / they strode into the space between the Achaians and Trojans, / looking terror at each other; and amazement seized the beholders, / Trojans, breakers of horses, and strong-greaved Achaians. / They took their stand in the measured space not far from each other / raging each at the other man and shaking their spearshafts" (3.340–45). Just as Homer makes no distinction between their armor, he presents their actions (3.341, 344, 345) and sentiments (3.342, 345) with common verbs, making it understood that the two are engaged in equivalent ritual gestures. The same "amazement" seizes the beholders of both armies (3.342), recalling the equal joy they shared when the duel was first proposed (3.111–12). Instead of only Paris, the individual responsible, a whole people will pay for his crime—just as all the Achaians suffered for Agamemnon's insult to Chryses. Not Menelaos alone, but his whole nation, will take part in the return of Helen; so that victory is necessary to restore harmony not only to his house and to his πόλις *pólis* ("city"), but to the whole of Argos as well. What is to come, we know, will contradict the balance of this scene. For the Trojans will lose because they are, without Hektor, unequal to the Achaians led by Achilles. The opportunity for a fully bilateral arbitration will never come again.

Before the duel scene closes, however, the poet draws our attention once more to Paris' arms by describing the "broidered strap under the softness of his throat" (3.371) which would have strangled him had not Aphrodite intervened. The "broidered strap" draws our attention to the physical delicacy, ἀπαλὴν *hapalēn*, of Paris—the gift of the goddess which he can only accept (3.65–66). Even when Paris is most warlike, donning his "glorious armour with bronze elaborate" (6.504) to join Hektor in leading the battle with apparent equality in Book 7 ("shining in all his armour of war as the sun shines," 6.513), a jarring undertone emphasizes how extraordinary is this eagerness for combat on the part of Alexandros. We are meant to recall that Paris can never be identified truly as a heroic warrior like his brother. His raiment is more characteristically of a peace- and leisure-loving nature—his fighting spirit of the bedroom variety. Aphrodite tells Helen she will find her husband, newly escaped from the duel, " 'shining in his raiment and his own beauty; you would not think / that he came from fighting against a man; you would think he was going / rather to a dance, or rested and had been dancing lately' " (3.392–94). And the boudoir again colors his warlike foray with Hektor in a scene which, by associating Paris' armor with womanly artifacts, undermines the virility usually symbolized by war-gear. Hektor's stalwart appearance in his brother's bedroom heightens the effect.

> There entered Hektor beloved of Zeus, in his hand holding
> the eleven-cubit-long spear, whose shaft was tipped with a shining
> bronze spearhead, and a ring of gold was hooped to hold it.
> He found the man in his chamber busy with his splendid armour,
> the corselet and the shield, and turning in his hands the curved bow,
> while Helen of Argos was sitting among her attendant women
> directing the magnificent work done by her handmaidens.
>
> (6.318–24)

Homer here elaborates the armor of each brother—but with how different an impact! We never doubt Hektor's fighting spirit and ability, whether he is in a bedroom, on the wall with his wife and child, or actually on the field. We will see him leaning upon this same spear (its description repeated verbatim, its sexual symbolism a blatant contrast to Paris' boudoir sexuality) in firm command of his troops at the very height of victory (8. 493 ff.).

At the same time, we will notice that the weapon of Paris here singled out by the poet, the "curved bow," will be associated elsewhere with his unwarlike beauty and love of women. Directed, with childlike eagerness, against Diomedes, his bow not only fails to kill, but also becomes the occasion for a long tirade from the would-be victim which brutally identifies Paris with his ineffectual military pose. Then Diomedes bluntly associates Paris' ineffectual bow with his general social impotency (11.369–95). The two passages are closely related; in both, Paris is connected with the bow, with beauty, and with women; in both he is set opposite an exemplary heroic character. This associative process presents Paris as a pathetically well-meaning man who cannot, despite his good intentions, escape from being identified as an unwilling scion of Aphrodite, like his wife. His erotic identity, so understood, is one with Paris' role in the poem's world; like Helen, he has allowed himself to be possessed by the blind force of passion that began its work of disorder at Thetis' wedding feast—and will end it, despite his present good intentions, only with the simultaneous deaths of Achilles and of Troy.

Throughout the *Iliad* Paris is called the "lord of lovely-haired Helen" (as in 7.355, 8.82). The epithet appears for the first time in 3.329 where it is in striking juxtaposition with the warlike arming process, reminding us of the incongruity of Paris' preparations for manly combat. Paris' most familiar epithet identifies him by his role as Helen's illicit husband—and in conjunction with her beauty. Unlike the familiar patronymic, which marks a man's status in the Iliadic world by reference to historical or genealogical order, this traditional epithet describes a social relationship with only *present* validity. That Alexandros is the son of Priam is, of course, significant; but his paternal identification is relevant only because Paris is, at this point in the life of Priam's city, the husband and abductor of Helen. Another kind of epithet commonly applied to specific heroes identifies them by their present *function* in communal action. Aias, for example, is called "bulwark of the Achaians." But the epithet for Paris is not descriptive in this sense, and with good reason. For the *Iliad* is concerned not with the contemporary acts of Paris, but with the present repercussions of his completed action in the past. Like the stone tossed into a pool, Paris, as Homer presents him in the poem, is the now inactive cause of the ever expanding circle of events that radiates outward, equally in all directions, to the very boundaries of the universe.

This momentarily convenient oversimplification of Paris' significance in the *Iliad* need not blind us to the complexity and subtlety of his character. Homer does not leave Paris simply typical or one-dimensional. As his appearances in Book 3 show, Paris can be as intriguing as Helen in his own peculiar way, even though his interest as a character is defined by Helen's force field. Like Helen, Paris is associated with extraordinary physical beauty, with self-consciousness and remorse, with the futile desire to better his regard among men, and with a certain extrinsically arranged detachment from reality. Paris is both active by ambition and passive by destiny, rebellious and resigned, shameful and ashamed, beautiful and sinister, innocent and guilty, egocentric and socially concerned. His tragedy is that these contradictory elements are never resolved, that he must persist in enduring their unrelenting tension.

The opening of Book 3 reveals his diversity in action: the beauty inspiring wonder and loathing, the desire to act heroically and its futility, the partial detachment from responsibility due to the manipulation of Aphrodite. As the two armies, just rallied by their respective leaders, clash for the first time in the *Iliad*, it is fitting that Paris be the first individual isolated on the stage. The wrath of Achilles has come to its first climax and the poet must now turn to the larger setting within which that wrath-story is contained, to provide the necessary foil for its development. Paris, the cause of the war, comes naturally to center-stage: "Alexandros the godlike leapt from the ranks of the Trojans, / as challenger wearing across his shoulders the hide of a leopard, / curved bow and sword; while in his hands shaking two javelins / pointed with bronze, he challenged all the best of the Argives / to fight man to man against him in bitter combat" (3.16–20). This brave image does not last long. Paris shrinks in craven terror behind the crowd of his companions the moment Menelaos, his counterpart, accepts the challenge (3.30–31). To emphasize the significance of Paris' finding refuge in the communal presence Homer employs a simile (3.33–36); despite the warlike boast, "godlike Alexandros" is incapable of redressing the social disorder he has wrought.

Hektor's rebuke angrily associates Paris' beauty with feminine and sinister elements: " 'Evil Paris, beautiful, woman-crazy, cajoling, / better had you never been born, or killed unwedded' " (3.39–40). Here again, Paris' singularity is defined in terms of his marriage to Helen (just as Menelaos will become immortalized by *his* marriage to her). Because he has entered into a contract which he himself cannot support, his people must risk their very existence to protect him. Paris is a thing of shame to the Achaians for his deed, to the Trojans for his inability to defend its repercussions, and to himself for being unable to control his own acts and emotions. In a sense Book 3 is unified by the uncontrollably passionate nature of Paris; it opens with his terror of battle and closes with his lust for a very different kind of engagement. And in the middle, the duel proves that his ineffectiveness in warfare is not solely his responsibility. The object of his first emotion is the manly Menelaos; of the second, Helen. And Aphrodite, possessing them both, assures this emotion's consummation.

Hektor's rebuke reveals the ambivalence of his brother's beauty. Unlike the distinctly functional beauty of Achilles on the ramparts in

Book 18, the beauty of Paris is sinister because it has no relevance to
orderly action. Hektor can distinguish between the beautiful appearance
of bravery and Paris' manifest lack of its essence: " 'Surely now the
flowing-haired Achaians laugh at us, / thinking you are our bravest
champion, only because your / looks are handsome, but there is no
strength in your heart, no courage' " (3.43–45). In wartime, the beauty of
peace cannot save an embattled society. All his associations with the arts
of leisure would be sadly ineffective in helping Paris dutifully confront
Menelaos on the battlefield: "The lyre would not help you then, nor the
favours of Aphrodite, / nor your locks, when you rolled in the dust, nor
all your beauty" (3.54–55). Paris' retort is to excuse himself by reference
to the moral ambiguity so characteristic of his relation to Helen. Paris
argues that Hektor's judgment must be qualified by the recognition that
human will can be suspended by the agency of divinity: " 'yet do
not / bring up against me the sweet favours of golden Aphrodite. /
Never to be cast away are the gifts of the gods, magnificent, / which they
give of their own will, no man could have them for wanting' " (3.64–66).
Although Paris may be guilty of enjoying, as he sometimes does, the
benefits of his disorderly role, he insists that he has been cast for the part
by a divine director whose plan for the play cannot be fathomed by
mortal actors. He is unable to apply his will to the present course of
events because Aphrodite predetermined history when she usurped his
will to arrange the abduction. There is in Paris' speech a subtle implication that apparently disorderly things may be part of an orderly pattern
so large in its design that the part cannot be judged except from the
viewpoint of the whole. Even beauty which is sinister, viewed in
isolation, may be wholesome from another angle—in the perspective of
the cosmic song. All of this is true, of course, without exonerating Paris
entirely from a degree of personal blame—even though we may not be
able to determine the exact degree.

   Paris' ambiguous detachment is embodied in the artifacts with which
he is associated. Just as the bow marks him apart from the heroic norms
of combat represented by Hektor's massive spear, and just as the lyre and
his raiment like a dancer's dissociate him from war, so, too, Alexandros'
house is an identifying image. It stands in contrast with the two other
houses described in any detail in the *Iliad*: the palace of Priam and the
lodge of Achilles. Paris' house embodies his selfish orientation. It is
remarkable that Homer makes Paris an artist; although he is not the sole
architect of his own fate, he at least built the house in which he and Helen
live while the fate initiated by Aphrodite's passion is working itself out.

   The scene with Hektor in the bedroom is introduced with a description
of "the house of Alexandros, / a splendid place he had built himself, with

the men who at that time / were the best men for craftsmanship in the generous Troad, / who had made him a sleeping room and a hall and a courtyard" (6.313–16). Paris' ability to call upon the best craftsmen available in the Troad, like Menelaos' access to the best armorers in Argos, identifies him as a royal individual. There is fine irony in the fact that this archetypal homewrecker should be a domestic architect. Paris' association with a distinctively personal house is criminal because the city, which alone can offer a safe environment for family life, is put in jeopardy by the selfish attitude housed within it.

Paris' splendidly wrought house is first mentioned in Book 3, when Aphrodite accompanies Helen home (3.421). As other artifacts have dissociated Paris from the war, the house furthers the process by connecting him with domestic tranquillity. His detachment from the world of action is presented as a matter of substituting a solely domestic orientation for a communal one: the opposite of Hektor's sacrifice of family. When others are engaged in preserving the political environment which makes the family secure, Paris is enjoying—without earning—the fruits of their labor. The artistic beauty of his house, in itself wholesome, is sinister because it symbolizes—through its association with its maker and user whose behavior is ignoble—not commitment to, but escape from, social responsibility.

The house is a fitting structure for the marital artifact it contains: the bed of Paris, the definitive image connecting him with the disorder of Helen's galaxy. Aphrodite addresses Helen on the wall: " 'Come with me: Alexandros sends for you to come home to him. / He is in his chamber now, in the bed with its circled pattern, / shining in his raiment and his own beauty; you would not think / that he came from fighting against a man; you would think he was going / rather to a dance, or rested and had been dancing lately' " (3.390–94). Despite her reluctance, Helen "went to the high-vaulted bed-chamber" (3.423). There Paris is waiting: "Speaking, he led the way to the bed; and his wife went with him. / So these two were laid in the carven bed" (3.447–48). Just as Paris' is the most emphatic house-image in the poem, it is *his* bed (parallel to Zeus' at the end of Book 1) which provides the key to the thematic pattern based on the association of this artifact with various characters in the *Iliad*. Like his, all other conjugal couches in the poem are disorderly in one way or another; causation of disorder is reciprocal among them. But the crucial bed is that of "Alexandros, for whose sake this strife has arisen" (3.87). While Homer's singular elaboration of Paris' bed accurately reflects the consciousness of his characters, his recurrent reference to beds suggests that the poet himself perceives the human disorder of the *Iliad* to be more ambiguous in origin, more inextricably a part of man's existence, than do any of his characters. The image of the bed looms in the background of events, no less sharply a focus of thematic conflict for being outnumbered by images of war.

What does the bed-image tell us about the theme of the *Iliad*? Implied in the clash of the two armies on the Trojan plain is the conflict between Helen's two beds, of Menelaos and Paris. The war itself will resolve the imagistic conflict by assuring the reestablishment of one marital couch or the continuity of the other, just as the wrath-motif will conclude only when Briseis has been assigned definitely to Agamemnon's or to Achilles' cot. Homer makes artistic images out of the very stuff of life. The bed is an intergalactic image having a common significance to men on either side of the struggle. Like the familial context which it represents, the bed signifies a more essential level of humanity than do political or national distinctions.

Considering Paris' bed on such an essentially human level suggests the relationship between selfishness and sterility. Although he has been married to Helen for nine years, Paris is without issue—Homer's silence is sufficient evidence. Within the social system of the Iliadic world the sterility of the marriage proves that it is disorderly—centripetal rather than properly centrifugal. For in the world of the poem the familial context, established by a marriage, is not an end in itself, but one more link in the hierarchical social chain. Paris' love for Helen is regarded as unnatural because she was the wife of another man, just as Agamemnon's love for Chryseis is "unkingly," as Thersites bravely (though impudently) declares (2.232–33), because it jeopardizes the stability of the army, and therefore of Argos (where Klytaimestra waits). It is significant that Paris expresses his passion for Helen in exactly the same words as those of Zeus for his wife (3.466; cf. 14.446). The consummation with which Book 3 concludes, then, violates the orderly nature of legal marriage which has for its social object the contribution of new individuals to the community.

And so we are prepared for the final outcome of the duel, knowing that in the Iliadic world the sterility of Paris' marriage is one more indication of his inequality to Menelaos. The opposition between the two men is indicated further by Menelaos' unqualified eagerness to risk his own individuality to restore his social context and by Paris' attempt to enjoy a fully-defined status without earning it. Menelaos' marriage was properly fruitful. Because Paris will not risk his own life to maintain his marriage he cannot pass on the gift of life to others.

The image of the bed helps to focus the roles played by Paris and by Menelaos in the thematic pattern of the *Iliad*. In the case of Menelaos a royal community (Sparta) has been disordered by the loss of its queen, both regal mother (whose womb potentially bears the continuation of Menelaos' line) and queenly wife (whose fruitful position by her husband's side represents the stability of the state). Because Agamemnon, the king of kings, is his brother (that is, because of the strength of the fraternal clan relationship), the entire Argive nation is disordered. Recovery of Argive honor necessitates recovery of Spartan honor; the latter, in turn, is equivalent to insuring the physical survival of Menelaos' line. The continued health of society on all levels demands nothing less than the annihilation of the alien Trojan society—since Helen has been made, unnaturally, a part of it. Accordingly, in the case of Paris, the community (Troy) has been disrupted by the introduction of an alien queen and wife. That Helen is not seen as a Trojan mother symbolizes the consequences of a royal figure contracting an adulterous and exogamous alliance. Because Paris is the princely son of Priam, his marriage to Helen is not only sterile in itself, but also suigenocidal: Troy itself is made impotent. In this way the social role of Paris (his familial and political status) is symbolized by his bed.

Paris' role is determined simultaneously by reference to the bond of guest-friendship. The bond itself is based, as I've argued, on the universal human need for familial and political coordinates, whether inherited or constructed; it is made effective precisely because the host possesses the necessary coordinates and can extend the protection and security they insure to his less fortunate guest. For a guest to violate the coordinates of his host, therefore, is for him to jeopardize his own definition—a truly absurd crime that undermines the social order of human existence.

Because of Paris' violation of the guest-friend relationship Menelaos curses all the Trojans. He declares that his authority for doing so is divine, since Zeus protects the relationship (13.620–27) as surely as he protects kings. Menelaos' description of Helen's role in the hospitality only compounds her ambiguity: " 'You who in vanity went away taking with you my wedded / wife, and many possessions, when she had received you in kindness' " (13.626–27). He associates Helen with himself as an injured party; Paris is isolated as the sacrilegiously ungrateful guest.

Hektor's rebuke to Paris enlarges our view of the nature of the crime. He points out that Alexandros' cowardice on the field is very different from the nerve he mustered to abduct Helen: " 'Were you like this that time when in sea-wandering vessels / assembling oarsmen to help you you sailed over the water, / and mixed with the outlanders, and carried away a fair women / from a remote land, whose lord's kin were spearmen and fighters, / to your father a big sorrow, and your city, and all your people, / to yourself a thing shameful but bringing joy to the enemy?' "

(3.46–51). Once again Homer reveals to us the existence of a common human dimension uniting both parties in the war. Both Achaians and Trojans enjoy a self-contained hierarchical social mode of existence which depends, for its autonomy and survival, upon a common respect for endogamy and for the guest-friend relationship. The result of Paris' crime is nothing less than total social dissolution; that is the point of Hektor's detailed analysis of the various hierarchical levels which will be affected by his brother's deed: familial, political, national, and individual (3.50–51).

Although they certainly do not *condone* him—even Hektor says Paris should have been stoned for his deed (3.52–53)—the Trojans stand by him because the very social norms he has dishonored dictate that society must protect the individual who now invokes them, however unnaturally. For Paris is a royal son, Helen both his wife and a guest-friend in Troy. Yet because of this forced concurrence they share the responsibility for their fate.

Paris, in his association with Helen, symbolizes the ambiguity of the human influence on a revolutionary historical development. It may be that he represents the eclipse of a communal consciousness by individualistic interests, the replacement of a familial motivation with a more self-centered heroic aspiration; for if there is a balance in the *Iliad* between these two modes of human life it has been provided only by the poet himself, perhaps composing in an age when a proper perspective of their reciprocal relationship has been restored. In the chaotic world of the *Iliad*, being a man is equivalent to being a *warrior* on one side or another. For until social harmony is reestablished by Helen's return, social interests must control the consciousness of individuals. Agamemnon's selfishness is peculiarly heinous because he is the chief representative of social consciousness; Achilles rightly calls him, as Agamemnon persists in his egocentric attitude, " 'King who feed on your people, since you rule nonentities' " (1.231) and dog-eyed and deer-hearted (1.225) because he doesn't understand the order over which he is supposed to rule (a passage ironically looking forward to the time when Patroklos will direct the same charges at Achilles). And Paris appears similarly, but more consistently, anomalous. While others are fighting with spears and shields, he fights—and ineffectively—with a bow. His efforts to pursue a proper social orientation are emphatically fruitless. While others are engaged in deadly man-to-man combat, he is making love with Helen in his elaborate bed (something Odysseus will do, with Penelope, because he has earned the right). While the beauty of Hektor and of Diomedes is the orderly manifestation of martial valor and virility, that of Paris is associated with an illusory domesticity, with peaceful pleasure, with the boudoir. It is a sterile, sinister beauty because it embodies the disordering of human equilibrium by the gods, or by an excessive devotion to one divine power, or by an improper balance of soul (in that Paris is as much blinded by Aphrodite as Agamemnon says he has been by Delusion, 19.91 ff.).

Paris' actions in Book 3 clearly define his ambivalent character in their paradoxical movement from cowardice to bravery, from defiance to remorse, from dutifulness to irresponsibility, from involvement to detachment, from innocence to guilt, from natural enmity and war to unnatural peace and love. The multiplicity of attitudes and emotions characteristic of Paris is emphasized by their opposition to the singleminded stance of Menelaos.

Aphrodite's Robe

As her womanhood is defined by contrast with that of Andromache, Helen's divinity is brought into focus by reference to the goddess of love and desire who has arranged her marriage with Paris. That is why Helen so easily penetrates the goddess' disguise in Book 3. Helen, after all, knows all about the business of weaving; Aphrodite has chosen, therefore, a peculiarly translucent mask, "likening herself to an aged woman, / a wool-dresser who when she was living in Lakedaimon / made beautiful things out of wool, and loved her beyond all others" (3.386–88). Heroine and goddess are related in the image of the loom, both associated regularly with splendid garments (3.141, 419; 5.315, 424).

Aphrodite seems a determined partisan in her several appearances in the *Iliad*. She rescues Paris from the wrath of Menelaos (3.374 ff.); she guards Hektor's body from the dogs (23.185). Nor is Paris the only Trojan transported from danger to security by her intercession; she performs the same service for Aineias (5.311–18). Aphrodite's active concern for her son in this episode is in contrast to Zeus' reluctant detachment from the fate of Sarpedon, and serves to emphasize the mysteriously unique position of Aineias. When Poseidon rescues him from the onslaught of Achilles (20.330 ff), we learn that Aineias is destined to survive the fall of Troy, and to reestablish the line of Dardanos after Priam's branch of it has perished. Homer's singular reference to the continuity of the Trojan race makes it clear that the forces represented by Aphrodite, in this case through her son, will transcend the contemporary international imbroglio.

But if the portrait of Aineias is extraordinary—showing him suspended from the rigors of the present, for ulterior motives—the ordinary is Aphrodite's unthinking involvement in momentary mortal affairs which symbolizes the total chaos of the human condition in the historical period recorded by Homer's epic. Diomedes attacks and wounds her in Book 5. As his spear passes "through the [ambrosial] / robe that the very Graces had woven for her carefully" (5.337–38), the vulnerability of the invulnerable artifact illustrates the bizarre nature of a physical conflict between gods and mortals. Diomedes' taunt to the wounded goddess marks the irresponsibility of her physical intervention in human affairs: " 'Give way, daughter of Zeus, from the fighting and the terror. It is / not then enough that you lead astray women without warcraft?' " (5.348–49). The present chaos makes Dione recall the primitive ways of the arcane deities who fought with each other physically before Zeus' establishment of conventional order on Olympos (5.373–74).

Aphrodite's character in the *Iliad* is informed by association with this prehistoric chaos; she behaves in the manner of the amorphous Uranian gods, not as a civilized Olympian. Her disorderly willfulness can be judged by her reply to Dione. She sees nothing unnatural in her action on behalf of her beloved son (5.377–78), but instead finds disorder in Diomedes' attempt to thwart her: " 'so now this is no horrible war of Achaians and Trojans, / but the Danaans are beginning to fight even with the immortals' " (5.379–80). It is indeed unusual for men to fight with gods. But desire, unnaturally arranged by a goddess, caused this war (24.30); so the goddess of desire herself is made to taste the physical fruits of human strife, for however brief a moment.

The exception which proves the rule is Aphrodite's relationship with Hera, her immortal mortal enemy, in Book 14. Aphrodite lends the wife of Zeus her girdle of love and desire. Here she is presented behaving with neutrality, in a mode of existence midway between the primeval Uranian chaos and the present disorder. She acts, in other words, in a way that suggests that Zeus' Olympian order controls her behavior. Moreover the disorder prevalent in the Iliadic world has come about precisely because Aphrodite has departed from her neutral position as arbitrary dispenser of desire and love to bestow her passionate gifts with a particular political purpose, based on the fulfillment of her own selfish vanity (to be the recipient of the golden apple, marked "To the fairest," thrown by Strife into the marriage feast of Thetis and Peleus). Love, which by her agency was meant to serve the well-being of all men, has been perverted, by her rewarding of Paris (who chose her promise of beauty over Hera's offer of power, and Athene's of wisdom), to the vainglorious ambitions of the agent goddess herself. Her disorderly intervention is not tragic for her, but it has mortal effects upon men. The gods may consider her wounding by Diomedes or her adultery with Ares laughing matters; but the *Iliad*, like the *Odyssey* (with the matter of

Klytaimestra's adultery), proves that it cannot be taken lightly by mortal men.

Aphrodite's divine role in the *Iliad*, then—like Helen's human role—is a center of paradox: fertility is made barren, birth made death, joy made grief, marriage made funeral; love turns into war, and the origins of a race are combined with racial annihilation. All of these antitheses are revealed in Aphrodite's argument with Helen on the wall in Book 3. Her sexual role is defined in its ambiguity as Homer portrays Aphrodite's movement from the field of war (with Paris) to the bed of love (with Helen). Her actions in Book 3 are witnesses to one of the grandest ironies in the *Iliad*, Zeus' later consolation of the wounded goddess: " 'No, my child, not for you are the works of warfare. Rather / concern yourself only with the lovely secrets of marriage, / while all this shall be left to Athene and sudden Ares' " (5.428–30). What the *Odyssey* makes explicit, the *Iliad* implies: the intimate union of Ares and Aphrodite, war and love. For, as Zeus speaks, Homer has made his audience well aware of the fact that it is precisely because Aphrodite is determined to interfere in human affairs that marriage and war are related vitally in the *Iliad* and cannot be separated. Havoc, not harmony, is Aphrodite's theme.

And it is this disorderly involvement in alien affairs which defines Helen's role in the Iliadic world. Through the manipulation of the goddess, Helen has become, her own will suspended, a passive counter in Aphrodite's effete game. So suspended from that ability to act which is generally associated with heroic character, Helen stands between Aphrodite and her desire.

> 'Strange divinity! Why are you still so stubborn to beguile me?
> Will you carry me further yet somewhere among cities
> fairly settled? In Phrygia or in lovely Maionia?
> Is there some mortal man there also who is dear to you?
> Is it because Menelaos has beaten great Alexandros
> and wishes, hateful even as I am, to carry me homeward,
> is it for this that you stand in your treachery now beside me?
> Go yourself and sit beside him, abandon the gods' way,
> turn your feet back never again to the path of Olympos
> but stay with him forever, and suffer for him, and look after him
> until he makes you his wedded wife, or makes you his slave girl.'

> (3.399–409)

Like every speech Homer gives her, this one expresses the paradox of Helen's character. It opens with a reference to the superhuman status and closes with the subhuman (as slaves were regarded). The tragedy of her being δῖα γυναικῶν *día gunaikōn* ("divine of women") is that Helen may

speak so brazenly, although still ineffectively, to a divinity, revealing as
she speaks her awareness of the profoundly disorderly implications of
Aphrodite's behavior. Helen's suggestion that Aphrodite in person
should fulfill her desire for Paris points up the unnaturalness of the
goddess's intervention in human life. But, as her words also recall
Aphrodite's tryst with Anchises, they further emphasize the goddess's
characteristic selfishness. Using Helen to achieve her satisfaction is
obviously in Aphrodite's greater interest since she may thereby enjoy
involvement and pretend aloofness at the same time. As for Helen, she
sees herself hopelessly ensnared in an inexplicable fate. Like a virus,
indeterminably chemical or organic, Helen can't be defined as goddess
or as woman, as proper wife or as slave-girl, as Argive or as Trojan. She
can be defined only by the disorderly effect of her presence in the body
politic. The desire to resolve her human identity which Helen expresses
here, her wish to return to Sparta, cannot countermand the purpose
Aphrodite has in mind for her; that is, that she return to the bed of Paris,
to become anew, for the duration of the poem, Helen of Troy—in a poetic
reenactment of her original crime. Against Helen's inclination toward
order Aphrodite reasserts Helen's fateful affinity with disorder, enforcing her tragically ambiguous definition in the poem's world. When
Pandaros' arrow, ending the truce, shows him the role of a new Paris, it is
Helen herself who must play the part of Helen.

For Aphrodite here betrays the effect of her divine ambition on Helen's
character: to make the woman as confused in orientation as she herself
is—a goddess who loves a man, an Achaian who loves a Trojan. Homer
will not allow Helen to escape the ambiguity of her mythic character, and
strengthens her entrapment by emphasizing the ambiguity of Aphrodite. So Aphrodite's callous warning proves that Helen's disobedience to
her would offer no amelioration of her status: " 'Wretched girl, do not
tease me lest in anger I forsake you / and grow to hate you as much as
now I terribly love you, / lest I encompass you in hard hate, caught
between both sides, / Danaans and Trojans alike, and you wretchedly
perish' " (3.414–17). There can be no reply to such divine illogic, since
the position Aphrodite threatens to impose scarcely differs from Helen's
present one. Helen makes no rebuttal. Homer tells us only that she is
frightened (3.418), perhaps by the irrevocable absurdity of her fate,
perhaps by a sudden sense that the goddess is inside her—Helen calls
her δαιμόνιη *daimoníē* ("demon"), the only time Homer uses the term
(later used by Socrates to discuss the personal god that possessed him) to
mean a particular divinity (3.399, 420)—and there is nothing she can do.
There is an element of force in Aphrodite's threat which doesn't fail to
impress Helen. It is true that the goddess' indeed terrible love has

trapped Helen symbolically already between both sides. There remains to her, however, both an immediate and a transcendent hope for definition. She may still, as a guest and royal wife, invoke the protection of Priam. Aphrodite can coerce Helen by threatening to deprive her of this single vestige of contemporary identity. But a more significant, and more desperate, hope is that Helen may be defined in the song of men to come as the woman who bore her enigmatic burden to the end, who did not shirk from confronting the absurdity of her ambiguous status among men. To realize this transcendent definition, Helen must allow herself to remain the symbol of the present conflict. So Aphrodite succeeds in making Helen cling to her tenuous contemporary definition, to remain a pseudo-Trojan, to allow gods and fate rather than only men to determine her final identity.

At the same time that Aphrodite reinforces Helen's connection with Paris and with Troy, the goddess's role is related to Helen's artistry. When Aphrodite takes Helen away from her visionary perspective on the wall, she is proving that the creation of Helen's loom is once again an accurate reflection of reality. Another divine agent, Iris, had interrupted Helen's weaving because its art was on the verge of becoming inaccurate; because of the arrangement of the duel, men were no longer fighting collectively as Trojans and Achaians. With the failure of the duel, however, the fighting will be renewed, the weaving once more accurate. Because Paris has escaped the consequences of manly combat, Achaians and Trojans will fight again on the plain for Helen's sake. That Aphrodite returns her not to the loom but to the bed of Paris suggests the primacy of the latter in Homer's causal association of the two artifacts. The disorder of the bed is the reason for the war which the loom records. As the duel and sacred truce to bring an orderly peace fail, the Trojan War starts again, from a new beginning. Homer stresses the drama of this moment—especially crucial in a poem which doesn't report the actual beginning of the war—by presenting the bedding-down of Helen and Paris. The image of their bed underlies Homer's version of the Trojan War story, just as Briseis' bed is the implicit central image of the wrath-story. Paris and Helen enact, in the final scene of Book 3, Aphrodite's own predilection for sexual alliances that show no care for order—with the widest of thematic implications and the deepest of paradoxical connotations.

Helen and Her Galaxy: 2

Priam Brings Gifts

Each time Priam appears in the *Iliad* his characteristic ambivalence, forged by the decline of Troy, is made apparent. The artifact-images that identify Priam as a member of the galaxy of disorder are those of the house and robes. All members of Helen's galaxy display an ambivalent orientation in one way or another: Paris is characteristically torn between individual and communal modes of action; Aphrodite, between divine and human, Olympian and Uranian. The ambiguity of Priam's character is determined by the opposition between his inclination to pursue a purely familial, paternal role and his responsibility as the nominal head of the Trojan hierarchy. The first significant reference to him is Menelaos' demand that, for the arrangement of the truce and the terms of the duel, the Trojans must " 'Bring, that he may seal the pledges, the strength of Priam: / Priam himself, for his sons are outrageous, not to be trusted' " (3. 105–6). From Menelaos' perspective Priam is regarded as the one valid spokesman for Trojan society. In this sense he is parallel to Agamemnon. Yet there is a proleptic irony in Menelaos' reference to Priam's "strength." As the outcome of the duel (Paris' unheroic escape) and of the truce (Pandaros' ignominious deed) will soon prove, that strength is insufficient to enforce the kingly authority with which it is associated.

Priam's kingship is weak for two reasons: the inevitable debility of his old age; and, related to this, the outrageousness of his sons. Troy's present jeopardy has come about because Priam was unable to prevent the disruptively selfish action of Paris. Pandaros' deed, moreover, suggests that Priam's ineffectiveness as a father to Paris is general—related directly to his political ineffectiveness. His sacred personal pledge does not bind the Trojans. Ideally it should; actually it cannot. Menelaos' statement, therefore, offers a framework for interpreting the ambivalence of Priam's character. As long as circumstances demand that he maintain kingship and fatherhood simultaneously, because of Paris' disorderly act, Priam cannot function effectively. The maintenance of both roles requires a division of his loyalties. Whereas Hektor and Paris, each in his own way, may be able to endure an ambivalent existence, Priam is not. That is the pathos of his situation. When paternal instinct conflicts with kingly responsibility, the royal role is slighted. Only when he relinquishes that role entirely does Priam find the potential for glorious deeds that he enjoyed as a youth.

The disorder at the heart of things in the Iliadic world makes it impossible for Priam to maintain effectively what should be his primary role as the head of Trojan society. Only Hektor's life stands between Priam's kingship and regression to a purely familial mode of existence. As long as Hektor lives, Priam remains king; Troy can survive as a society intact. But when its bulwark topples, Troy must cease to exist, leaving Priam no active recourse but a parental response. Priam's greatness in the poem is that he finds nobility and renewed effectiveness in pursuing that more basic human course—nobility he could not achieve as a king because his own princely son, Paris, had undermined the foundations of his kingship. The artifact-images associated with Priam bring focus to the process by which his societal identity disintegrates until Priam is defined, in the end, simply as a father.

Thematically the most important exchange of gifts in the *Iliad* is that initiated by Priam to win back the body of his heroic son.

> He spoke, and lifted back the fair covering of his clothes-chest
> and from inside took out twelve robes surpassingly lovely
> and twelve mantles to be worn single, as many blankets,
> as many great white cloaks, also the same number of tunics.
> He weighed and carried out ten full talents of gold, and brought forth
> two shining tripods, and four cauldrons, and brought out a goblet
> of surpassing loveliness that the men of Thrace had given him
> when he went to them with a message, but now the old man spared not
> even this in his halls, so much was it his heart's desire
> to ransom back his beloved son.
>
> (24. 227–36)

Certainly we are impressed with the Trojan king's wealth; his was the kind of royal treasure room that might have included a Maionian cheekpiece. Not far from our thoughts, perhaps, is the suppliant who appeared at the opening of the poem with "gifts beyond count" (1. 13).

If we associate this imagistic context with others in which the ransom-artifacts are mentioned, we see that the enumeration here effectively produces a *general* impression of richness. When he presents the gifts to Achilles, Priam proves that his generosity is no less than that of

Chryses: " 'I bring you gifts beyond number' " (24. 502). Neither Priam, nor Achilles, nor Homer means to put a specific price on Hektor's head; important only is the magnificence of the gifts: " 'Accept the ransom / we bring you, which is great. You may have joy of it' " (24. 555–56). Automedon and Alkimos "from the smooth-polished mule wagon / lifted out the innumerable spoils for the head of Hektor'" (24. 578–79). Twice, then, the traditional formula quietly underlines the unstinting largesse of Priam's offering.

There is no doubt in Achilles' mind that the proffered ransom is appropriately grand. He pleads with the spirit of Patroklos to understand why he returned Hektor, " 'for the ransom he gave me was not unworthy' " (24. 594). Yet were it not for the symbolic function of these artifacts Achilles' consideration of the ransom might seem disconcerting, especially when we recall the mighty list of gifts presented by Agamemnon's ambassadors in Book 9 but rejected by Achilles. Here it is nothing materialistic which influences him, which incites his mercy; only that Priam, unlike Agamemnon in Book 9, has humbled himself before Achilles and has recognized the hero's values as transcendent of the feudal spoils-system which limits Agamemnon's vision. The ransom, then, symbolizes what the Myrmidon king admires in his guest-suppliant: coming to his tent as a stranger, Priam has willingly separated himself from the context by which he is defined in the Iliadic world. It is not the national leader Achilles hosts now, but a father like his own. Priam has reduced his own definition, so to speak, to a more basic human level. For a king to do this is great-hearted indeed.

> 'How could you dare to come alone to the ships of the Achaians
> and before my eyes, when I am one who have killed in such numbers
> such brave sons of yours? The heart in you is iron. Come, then,
> and sit down upon this chair, and you and I will even let
> our sorrows lie still in the heart for all our grieving. There is not
> any advantage to be won from grim lamentation.
> Such is the way the gods spun life for unfortunate mortals,
> that we live in unhappiness.'
>
>   (24. 519–26)

Achilles' generalization about the status of mankind (24. 525–26) acutely expresses his awareness of the social sacrifice entailed by Priam's appearance before him; it also recalls Glaukos' pessimistic simile, just as this exchange of gifts reflects the earlier one. The common nature of their grief here transcends Achaian and Trojan distinctions, as an essentially human emotion which transforms their enmity into a truly universal brotherhood. The chair upon which Priam now sits is very different from his accustomed one in the citadel; yet it is even more glorious.

The exchange between Priam and Achilles, then, is evenly balanced not through any materialistic evaluation, but because it represents one iron heart revealing its basic humanity to another, abandoning "heroic" honor. That Priam has given his all in the bargain is also suggested by Homer's description of the "goblet / of surpassing loveliness" (24. 233–34)—the one artifact in the inventory treated with significant elaboration. The goblet symbolizes the wholeheartedness of Priam's offering; for it is associated with the old king's heroic identity. Like the cup in the halls of Diomedes, the Thracian artifact here is mnemonic externalization of Priam's personality. Yet he gladly includes it with the other treasures, "so much was it his heart's desire to ransom back his beloved son" (24.236–37). Referring to him as ὁ γέρον *ho gérōn* ("the old man") Homer emphasizes even more strongly the quality of Priam's sacrifice. The implication is that Priam is now too old actively to engage in deeds that might merit such beautiful and individualizing trophies. Relinquishing the physical proof of his former prowess is a poignant gesture; he sets aside his former heroic identity. Yet that gesture alone wins for him the most desirable trophy: the body of his son in exchange.

Achilles' gesture is equally powerful. When Automedon and Alkimos are delegated to unload the wagon's treasure, they "left inside it two great cloaks and a fine-spun tunic to shroud the corpse in" (24. 580–81). The gesture reasserts the supraoccasional value of the ransom artifacts, showing that Achilles' motivation is anything but materialistic (recalling the narrator's comment about Glaukos' exchange). His generous gesture symbolizes the essentially human communication between the two men. When the body of Hektor returns to its proper social context, its bier in Troy, it will be accompanied by a token of Achilles' own identity—a voluntary return to Troy of things that were his in the first place. He is merciful to Priam not as an Achaian, but simply as a man. By presenting us with this reverse exchange Homer has sharpened our awareness of the symbolic pattern previously seen in the exchanges between Aias and Hektor, Glaukos and Diomedes.

Hekabe's actions in Book 6 parallel Priam's in Book 24, but with a very different outcome. Helenos advises Hektor to bid his mother offer from her " 'sacred chamber . . . a robe, which seems to her the largest and loveliest / in the great house, and that which is far her dearest possession' " (6. 89–91), to Athene in her temple, that the goddess may hold back the onslaught of Diomedes. His counsel suggests, as does Priam's catalogue of treasures in Book 24, that the suppliant must be willing to sacrifice his all. Hektor repeats the instructions of Helenos verbatim to his mother (6. 271–72). The "largest and loveliest" robe which is "far her dearest possession," then, symbolizes generally the wholehearted nature of the propitiatory gift. But as he describes Hekabe's action itself, the poet makes the artifact both more specifically symbolic (functionally appropriate to Hekabe in this particular situation), and more explicitly associated with the central theme of the epic (by the artifact's connection with Paris and Helen).

Instead of another verbatim repetition, Homer elaborates the formulaic pattern:

> she descended into the fragrant store-chamber.
> There lay the elaborately wrought robes, the work of Sidonian
> women, whom Alexandros himself, the godlike, had brought home
> from the land of Sidon, crossing the wide sea, on that journey
> when he brought back also gloriously descended Helen.
> Hekabe lifted out one and took it as gift to Athene,
> that which was the loveliest in design and the largest,
> and shone like a star. It lay beneath the others.
>
> (6. 288–95)

Although these lines, considered as a unit, are unique in the *Iliad*, they closely resemble those in the *Odyssey* which describe Helen's choice of a robe for Telemachos. Sidon is mentioned in both passages, suggesting yet another connection between Paris and Menelaos by reference to Helen. *Iliad* 6. 288 and *Odyssey* 15. 99 differ only with respect to gender; and lines 6.294–95 are identical with *Odyssey* 15.107–8, where the robe is portrayed as being extraordinary because it was made by Helen herself. But the resemblance between the two passages, compared with the particular discrepancies, only reasserts the fact that Homer, like a tailor, often customizes standard patterns. The identical lines, in the *Odyssey*, relate the special quality of the robe to the mystery of Helen's creative character; in the *Iliad*, to the suppliant role that Hekabe is enacting. The particularization is seen in the simple formulaic substitutions by which the lines preceding the identical ones are differentiated:

> τῶν ἕν' ἀεφαμένη Ἐλένη φέρε, δία γυναικῶν,
> τῶν ἕν' ἀειραμένη Ἑκάβη φέρε δῶρον Ἀθήνῃ,
> tôn hén' aeiraménē Hēlenē phére, día gunaikôn (*Odyssey* 15.106)
> tôn hén' aeiraménē Hekābē phére dôron Athéne (*Iliad* 6. 293)
> And Helen, shining among women, lifted out one of them
> Hekabe lifted out one and took it as a gift to Athene

The Odyssean line introduces the robe by reference to the mysterious nature of its maker. But the Iliadic line suggests the way in which the robe defines the suppliant role Hekabe is playing—by proceeding to the goddess who comprises the other half of that relationship.

In each case, therefore, the artifact becomes an individualizing mechanism, here by symbolizing Hekabe's supplication. The robe is simultaneously, and on two levels of symbolic association, a mnemonic device: within the framework of the fictive world it is a concrete token, by the narrator's reference to its origins, of the fateful abduction; within the framework of the poem it functions mnemonically to recall to the audience the regular association of Paris and of Helen with robes. Homer insists upon the mnemonic force possessed by the artifact-image on this occasion; for the failure of Hekabe's supplication is caused by her unmindfulness of an object's power to inspire recollection. "Pallas Athene turned her head from her" (6. 311). The narrator need not explain the goddess' reaction; the artifact itself displays the reason for it: the robe, because of its origins and associations, only serves to remind Athene of why she hates Troy in the first place.

Hekabe's action in this episode, then, though it resembles Priam's in Book 24, is distinguished from his by its unsuccessful outcome. Yet there is an even more basic difference between the two supplications. The differing results of their actions can be explained by the fact that each suppliant is acting on a different level of hierarchical motivation. Hekabe is playing a queenly role in Book 6, as a representative of the πόλις *pólis* ("city"), the communal form of human existence for which she is responsible; she prays that Athene will defend, against Diomedes, " 'the town of Troy, and the Trojan wives, and their innocent children' " (6. 310), and her gesture is unacceptable precisely because it is a social one; for the robe symbolizes everything Athene opposes *politically*. Because her divine opposition, moreover, is destined to succeed in destroying Troy as a political entity, the primary representatives of that society, Priam and Hekabe, must be ineffective *when they act from social motivations*. Priam, on the other hand, succeeds in his mission because he acts on the familial, paternal level only. In Book 24 the robes symbolize the exchange of social (Trojan) disorder for social (Achaian) order. What Paris stole unnaturally from Argos is now returned for the life of Hektor which Achilles took naturally, and precisely *because* Paris had taken the robes and Helen.

Priam's house has a similar symbolic function, in this case a function derived from physical description and from dramatic position in the narrative rather than from mnemonic or historical import. Whereas the poet's employment of the robe-image demonstrated "the law of narrative relevance," Homer's attention to the palace of Priam displays the striking effect that can be achieved when that law is suspended. When Hektor

comes to instruct Hekabe about the offering of the robe, we are given a
seemingly gratuitous description of the royal palace:

> Now he entered the wonderfully built palace of Priam.
> This was fashioned with smooth-stone cloister walks, and within it
> were embodied fifty sleeping chambers of smoothed stone
> built so as to connect with each other; and within these slept
> each beside his own wedded wife, the sons of Priam.
> In the same inner court on the opposite side, to face these,
> lay the twelve close smooth-stone sleeping chambers of his daughters
> built so as to connect with each other; and within these slept,
> each by his own modest wife, the lords of the daughters of Priam.
>
> (6. 242–50)

Priam's palace has no critical part in the story, no immediate literal
function. Yet, by presenting it so artistically, Homer insures that the
palace plays a definite symbolic role. The image of Paris' house acts
simultaneously on the immediate and on the transcendent thematic
levels, and provides what might be called a technical norm. More
comparable to Priam's is the house of Poseidon, "built in the waters'
depth, glittering with gold, imperishable forever" (13. 21–22). Here the
artifact, with its watery environment, is presented as being specifically
appropriate to the sea-god; but it has no "higher" symbolic
implications—its significance lies on the immediate narrative level only.

By contrast with the sketchy reference to Poseidon's house, the presentation of Priam's palace is an imagistic device with wide-ranging symbolic significance. The images achieve this impact through the elaboration of detail, and because of the description's peculiar emphasis proceeding rapidly from the general whole (6. 242) to the particular parts
Homer means to isolate for the attention of his audience: the connecting
walks (6. 242, 245, 249) and the bedrooms which they connect (6. 243–50).
The visualization of the house-artifact, remarkable for what it neglects as
well as for what it emphasizes, impresses us with the stability (a
specifically sexual, marital, familial equilibrium) of the household—and,
because this is the royal household, of the πόλις *pólis* ("city") as a social
entity (of the Troadic hierarchy itself). Priam's palace is, therefore, an
image of things as they should be, when society is well-established
because of the harmonious interrelationship of its various levels. As such
the image of the house reflects the orderliness of the peaceful scenes on
Achilles' shield.

But the impression created by this description of the palace is made
thematically forceful only by juxtaposition with other contexts which
reveal the stability it symbolizes to be illusory and unrealistic. Priam's

speech in Book 24 reveals that equality among his sons is only ideal and is unrealized in fact. But imagistically the equality is already undermined in Book 6. For subsequent to the description of Priam's palace is that of Hektor's and of Paris'. The two most important sons, the most consequential individuals in Troy, have separate abodes; and their personalized residences suggest why the stability of Priam's house is itself in jeopardy. The physical separation of each house from the hierarchically constituted household of the king is an imagistic parallel to the fact that Hektor and, more drastically, Paris are dissociated from the social harmony by their attitudes. Paris has, in effect, replaced a balanced social perspective with an unnatural individualistic one. His behavior has caused Hektor's conflict of interests, between familial and political loyalties. Counting on his audience to remember each context in which the house is visualized, the poet implies that the unity of Priam's palace is only an apparent one. The unity symbolized by the artifact in this scene, like the strength of Priam's kingship, is, lamentably, a thing of the past. The only kind of domestic unity established now in Troy is disorderly and artificially contrived: the unity symbolized by the bedding-down of Paris and Helen.

Priam appears in person for the first time with Helen on the Trojan wall. After the elders of the city have expressed their wonder at Helen's beauty, they conclude that, nevertheless, she should be returned to Argos for the trouble she has brought Troy. But Priam, regally disdaining even to address a reprimand to them, reaffirms his determination to protect her: " 'Come over where I am, dear child, and sit down beside me, / to look at your husband of time past, your friends and your people. / I am not blaming you: to me the gods are blameworthy / who drove upon me this sorrowful war against the Achaians. / So you could tell me the name of this man who is so tremendous. . . .' " (3. 162–66). In a merely logical sense, this vision of the king himself sheltering the individual who embodies disaster for his royal domain implies weakness. But Homer's art consistently complements the inner logic of his world with reminders of the continuity of human nature striving to transcend events that threaten its orderly environment. This is what makes the *Iliad* realistically human, tragically authentic. The relationship between Priam and Helen is defined, then, only from the semidetached perspective of the poet whose view is both within the created world and within the real world of the audience.

Priam, in this scene, is portrayed as attempting to sustain the royal role with a gentleness and vigor unaccommodated to the precariousness of his tenure. He directs his attempt to the very social institution which, dishonored by Paris, first precipitated, in its disintegration, the inevitable dissolution of all other social bonds: the guest-friend relationship. It is in the role of a securely-based and self-assured royal host that he would offer the comfort of a socially defined position to this vulnerable guest. Priam knows that Helen is not personally responsible for her presence in Troy, that the gods have intervened to compel her unhappy deed. Maybe it is because he so rises above the consequences of present events that Priam cannot function as a king to protect his city.

Perhaps the seduction of old age by youthful beauty ("dear child" 3. 162) explains Priam's grand but ultimately futile gesture toward Helen. Or perhaps Homer meant the explanation to reside in Priam's last, most touching, efforts to play the king—to protect the sacred institutions which insure social order. Yet here there is already the suggestion that Priam is reverting to a mode of action which will become definitively paternal. He loves Helen because she is the wife of his son; his reference to her Achaian lord as a "husband of time past" (3. 163) proves that Priam has accepted her, without reservation, into his own family. His motives for defending Helen, then, are identical with those of Menelaos for accomplishing her return. Priam and Helen are allied by reference to the two most essentially human bonds: that of fatherhood and that of guest-friendship.

Helen is even more intricately involved in defining Priam's role than these general considerations suggest. He calls upon her to provide him with a catalogue of Argive identities (3. 166 ff.), as if he wished to be introduced beforehand to the warriors he will soon be asked to meet in the field. His request is structurally significant, part of Homer's charac-terization of Helen, and at the same time a reconfirmation of Priam's character and role. For Helen's identification of the more important Danaan heroes is the fourth and final element in a remarkable hysteron proteron which, considered in its entirety, reveals the distinction that exists between Trojans and Achaians specifically with respect to the warrior-king relationship. Book 2 concludes with the catalogues of Argives and of Trojans, in that order; the armies are marshaled by Agamemnon and by Hektor. Before introducing Priam himself in Book 3, Homer abruptly lists the elderly statesmen who sit beside the king on the wall (3. 146 ff.). First, then, we see all the Achaians and all the Trojans; then, the most important Trojan counselors and the most outstanding Achaian fighters (as Helen identifies them). Now we understand the critical distinction. In Argos there is no division between ruler and fighter, king and combatant; Agamemnon himself musters and leads his army. Priam's address to Agamemnon from the wall indicates his own awareness of this distinction between their roles; he calls Agamemnon "blessed, child of fortune and favour" (3. 182) because the Greek king himself is able to command his men in the engagement. In Priam's eyes it is the mere presence of Agamemnon, sharing the physical danger of battle, that unifies Argos, making society and its protecting army synonymous. On the other side, as Homer explicitly remarks (3. 151), it is Priam's misfortune that old age dictates for Troy a separation of powers. Speakers of words there are not doers of deeds. Priam heads the council but Hektor must lead the troops.

The contrast between Priam and Agamemnon is evident, too, in the speeches made by both kings at the arrangement of the truce. Agamemnon's prayer to Zeus concludes with his promise that "I myself shall fight" (3. 290), proving his ability and willingness to enact the role of the warrior-king. But Priam's words imply a weakness which, although related to the ordinary pressures of old age, goes beyond them. For despite his equally insistent age, Nestor would never say, as Priam does, " 'Now I am going away to windy Ilion, homeward, / since I cannot look with these eyes on the sight of my dear son / fighting against warlike Menelaos in single combat. / Zeus knows—maybe he knows—and the rest of the gods immortal / for which of the two death is appointed to end this matter' " (3. 305–9). Nestor is capable of action still because he, unlike Priam, belongs to an orderly society. For Priam the weakness in his eyes is connected with the weakness in his line—the inability of Paris to accept responsibility for his crime. It is as if Priam knows that his unruly son must bow before the orderly nature and position of Menelaos. Yet his speech also suggests that Priam consciously chooses a paternal role as alternative to his deteriorating kingly position. He refers to Paris here as "my dear son" (3. 306), as though to console himself by redefining the destroyer of political stability in a purely filial context.

Finally the concluding lines of Priam's speech (3. 308–9) reveal his total inability to find an effective mode of glorious action that would reconcile his royal and paternal responsibilities. Action becomes noble when a hero finds within himself the determination to engage in socially-beneficial deeds despite his awareness of the indeterminable influence of the gods. Finding uncertainty even in divine intervention, Priam can approach nobility only by honestly admitting his passive kingship, by openly preferring to pursue paternal motivations. Because while Hektor lives, and Priam is still a king, he must allow the duel to take place; his communal responsibility prevents his disapproval. But as a father he refuses to watch it; he cannot bear to see the outcome. Homer makes a point of narrating Priam's return to Troy when he might, as he does so often, have forgotten him in the onrush of events. The poet will not allow Priam in battle.

The king can find sanctuary in fatherhood only because Hektor is there to take his place. Hektor remains to officiate the duel—Hektor, that is, "the son of Priam" (3. 314). Without Hektor Priam can continue to play the role of father only by abandoning his claim to kingship. Hektor is at his most valiant when he confronts Achilles. From the wall, "the aged Priam was the first of all whose eyes saw him" (22.25). The image of vision, so often associated with Priam, is here strikingly paradoxical. In contrast with his physical debility, connected with Priam's royal role, is the sharpness of his paternal vision. He is the first to see Hektor. Wanting, above all, to preserve his family intact, while yet hoping to protect his city, Priam calls to Hektor with strange and ominous logic. He recognizes that Hektor is the single force remaining between life and death for Troy; his royal role demands that he apply this force.

But because he knows that the end of Troy is predestined, the king is hesitant to deploy his last resource since that will result in his family's ruin as well. Priam's hesitancy is expressed in a most ambiguous invocation of social and personal values. The result is a moving lament for the death of a city, a people, a family, and of a king who is also a father:

> 'Come then inside the wall, my child, so that you can rescue
> the Trojans and the women of Troy, neither win the high glory
> for Peleus' son, and yourself be robbed of your very life. Oh, take
> pity on me, the unfortunate still alive, still sentient
> but ill-starred, whom the father, Kronos' son, on the threshold of old age
> will blast with hard fate, after I have looked upon evils
> and seen my sons destroyed and my daughters dragged away captive
> and the chambers of marriage wrecked and the innocent children taken
> and dashed to the ground in the hatefulness of war, and the wives
> of my sons dragged off by the accursed hands of the Achaians.
> And myself last of all, my dogs in front of my doorway
> will rip me raw, after some man with stroke of the sharp bronze
> spear, or with spearcast, has torn the life out of my body;
> those dogs I raised in my halls to be at my table, to guard my
> gates, who will lap my blood in the savagery of their anger
> and then lie down in my courts.'
>
> (22. 56–71)

Priam's purpose would seem to be the postponement of the final reckoning. His request—it has not the strength of a command—of Hektor is proven unrealistic by the fact that the imagined consequences of the warrior's return to Troy are unrealizable. Hektor does indeed symbolize the security of the city; but his symbolic role depends upon his acting in the present; without actually fighting he cannot remain the symbol of Trojan stability. Hektor's return would be unheroic retreat. Priam's advice is therefore quite unkingly, and this speech marks the process by which his royal stance dissolves first to a paternal, then to a merely personal, motivation. As a king he must make the ultimate sacrifice—Hektor's death—for his people. As a father, because he knows it will be made in vain, he shrinks from doing so.

As in the scene with Helen here Priam is portrayed as the observer—by the reference to his eyes and to the visions they will behold (22.60–61; cf. 24. 244–45). Priam perceives the relationship between the city's disruption and the inevitably simultaneous dissolution of the family. He communicates his perception through the image of the marriage chambers in his palace (22. 62). The house of Priam is thereby acknowledged as a symbol of unity at the same time as it is revealed in its true chaotic condition. Knowing that the loss of Hektor will strip him of his royalty (since then the city will fall), Priam fears it will deprive him of his paternal role as well (since his children will be scattered). He will be left, he knows, to face death as an isolated individual, undefined by the natural social coordinates of human existence (22. 66 ff.). The image of the ungrateful dogs is the final, total symbolic inversion of institutional well-being and identity. Priam is now a stranger; the dogs are his inhuman hosts.

Since the confusion in the Iliadic world affects even the animal kingdom, as this image of the dogs makes clear, it may be useful to pause here long enough to trace in detail Homer's equal-handed and characteristically thorough attention to the subhuman realm. Doing so, we discover that the disorder prevalent among gods and men is reflected in the animal kingdom—and not by coincidence. When the orderly truce between Achaians and Trojans breaks down in Book 3 through the intervention of Aphrodite, Homer leaves us with the image of furious Menelaos, ranging "like a wild beast up and down the host, to discover / whether he could find anywhere godlike Alexandros" (3. 449–50). Simile and epithet refer to animal and divine life, but human order has failed (precisely because of an interfering divinity) and men, as a result, are maddened and made less than human. So extraordinary is the wrath of Achilles as he arms himself, finally, to reenter the battle, that his faithful horse, Xanthos (empowered by a goddess, Hera) prophesies his master's death (19. 405 ff.). The confusion of living kingdoms continues when Achilles, confronting Aineias in his rage, is compared to

> a lion against him,
> the baleful beast, when men have been straining to kill him, the country
> all in the hunt, and he at the first pays them no attention
> but goes his way, only when someone of the impetuous young men
> has hit him with the spear he whirls, jaws open, over his teeth foam

breaks out, and in the depth of his chest the powerful heart groans;
he lashes his own ribs with his tail and the flanks on both sides
as he rouses himself to fury for the fight, eyes glaring,
and hurls himself straight onward on the chance of killing some one
of the men, or else being killed himself in the first onrush.

(20. 164–73)

No human comparison is adequate at the point when, possessed by emotions that serve the ordering force of Zeus himself, Achilles reinserts himself into society to change the course of history.

We can more fully focus our critical appreciation of Homer's treatment of animals by considering references to dogs throughout the poem, traced by my student Doug Lohmar. The dogs of the *Iliad* are not the faithful, long-suffering pets (like Argos, who waits to see Odysseus home again before he dies) nor the artificial supernatural hounds (created by Hephaistos to guard the palace of Alkinoös) of the peacetime *Odyssey*. Instead they are the derelicts and scavengers of the battlefield, whose mere presence constantly warns the warriors of the necessity for heroic self-defense—and for social cooperation to protect their dead bodies from the hunger of these animals, more wolves than dogs. Dogs appear in the opening lines of the poem, when Homer outlines the repercussions of Achilles' wrath, that "hurled in their multitudes to the house of Hades strong souls / of heroes, but gave their bodies to be the delicate feasting / of dogs, of all birds, and the will of Zeus was accomplished" (1. 3–5). The eery combination of human, divine, and animal orders so early in the epic foreshadows Homer's theme of order and disorder; if men are inhuman (as Achilles, sulking, clearly is, by Patroklos's own accusation, 16. 34–36) Zeus feeds them to animals. And the animals are ready to eat; wild dogs roam around the battlefield, disposing of the bodies of the slain who could not be given honorable burials. These scavengers may have been brought with the Achaians, either as hunting dogs or as camp pets, when they came to Troy; they are the first object of Apollo's fatal arrow (1. 50). But, as Priam's speech indicates, they are also household pets in Troy, watchdogs who guard the doorway (22. 66), at least until the master is dead. The guest-host relationship extends even to the canine level; the dogs are the guests of their human host, receiving their domestic identity from him.

When a dog's master dies, the dog, like a man in a similar situation, has two alternatives: he can find a new host, thereby establishing a new identity (as Andromache does with Hektor, or Patroklos with Achilles); or he can become a nameless wanderer, drifting between the camps. In either case, the dog must eat. Those that found new hosts would be fed by them; the others would have to find food on their own. And freshly killed meat was plentiful on the Trojan plain. The bloody horror of that plain comes home in Priam's prediction of his own fate (22. 65–70, quoted above). Similarly the disorderly slaying of Patroklos by Hektor is expressed by a reference to Hektor's dishonorable treatment of his noble foe's body, which he drags off to give to "the dogs of Troy" (17. 127). Hektor, then, is not altogether blameless for the unhappy fate that befalls him in the poem; he lapses in his adherence to the code of honor that Achilles, before his fight with Agamemnon, illustrated in his courteous treatment of the vanquished Eëtion (5. 416–20). Hektor should have given Patroklos an honorable burial, as Achilles did Andromache's royal father, and as Achilles allowed Priam to do for Hektor himself. When we contrast Hektor's inhuman behavior here with his otherwise orderly comportment, we realize that he, like Achilles in Books 19–22, has allowed himself to be possessed by the spirit of battle—the delusion that makes him at least partly responsible for his own tragic death. The image of dogs rending Patroklos' body, in fact, is used by Iris to rouse Achilles into action, even before his divine armor is finished (18. 179–80); at the behest of the messenger-goddess sent by Hera, and with the aegis instantly provided by Athene, Achilles goes to the ditch and howls his anguish and hate across to the Trojans who have dehumanized the war by Hektor's threat (18. 205 ff). When the new armor is delivered by Thetis, we are not surprised to find that dogs are depicted on it—hounds who are afraid of the lions (18. 580)—and that Priam sees the shield advancing fatally against Hektor, "like that star / which comes on in the autumn and whose conspicuous brightness / far outshines the stars that are numbered in the night's darkening, / the star they give the name of Orion's Dog, which is brightest / among the stars, and yet is wrought as a sign of evil" (22. 26–30). The old man groans aloud to see Dog-Star-like Achilles (who is crossing the space between the armies exactly like one of the ravenous wild dogs), answering Achilles' earlier doglike howl at the ditch, grief for grief (22. 33); and Priam's keen vision must comprehend the fatal irony of the starlike hero who carries a shield displaying the star itself upon its shining surface. So the speech begging Hektor to return within the wall begins and ends with the image of the dog.

At their previous confrontation, which ended when Apollo rescued Hektor in a cloud, Achilles had even called the Trojan "dog" (20. 449), an epithet appropriate not only because of Hektor's implied cowardice of the moment, but also because of his declared plan for Patroklos' body (and the disorderly pride motivating that plan)—and, in an even wider sense, because of Hektor's basically disorderly role in the world of the poem, as the bulwark of a guilty city (recalling that Achilles also calls Agamemnon "dog" (1. 225), when he wants to point to the king's antisocial behavior). The animal imagery dominates their final meeting, too. First, Achilles refused Hektor's plea for an agreement about the disposition of his body (22. 261–65), responding to the Trojan's prior lack of humanity with an even stronger, because intentional, rejection of human brotherhood:

> 'Hektor, argue me no agreements. I cannot forgive you.
> As there are no trustworthy oaths between men and lions,
> nor wolves and lambs have spirit that can be brought to agreement
> but forever these hold feelings of hate for each other,
> so there can be no love between you and me, nor shall there be
> oaths between us, but one or the other must fall before then
> to glut with his blood Ares the god who fights under the shield's guard.'
>
> (22. 261–67)

Hektor's sin against Patroklos will be repaid in kind—but not human kind. Achilles here is conscious brute force. The dog-image returns as Achilles taunts the dying Hektor with his stupidity in thinking he could treat Patroklos inhumanly without retaliation: " 'O fool, for an avenger was left, far greater than he was, / behind him and away by the hollow ships. And it was I; / and I have broken your strength; on you the dogs and the vultures / shall feed and foully rip you; the Achaians will bury Patroklos' " (22. 333–36). Hektor's response is strangely akin to the persuasive argument used by Patroklos against Achilles' isolation, in Book 22, when he had accused the Myrmidon king of being inhuman, without mother or father; " 'I entreat you, by your life, by your knees, by your parents, / do not let the dogs feed on me by the ships of the Achaians' " (22. 338–39). Achilles' retort expresses the excess of his wrath in cannibalistic brutality:

> 'No more entreating of me, you dog, by knees or parents.
> I wish only that my spirit and fury would drive me
> to hack your meat away and eat it raw for the things that
> you have done to me. So there is no one who can hold the dogs off
> from your head, not if they bring here and set before me ten times
> and twenty times the ransom, and promise more in addition,
> not if Priam son of Dardanos should offer to weigh out
> your bulk in gold; not even so shall the lady your mother
> who herself bore you lay you on the death-bed and mourn you:
> no, but the dogs and the birds will have you all for their feasting.'
>
> (22. 345–54)

Of course there is no human justification for the gruesome feast Achilles invites Hektor to—any more than there is for Hekabe's cannibalistic curse of Achilles, which mentions again the "dogs with their shifting feet" (24. 211); human beings are most bestial when they are most emotional. The passions felt and expressed by Hektor, by Achilles, and by Hekabe are the consequences of the disorder at the heart of things in the Iliadic world, consequences that generally, in human experience, have excessive consequences of their own. Hekabe, for example, predicts the canine feast that Achilles will provide with her son's body (22. 89). The majesty of Homer's epic is that, in the end, normal savagery is reversed.

The reversal comes, as order is restored among gods, men, and dogs, in Books 23 and 24. Of the nine "dogs of the table that had belonged to the lord Patroklos," Achilles slit "the throats of two, and set them on the pyre" (23. 172–73). Unlike Priam (in his nightmare prediction) Patroklos, in death, remains the master of his hounds; they accompany him faithfully as companions to the house of Hades. Man is superior, as he should be, on the great chain of being. So far, Achilles is orderly in his actions. But the inversion of Achilles' farewell prayer for Patroklos provokes an immediate angry rejection from the gods, indicating that it is as disorderly as was Hektor's plan for Patroklos: " 'But I will not / give Hektor, Priam's son, to the fire, but the dogs, to feast on.' / So he spoke his threat. But the dogs did not deal with Hektor, / for Aphrodite, daughter of Zeus, drove the dogs back from him / by day and night . . ." (23. 183–86). Later, when Apollo points out to them that Achilles is behaving more like a lion than a man (24. 41), all the gods agree that it is time for him to be human again. Their agreement—the rehumanization that Achilles accepts as suddenly as he had allowed wrath to possess him (24. 139–40)—is expressed in the voluntary return of Hektor's body, saving it from the dogs, not for " 'ten times / and twenty times the ransom, and . . . more in addition' " (22. 349–50), but for a "ransom past counting" (my translation—24. 502) because both Priam and Achilles finally realize that counting is not the point. The poem that began with multitudes of Achaians becoming extraordinary dog-food (1.5) ends with the humanly dignified burial of a Trojan who was known among men as a great "breaker of horses" (24. 804)—the same horses who, "each beside his chariot, champing white barley / and oats . . . waited for the dawn to mount to her high place" (8. 564–65) in the orderly heavens where the Dog Star forever follows his master Orion, keeping his proper place in a world at peace (see Appendix 2).

The image of the ungrateful dogs with which Priam ends his outcry from the wall, then, is yet another stunningly appropriate expression of the overriding theme symbolized by the advancing shield of Achilles that Priam sees accurately, "wrought as a sign of evil / . . . for unfortunate mortals" (22. 30–31), to cause the bestial groan which incites the old man's desperate petition and dire prediction. Priam has reason to be terrified; Orion's dog has fallen on the Trojan plain. Just as the Trojan king's vision is not dimmed by age, there are no holes in Homer's poetic vision; everything fits with everything else. So it is all the more patheti-cally ironic that Priam performs his final royal act involuntarily. Hektor's will prevails; the warrior remains on the plain to fight in defense of the city (22. 91). In tacitly allowing Hektor's decision to stand, Priam appears most regal and most unfatherly. Yet his silence, in a sense, marks the moment of succession in which Hektor becomes the royal head of Trojan society—only to die immediately, as that society itself must, as a result of his death, die soon. In another sense, Priam's misfortune is that at the moment of truth for the existence of Troy he, because of the determina-tion of his now-orderly son, must play the king willy-nilly, when he would rather play the father. The fulfillment of Priam's paternal instincts must wait until Hektor is dead, since while Hektor lives Troy survives. As he mourns for his heroic son, Priam is "his father" (22. 408), not "the king."

Priam's lament for Hektor (22. 412–28) makes it clear that the now certain end of Troy means his own reversion—to being an ordinary family man. Yet he greets this change in status with new-found equanimity, as if aware that his new status offers him a chance to act effectively again. The speech also suggests that the transformation from a political to a domestic viewpoint is at the same time a movement toward essential human action. As he invokes the paternal-filial bond common to all men by which he hopes to move Achilles (22. 415), Priam is symbolically dismantling his national role, which has been revealed by Hektor's death to be more tenuous, more accidental, than the familial role. In fact he has no alternative than to stir in Achilles a recognition of their common humanity; for the old man no longer has a political position from which to argue (22. 420). With no society of his own, Priam must rely upon that of his host Achilles.

Priam's lament concludes with a poignantly concrete image that sum-marizes the relationship between the family and the πόλις *pólis* ("city") as it should be in an orderly society. He wishes that Hektor had died in his arms (22. 426–28). The encircling parental arms represent the secu-rity provided for the individual from birth to death by a stable familial environment. In the natural way of things, that circle may be opened to allow the individual to function on behalf of society. Social stability, after all, is necessary for the family's well-being. Yet when society is itself harmonious and well-off, society will insure the individual's return to the bosom of his family. There will be no conflict of loyalties such as the one so painfully expressed in Hektor's last meeting with Andromache and Astyanax. No such cyclic reciprocity, however, is insured for Hektor when his family circle releases him to serve the city. For another individual from the same family—Paris—had acted without a proper social perspective to undermine the entire system. Because of his disorderly deed every level of society must collapse, from bottom to top.

Priam's final concern in the *Iliad* is to reestablish that basic human circle, the family. He knows his particular family must perish; his only ambition is that it may perish symbolically intact. When Priam turns from a regal to a paternal orientation, then, his purpose is perfectly orderly. The result of Priam's deed is noble and harmonious. He goes to Achilles not as a king accompanied by a vast retinue but as an individual father (24. 148)—and not to the camp of another people, but to the lodge of another man. Hermes' greeting makes Priam's present role clear: " 'You seem to me like a beloved father' " (24. 371). And Priam's newly effective action on the familial level becomes a microcosm and a recollection of his former glorious action on the political level. Priam's old age—also emphasized in the meeting with Hermes—has been rejuvenated by Hektor's death because that death releases Priam to act on a level within his competence and desire.

Priam's protection of Helen in Book 3 must be considered in light of his final evaluation of Paris. The "dear son" of the duel scene is included in Priam's comprehensive curse of his surviving children:

> 'Get out, you failures, you disgraces. Have you not also
> mourning of your own at home that you come to me with your sorrows?
> Is it not enough that Zeus, son of Kronos, has given me sorrow
> in losing the best of my sons? You also shall be aware of this
> since you will be all the easier for the Achaians to slaughter
> now he is dead. But, for myself, before my eyes look
> upon this city as it is destroyed and its people are slaughtered,
> my wish is to go sooner down to the house of the death god.'
>
> (24. 239–46)

It is clear now that if Priam plays the father's role he plays it only to Hektor. The speech reveals the cause for his exclusiveness: the chief representative of social order has witnessed the disordering of his civilization by aberrant individuals, especially Paris and Pandaros. Among Priam's sons only Hektor acted in an orderly manner. Only with respect to Hektor, consequently, can Priam hope to reestablish an orderly familial structure.

The others may be excluded—just as Troy itself has been—from Priam's loyalty: "He was scolding his children / and cursing Helenos, and Paris" (24. 248–49). He does not spare their feelings: " 'Make haste,

wicked children, my disgraces. I wish all of you / had been killed . . . in
the place of Hektor' " (24. 253–54). These are individuals who reap the
benefits of social cooperation without themselves contributing: " 'all
that are left me are the disgraces, / the liars and the dancers, champions
of the chorus, the plunderers / of their own people in their land of lambs
and kids' " (24. 260–62). The orderly father must dissociate himself from
unruly offspring if the family and society are to remain secure. Priam has
come to this knowledge too late; his words here suggest that he is now
aware of the impropriety of his royal protection of Paris. For it is clearly
Paris who is described in these lines physically as he appeared in Book 3,
and symbolically as we know his role to have been from the start of the
war. Priam sees that his personal failure to refute the unnatural deed of
Paris led directly to Hektor's death. He has learned that the orderliness of
one man is not sufficient to prevent the disorderliness of many from
destroying order itself.

　　Although Priam will enter the camp of Achilles unaccompanied, the
splendid preparation of his wagon and team reinvokes his regal status.

> So he spoke, and they in terror at the old man's scolding
> hauled out the easily running wagon for mules, a fine thing
> new-fabricated, and fastened the carrying basket upon it.
> They took away from its peg the mule yoke made of boxwood
> with its massive knob, well fitted with guiding rings, and brought forth
> the yoke lashing (together with the yoke itself) of nine cubits
> and snugged it well into place upon the smooth-polished wagon-pole
> at the foot of the beam, then slipped the ring over the peg, and lashed it
> with three turns on either side to the knob, and afterwards
> fastened it all in order and secured it under a hooked guard.
> Then they carried out and piled into the smooth-polished mule wagon
> all the unnumbered spoils to be given for the head of Hektor,
> then yoked the powerful-footed mules who pulled in the harness
> and whom the Mysians gave once as glorious presents to Priam;
> but for Priam they led under the yoke those horses the old man
> himself had kept, and cared for them at his polished manger.
>
> 　　　　　　　　　　　　　　　　　　　　　　　(24. 265–80)

This description of the wagon-artifact also defines the familial auspices
under which Priam's journey takes place; the wagon is prepared not by
servants, but by his princely sons. Yet even here there is a deeper
significance. For these sons are the "disgraces" (24. 260), and to Priam
their survival serves only to deepen his anguish over the loss of Hektor
(24. 495–500). The elaboration of the wagon, then, has the effect of
making it appear a worthy vehicle for bearing not only the "countless
ransom" but also for returning to Troy Hektor's body. The ritual prepara-

tion initiates a funeral ceremony; the outfitting of Priam's "newly fabricated" wagon is the beginning of the end of the poem.

Old age is given its greatest moment in the *Iliad* when, in Priam's meeting with Achilles, Homer makes us understand that age, too, is an accidental distinction which does not prevent communication on a more essential human level: that of the father-son relationship and of the guest-friend bond. Priam enjoys a peculiar suspension of normal reality in his meeting with Achilles deriving from his psychical detachment from his own welfare. His own life is of no concern to him unless he recovers his son's body. What Hektor shares with Helen at the moment of his death—a vision of the poetic, memorial significance of his acts—Priam now shares with them and with Achilles in the Myrmidon camp. Because he possesses that vision of essential humanity while he is still alive, Priam, despite his age, is more fortunate than Hektor. For the king is now able to direct that vision toward informing action—the successful return of the body.

Like Helen, Priam is portrayed as attempting to find an orderly mode of acting amidst the ruins of the Trojan social system. Priam is more fortunate than Helen in this respect; he finds an effective role when he becomes a guest-suppliant. Willingly detached from his customary identity, Priam finds a certain resolution to the anguish which besieges him throughout the *Iliad* by placing himself at the mercy of the gods— and of human nature itself, whose essential forces the gods seem to both embody and represent. When he dares to face the wrath-forged, fire-refined humanity of Achilles, the beautiful characteristic paradox of Homer's Priam is that the most venerable king achieves nobility and glory in the ironhearted abnegation of his kingship.

Hektor of the Shining Helm

Hektor's dilemma is that of the individual indispensable to his personal family and at the same time indispensable, actually and symbolically, to the city which provides *all* families with a functional environment. His anguish arises from the predestined futility of his service to the Troadic nation. Yet if he would preserve a personal honor which depends upon social approbation, he has no honorable alternative but to fight. Hektor's characteristic activity is, therefore, fatally absurd; when society is doomed, fame is meaningless. But in subordinating both his personal and his family's interests to the fulfillment of his orderly social function, Hektor finds another kind of glory accessible to him—glory which transcends a particular human society like Troy, to define its value on a universally human level. This kind of glory—characteristically

associated with Helen's knowledge of it—promises a mnemonic immortality to the individual who merits it by his actions. It does not depend
upon the survival of Troy, but only upon the continuity of humankind
and the Muses of Memory.

Each artifact associated with Hektor—the loom, his shining helmet,
the marriage bed and funeral bier, his dazzling armor, the Trojan
washbasins, and song—marks his character as a center of social definition disordered by the breakdown of society. Into Hektor's character, his
attitudes and emotions, Homer has woven the intricate, mutually reciprocal, interrelationships between the individual and the communal
dimensions of human existence in a way as comprehensive as the Iliadic
vision itself. It may be true that Hektor, as a leading character, was
Homer's invention. Hektor, in contrast to Paris, is the strong and orderly
individual whose role it is to hold together both his personal family and
the πόλις *pólis* ("city"), ruled by his father's royal house. Like Paris,
Hektor falls into error; but he reverses his delusion and thereby surpas-
ses his brother. It is characteristic of the galaxy to which he belongs that
Hektor's reversal comes too late to change the conditions of his life—
comes only at the moment of death. He is distinguished, then, from
members of the galaxy of order (like Achilles and Nestor), who are
characteristically turned from error to orderly action, only by the fact that
Hektor's last minute change of heart cannot reverse the disorderly
consequences of his error. His poetic role is all the more exemplary for
the futility of his real-life role. Illustrating the interaction between
individual and community Hektor's character asserts that neither is well
off unless the other is at the same time. Only through this natural
balanced perspective is the order willed by Zeus maintained.

Hektor, like Paris, is characteristically shown in proximity with wom-
en. But unlike his self-serving brother, Hektor respects and protects the
feminine principle in human life; Paris never mentions children, but for
Hektor femininity and motherhood go together. In the embattled city,
the distinction between warriors and the values they defend, between
active and passive individuals, is not only one of age, but is also a matter
of gender: "Now as Hektor had come to the Skaian gates and the oak
tree, / all the wives of the Trojans and their daughters came running
about him / to ask after their sons, after their brothers and
neighbours, / their husbands" (6. 237–40). Because of his double image
as a family and national leader, Hektor is the interpreter between the two
sexes. His virility and his domesticity are complementary; his heroism
arises directly from his gentleness. Of the two formal prayers for a loved
one in the poem, one is Hektor's for his son (the other Achilles' for

Patroklos). Even Zeus' unique address to Hektor includes a reference to Andromache (17. 206).

Hektor's commitment to the city, through a prior responsibility to his father's royal house, demands an unbearable sacrifice of him: " 'For I am going first to my own house, so I can visit / my own people, my beloved wife and my son, who is little, / since I do not know if ever again I shall come back this way, / or whether the gods will strike me down at the hands of the Achaians' " (6. 365–68). What makes the denial of family so poignant is that Hektor is as indispensable domestically as he is nationally. Priam has recognized him as the only orderly individual in Troy, upon whose orderliness the city depends for its existence; Andromache declares that Hektor is all the family she has (6.430 ff.)—in his absence she is undefined, and ultimately doomed.

Hektor's personal anguish, then, is deepened on the one hand by his emotional attachment to his family and on the other by his awareness of the inevitable failure of his military goals. Like Achilles he harbors no personal animosity against the national enemy; his address to the Trojan allies insists that no self-interest motivated his gathering of the tribes, but simply the necessity of defending the helpless wives and children of Troy. This task has resulted in the steady depletion of the city's resources (17. 220–28). The bleeding of Troy's material resources is just one indication to Hektor that his efforts are to be in vain. There is also the dissension over Helen, the ignominious deed of Pandaros, the loss of so many brave men, the enmity of the gods. Most ominous, of course, is the weakness he sees in the royal family, one which will eventually affect even him. In Helen's bedroom the strong and orderly individual confronts, in Paris, the disorderly truant: " 'Strange man! It is not fair to keep in your heart this coldness. / The people are dying around the city and around the steep wall / as they fight hard; and it is for you that this war with its clamour / has flared up about our city. You yourself would fight with another / whom you saw anywhere hanging back from the hateful encounter. / Up then, to keep our town from burning at once in the hot fire' " (6. 326–31). Paris must be out of his mind (the Greek word δαιμόνι daimóni, used to address Paris, strongly implies possession) not to know, as Hektor does, that all able bodies, young and old, must cooperate, each in the way proper to his station, if the city is to ward off annihilation: " 'And let the heralds Zeus loves give orders about the city / for the boys who are in their first youth and the grey-browed elders / to take stations on the god-founded bastions that circle the city; / and as for the women, have our wives, each one in her own house, / kindle a great fire; let there be a watch kept steadily' " (8.

517–21). Only if there are no laggards among them may the Trojans
" 'drive from our place these dogs swept into destruction / whom the
spirits of death have carried here on their black ships' " (8. 527–28).

Equal to the decadence displayed by members of the royal family is the
weakness which Hektor gradually recognizes as the irreversible characteristic of old age. Homer makes this clear in the scene where Priam and
Hekabe plead with him from the wall to return to the illusory security
within. Similar to Priam's attitude is that of Hekabe in this scene. She no
longer enacts her queenly role. Instead, she invokes primal motherhood
by baring her breast and begging her son to turn back (22. 79–83)—
reverting to the irrevocable time of Hektor's infantile dependence upon
her, at the very moment when society most emphatically depends upon
his mature action outside the family's sheltering arms.

With society crumbling around him, as his parents' speeches proclaim, the socially-motivated individual can only be perplexed—as Hektor is. The aspiration for honor inspires orderly behavior; but now that
the source of honor is in jeopardy, its value has become questionable. In
this light, Hektor's rhetoric sounds ominously hollow: " 'Fight on then
by the ships together. He who among you / finds by spear thrown or
spear thrust his death and destiny, / let him die. He has no dishonour
when he dies defending / his country, for then his wife shall be saved
and his children, afterwards, / and his house and property shall not be
damaged, if the Achaians / must go away with their ships to the beloved
land of their fathers' " (15. 494–99). The source of Hektor's vacillation is
the equation he makes here between the validity of personal glory and
the survival of the particular community by which glory is recognized
and inspired. He has not envisioned clearly enough yet a glorious way of
acting which finds its inspiration not in a single mortal city, but in the
undying memory of mankind.

Judging glory as a national value leads Hektor to the logical conclusion
that its achievement can no longer be associated with the national realm
when that realm is imminently doomed. The first alternative which
occurs to him is physical immortality—a wish that must appear unrealistic even to himself: " 'Oh, if I only / could be as this in all my days
immortal and ageless / and be held in honour as Athene and Apollo are
honoured' " (8. 538–40; cf. 13. 824 ff.). Against this unrealizable alternative Helen will offer Hektor a more certain, more attainable one: the
promise of enjoying immortality in the memory of *all* men. Hektor's
name, although it cannot be memorialized by Troy, which will die, will
live nevertheless, as long as there are human beings to sing.

But Hektor's honor will be memorialized in song only if he continues
to act in an orderly social way, for only by so acting will he become a

communicable model of proper human behavior—an inspiration to any man, in any age, to recognize the essential human rightness of communal responsibility. So when Hektor expresses the wish to act individualistically he jeopardizes the very goal he prizes above all others. It is his misfortune that Hektor allows his disorderly impulse to be realized in action, when he goes against the counsel of Poulydamas to become the aggressor, to slay Patroklos, and to don the armor of Achilles. He has no proper right to such action; he ought to remain the protector, in keeping with Zeus' plan which designates that he play a part only in the defense of Troy (12. 241–43). Allowing himself to be blinded momentarily, as Pandaros was, by the joy of his own strength, Hektor has allowed his political responsibility to lapse; and that lapse is the beginning of the end for Troy, since it makes inevitable the loss of the city's mightiest protector. Now that he has slain Patroklos there is no way for Hektor to save his country. Not even the return of Helen, which he considers in his desperation (22. 111–12), will be helpful now. The vengeance of Achilles has no immediate bearing on her plight. Achilles' wrath is the critical determinant of the war's outcome, because it leads to the death of Hektor. In this way, too, Homer contrives to have men share responsibility for misfortune with the gods. For by the implicit logic of the Iliadic world the Achaians are rightfully fighting for Helen's return; it is therefore wrong for Hektor, a Trojan, to take the offensive.

Hektor is redeemed, however, because he finally recognizes and admits the folly of his blind pursuit of egotistic glory. He rededicates himself, with full acceptance of futility, to a responsible communal role. Hektor has no assurance that this renewal of his national commitment will enable him to achieve glory despite his single lapse; but he knows that he has no other honorable course of action. To persist in his blindness would be to identify his deeds with those of Pandaros and Paris. So he replies to Priam's and Hekabe's pleas from the wall: " 'Now, since by my own recklessness I have ruined my people, / I feel shame before the Trojans and the Trojan women with trailing / robes, that someone who is less of a man than I will say of me: / "Hektor believed in his own strength and ruined his people." / Thus they will speak; and as for me, it would be much better / at that time, to go against Achilleus, and slay him, and come back, / or else be killed by him in glory in front of the city' " (22. 104–10). In Homer's view, every human action, no matter how small or unique, has an irreversible effect on character and circumstances. The consequences of Hektor's single lapse from a social orientation cannot be underestimated. Because of it, Achilles, the one man who has the human and divine power to destroy him and his city, has reentered the war.

Hektor's own deed, therefore, has destroyed the forum by which honor is normally assigned to the orderly individual; he himself, no less than Paris, has jeopardized Troy's stability. In one moment of weakness Hektor became, no less than his brother, an unnatural Trojan, inimical to his own people (22. 105–7). It is pathetically ironic that Hektor had to be "undefined" as a Trojan in order to find his definitive, glorious, identity as a hero. For Hektor is well aware, from Patroklos' dying words (16. 844–54), that the first alternative he mentions (22. 109, above), is impossible; and the second will be the ruin of his city (22. 110). As he confronts his last antagonist, therefore, Hektor must appeal to the tribunal of human nature itself. Hektor's role has been paradoxically transformed. His every living deed had actual, historical import for Troy; but Hektor's final gesture, deprived of its potential to influence present events, appeals to a trans-political, purely symbolic, level. In his death Hektor reaches beyond the Iliadic world to that real future in which he will be memorialized in the memory of men unborn, in the song of Homer.

Hektor's reference to the loom is in keeping with his consistent association with domesticity in general, and the feminine in particular. He tells Andromache that no other grief—political (6. 450), parental (6. 451), or fraternal (6. 452)—equals that which he feels over what will become of his widow, " 'when some bronze-armored / Achaian leads you off, taking away your day of liberty, / in tears; and in Argos you must work at the loom of another' " (6. 454–56). Here the alien loom symbolizes to Hektor his own insufficiency as the guardian of his family's safety (6. 463). When Andromache's outspoken grief leads Hektor to comfort her with brave but false hope, the loom is used to symbolize the normal order of human life—when the woman minds the hearth, while the man, in cooperation with his comrades, defends the city: " 'Go therefore back to our house, and take up your own work, / the loom and the distaff, and see to it that your handmaidens / ply their work also; but the men must see to the fighting, / all men who are the people of Ilion, but I beyond others' " (6. 490–93). Shortly before this scene, Hektor had removed Paris from his indolent observation of Helen's distaff activities. The loom is associated with the stability of the home; its recurrence here relates the unnatural, artificial order of Paris' domestic situation to the consequent real disruption of Hektor's. Homer will later present Andromache weaving her husband's shroud.

While the loom is an image common to both fraternal families, although its symbolic function is characteristically different for each, the shining helmet is the special artifact associated with Hektor's personal family, identifying it as an orderly relationship threatened by chaos. The artifact's use identifies its symbolic significance; the helmet protects Hektor as he protects his family.

Throughout the *Iliad* Hektor's traditional epithet is "Hektor of the shining helm." Were it not for the appearance of his shining helm in the famous scene on the wall in Book 6 we might be led to dismiss the recurrent epithet as displaying nothing more than formulaic convenience. Yet this particular traditional image caught the imagination of Homer, inspiring him to focus the character of one of his favorite heroes through an inventive expansion of the image. In this scene he enhances the helmet's normal combat role with a momentary dramatic function which reveals the effects of war upon the family. Homer's genius has made this visual unit, the helmet, forever mnemonically associated with Hektor's farewell to wife and son:

> So speaking glorious Hektor held out his arms to his baby,
> who shrank back to his fair-girdled nurse's bosom
> screaming, and frightened at the aspect of his own father,
> terrified as he saw the bronze and the crest with its horse-hair,
> nodding dreadfully, as he thought, from the peak of the helmet.
> Then his beloved father laughed out, and his honoured mother,
> and at once glorious Hektor lifted from his head the helmet
> and laid it in all its shining upon the ground. Then taking
> up his dear son he tossed him about in his arms, and kissed him.
>
> (6. 466–74)

The cohesive function of the artifact as a structural device is especially striking. The image of the helmet draws our attention to Astyanax, who tosses like its horse-hair crest (6. 470, 474)—a visual contrast between political war and domestic peace. Indeed the very name of Hektor's son ("lord of the city," 6. 400–403) suggests his father's conflicting loyalties. If the natural order were to prevail Astyanax would be someday the "lord of the city" because his father's strength would have insured the continuity of Trojan society.

But while the boy's name signifies Hektor's political role, Astyanax's actual behavior in this scene symbolizes the unnaturalness of Hektor's enforced detachment from the paternal duties so dear to him. Bound to his political role, Hektor can't allow the personal, familial instincts, which he feels so strongly, to influence him beyond this momentary indulgence. Hektor carefully removes his helmet. If he is allowed to forget, for an instant, its usual warlike function, Homer does not allow us to; even on the ground the artifact is "all shining" (6. 473). And just as Hektor's willing despoilment of his own combat gear in this scene predicts the ultimate involuntary stripping of his armor by Achilles, so Astyanax's terror at the unfamiliar appearance of his father is an apocalyptical foreshadowing of the final, irrevocable separation of father and son. The war loosens familial bonds; Hektor's single egocentric deed will make it impossible for his own family to survive the loss of its father. Another poet might have brooded, self-consciously, over the tragic implications of this scene. Homer, instead, reenforces fatality with laughter.

The laughter of Hektor and Andromache not only contrasts with the anguish of their situation, it also serves a thematic purpose, signifying the integrity of their family relationship which endures on the very brink of disruption. It is indeed a fleeting happiness which Hektor finds in the company of wife and son, but not, for being so, illusory. Homer's greatness lies in the fact that he is able, despite the sweeping grandeur of his perspective, to appreciate and communicate the unique beauty of each element in his creation. In this scene it is the value of an orderly marital and paternal emotion that the poet analyzes and portrays. Hektor's unselfish prayer for his son (6. 476–81) is that Astyanax might be a better man than he is. The orderly father understands that he must submit his offspring to the service of his people.

At the very moment when Hektor, the bulwark against the common enemy, is on the verge of being toppled, the poet presents a contrast: of imminent death with life at its most serene and secure. The symbolic effect is all the more startling and poignant for the simplicity of the artifact-image used to accomplish it. The racing warriors, pursuer and pursued, pass close by "the washing-hollows / of stone, and magnificent, where the wives of the Trojans and their lovely / daughters washed the clothes to shining, in the old days / when there was peace, before the coming of the sons of the Achaians. / They ran beside these, one escaping, the other after him" (22. 153–57). On his way to die, Hektor runs past domestic monuments of the civilization he defends. Moreover these tokens of Troy-past, the basins, are related by their natural function to the distaff side of the family with whom Hektor has been regularly juxtaposed. How different is this deadly course from the footraces of peacetime games! "As when about the turnposts racing single-foot horses / run at full speed, when a great prize is laid up for their winning, / a tripod or a woman, in games for a man's funeral, / so these two swept whirling about the city of Priam / in the speed of their feet, while all the gods were looking upon them" (22. 162–66). As Achilles pursues Hektor around and around the walls of Troy, the two enact an archetypal drama in which man's social way of living is clearly visualized. The individual warrior, Hektor, is something like the valence electron in an atom's outer shell by which that atom is able to combine with other atoms. Societies do not contact societies; individuals confront individuals. So the circling individual has an ambivalent function: contact or protection. When, moreover, an alien individual would intrude, the protecting individual must defend the nuclear collective (within the walls) *through contact.* The orbit of the circling individual, in another analogy, is a semipermeable membrane which bars lethal influences from entering at the same time that it allows beneficial influences in. If, in the contact with an attacking individual, the circling individual is defeated—the shell broken, the membrane rent—there is nothing left to prevent destructive penetration by the alien. There is no doubt that Troy will fall once Hektor is slain.

These simplified cellular or atomic analogies also apply to the sexual element of the Trojan conflict. Because an individual, Paris, did not perform his filtering function properly, but attacked an alien organism instead, Troy has been undermined from the start. Paris willingly invited an alien individual, Helen, into his own city. Similarly Hektor's moment of hubris which leads to the death of Patroklos proves to be the fatal flaw in his individual character making him an ultimately ineffective defender of the community. When the shell is weakened, the collective nucleus will soon be destroyed. So Homer's vision asserts the crucial importance of the individual at the same time that it defines individuality as a function of the social collective. Achilles shows he's aware of the reciprocal configuration between citizen and city when he refuses to let Hektor reenter Troy (22. 194–98). Achilles insists that his opponent must function in his communal role by confronting, at this precise moment in history, the fatally designated representative of the Achaian community. Moreover Achilles emphasizes the indispensable value of the individual. Hektor calls on his fellow Trojans for relief whereas Achilles warns his people to leave the outcome entirely to him (22. 205–7). As far as individuality is concerned Achilles is not only the stronger but is also the more righteous—since all Trojans are vulnerable because of Paris' deed, all Achaians rightfully vengeful. Therefore Achilles can stand alone against Hektor while Hektor fears his own insufficiency. In the end Achilles, from the circle of the besieging Greeks, overcomes Hektor, from the besieged circle—until the outer circle contracts to explode the inner, Troy. As early as Gilgamesh, poets have recognized the correspondence between the circularity of city walls and the individual's relationship with his society. In this great race around Troy, no prize artifact is at stake for the winner (22. 159, 164): "No, they ran for the life of Hektor, breaker of horses" (22. 161). By his reference, then, to pre-Achaian Troy (22. 156) and by his employment of the epithet with which the poem itself will terminate (24. 804), Homer contracts into a single image the entire span of human history from which his poem derives.

Just as he is related to Helen through the image of the loom, so, too, Hektor is associated with his extraordinary sister-in-law by reference to the bed. The image of the bed in Book 24 becomes the meeting place of life and death, and so fulfills the symbolic implications of Paris' elaborate bed in Book 3. For Hektor the cycle of human life is completed when Priam restores his body to Troy. Crib and marital couch alike have been transformed into the funeral bier: "And when they had brought him inside the renowned house, they laid him / then on a carved bed, and seated beside him the singers" (24. 719–20). Andromache, in the first of three laments over the warrior's body, expresses the tragedy of his death as a familial, marital one: " 'for you did not die in bed, and stretch your arms to me, / nor tell me some last intimate word that I could remember / always, all the nights and days of my weeping for you' " (24. 743–45). Andromache's visualization of the physical gesture which her husband was not able to make toward her in his final moments makes the unnaturalness of Hektor's death all the more grievous; it is the very same gesture that Homer portrayed in the scene with Astyanax (6. 466): stretching out his arms. So we remember it as clearly as she longs for it.

Helen's lament is dramatically last. Her speech marks her special intimacy with Hektor; a common fate, beyond their control, has made them kindred spirits (24. 763). Her involuntary role in Trojan affairs does not remove from Helen the burden of feeling somehow responsible for Hektor's death. Here, too, the significance of her crime is stressed; she is an expatriate whose forced alienation from her natural environment has caused all this turmoil (24. 765–71). Hektor above all others made it possible for her to enjoy the definition, however tenuous, allowed her in Troy. Therefore his death is doubly lamentable; she mourns not only Hektor but also herself, since " 'There was no other in all the wide Troad / who was kind to me, and my friend; all others shrank when they saw me' " (24. 774–75). With the loss of Hektor, Helen is deprived of her last hope for a secure social identity.

The tripartite hierarchical pattern of the laments illustrates the ritual aspect of the funeral which makes it a primary form of continuity. Yet Hektor's funeral is different from that of Patroklos. The funeral games of Book 23 promise the restoration of Argive social order as the proceedings for Hektor cannot promise for Troy. But Priam's voluntary dissociation of his fatherly from his kingly role has indicated already that we are witnessing a mode of behavior which is somehow more basic than the nationalistic mode. The mourning women are not portrayed as queen and princesses: they are wife, mother, and sister-in-law. The family of Paris, in burying Hektor's body, buries its royalty as well. What survives is human, not Trojan, domesticity. It is therefore man, in the generic sense, who in this moving expression of the Iliadic vision is able to cope with death; this is the transcendent lesson that shapes, in Book 24, so sublime an ending to the *Iliad*. Hektor's burial occurs at the same level of action as does his final heroic act: the purely human.

Hektor's deathbed is surrounded by singers (24. 720–22) and Andromache complains that her husband had given her no "special word" by which to remember him (24. 744). Homer is aware of the analogy between the image of tales, songs (as memorable, remembered word) and the artifact-images we are examining. More than any other image, that of remembered tales unites the two thematic galaxies under the auspices of a common humanity. On the transcendent poetic level (where the Muses are the daughters of Zeus and Memory, the source of order allied with the agents by which order is normally communicated among men), the recollected tale is what the bed is on the immediate thematic level: a universal image. Remembered words, in the exchange between Glaukos and Diomedes, brought living order to an otherwise fatal encounter. Like the funeral and like Hektor's final heroic action, memory communicates the promise of continuity on an essentially human level.

Helen always, in the *Iliad*, understands the unique quality of song, having reached, long before Hektor, the depths of despair. Helen knows that their present misery will not be alleviated within their lifetimes or by any acts of their own, that the glorious reward for defending Troy will not be actually enjoyed by the man destined to the task. Hektor therefore must be satisfied with the foreknowledge of his transcendent glory in the songs of memory (6. 343 ff.). Hektor will not at first accept the attraction of this distant promise because he retains the illusory hope of still being able to alter the course of history. So he rebukes Helen for suggesting that he even briefly share her detachment from events on the plain (6. 359).

Still striving to influence national events he is not convinced yet that he must settle for identity in the memory of poets (6. 359). But as his illusions dissolve—after his temporary blindness leads him, once it is lifted, to accept his fate—Hektor begins to understand Helen's poetic viewpoint. He shares with Helen intimations of immortality realized on a more essential human plane than that on which the others fight for Troy. Theirs, Hektor and Helen's, is an affinity of spirit which Homer ingeniously leaves in mystery. The poet must feel, as Helen's words to Hektor suggest she does as well (6. 357–58), that the lives of some individuals may be explained only by mankind's need for inspiration and evidence of nobility which the song of memory alone provides. The gods, in suspending Hektor's effectiveness in contemporary reality and making him live out a futile life involuntarily, are identical with the spirit of poetry. What motivates Hektor, like Sarpedon in Book 12, is a rudimentary but nonetheless clearly focused confidence in the future continuity of mankind undiminished by the insecurity of particular societies or nations.

So Hektor appeals, in his dying words, to Achilles' essential humanity. His plea that proper reverence be given to his body will be realized, despite Achilles' impassioned denial, when Priam, too, acts on a purely human level. Future generations will recall Hektor's futile but brave death in conjunction with the honorable burial. The burial proves that Troy, despite the imminence of its destruction still honors the common rituals of humanity. And the funeral is made possible by the communion of spirit between two deadly enemies. The unresolved fate of Troy with which Homer's own "song" concludes, in juxtaposition with the completion of the funeral rites, is Homer's way of communicating his visionary perspective that, while historical peace may be ephemeral and rare, human peace is not only possible, but also truly realized, in the poems of memory. Even the man for whom war is the reality, therefore, can find peace in his appreciation of the poem. The special quality, the definitive beauty, of this ultimate Homeric glory, symbolized by the ritual burial of Hektor, is that it is both social and religious, human and divine, at the same time, since it is with the gods' help that the poet records heroic deeds for posterity—just as the gods willed Hektor's honorable last rites but insisted that Achilles make them possible. This special glory is actualized by Hektor's performance of exemplary action; it is immortalized when Hektor's example, recorded in memory and communicated in song, becomes the inspiration for deeds modeled upon his own, in future situations of social crisis.

Hektor, who was ineffective in accomplishing his historical ambition, receives, as the reward for his dutifulness, the memorial power of moving individuals yet unborn toward orderly action. The memory of his name becomes a shaping force in future human events. Hektor's final mystery, his ultimate poetic magnificence, lies in his becoming an example. In death the Olympians attend him as they did not in life. Their attention to his mortal remains is Homer's way of symbolizing the transcendent value of the individual. The human spirit of poetry, like their immortal vigilance, will issue in the mnemonic perpetuation of Hektor's name. Just as their physical service prepares his body for an historically glorious funeral, the singer's craft attaches to Hektor's name the honor it deserves—in the memorialization of the song. However subject to the erosion of physical change may be the hero's barrow, the poem will contain the name of Hektor securely for as long as mankind. Memory shields the individual from death.

Andromache's Headdress

If the name of Andromache at once calls to mind the image of her tearful smiling, then Homer's song of memory has preserved the essence of her character. Never in the *Iliad* is Andromache far from tears. Once only does she smile. Yet, despite this quantitative disproportion, the paradox of her role is balanced. The smile is as important to Homer's definition of Andromache's character as are her countless tears. Against the disorder of all her other social ties represented by the tears, Andromache's unique smile symbolizes the order of her existence that has been established through her perfect marriage to Hektor. One man gives her existence meaning which one smile expresses. Yet precisely because she values, so much more strongly than others whose identities are defined through multiple relations, the orderliness which her husband embodies, Andromache must let Hektor risk his life—and so her own life as well—in order to preserve it. Even the single smile is mingled with tears.

Unlike Helen, Andromache is voluntarily and naturally defined only as a Trojan in the *Iliad*. Her affinity with Helen's galaxy of images and characters is more circumstantial than essential; it is expressed in Andromache's divided loyalties, more toward husband than toward city, which have resulted from the disorder of current Trojan circumstances. But Homer wasn't interested in expressing the aversion Andromache might well have felt toward the society for which her husband—whose ambiguous motivation the poet does explore exhaustively—fought; we never hear her speak against Troy in general, or Paris in particular. Rather, the composer of the *Iliad* consistently emphasizes Andromache's single-minded and unswerving dedication to Hektor, as a contrast with Helen's more evenly ambivalent attitude. Homer lets his listeners draw their own conclusions about her silence concerning anything outside her family. Andromache speaks, in the *Iliad*, to no one but her husband.

Andromache is related to Helen through the images of the loom, the bed, the headdress, and memory. The thematic importance of the meeting on the wall in Book 6 is defined by Andromache as much as by Hektor. To begin with, Homer emphasizes the family's appearance together by juxtaposing it dramatically with the furious battle; dramatic impact is enhanced by the fact that the scene immediately follows the encounter between Glaukos and Diomedes. In the context of that exchange Homer revealed the way in which personal experience, the genealogically-revealed relationship between the two warriors' families, might relegate war temporarily to the background of man's concern. But the poet quickly reasserts the major theme by showing the even closer relationship between Hektor and Andromache overshadowed, and unalterably influenced, by the presence of war: when Astyanax is terrified by his father's helmet. Battle and death, suspended temporarily in the understanding between Glaukos and Diomedes, once again prevail.

Andromache is a figure whose total propriety heightens our recognition of Helen's unnatural position. She, like Helen, is shown on the Trojan wall, but for such different reasons, such unmixed emotions. Andromache is absorbed in her husband and home. Hers is not the selfish attitude of Paris, nor the communal motivation of her Hektor, nor the transcendent perspective of Helen; hers is purely familial: Andromache is wife, mother, and widow. So comprehensively domestic is her relationship with Hektor that she even tends his horses (8. 187). Andromache's singular mode of behavior is explained by the fact that she is, like Helen, an expatriate—an element in Andromache's characterization which has the widest implications, associating her also with Chryseis and Briseis. Achilles was responsible for the alienation of all three women from their homelands. Andromache's formal introduction as the daughter of Eëtion (6. 395) contrasts the normal multiplicity of her former identity (as sister, child, and princess) with the present one-sided definition she possesses as a guest-bride in a foreign society.

The relationship between Andromache and Hektor in Book 6 contrasts strikingly with that between Helen and Paris in Book 3. The superficial resolution of the disorderly marriage in Book 3 (recalling the equally superficial resolution implied in Hera and Zeus' bedding-down at the end of Book 1) is very different from the fatally interrupted orderly marriage in Book 6. Hektor's two references to the loom symbolically frame the possibilities for Andromache. His first mention of the artifact, when he predicts that Andromache will serve at the loom of an alien warrior (6. 456), makes it an image of their disrupted domestic harmony. In fact, Andromache is not found at home where Hektor expects her (6. 371); her absence from the household is ominous.

Hektor's second mention of the loom marks a momentary alteration in his doomsday outlook to a more hopeful one, no doubt explained by his wish to alleviate Andromache's grievous reaction to his first prophetic speech. Here the artifact symbolizes the stability of the family and the order of their marriage (6. 491); Hektor includes weaving in his delineation of the appropriate duties for women within an orderly society (6. 492–93). Since their relationship has produced a son who may continue their orderly mode of action, Hektor's optimism may have some ground. Neither he nor Andromache knows for sure at this moment which of the two outcomes, symbolized by each image of the loom, will in fact occur. In the meantime Hektor fights for the preservation of order; and Andromache must return to her loom which is still her orderly work. The scene concludes with the tacit agreement that each will persist in unselfish activity. Helen and Paris come together, Hektor and Andromache go apart, when, in each case, the movement should be the opposite. Andromache complies with her husband's decision, although she does not share the process of its making. Andromache plies her loom, not self-conscious of her own importance, but solely in the hope that her beloved domestic stability will continue—through Hektor's political success.

Andromache is at her loom when she receives the dreaded news of Hektor's death; the imagistic continuity is an example of the psychology of memory, leaving us with the impression that in the time that has passed between their meeting in Book 6 and the events here in Book 22 Andromache hasn't once moved from the family hearth, where, obeying her husband, she persists in maintaining domestic order. Now there is no doubt which symbolic meaning of the artifact has been realized on the plain:

> but the wife of Hektor had not yet
> heard: for no sure messenger had come to her and told her
> how her husband had held his ground there outside the gates;
> but she was weaving a web in the inner room of the high house,
> a red folding robe, and inworking elaborate figures.
> She called out through the house to her lovely-haired handmaidens
> to set a great cauldron over the fire, so that there would be
> hot water for Hektor's bath as he came back out of the fighting;
> poor innocent, nor knew how, far from waters for bathing,
> Pallas Athene had cut him down at the hands of Achilleus.
> She heard from the great bastion the noise of mourning and sorrow.
> Her limbs spun, and the shuttle dropped from her hand to the ground.
>
> (22. 437–48)

It is pathetically ironic that Andromache is introduced here simply as "the wife of Hektor" (22. 437) at the very point when she has lost her primary identity, and it is tragically ironic that Hektor's wife is the last to know about his death. Homer emphasizes Hektor's compulsion to act on behalf of his nation by having the news come first to king and queen. Hektor's death, after all, signals the end of Troy. Only after the representatives of society have expressed their initial grief does Homer turn to narrate the reaction of Andromache. But how much more fully he elaborates her reception of the news, how much more extensively he concentrates upon her actions! As if to compensate her somehow for being the last to know, the poet employs the strangely equivocal adjective ἐτήτυμος *etḗtumos* ("true, truthful, real") to describe the messenger *who did not come* to Andromache. The impression so created is that Hektor's wife possessed the knowledge of his death mysteriously, but no less certainly, through some extraordinary manner of cognition. Her first words all too accurately reflect the reality which she has feared for so long (22. 449 ff.).

Yet despite her premonitions, Andromache has persisted in her weaving. Homer portrays her pursuing a course of action no less futile, with respect to family well-being, than are Hektor's own final acts, with respect to social stability. Quietly reflecting her husband's pursuit of transcendent glory, Andromache becomes herself the symbol of wifely devotion (like Penelope, whose patient weaving has a happier reward). Without elaborating its subject matter, Homer makes the robe she weaves nevertheless special, as a symbol of her dutiful fulfillment to her husband's exact wishes; her subsequent orders for the building of the bath-fire indicate that her obedience is complete—extending to Hektor's general wishes as well as to his detailed commands. Long before, Hektor had outlined the proper behavior for all Trojans to pursue (8. 517–20), dictating that each wife, in her own house, should kindle a fire. He did not mention, then, what purpose their fires should serve; here, at the most dramatic moment possible, their function is emphatically familial. As it washes the soil of battle from the weary soldier, the household bath simultaneously cleanses him of his outside, national responsibilities. The tragedy of Hektor's conflicting loyalties is that he fell "far from waters for bathing" (22. 445). The attentive efforts of his wife have been in vain; the narrator's comment heightens the poignancy of Andromache's futile preparations (22. 445).

Andromache drops the shuttle from her hands (22. 448). The sudden interruption of the artifact's creation directly reflects not only the disruption of the marriage, now final, but also of Andromache herself who is, by Hektor's death, undefined. The composer's attention to this particular detail of the image—the actual cessation of the weaving—is another contrast with his treatment of the loom of Helen. The loom of Andromache is meant to be associated particularly with the dissolution of the family; with the husband and father dead, the loom's function, both actual and symbolic, ends. Helen's loom, on the other hand, symbolizes the general breakdown of human society—Trojan and Achaian together.

Still, the two Trojan wives (in Book 3, and in Books 6 and 22) behave in similar ways. Both women, for example, are shown twice at the wall.

Helen was led there, the first time, by Iris to witness the hoped-for restoration of order, through the arrangement of the truce and duel; and order was the keynote of Andromache's first appearance on the wall with husband and son. Now, however, the wife of Hektor leaves her household behind once more, but this time with symbolic finality; the potential of order has been lost, the probable disorder realized. Instead of a living Hektor she sees at the wall a husband dead and cruelly dishonored (22. 462 ff.). Andromache reflects her husband's mortality, so allied with her identity, when she faints (22. 467). Andromache's swoon is the physical gesture that complements the namelessness with which Homer had introduced her in this scene. In much the same manner Helen was led away by Aphrodite from her position next to Priam on the wall; here, too, the movement is from the unrealized potential of order to the renewal of actual disorder, in the daemonically enforced bedding-down with Paris. The relationship between the two wives, with respect to their appearances on the wall, is that of cause and effect: Helen's involuntary reaffirmation of disorder leads directly to Andromache's brokenhearted experience of domestic disintegration. Helen's return to her unnatural home has caused Andromache to be separated forever from her natural one. So house is set against house, bed against bed.

In the lines that follow the fainting scene, Homer associates another artifact, the headdress, with Andromache, to form an image that serves to focus her present grief in a gesture, to recall the depth of her emotion in a history of the artifact's origin, and to heighten the emotional impact of the poem's major theme by evoking our visual memory of a similar artifact treated in a similar way for an entirely different reason—Hektor's shining helmet. Her first experience of grief recalls to Andromache her wedding:

> The darkness of night misted over the eyes of Andromache.
> She fell backward, and gasped the life breath from her, and far off
> threw from her head the shining gear that ordered her headdress,
> the diadem and the cap, and the holding-band woven together,
> and the circlet, which Aphrodite the golden once had given her
> on that day when Hektor of the shining helmet led her forth
> from the house of Eëtion, and gave numberless gifts to win her.
>
> (22. 466–72)

First the poet reiterates Andromache's imitation of her husband's death (22. 466–67), reminding us of Hektor's identifying role in their intimate marriage. Her ritual despoilment of the headdress recalls the previous dropping of the shuttle, but even more strikingly, Hektor's voluntary removal of *his* headgear for the benefit of their son. But Homer contrasts the two acts with precision. Here is no careful displacement to signify, in the case of Hektor, a retention of respect and value for the object; instead, the headdress is relinquished definitely, forever—its usefulness, like that of the loom, at an end. In the visual imagination, the difference between the two gestures is as stunning as it is precisely drawn.

Yet even displaced, the headdress works mnemonically to associate Andromache with Aphrodite, with her wedding, and with her expatriate status. The manner in which she left the house of Eëtion, through the propriety of Hektor's "numberless gifts" (22. 472), stands in sharp contrast with the disorderly abduction of Helen by Paris. Hektor's wooing is the exemplary standard by which others, like Othryoneus' of Kassandra, or even Achilles' of Briseis, are to be judged; and Andromache is the symbol of ideal marriage. Andromache's newly symbolic role, on the essential human level, is confirmed in the image of her almost ritual elevation: "And about her stood thronging her husband's sisters and the wives of his brothers / and these, in her despair for death, held her up among them" (22. 473–74). The gesture of her in-laws seems to say, Look what war has wrought upon the family!

When Andromache recovers from her swoon, her speech expresses explicitly what the imagery has implied. Recalling the temporary disruption of her family in the scene in Book 6, she declares, in the superfluous catechism of extreme emotion, that the reciprocal relationship between father and son is now destroyed conclusively. Hektor can no longer help Astyanax; nor can the son serve his father (22. 485–86). Her prophecy of his certain fate is vivid (22. 488 ff.). And her speech ends with a poignant evocation of lost domesticity, focused on the same art-images associated with her bath-fire at the opening of the episode: " 'But now, beside the curving ships, far away from your parents, / the writhing worms will feed, when the dogs have had enough of you, / on your naked corpse, though in your house there is clothing laid up / that is fine-textured and pleasant, wrought by the hands of women. / But all of these I will burn up in the fire's blazing, / no use to you, since you will never be laid away in them' " (22. 508–13). Her carefully prepared fire will now fulfill a purpose very different from that for which it was originally intended. All images of the peaceful hearth are inverted. Sure that Hektor will have no honorable funeral, Andromache resigns herself to carrying out the ultimate duties of a loyal wife. Priam's faith in human nature and his ability and determination to test it are not granted to Andromache. She finds no consolation in the discovery of a new, meaningful way of acting; yet she remains stolidly content in the knowledge that her symbolic gestures will be meaningful enough. Because of Priam's unexpected success, however, Andromache will appear one last time with her dead husband, in Book 24. Homer recapitulates her characterization in her bedside attention to Hektor. The image of the funeral bed reverses the order of thematic implications which had been suggested by the head-dress in Book 22. There the death of Hektor led to recollection of their wedding; here the wedding bed has become the funeral bier.

Andromache finally stands juxtaposed with Kassandra, whose outcry over her greatest brother defines in the most general terms the political role of the primary Trojan warrior: "She cried out then in sorrow and spoke to the entire city: / 'Come, men of Troy and Trojan women; look upon Hektor / if ever before you were joyful when you saw him come back living / from battle; for he was a great joy to his city, and all his people' " (24. 703–6). What Kassandra only implies in her own general social role, as futile as that of Hektor, Andromache will make explicit. She, like the others, recognizes the national importance of Hektor's death and of the role he played in life. But when the meeting between Priam and Achilles reveals that it is the familial structure which will survive the particular catastrophes of history that conclusively destroy one society or another, we understand that Andromache's view is closer to the heart of Homer's vision. So Andromache speaks of the widow and the orphan, who will bear the sufferings of social disruption. Because Troy must now fall, Astyanax will die. And she reminds us that Hektor's protection of the city was just the general way of referring to his defense of individual wives and children who must now be separated from their nourishing and identifying habitat (24. 725–43). For humankind experiences anguish only when the individual human being is touched by pain and grief. The disaster of social disorder is, then, in the last analysis, intelligible only in the sorrow of each person who has been separated unnaturally from the stability of a social system. Andromache's lament concludes with the image of the marriage bed deprived of its natural occupant. It is in this way that Homer communicates his characteristically social perspective: that war ends, as it begins, with conjugal disorder.

4

The Central Weaving

What sets Helen apart, even from the galaxy of characters intimately related to her, is simply that *her* social ambiguity is the human cause of the disorder experienced by everyone in the poem's world. And because Homer leaves Helen's fundamental ambiguity unresolved, she embodies the great thematic tensions which give form to the *Iliad*. The primary tension is the conflict between two forms of social order, the heroic and the familial systems; and for Helen Homer reserves the "poetic" function of representing by her special ambiguous existence the anguish experienced by the individual caught between these two systems. Helen therefore is allowed no identifying outlet, no expression of will, in action. The conflict remains pent up within her character through the very end of the epic. The essential characteristic of Helen's role in Homer's poem, appropriate to her mythic character, is its ambivalence.

Aphrodite is a divine agent of the cosmic disorder in the *Iliad*; Helen is a human, and most important, counterpart of cosmic and divine disorder. She alone remains a passive character throughout the poem. The mysterious quality of her symbolic status is carefully kept intact. Because Helen's will has been suspended, her own control of it denied, she can find an *active* identity only outside the contemporary fictional world—in future song.

Yet, ironically, all the action of the epic centers around Helen's passive status. On one hand, she symbolizes an historical challenge to the familial society—the system based on kinship—on every level (political, familial-parental, familial-conjugal, and so on) by the heroic code of behavior (personal and national). On the other hand, Helen signifies the continuing ordering force of familial relationships. The disorder Helen embodies has such a disastrous impact on the entire human world because she embodies it paradoxically under the auspices of order. Priam's and Hektor's courtesy toward and protection of her validate Helen's claim to the protected status of guest-friend. Moreover, because she has been accepted as a royal wife, an integral member of Priam's family, Helen is defended by the representatives of Trojan society despite the hatred some Trojans bear her. Paris' violation of Menelaos' hospitality has not nullified Helen's right to demand the benefits of that sacred bond; Paris' princely station makes it all the more necessary that Troy duly honor and protect Helen.

Yet Troy's official recognition of her marriage to Paris is the cause of the war. When the city ratifies an illegal conjugal alliance, the entire social system is threatened. The autonomy of one society depends on its respecting that of another; only by remaining separate can the two Iliadic societies, Troadic and Achaian, be securely equal. Accepting Helen, and refusing to return her, the Trojan nation is attempting to maintain a vital order from lethal components: it has undermined the stability of an alien society. And because the Achaian system is able to enforce its solidarity by commissioning an army to restore the abducted member, Troy's own security is jeopardized, as Hektor explicitly recognizes (3. 49).

Helen's presence in Troy, then, represents a double social and genealogical threat. It threatens, on one hand, the family and kingdom of Menelaos and the national integrity of Argos; the disruption of a single Achaian family causes total social disarray—suggesting that all social entities derive their basic vitality from the security of the primary marital relationship. On the other hand, Helen's unnatural, sterile marriage with Paris affects Priam's city and the Troad nation itself, both in the future (since it precludes physical continuity) and in the present (since it invites military destruction). In this way, Helen is the symbol of fundamental disorder which encompasses all mankind and even extends to the gods; she is the focus of the poem's major theme. Zeus' first words in the *Iliad* reveal his marital problems with Hera (1. 493–530). Hera herself reports that, on the shadowy archaic level of primordial cosmic deities, Tethys and Okeanos are no longer sleeping together (14. 205–7). There are suggestions of continuing sibling rivalry between Poseidon and Zeus. Then, on what might be called the level of Fate (defined as such by the exchange between Zeus and Hera concerning the destiny of Sarpedon, and their bargaining over favorite cities) there is the conjugal squabbling between the two chief Olympians, with disastrous implications for gods as well as men (1. 573–75). On a familial plane, there is sibling rivalry between Athene and Hera, on the one hand, and Athene and Aphrodite on the other (also the love-hate between Aphrodite and Ares). Even on the personal level Zeus, Aphrodite, Achilles, Hektor, and others display self-contradictory behavior. Helen's extraordinary status in the Iliadic world, therefore, suggests that what is at stake is the continuation of the social system itself—the human condition proven to be most orderly for all, but now threatened at its basic sexual roots. The *heroic* attitude exemplified in the selfish deed of Paris, and in Helen's divinely-forced cooperation in it, may overturn the familial system which seems to be, in Homer's history, the prior and more essential standard.

From this widely social perspective we can best appreciate the profound significance of the disorder Homer embodies in this characterization of Helen—and how humanly crucial are the social issues faced by all the Iliadic heroes. Helen is human progress itself, vacillating between two orders, waiting in suspension for a continuity that will come only when their conflict has been transformed into cooperation, their antithetical potentials synthesized. The fact that Helen's individual will is suspended but that her actions, although involuntary, have collective repercussions which are material for memory reveals Homer's refusal to accept either norm, the heroic or the familial, as sufficient; neither, alone, provides man with a divinely-sanctioned order for social well-being, or even for social survival. Inasmuch as he rejects both purely communal and purely personal motivations, Homer stands as a prophet of the great Athenian phenomenon which managed to gloriously combine the γνῶθι σέ αὐτόν *gnōthi sé autón* ("know thyself") of Socrates with the holistic spirit of Plato's *Republic*. When a balance is maintained between these two orientations, human nature achieves its fullest, most nearly divine expression.

To Homer's audience Helen's tragic inability to act becomes, then, an inspiration to act; she is an anti-exemplum. The audience must prevent a recurrence of Helen's impotent dilemma in real life by insuring that the system they subscribe to has sufficient power to define each of its members unambiguously. In this broad sense, Havelock is right in speaking of the Homeric epic as didactic in impact and intention. The image of Helen's weaving, as central to the symbolic pattern of artifacts as is Achilles' shield, tells us much about Homer's own art:

> Now to Helen of the white arms came a messenger, Iris,
> in the likeness of her sister-in-law, the wife of Antenor's
> son, whom strong Helikaon wed, the son of Antenor,
> Laodike, loveliest looking of all the daughters of Priam.
> She came on Helen in the chamber; she was weaving a great web,
> a red folding robe, and working into it the numerous struggles
> of Trojans, breakers of horses, and bronze-armoured Achaians,
> struggles that they endured for her sake at the hands of the war god.
>
> (3. 121–28)

The poet's emphasis on this weaving image is revealed by the fact that he presents here not only art—and art in the making—but also the historical subject from which the woven product derives its thematic form. This special attention to content, as well as to style (the color of the robe, its intricacy of design) and process, distinguishes Helen's loom from all other looms in the *Iliad*. The others are "secondary" images, in the sense that their symbolic force derives from that of Helen's loom. Agamemnon's reference to Klytaimestra's loom, for example, which he wishes Chryseis to take over, deepens our appreciation of the king's profoundly disordered attitude which shapes the wrath-story (1.3); but it has this effect on us because of Helen's association with the same artifact. Yet neither Klytaimestra's loom, nor the description of creative weaving (in process) in connection with Andromache, includes a reference to the artistic human theme of the craftsmanship. Andromache does not weave history. Even though her weaving displays stylistic elaboration, the formulaic resemblance between it and the lines in which Helen's appears is limited to the technical aspects of the artistry: "but she was weaving a web in the inner room of the high house, / a red folding robe, and inworking elaborate figures" (22. 440–41). Like Helen's, although Andromache's web is not described as being "great" (3. 125), Andromache's artifact is purple in color and double in fold. But if the single adjective is not enough to suggest a distinction in scope and symbolic importance between the two looms, the distinction is proved definitively by contrasting Helen's "numerous struggles" with Andromache's "elaborate figures." Homer's material description of the human events taking memorial shape upon Helen's loom uniquely defines her thematically central role in the poem. Helen's loom, like Homer's poem (and like the Hellenic potter's art—suggesting a symbiotic relationship among all three art forms), records history, its essential mythic patterns. Homer's memory may have been supported by seeing such tapestries as Helen's hanging on the walls of royal courts, tapestries which in turn were rewoven, when they grew worn from age, by the new queen as she listened to the old court poet singing.

The dramatic effect of Helens' weaving is also achieved by its strategic position in the narrative. The symbolic import of the image relies to a remarkable extent on the narrative elements which comprise the context surrounding it; at the same time, the thematic significance of those elements is deepened by their association with her weaving. For example, Iris' appearance here is most unusual. In the eleven contexts presenting her in action, Iris is a messenger in all but one (when she escorts the wounded Aphrodite to Olympos, 5. 353 ff.). The pattern of her courier role is for Iris to be sent by Zeus, or at his behest, to gods or mortals, without disguise; in this way, he sends her to the Trojan assembly (2. 786 ff.), to Hera (8. 398 ff.), to Hektor (11.185 ff.), to Poseidon (15. 206 ff.), and

to Priam (24. 117 ff.). The pattern is broken only in connection with
Achilles and with Helen. In Book 18 *Hera* sends Iris to induce Achilles to
fight (18. 166 ff.), the goddesses strangely seeming to have forgotten his
lack of armor until he reminds Iris of it. Only once in the *Iliad* does a
mortal commission Iris; Achilles himself, in Book 23. 198 ff., sends her to
the winds to provide the fire for Patroklos' bier. The appearance of Iris to
Helen, then, is extraordinary for two reasons: only this once does Homer
fail to report the originator of the goddess' mission; and only here does
the poet present Iris in disguise. Homer alters Iris' role only in connection with the central weaving and the all-embracing shield.

The first alteration poses the question of who sends Iris to Helen. We
recall the adjective used to describe the messenger who did not come to
Andromache with the news of Hektor's death: ἐτήτυμος *etétumos* ("true,
truthful, real"—22. 438); yet Andromache's actions and her words indicate that she nonetheless knew of it somehow—she is, after all, weaving
a purple robe. The domestic act of weaving itself, as ordered by Hektor
in Book 6, seems to have given Andromache an inkling of the doom
which has now fallen upon her household. Similarly, Iris' appearance to
Helen suggests the immediate presence of the poet's hand, since Iris
comes to her by no fictional command, yet comes disguised as a fictional
character. The second alteration of the familiar pattern, Iris' disguise and
its detailed description by the narrator, symbolizes the social significance of Helen's role. Iris comes as Laodike, Helen's sister-in-law, whom
the narrator defines by reference to her natural social coordinates: her
own father (3. 124), her father-in-law (3. 122–23), and her husband (3.
123). The naturalness of Laodike's relations are a contrast to Helen's
social ambiguity; for Helen has two fathers-in-law, two husbands. But
Helen shares one coordinate with Laodike (Priam), proving her integration into Trojan society. The choice of disguises is even more specifically
appropriate. As the loveliest of Priam's daughters (3. 124) Laodike's
natural, orderly beauty stands in contrast with Helen's disorderly,
somehow unnatural beauty. By the same logic, the loom is connected
with the image of Paris' bed, as the parallel between Iris' appearance to
Helen and Aphrodite's in such narrative proximity emphasizes. Iris
represents the influence of the orderly principle (the divine spirit of
poetry, the art of memory). Aphrodite, in contrast, is the historical
disorder of the Iliadic world daemonically personified.

Helen's weaving in Book 3 contrasts with other weaving scenes as Iris'
appearance here differs from her other annunciations. The image of
Helen at the loom is not that of wifely dutifulness evoked by Andromache's activity in Book 22. Andromache's directs her weaving, and
the fire making associated with it, toward the maintenance of domestic

well-being. Ironically, the cloth she weaves will probably be Hektor's shroud; since the immediate context of her weaving emphasizes her unselfishness and the harmony of their marriage. Helen's artistry has no such implications; here there is no reference to Paris, no connotation of domesticity. Helen's art deals with the struggles "that they endured for her sake" (3. 128) on the Trojan plain. Yet the immediate drama of Helen's weaving is that it symbolizes imagistically the potential for peace expressed discursively in the preceding speech of Menelaos (3. 97 ff.) and conveyed emotionally in the common joyful reaction of both armies to the proposed truce (3. 111 ff.). Homer's introduction of the loom at this point, and the ensuing episode with Priam and the elders on the wall, complicates the usually straightforward narrative development—and results in emphasizing the element that causes the complication, the entire Helen episode. Homer sends Iris at the very moment when Hektor sends the two heralds to summon Priam to the place of arbitration (3. 116 ff.). The technical skill of the composer is revealed in the fact that the scene at the loom and the whole episode on the wall take place while the heralds are en route. The suspension of linear narrative time dramatically asserts how far the potential and the actual are separated; simultaneously it signifies the monumental importance of the movement from unruly war to the legally-based duel from which orderly peace might issue. The scene, then, reflects Helen's own unresolved position between potential and real action. The movement is from action to the contemplation of action, from the artistic detachment of the weaver to the physical aloofness of Helen and Priam observing the Achaians from the wall. The subject of her weaving is war. But her ceasing this activity introduces a momentous thematic turning point, a momentary possibility of peace—momentarily realized in Priam's courtesy and objectivity toward her, and in their joint vision of the quietly expectant warriors.

The subject matter of Helen's woven artistry is directly related to her descriptive catalogue of the Achaian warriors for Priam. In both places, at the loom and on the wall, Homer presents a methodology of naming; and the significance of the heroic or individualistic nature of the latter is influenced by reference to the *generalized* nature of the loom's method of nomenclature. Only Achilles' shield will be an artistic expression of both methodologies, individual and collective together. Helen is associated with well-wrought robes even here on the wall (3. 141, 385). The shimmering robe she wears to her meeting with Priam suggests the nature of the one Iris finds her making. Moreover Aphrodite's appearance is related imagistically to that of Iris through the poet's detailed observation of the way in which the goddess gets Helen's attention: "She laid her hand upon the robe immortal, and shook it" (3. 385). The eternal aspect of the artifact is related to the nature of Helen's artistry. The bed is the imagistic coefficient of the loom: what the loom symbolizes on the transcendent, eternal plane of memory, the bed represents within the temporal arena of action.

The relationship between the two images is suggested by Aphrodite's plucking the robe and by her appearance to Helen on the wall in the likeness of an aged wool-dresser, especially loved by Helen (3. 386–88). Aphrodite's disguise is a striking contrast to Iris' in its mnemonic reference to Helen's former Lakedaimonian social identity (3. 387). In this way Homer heightens the poignancy of the fact that Helen must now—since the duel has been aborted—remain in her present unnatural situation. Her involuntary involvement in disorder and the concommit-ant indefiniteness of her being, renewed at this point by Aphrodite's command that she return to the bed of Paris, had caused Helen to seek the consolation of her weaving. Only in this "poetic" action is Helen defined, for future men to know, as the woman for whom these particular men and nations once fought. In real life she must sleep, indefinite, beside Paris; but she will rise from that disorderly bed once again to pursue her search for identity in the creativity of her weaving. Helen's loom radiates symbolically outward to recall, and then to focus in itself and Helen, the major theme of the *Iliad*. Looms generally symbolize the domestic and social harmony which comes when the partners in a marriage act in an orderly fashion; as a corollary to this typical signifi-cance, the loom may represent disorder if its domestic position is unnatural. In this sinister sense, Agamemnon envisions Chryseis and Hektor envisions Andromache plying someone else's loom. The sym-bolic impact of the image is different in each case only because the attitudes of Hektor and Agamemnon toward the loom are different: one is disorderly, the other orderly. Agamemnon desires the establishment of unnatural domesticity (1. 31), whereas Hektor obviously does not (6. 456). So it is that Hektor's image of the foreign loom is countermanded by an image which reveals *his* desire; he sends Andromache back to her proper loom, his own (6. 491). There, fulfilling the appointed respon-sibilities of a wife, she loyally remains (22. 440). Helen's loom alone is not identified strictly by a domestic framework.

Instead the self-consciousness of her weaving suggests Helen's poetic mode of existence, unique among Iliadic mortals. That Helen's self-awareness, moreover, is an artistic characteristic (like Achilles' singing) is implied by the relationship between the subject matter (the fictive "fictional reality") of the loom and the fictional reality of the *Iliad*. Here traditional formulaic repetition serves a particular thematic purpose. Homer himself has told us that Helen was weaving the many battles "of Trojans, breakers of horses, and bronze-armoured Achaians" (3. 127). When Iris describes the reality outside Helen's chamber, she uses the identical words:

> 'Come with me, dear girl, to behold the marvellous things done
> by Trojans, breakers of horses, and bronze-armoured Achaians,
> who just now carried sorrowful war against each other,
> in the plain, and all their desire was for deadly fighting;
> now they are all seated in silence, the fighting has ended;
> they lean on their shields, the tall spears stuck in the ground beside them.
> But Menelaos the warlike and Alexandros will fight
> with long spears against each other for your possession.
> You shall be called beloved wife of the man who wins you.'
>
> (3. 130–38)

The great irony in the parallel between Iris and Aphrodite is that Helen will, in the end, be called the beloved wife of the man who did *not* win her. The single repetition in Iris' speech (line 127 = line 131) suggests a correspondence between Helen and the poet of the *Iliad*: she has made herself inform the doubly fictional woven war just as Homer, through shaping her character, has made himself inform the primary Iliadic war.

By comparison with international war and its threat to both societies, the duel is an orderly alternative. The two individuals for whom the stake is personal have agreed to isolate their particular problem from the community; in agreeing to the duel they have discovered a way of preventing their individual disorders from fatally affecting the order of their societies. This is the great potential of the truce (expressed in the orderly arbitration Hephaistos depicts on Achilles' shield). And Helen must see for herself whether it will be realized (3. 130)—and she herself defined by an orderly conclusion (3. 139). By having her move to the visionary perspective of the wall, Iris insures the continued aesthetic integrity of Helen's craft.

The symbolic significance of Helen's loom, then, is that its art is historically realistic. Others have been impressed by this quality of her weaving, even to the fanciful archaeological speculation of the Scholia of Venice, faithfully reporting the opinion of Aristarchus that "from the scenes embroidered on this web . . . Homer took the greater part of his history of the war." Indeed Eustathius went so far as to declare that Homer transcribed exactly what he saw sewn upon this marvelously historical artifact. But we don't need a miraculous textile discovery by a modern Schliemann to conclude safely that, in Homer's view, art records actual human events. Helen's web, as Havelock calls the epic (p. 66), was a kind of cultural encyclopedia.

The components of this view of art's relationship to reality are apparent in the wall catalogue provided by Helen. The artist's visionary perspective must be detached from the reality it records—just as Helen and Priam can observe all on the plain as they look down from the high wall of Troy. Helen is also detached in her ability to make art from a subject with which she is so personally involved. Her social ambivalence makes her weaving poetically special for the same reason that her vision from the wall is superior to Priam's—for whom she identifies the Argive leaders. He merely sees; Helen sees and knows, and tells. In Helen, Homer has expressed the poet's extraordinary insight, inspiration, or talent—to see men and gods and their deeds with the knowing vision by which their true identity and essential meaning can be communicated to his audience for the sake of order.

The scene, after all, is Homer's formal introduction of the Achaians in his poem. We've seen them in action, we may have heard of them already, but we've never been properly introduced. Now, for our benefit (as Homer's special audience for the wrath-story he has fashioned), the narrator and Helen introduce them simultaneously (just as Odysseus and the narrator become one in Book 9 of the *Odyssey*). They are naming from memory together. We are bound by the poetic spell so successfully that we ignore the suspension of narrative logic: after nine years of painful observation, and the Achaian embassy to Troy (3. 205–6), Priam knows these warriors well enough already. But Homer presents his characters to us through Helen's eyes because she knows them more intimately, and on their own grounds; and seeing them through her eyes we feel ourselves the profound ambivalence of her unique perspective. Homer explicitly reveals here what is only implied in the image of the loom: the precise manner in which the artist obtains his subject matter and theme. Like the poet, Helen, a true composer of memory, is not only the detached observer but also one who possesses insight, from experience. Her detachment is the accidental consequence of physical separation; the narrator's is that of temporal distance. Yet the narrator and the artist-heroine are nonetheless emotionally involved in the characters and deeds they witness and record. Helen's involvement, like her inside information, comes from being, unnaturally, both Argive and Trojan. Homer's intimate knowledge of his created world comes from his being imbued with the unbroken tradition which gives him (and us, through him) access to this crucial moment in human history; his emotional involvement, by which the poem captures and communicates the essence and meaning of that moment, comes from being, voluntarily, possessed by the Muse—who is the child of Zeus (as the principle of order) and Memory (the conveyor of the principle). The poet's inspiration differs from Helen's because his is a voluntary, active possession, hers an involuntary, passive one; the result of this difference between the two is the contrast between the poignant ambiguity of Helen's introspective admission of her personal disorder and the compelling clarity of the poem's public affirmation of hierarchical order. One brings only sorrow and resignation; the other brings, out of the sorrow, joy and hope.

Helen weaves, but then is made to desist. Her weaving treats only of societies and nations, not at all of individuals, and is an incomplete, ultimately inadequate art by Homer's standards. The juxtaposition of the familial and individual names on the wall complements her weaving, as does Iris' prediction of the man-to-man combat. Helen's concentration on collective human life is, then, insufficient from the implied Homeric viewpoint insofar as it is too naïvely conclusive. She is still an apprentice, ineffective even in artistic activity (compared to her artistic proficiency in the *Odyssey* where her identity is finally settled). The inadequacy of her art, compared with that of the epic poet, is suggested even more revealingly in another way. Helen was, after all, herself part of her woven subject (3. 128). The loom's art is also too personal. The robe does not portray the fullness of human life—transcendent as well as transitory—found in the epic poem, the essential imitation by which the poet confirms values as he records deeds, and moves individuals to concern about those values—and represented, within it, with greater adequacy, by Hephaistos. Including many individuals and several collectives, but refusing to give them specific names, the shield expresses the essentially—or typically, or ideally—human. Homer's poem, however, does both, presenting particular individuals and societies and, underlying them, essential human nature as well. As the *Iliad* succeeds in conceptualizing—through its artistic imagery—this total cosmic vision, we come to recognize that the poet, possessed by memory, is the self-acknowledged legislator of his society, the agent on earth of Zeus' Olympian order. Helen's weaving bears witness to Homer's awareness of his social role and pride in his own workmanship. But Helen herself must intend her history-recording robe to be an inspiration for men to come, one by which her painful identity will be communicated and preserved. In this sense, the weaving expresses a characteristic tension between process (of creation) and stasis (the continuing memorial influence of the completed robe).

Homer's emphasis on the process of Helen's weaving defines the

direct relationship between art and reality; Helen is the type of the epic
singer. Her responsibility, indeed her only clearly definite role, is to
know the facts. Iris (as divine or poetic authority) makes sure that Helen
will have direct access to the knowledge she needs for her art. Helen is
distinguished, in the *Iliad*, as the only mortal artist whose art is presented
in all its essential aspects: its technical process, as well as the nature of its
vision with respect to knowledge and memory. As a consequence, if
Helen can be said to be defined in any sense within the Iliadic world, it is
only as an artist that her identity is revealed—and it is a peculiarly poetic
one. The artist's extraordinary position is that he is identified not by
glorious deeds, but by his technical ability, through his powerfully-
ordered words, to move men to action.

The divine shield, another reflection of the mimetic art of Homer, may
be distinguished from the loom's art on the same basis by which
Aristotle contrasts history and poetry: "The difference between an
historian and a poet is . . . that one tells what happened and the other
what might happen. For this reason poetry is something more scientific
and serious than history, because poetry tends to give general truths
while history gives particular facts" (*Poetics* 35.9). Helen's ready assumption that the war she depicts on her loom was fought for her sake seems
simplistic by comparison with Homer's view of the *casus belli* in the
poem itself (not to mention Herodotus' dismissal of her minor role in the
ancient conflict between Europe and Asia). The poet carefully refrains
from judging Helen, even though he lets his characters judge her; indeed
the variety of their opinions proves the elusiveness of causality. It is
never certain whether we are to blame Helen, Paris, or Aphrodite for the
worldwide disorder; Zeus and Hera are also involved, as are Okeanos
and Tethys, Peleus and Thetis, Agamemnon and Artemis, Iphigeneia
and Klytaimestra—and many others, back to Strife, who dropped the
fateful apple on the dance floor. What sets the *Iliad* apart is that it
manages to combine a particular with a general viewpoint, the concrete
with the ideal, as well as history with imaginative poetry; the result is its
simultaneous realism and universality.

Helen is also distinguished from others by her singular self-
consciousness, deeper and more consistent than that displayed by any
other mortal. Even the self-consciousness of Achilles issues, finally, in
action. Helen can only contemplate action and the repercussions of
action. Consider her reply to Priam, after his courteous gesture toward
her, on the wall: " 'and I wish bitter death had been what I wanted, when
I came hither / following your son, forsaking my chamber, my
kinsmen, / my grown child, and the loveliness of girls my own age. / It
did not happen that way: and now I am worn with weeping' " (3.

173–76). As her weeping is apart from her coming to Troy, so is Helen's present inability to act separated from her past way of life. She lives now with the consequences of action only. Helen here appraises her own beauty from a perspective different from that of the elders, who do not see the deterioration she speaks of; or what they see is the uncanny effect of Helen's beauty, its transformation into something superhuman, wondrously mysterious (3. 158). Her beauty is indeed, by comparison with the "loveliness of girls," "terrible"—and it is a proof of Homer's genius that when he comes to describe the most beautiful of all women, he does so only by reference to the effect of her beauty on the experienced elders, using with stunning ironic impact the same adjective (δεινός deinós, "terrible") he will later apply to Athene's terrifying aegis. Helen's words neither prove her conscious guilt nor deny it; but they indicate, in their orderly reference to the various levels of now disordered society, her awareness of the communal implications of individual action. And so her regret for that action, because its repercussions are irreversible (unless the duel succeeds), is regret for her very existence. For this reason, she calls herself "dog-faced" (3. 180), whom the narrator calls "divine of women."

In the same vein, Helen's speech to Aphrodite suggests that she values honor more than does her Trojan husband, or even the goddess herself: " 'Not I. I am not going to him. It would be too shameful. / I will not serve his bed, since the Trojan women hereafter / would laugh at me, all, and my heart even now is confused with sorrows' " (3. 410–12). Here self-consciousness is related to self-respect. But with Hektor, Helen's self-consciousness becomes centrifugal, leading her to express her awareness of and sorrow for the suffering she has caused others:

> 'Brother
> by marriage to me, who am a nasty bitch evil-intriguing,
> how I wish that on that day when my mother first bore me
> the foul whirlwind of the storm had caught me away and swept me
> to the mountain, or into the wash of the sea deep-thundering
> where the waves would have swept me away before all these things had happened.
> Yet since the gods had brought it about that these vile things must be,
> I wish I had been the wife of a better man than this is,
> one who knew modesty and all things of shame that men say.
> But this man's heart is no steadfast thing, nor yet will it be so
> ever hereafter; for that I think he shall take the consequence.
> But come now, come in and rest on this chair, my brother,
> since it is on your heart beyond all that the hard work has fallen
> for the sake of dishonoured me and the blind act of Alexandros.'
>
> (6. 344–56)

We see that Helen's self-consciousness, in keeping with her nature, is ambivalent, directed toward others as well as toward herself. Regretting her very existence once again, Helen speaks in the manner of an author in search of a metaphor (6. 345–48). She knows the gods are involved in her present circumstances in which she exists without a will of her own (6. 349); but she also understands the criminal nature of Paris' breach of order and its inevitable repercussions on him and on others (6. 351–55). Her last sentence seems to contrast her own involuntary action, its passive nature, with the willful blindness of Paris (6. 356). But there is nothing equivocal about the depth of her regard for Hektor; her gesture, and the repeated address δᾶερ *dâer* ("husband's brother"), show her sincerity (6. 354–55). Her special affection for Hektor is her recognition that he is all that Paris is not, a civic-minded husband and dedicated warrior. Perhaps she implicitly associates Hektor with Menelaos as well, who is consistently described as warlike. Hektor combines in his character the finest qualities of war and peace, combat and love, political commitment and domestic propriety. Both Paris and Menelaos suffer by comparison with him.

Helen's words, then, express the same bilateral self-consciousness that her weaving presents. Her poetic self-awareness perceives "self" and "others" both separately and in their inevitable interrelationship. The ecphrastic (poetic description of a plastic work of art) nature of Helen's loom, therefore, in its association with her characteristic self-consciousness in Homer's poem, displays what Lowry Nelson, Jr., has called "an inward-turning self-reflexiveness: the poem commenting on itself . . . a playing with the reality of the fiction, or, more strongly, the exposure of the fiction to the end, paradoxically, of reenforcing it" (p. 173). In the image of the loom, Homer reminds his audience that the poem of memory itself, like the weaving which imitates it, is both a part of everyday reality and apart from it. That is why the poem is didactically effective—because we recognize it as a communication of essentials.

Perhaps her beauty appears so enigmatic and so characteristically poetic because Homer has granted Helen only this one luxury, her physical distance from all contemporary and ephemeral objects and events. She need not fear a greater harm from men or gods than that which she experiences already. She can address Aphrodite and Paris alike with impunity and without a sense of shame. Her beauty is the objective correlative of this physical aloofness from others, her poetic, transcendent position. In the words of Bespaloff: "In the depths of her wretchedness, Helen still wears an air of majesty that keeps the world at a distance and flouts old age and death" (p. 68). This is the essential meaning of her paradoxical epithet, δῖα γυναικῶν dia gunaikōn ("divine of women"). The ambiguity of her beauty—inhuman, like that of a goddess; but not purely divine, like that of a woman—embodies the strangeness of her relationship with the social structure of the Iliadic world which she unites, symbolically, with the world of Homer's audience. For although her beauty has a definite effect, upon the Trojan elders on the wall, that beauty is defined generally only by reference to its public effect. Homer means his audience to react just as emotionally to his portrait of Helen as he has reacted to her mythic image. Our reaction to Helen should be comparable to the marvel with which Achilles accepts the glorious divine armor from the hands of his mother, to the awestruck wonder of the elders on the wall. Like Helen's beauty, Homer's epic rises above time. Nothing and no one can quite compare with Helen; the *Iliad* alone is equal to her. Helen's ultimate identity is derived from outside her world, in the future of Homer's poem, the future invoked by her weaving. This is what Helen means when she marks her resemblance to Hektor by saying: " 'us two, on whom Zeus set a vile destiny, so that hereafter / we shall be made into things of song for the men of the future' " (6. 357–58).

Homer has created this special role for Helen in his poem by explicitly recording her dual affiliations: with Hera *and* Aphrodite, Menelaos *and* Paris, Andromache *and* Briseis, Agamemnon *and* Priam. At the same time, he provides contrasting figures whose social status serves to define her own lack of a certain one. These are the expatriates who take on new identities that are unfamiliar, but successfully unilateral: Briseis, Andromache, Patroklos, Phoinix. Their new identification is successful because they have an orderly right to it and a natural necessity for assuming it, since their former social coordinates have been dissolved in one way or another. But Helen's have not; Menelaos and the Achaians will not let go. So it is that she is *undefined* precisely by virtue of being overdefined. And when her suspended will is allowed the restricted expression of speech, we see that her loyalties, like her self-conscious emotions, remain divided:

> and Helen, daughter of Zeus of the aegis, took her place there
> turning her eyes away, and spoke to her lord in derision:
> 'So you came back from fighting. Oh, how I wish you had died there
> beaten down by the stronger man, who was once my husband.
> There was a time before now you boasted that you were better
> than warlike Menelaos, in spear and hand and your own strength.
> Go forth now and challenge warlike Menelaos
> once again to fight you in combat. But no: I advise you

>rather to let it be, and fight no longer with fair-haired
>Menelaos, strength against strength in single combat
>recklessly. You might very well go down before his spear.'
>
>   (3. 426–36)

Andromache would never have spoken to her husband in such terms. But despite Helen's tone of voice, her words themselves effectively prove that her heart goes out to both husbands, as it does to both brothers-in-law, both kings. In a very real sense, Helen's sympathy for the plight of human beings is universal, because she sympathizes with herself—and she, like Achilles, is at the human center of the poem.

Helen's poetic role in the *Iliad*, then, is expressed in her three functions as 1) the knower of names (human and divine), 2) the recorder of human events, and 3) the agent of inspiration by which we are put in touch with the transcendent divinity of our human nature—the divinely inspired poet who fashions her poetic character. Helen's function as knower and interpreter of identity recalls her immediate recognition of Telemachos in the *Odyssey*; in the *Iliad* Helen recognizes Aphrodite even though the disguises of the gods are impenetrable to ordinary men. This is the service Helen performs for Priam on the wall. As she names the chief Argives for Priam, she reveals each individual's intrinsic character. Helen says of Agamemnon, for example: " 'That man is Atreus' son Agamemnon, widely powerful, / at the same time a good king and a strong spearfighter, / once my kinsman, slut that I am. Did this ever happen?' " (3. 178–80). Her introduction summarizes Agamemnon's social responsibilities, delineating the particular social coordinates which distinguish him; even his reason for warring against Priam is revealed in the process: he was her kinsman. Helen does for Priam, then, the same service that Homer does for his listeners when he tells them the names of the Trojan elders on the wall or when he presents the catalogue of ships. Helen's knowledge, and her ability to communicate her knowledge, suggests Homer's own.

But Homer distinguishes his knowledge of human events from hers; his perspective, after all, is later and therefore more complete. An example is the narrator's deeply poignant interjection after Helen notices the absence of her brothers from the plain beneath the wall:

>   'I see them
>all now, all the rest of the glancing-eyed Achaians,
>all whom I would know well by sight, whose names I could tell you,
>yet nowhere can I see those two, the marshals of the people,
>Kastor, breaker of horses, and the strong boxer, Polydeukes,
>my own brothers, born with me of a single mother.

Perhaps these came not with the rest from Lakedaimon the lovely,
or else they did come here in their sea-wandering ships, yet
now they are reluctant to go with the men into battle
dreading the words of shame and all the reproach that is on me.'
    So she spoke, but the teeming earth lay already upon them
away in Lakedaimon, the beloved land of their fathers.

(3. 234–44)

With so delicate a stroke, Homer shows his greater knowledge, thereby adding to our appreciation of her anguished separation from her natural environment; for that environment is now irretrievable.

Helen's interpretative function makes her recording role possible. Her weaving is intended to memorialize the content of her speech to Priam, to make it known to others whom she cannot address in person. Therefore, if Homer is the "imaginary spectator," as Ezra Pound terms him, he is so only inasmuch as we can distinguish his manner of recording from Helen's. Mainly, of course, it is more objective than hers; she, after all, refers to herself openly in her weaving. Because "the poet tells us nothing about himself we are left to draw our conclusions from analogies," as Maurice Bowra remarks (*Tradition and Design in the "Iliad,"* p. 7). Yet Helen's importance to the curious reader is that her weaving offers us a glimpse of Homer's artistic posture which might otherwise have remained more elusive than it is. Her weaving shows us that Homer considered the thematic materials of his art to be real human events. The significance of the loom, then, as a prefiguration of the shield and as a type of the poem itself, is that the warriors who move across the woven robe bear the same relation to the warriors who move in the Homeric hexameters as those warriors, and the loom itself, bear to Homer's contemporaries. If the art of the loom is less universal than that of the poem it is only because Helen, unlike Homer, has not yet seen all the repercussions of action before beginning to record them for posterity.

Helen's third poetic function in the *Iliad* is that of intermediary. Defining the human purpose of memory, in her weaving and in her references to song, Helen enhances the quality of human life and confirms divine values of order—to express meaningfulness, to shape nobility, to prophesy the immortality of glory. That is what the singer does, with the song of memory on which Homer bases his poem. The potential of the robe is revealed, by analogy, when Helen states that she and Hektor will be remembered in song—and Hektor comes to Helen as she is directing the handiwork of her maidens (6. 323 ff.). But Hektor does not understand Helen's suggestion that he should rest; he thinks that would be shirking his duty (3. 360). At this point in his own poetic

development he is an unappreciative audience. But we see that what
Helen's speech really suggests is a sympathetic recognition of the
psychical distance which he shares with her because the effects of his
present actions are beyond his control. After he has fallen from order and
is faced with a futile death, he comes to learn the lesson that Helen
teaches. Because Hektor knows, at last, that his honor is irretrievable in
the present, he voluntarily entrusts its realization, through the agency of
memory and song, to the future. At the moment of final vision Hektor's
poetic identity is born, when he understands the fatality shaping his acts
and the relative impotence of his personal will. He recognizes Deïphobos
as Athene, seeing through her disguise, too late, but now just as
knowledgeably as Helen:

> And Hektor knew the truth inside his heart, and spoke aloud:
> 'No use. Here at last the gods have summoned me deathward.
> I thought Deïphobos the hero was here close beside me,
> but he is behind the wall and it was Athene cheating me,
> and now evil death is close to me, and no longer far away,
> and there is no way out. So it must long since have been pleasing
> to Zeus, and Zeus' son who strikes from afar, this way; though before this
> they defended me gladly. But now my death is upon me.
> Let me at least not die without a struggle, inglorious,
> but do some big thing first, that men to come shall know of it.'
>
> (22. 296–305)

It isn't the gods that Hektor addresses here, nor only his own heart. His
words are spoken aloud to the bearers of memory, who alone can now
insure his glory. Only in the memory he leaves behind can there be a
final solace, a sufficient incentive for his orderly persistence to the end.
That end will be futile, therefore, only on the immediate level; it will be
gloriously effective, in the transcendent memory of poetry, in providing
an example for men to come. Hektor plays his last scene for us.

We know that the art of the poet is, like that of the weaver, a mnemonic
one whose technique is inspired by the gods to perpetuate human order.
To retain his gift of mnemonic artistry and his social effectiveness, the
poet must allow himself to be possessed by this inspiring spirit; to
express divine order fully, the poet must deny himself (the original sense
of ecstasy). Homer tells us this directly, when he refers to the fate of
another bard, in Dorion, where the Muses "encountering Thamyris the
Thracian stopped him from singing / as he came from Oichalia and
Oichalian Eurytos; / for he boasted that he would surpass, if the very
Muses, / daughters of Zeus who holds the aegis, were singing against
him, / and these in their anger struck him maimed, and the [divine

song] / they took away, and made him [forget his lyre playing]" (2.
594–600). The art of the lyre, like that of the loom, receives its communicative force from the continuity of memory under divine inspiration. Helen, like the Muse of song, is a κούρη διὸς *koúrē diòs* ("daughter of
Zeus"—3. 426). Homer has avoided Thamyris' Arachnean fate because
he records not his own greatness but, steadfastly, that of all men and of
humanity—interacting with the gods. The *Iliad* begins and ends with
ritual song: the Achaians' propitiation of Apollo and the Trojans' dirge
for Hektor. Throughout the epic singing is associated with communal
order, with the perpetuity of memory, with its supraindividual inspiration, with love and marriage, history and genealogy, the glory that can be
inspired by didactic exemplification, the ability to cope with death, the
renewal of spring, crimes against and honor to the gods, with mortality
and immortality alike—in short, with the entire span of human life
depicted on the great shield. Even more lasting than the monumental
bronze forged by Hephaistos are the memorable hexameters of Homer's
poem. Helen's tragedy is that, even as an artist, she is characteristically
subject to time. Her weaving survives only within the stronger shield of
memory, the poem itself.

5

The Queen of the Gods and the King of Men

Double-dealing Hera

Analyzing Hera's role in the *Iliad* provides a natural transition from Helen and her disorderly galaxy to that of Hephaistos and Achilles, maker and bearer of the great shield. Like the heroine whose adopted city she despises, the wife of Zeus is a mysterious figure in early Greek mythology—an ancient, pre-Hellenic deity of unknown, possibly chthonic, origins whose very name in Greek is only a title (meaning "lady"). H. J. Rose and C. H. Robertson speculate that Hera's relationship with Zeus may have come about because his worshippers, arriving on the Greek mainland, found her preexisting cult too strong to be displaced completely. So even though she was regularly, before, sexually unallied, the Greeks married her to their chief god in the usual way of invading religions. The quarrels between Zeus and Hera in the *Iliad* may reflect a time when their cults "were not fully reconciled" (*Oxford Classical Dictionary*, p. 497). Their domestic squabbles, then, are doubly significant: because they are the Olympian ruling couple, and because Hera is characteristically associated with sacred marriage rituals (in Argos and Samos, from most ancient times). Only Hera shares with Helen the epithet Ἀργείην *Argeíēn* ("Argive"). Whereas Aphrodite's associations with marriage are passionate and erotic, Hera's are more characteristically orderly; she generally represents, as a result, the power of the marriage bond, and often, sheer power itself and force of will. It is power that she offers to bribe Paris, which he rejects, along with Athene's offer of wisdom, in favor of the love and beauty promised by Aphrodite. But the distinction between these two goddesses was unclear even among the ancient Greeks; Pausanias records early statues of "Hera Aphrodite."

Hera is connected with both Helen and Hephaistos in a strange way; she is, in the *Iliad*, Hephaistos' only parent; and she is, by virtue of her marriage to Zeus, Helen's jealous stepmother. In one sense the smith-god's parthenogenesis is Hera's poetically just response to Zeus' infidelity with Leda; in another, it parallels his fathering of Athene, suggesting that she can do anything he can do. Hera's relentless enmity toward Helen's Trojan husband leads her to risk her own marital harmony in order to accomplish Zeus' cooperation in the fall of Troy, which will result in Helen's final Argive identity. Hera's peculiarly intimate relationship with her artisan-son is perhaps a reflection of her primitive associations with sacred shields in both Minoan and Mycenaean cults (as displayed in the Argive Heraia festival). Homer expresses their intimacy, in the *Iliad*, by the extraordinary technical assistance Hephaistos is willing to give his mother—as long as it does not contradict Zeus' order. Hephaistos has built her marvelous bedroom, with its magic doors (14. 168), and loyally dedicates his art to her wishes (14. 239). At her command, he intervenes against the river on behalf of Achilles (21. 330 ff.). Like Sleep in Book 14, Hephaistos reports that his willing service to his mother in the past has had dire repercussions on himself (1. 585 ff.).

All this makes it almost comically ironic that Zeus is regularly called "the thunderous lord of Hera" (13.154). His very dubious control over his royal consort, despite all his thundering, betrays the extraordinary character of their marital alliance; Hera, in fact, claims to be the equal of her husband (4. 58–64). In the thematic structure of Homer's poem, Hera is virtually Zeus' antithesis; for she is able to command an influence over human affairs as disorderly as his is orderly. And if it is sometimes difficult for us to interpret the words and deeds of Zeus as clear expressions of order, it is Hera's unruly presence that makes it so. Were it not for her interference, his benign and temperate plan for ordering both Olympian and human society would enable men to work out their destinies without the tragic fatality of war. In short, the character of Hera is a pivotal one, without which we would have a very different *Iliad*. As it is, studying Hera helps us understand that Homer's conception of the relation between order and disorder is far from being simple, neither right against wrong, nor god against man, nor Hera and Athene against Aphrodite, nor even Trojan against Achaian.

Hera's unruly nature is just as unalterable and intransigent as Zeus' love for order which leads him, as early as Hesiod, to be identified with mind at its best. Hera's hatred for Troy is so violent and unrestrained that we see Homer expressing, in her, the cosmic force of sheer passionate will; Zeus himself can liken it only to cannibalism.

> Deeply troubled, Zeus who gathers the clouds answered her:
> 'Dear lady, what can be all the great evils done to you
> by Priam and the sons of Priam, that you are thus furious
> forever to bring down the strong-founded city of Ilion?

If you could walk through the gates and through the towering ramparts
and eat Priam and the children of Priam raw, and the other
Trojans, then, then only might you glut at last your anger.'

(4. 30–36).

At the same time he realizes that he must allow her passion to be
satisfied; otherwise it will threaten his own tenuous, and perhaps recent,
primacy on Olympos (4. 37 ff.; 8. 205–6). Hera's determination to destroy
Priam's race at any cost reveals the fragility of order. When disorder,
with its centripetal action, chooses to flex its strength and prove its
independence, the stability of the universe is threatened from top to
bottom: "the lady Hera was angry, / and started upon her throne, and
tall Olympos was shaken" (8. 198–99). When Hera pits her will against
the will of Zeus, the harmony of the pantheon is disrupted.

Homer focuses this disruption in Hera's seduction of her husband,
with the help of Aphrodite and Sleep, in Book 14. Her purpose is to
suspend the operation of the principle of order so that she, with
Poseidon and their allies, can countermand Zeus' solemn promise to
Thetis to make the Achaians suffer for the slight to Achilles. To accomplish that aim Hera uses on Zeus the same self-centered passionate
love by which Agamemnon is blinded—as Thersites points out (3.
232–33)—and by which Paris desires the bedroom service of Helen at the
end of Book 3 (when his emotion is expressed in words nearly identical to
those used by Zeus—cf. 3. 442–46 and 14. 315–28). Hera accomplishes her
sinister plan with a great degree of craftiness: "And to her mind this
thing appeared to be the best counsel, / to array herself in loveliness, and
go down to Ida, / and perhaps he might be taken with desire to lie in love
with her / next her skin, and she might be able to drift an innocent /
warm sleep across his eyelids, and seal his crafty perceptions" (14.
161–65). The disorder in Hera's project is a wife's use of sex as a weapon
for selfish ends; as the symbol of sacred marriage, her selfishness
undercuts her own mythic character—so furious is her jealousy that it
blinds her even as she means to blind all-seeing Zeus.

The images Homer uses to describe her cosmetic preparations associate Hera with characters in both thematic galaxies. She dresses in the
chamber Hephaistos has fitted out for her with wonderfully intricate
doors which "no other of the gods could open" (14. 166–68). The doors
represent Hera's peculiar autonomy, comparable only to that of Zeus
among the gods; they also recall the doors to Achilles' hut, which only he
can open. The architectural description of the chamber associates
Hephaistos' work for his mother with Paris' craftsmanship. After anoint-
ing her body and arranging her hair (14. 169–77), Hera

dressed in an ambrosial robe that Athene
had made her carefully, smooth, and with many figures upon it,
and pinned it across her breast with a golden brooch, and circled
her waist about with a zone that floated a hundred tassels,
and in the lobes of her carefully pierced ears she put rings
with triple drops in mulberry clusters, radiant with beauty,
and, lovely among goddesses, she veiled her head downward
with a sweet fresh veil that glimmered pale like the sunlight.
Underneath her shining feet she bound on the fair sandals.

(14. 178–86)

My student Bennett Munsey has observed that Hera's toilet is an ironic parody of the famous partly-formulaic arming sequences in the poem—like those of Paris, Patroklos, Agamemnon, and Achilles. The scene in the bedroom follows the same orderly pattern, includes equally detailed descriptions of each item of Hera's apparel, and leads up to a turning point in the thematic conflict of order and disorder—which, by its very detail, the dressing scene dramatically highlights. The implications of Hera's robing are complex because in this most complete description of dressing in the poem, artifacts characteristically associated with one galaxy or the other are juxtaposed with elusive discrimination. In some ways, the scene, by its imagistic associations with both galaxies, represents the *intentional* aspect of art. For an artifact's functionality depends only upon its being well made, as all of these objects of dress are; but the will of its user determines whether the artifact will have an orderly or a disorderly effect.

Hera's gown was made by the artisan-goddess (the female counterpart of Hephaistos whose craftiness plays a central divine role in the *Odyssey*) who—unlike Aphrodite to whom Hera is about to speak—has been allied with the queen of the gods from the outset of the war. The image of the many-figured robe associates its maker, Athene, paradoxically with Helen and Andromache, the only women who weave in the *Iliad*. Woven by Helen and Andromache, the robe symbolizes domestic and political harmony disordered. To plead for the restoration of harmony Hekabe offers a robe to Athene—Priam, robes to Achilles; and to symbolize its ultimate reestablishment, Achilles returns two robes with Hektor's body. Athene's association with the robe, moreover, is logically consistent. Symbolizing order in her sponsorship of the Argives, Athene in the *Iliad* dissociates herself from the robe because war is necessary to restore equilibrium to Danaan society in particular and to the human condition in general. So she turns her head away from Hekabe's offering; and so she carefully removes her robe, to don the aegis of Zeus, whenever she leaves Olympos to go into battle (5. 734–35 = 8. 385–86); while Achilles awaits divine battle dress, Athene flutters the aegis over him to terrify the Trojans (18. 204). But Hera, in her characteristically willful fashion, perpetrates her deception, accomplishes her warlike intention, by pretending to the peaceful marital harmony which Athene's robe symbolizes. As Munsey points out, the consistent emphasis on delicate, fragrant, emphatically feminine clothing directly contrasts with the "powerfully masculine armor" of normal warriors; the contrast underlines the sinister nature of Hera's intent, upsetting our normal expectations as to what particular artifacts represent.

The brooch and earring are associated with Hephaistos, who learned the jeweler's art when Thetis and Eurynome protected him from the wrath of his mother (18. 395 ff.); Hera's devious exploitation of her son's artistry is implicitly contrasted with Thetis' orderly request for the shield. Hephaistos serves his mother because order dictates, on one level, that he should do so; it is not his fault if she turns his labors awry in her own pursuit of disorderly ambitions. Similarly, Hermes' sandals are associated with his orderly mission in Book 24, to accompany Priam; whereas here the sandals function very differently: to convey Hera on her maliciously sensuous journey. When Hera dons her headdress, the gesture symbolizes a marital arrangement which contrasts strikingly with that of Andromache as she dashes her bridal veil to the ground in Book 22—indeed, it is more like Hektor's gesture, as he recovers his helmet to enter battle. But Hera, unlike Hektor, enters battle in disguise, assaulting order by means of the "disorderly influence of feminine sensuality." The "pale sunlight" (14. 185) that bathes her "arming" is, as Munsey observes, a telling contrast to the radiance that shines about Achilles as he arms to reenter the war. Achilles' radiance comes from the divine order with which he is literally armed; Hera's, on the other hand, is artificial and disorderly.

Hera's double standard is revealed in her deception of Aphrodite. She manages to borrow the powerful girdle of the goddess of love—much more elaborate in its fabrication than Athene's (14. 215–17)—by appealing to Aphrodite on a level which transcends their mortal antagonism (14. 190–92)—the level of Olympian detachment. Not doubting Hera's good faith, or perhaps beguiled by her aura of power, Aphrodite responds in an orderly manner, on the same high Olympian level (14. 193–96). Then Hera furthers her deception by claiming that she intends to act on behalf of cosmic order, as if she means to reinstate the harmony among the gods by resolving the most fundamental divine conflict of all. As Hera requests the girdle, the narrator notes the deceit explicitly: "Then, with false lying purpose the lady Hera answered her: / 'Give me loveliness and desirability, graces / with which you overwhelm mortal men, and all the immortals. / Since I go now to the ends of the generous earth, on a visit / to Okeanos, whence the gods have risen, and Tethys our mother / who brought me up kindly in their own house, and cared for me' " (14. 197–202). The nobility of the goal she proposes only heightens the ignominy of Hera's true intentions. Hera plans to reassert not order, but disorder. She wins Aphrodite's cooperation through blatant flattery: attributing universal power to her over men and gods alike (14. 199). Hera's lying expediency is proved when she uses the exact same words to convince Sleep (14. 233), as well as to flatter Zeus (14. 309–11). Clearly she will stop at nothing to achieve her purpose. No power, no propriety restricts what she may say and do.

Hera's perfidy implicates the very heart of universal being, as well as her own essential identity as the guardian of sacred marriage. Only here in the *Iliad* does Homer refer directly to the disorder at the cosmic center. Hera's lying proposal, then, delineates the limits to which disorder has affected Iliadic reality. Okeanos "whence the gods have risen" (14. 201), will later be depicted by Hephaistos as the outer boundary of the world reflected on the great shield. We learn from Hesiod's *Theogony* (130–35) that Tethys is also his sister, both born from Gaia (earth) and Uranus (sky). So there is a temporal comprehensiveness to Hera's reference, as well. She speaks of the orderly function played by these archaic gods at the time when Zeus was in the process of establishing the present Olympian order (14. 202–4). Their temporal priority makes their present conflict profoundly symbolic of the disorder rampant in the Iliadic world. Moreover Hera's description of the present marital state of Okeanos and Tethys must be accurate; Aphrodite doesn't question it. The disruption of the ancient marriage bed symbolizes the underlying turmoil; a bedding-down between these two old gods would indeed accomplish, as well as symbolize, the restoration of cosmic equilibrium. Hera portrays her role as one of filial gratitude and familial peacemaking, like that played by Hephaistos at the end of Book 1. And Aphrodite's are the powers she needs to fulfill it successfully. The sad irony is that Hera wins Aphrodite's help with the "words made gentle" that Hephaistos, with orderly intention, advised her to use (1. 582).

Recognizing the comprehensive orderliness of Hera's assumed role, Aphrodite unknowingly reveals the false basis of the scheme: " 'I cannot, and I must not deny this thing that you ask for, / you, who lie in the arms of Zeus, since he is our greatest' " (14. 212–13). Aphrodite does not seem to be aware of the conflict between Hera and Zeus; her knowledge, in this scene, is oddly limited, especially since she is the goddess of love—just as her own unruly involvement in the affairs of mortals is not mentioned. Instead, this once, Aphrodite performs an orderly role: she serves the reinstatement of marital love whenever and however possible. The girdle she lends to Hera is Aphrodite's most characteristic artifact; and it is as if she is lending her very identity to the rival goddess:

> She spoke, and from her breasts unbound the elaborate, pattern-pierced
> zone, and on it are figured all beguilements, and loveliness
> is figured upon it, and passion of sex is there, and the whispered
> endearment that steals the heart away even from the thoughtful.
> She put this in Hera's hands, and called her by name and spoke to her:
> 'Take this zone, and hide it away in the fold of your bosom.
> It is elaborate, all things are figured therein. And I think
> whatever is your heart's desire shall not go unaccomplished.'
> So she spoke, and the ox-eyed lady Hera smiled on her
> and smiling hid the zone away in the fold of her bosom.
>
> (14. 214–23)

The poet's use of the present tense to describe the girdle suggests not only the artifact's eternal nature, but also the personally transcendent level of behavior on which Aphrodite acts in this scene. It is clear that Hera is acting on quite a different level, one of self-interested involvement, when we compare her far from innocent smile, so unlike Andromache's in Book 6, with the laughter of Aphrodite (14. 211). That Hera is the wife of Zeus magnifies the proportion of her deception of Zeus' daughter, and of Zeus himself. Given in an orderly spirit, the girdle is accepted in a spirit of disorder.

As a misappropriated ordering agent, the girdle is an antitype of Achilles' shield. Because the wills of the lender and borrower are at odds, the girdle will function with chaotic consequences. As its primary custodian Aphrodite instructs the borrower that, if the girdle is employed in keeping with its nature (14. 219) it can only be effective (14. 221)—in influencing natural, orderly action. Hera does follow Aphrodite's instructions exactly, hiding it in her bosom (14. 223). She learns the technique, but not the orderly spirit, of Aphrodite's art. The concealment of the girdle, which works its influence upon men without being seen, is in striking opposition to the openness of the shield image.

After her Hermes-like descent to Lemnos, Hera accosts Sleep, the brother of Death, promising him, if he will assist her, " 'gifts; a lovely throne, imperishable forever, / of gold. My own son, he of the strong arms, Hephaistos, / shall make it with careful skill, and make for your feet a footstool' " (14. 238–40). But Sleep has learned caution from experience: " 'any other one of the gods, whose race is immortal / I would lightly put to sleep, even the stream of that River / Okeanos, whence is risen the seed of all the immortals. / But I would not come too close to Zeus, the son of Kronos, / nor put him to sleep, unless when he himself were to tell me' " (14. 244–48). Like Hephaistos, Sleep is not quite so willing to help Hera as he once was. His past service to her has had unhappy repercussions (14. 249 ff.). It is ironic that he happens to mention Okeanos; for Hera has not told her lying story to him. Sleep implies that the power of the Olympian Zeus now takes precedence over that of the archaic gods, perhaps explaining why Hera is unable to exploit their predicament with impunity.

Hera's reply expresses the difference between her present motivation and that of Zeus. She has a personal interest in this war among mortals, which he has not (14. 265–66). Like a good politician she detects her victim's critical weakness. Sleep's well-founded objection is swept away by a well-placed marital bribe; she promises to give him Pasithea, the Grace he loves, for his wife (14. 267–69). Following her solemn Stygian oath to do so, Sleep eagerly agrees (14. 270–80).

Together they arrive at Ida. Zeus is stunned by Hera's fragrant appearance, as the girdle works the will of its user, not of its lender. Homer again explicitly marks the insincerity of her reply, as Hera repeats her false mission (14. 300–306). Her lies about leaving her horses below and about her professed subservience to his governmental order heighten the general effect of crafty deception (14. 307–11). She tells Zeus she came to ask his permission for her noble journey. As the girdle continues its influence, Zeus tells her that he is struck with a greater desire than he has felt before with her, or with anyone else (14. 313–17). To prove his point to her, he catalogues his many mistresses: Ixion's wife, Danaë, Europa, Semele, Alkmene, Demeter, and Leto. He seems to be going out of his way to show that Hera is now giving him no more than what he deserves for his past infidelities. Each of Zeus' sexual alliances is a fruitful one: Peirithoös, Perseus, Minos, Rhadamanthys, Herakles, Dionysos, and Apollo. But Hera is mother only to Hephaistos in the *Iliad*; and Zeus is not his father. The fertility of Zeus' improper alliances contrasts with the sterility of his proper marriage.

Hera's deception progresses when she claims that modesty forbids that she sleep with him in the open (14. 330–36). She asks her husband to return with her to the chamber Hephaistos built; but in describing her bedroom, Hera does not mention the doors which she alone can unlock (14. 337–40)—her verbatim repetition stops short of that most significant detail. The only qualification to the success of Hera's stratagem is the fact that Zeus, instead of returning to her closed chamber as she wishes, performs a miracle to display his might; he creates a marvelous cloud beneath which their bedding-down takes place. As a result Hephaistos is not associated with this disorderly sexual dalliance, in which both partners act solely from self-interest. Because Zeus does not return to the bedroom, he awakens earlier, the cloud lifted, to discover his wife's deceit. His awakening insures the ultimate triumph of order over disorder, his will over hers.

Their bedding-down (14. 346–51) is comparable to that of Paris and Helen in Book 3. While Hera is so occupied, Sleep informs Poseidon that Zeus is temporarily out of commission (14. 357–60). Consequently, despite the absence of Achilles, the Achaians carry the day. Here we see the connection between the will of Zeus and the theme of the *Iliad*, the glory of Achilles. For the effect of Hera's sinister art is to threaten the fulfillment of that will (the promise to Thetis). As Poseidon himself declares, Achilles will not need to be remembered in song—indeed will have no occasion to be—if the Argives can be victorious without him (14. 368–69). Somehow Zeus and Hera must be made to work together if Achilles is to be given the opportunity for memorable action. The Achaians must ultimately triumph, but only with the reemergence of Achilles from his unnatural seclusion. Hera's desire to have them prevail without their most important individual is emphatically disorderly, inasmuch as such a turn of events would exemplify no socially beneficial lesson. It would suggest that the individual's secession from society does not jeopardize both his own honor and the well-being of society itself.

But the poet reasserts control of his theme when Zeus awakens on Ida. The king of the gods reaffirms the priority of his order to Hera's by reminding her of his punishment of her in the past, referring to the same story recalled by Sleep (15. 14 ff.). Hera is frightened by the recollection, but avoids being punished for her present deception by compounding her falsehood: she blames the events Zeus now observes entirely on Poseidon. And her disorderly attitude toward their conjugal bond is recapitulated in her solemn oath by the primary symbol of that bond: " 'Earth be my witness in this, and the wide heaven above us, / and the dripping water of the Styx, which oath is the biggest / and most formidable oath among the blessed immortals. / The sanctity of your head be witness, and the bed of marriage / between us: a thing by which I at least could never swear vainly" ' (15. 36–40). With what effrontery the hypocritical oath is taken, and insolent disregard for all propriety! If the queen of the gods, the guardian of sacred marriage, can swear, no mortal blasphemy or discord may surprise us. Zeus, moreover, allows himself to be convinced by her lying oath; the state of order in the Homeric world is overwhelmingly tenuous. Disorder, holding no value ultimately sacred, cannot be chained; at best, Hera can be pacified. With her oath by the marriage bed, it becomes evident that disorder is rooted, sexually, in the very nature of things.

The result of Hera's seduction of Zeus, despite the immediate implications of disorder, is, ironically enough, the basis of a new divine order and harmony that will determine the ensuing course of events. Book 15 presents the reconciliation of the gods made possible by Zeus' acceptance of Hera's deceitful acquiescence to the will of her husband, inspired by fear of his power. It is not only because Hera has achieved her immediate purpose—the temporary victory of the Argives—that she pretends to support Zeus' order (15. 45–46). It is also because she senses that Zeus himself is ready to add his influence to her own to achieve a more permanent solution to the war, one in keeping with her ambition. The promise to Thetis has received sufficient fulfillment, and Zeus is free now to cooperate fully in the predestined fall of Troy. The explanation for this most significant thematic reversal can only be Hera's declaration of loyalty.

Zeus cares not for his wife's concealed motives, but is satisfied with her *apparently* orderly behavior. If she is willing to *act* in harmony with him, that is enough to assure the maintenance of his governmental role; even at the start of Greek culture, action precedes intention. And his new-found position of authority is reenforced when Zeus predicts to Hera future events as he sees them from his comprehensive perspective. Hera must be firmly reconciled to him when she learns that Zeus' plan for Troy is akin to her own, that his temporary opposition to her over the matter of Achilles was not, in fact, in contradiction to her will. First, then, he brings about the new Olympian stability by accepting her disclaimer at face value: " 'If even you, lady Hera of the ox eyes, hereafter / were to take your place among the immortals thinking as I do, / then Poseidon, hard though he may wish it otherwise, / must at once turn his mind so it follows your heart, and my heart' " (15. 49–52). The very act of accepting her professed loyalty works to insure that loyalty's practical effectiveness in forming a new government, hierarchically structured. Hera must now act as her husband dictates, if she is to maintain the original falsehood; she has been co-opted by her own deceit.

Zeus orders her to send Iris to remove Poseidon from the battle and to assemble " 'the generations of the gods' " (15. 54)—perhaps a veiled reference to her mention of Okeanos, since Zeus now controls all those who sprang from the older god Hera claimed to be serving. His authority reinstated, the orders Zeus issues are efficient and peremptory: Iris is to stop Poseidon (15. 56–58), Apollo is to reinvigorate Hektor (15. 59–61), Hektor will rout the Achaians (15. 62–63). The causality of the predicted sequence is what we would expect from the master of the golden chain. The Argive rout will cause Achilles to send Patroklos forth (15. 64); Hektor will then slay him (15. 65), avenging Sarpedon in the process (15.

67); Achilles, in turn, will kill Hektor (15. 68). Finally, the Achaians, with the help of Athene, will take Ilion (15. 71). Both Hera and Thetis, therefore, will be satisfied at one and the same time (15. 72–76).

As the final series of events is simultaneously predicted and set in motion, the superiority of Zeus' will is revealed to be in its expression of the collective nature of man, and of the spirit of poetry. Indeed his speech is a succinct outline of the remainder of the Homeric song. Zeus is both more foresighted than Hera, and less self-interested. Zeus' will, like hers, has the same ultimately orderly aim: the triumph of Argos. But his will is attuned to that aim in a way which makes its accomplishment a matter of transcendent human significance—through its provision of the occasion for the magnification of Achilles, his exaltation to ideal model of social man. For what makes an Argive victory possible is the reintegration of the errant primary individual into the communal consciousness. In Achilles' reintegration with Argos, the social nature of human existence is divinely sanctioned. And that sanction is the great poetic truth by which the race of mankind will be able to survive the fall of a great city; it is Homer's Zeus-given lesson, by which his audience is enabled to overcome any historical crisis. Hera's self-centered desire to have the Achaians prevail, even without Achilles, would have given to their victory a merely transitory significance. But Zeus is identified with the transcendent spirit of order, with the Olympian spirit of poetry, which forms a durable harmony from the opposition of transitory principles of disorder: Hera and Thetis.

The complex relations among Zeus, Hera, and Thetis show that the thematic interplay between order and disorder is far from simple. As the poem opens, Hera favors Achilles because he is the most important Argive warrior and is, at this point, attuned to the interests of the army she sponsors. She therefore inspires him to call the assembly to deal with the plague (1. 54). But the assembly results in Achilles' secession from the army; Hera no longer has interest in him now, seeming to forget that he is indispensable to Argos. Thetis, on the other hand, favors her son more than ever, in his present sorrow. Zeus is indebted to her for once freeing him from the bonds contrived by Hera (1. 400 ff.) and helping him to reestablish Olympian order. Honoring his debt, Zeus' promise to Thetis sets her at odds with Hera in the present, just as she had been in the past. We begin to understand how complicated is this matter of order and disorder when viewed from the perspective of human affairs.

In one sense, then, both Hera and Thetis are disorderly in their motivations. Hera's reason for favoring the Achaians is not based on human interests at all, but solely upon her jealous desire for revenge against Paris and Aphrodite. Not once does Hera mention her concern for the plight of Menelaos. Thetis, on the other hand, may be considered actively disorderly because she supports Achilles' wrongheaded desire to dissociate himself from the only context in which his identity can be defined meaningfully. But her disorder is more intrinsic to her circumstances than wilfully selfish; it arises from her unnatural marriage to a mortal. The mixture of two realms of being, human and divine, is the work of that underlying disorder (seen also in Aphrodite's alliances with Anchises and with Paris, or Helen's own birth); just as it was primitive Discord, though not invited to the wedding feast, who doomed the heroic product of Thetis' mating with Peleus to the agony described in Homer's poem.

It speaks well of Thetis that she has strong reservations about Achilles' proposed revenge on the army, and her own role in it (1. 415 ff.). For, in another sense, Hera's purpose is the proper one, from the human viewpoint. Since Argos is right and Troy wrong, Argos must defeat Troy. If Thetis would insure the glory of her son, she must ultimately favor the Achaian cause. And Zeus knows, as Hera apparently does not, that an Argive victory depends upon the integrity of the Achaian nation— demands the participation of Achilles. Somehow, therefore, Zeus must reconcile Thetis' request with Hera's intention; and he must do so despite his own personal preference for Troy. Perhaps it is precisely because of that preference, and his sorrow over Sarpedon's fate, that Zeus accomplishes Troy's ruin only after he has devalued the motives of each goddess, showing them to be too centripetal. When Achilles (and Thetis) sees the necessity of his orientation toward the community, when Hera admits that the gods must relinquish personal quarrels in the interest of universal stable government (the gist of Book 15), then only will Zeus manipulate an Argive victory. Then only will he bring about the fall of Troy. In the contrivance of Troy's doom, the superiority of his own will will be manifested; the destruction of the city of men will not prove to be a final disaster for the race of man. It is Zeus, after all, who sends Priam to Achilles; Zeus who inspires Achilles to accept the old man's gifts.

To approach the complex from another direction, there are two human disorders with which Zeus must deal: the disruption of Menelaos' proper marriage; and the continuance of Paris' unnatural alliance with Helen. Both disorders are resolved only when Zeus and Hera are themselves properly allied, only when their marital relationship is naturally effective, as it is after the deception, when Hera acquiesces to the will of her husband. With the gods reconciled, after the example of the royal couple, Helen can be restored to Menelaos. Paris will lose his unnatural wife. That order (the will of Zeus) can be restored by serving disorder

(Thetis and Hera) points to the chaos that results when gods and goddesses involve themselves in the lives of men and women.

The conversation between Zeus and Hera following the death of Patroklos is especially intriguing. The enmeshing of their wills, suggested by the words of Zeus attributing to Hera's influence events which he himself predicted and ordered in Book 15, illustrates the difficulty of a simplistic interpretation of Homer's employment of the gods to define his theme of order. The necessity for Troy's destruction seems to be based upon the natural superiority, or orderliness, of Argos—a superiority now reaffirmed by Achilles' imminent reenlistment in the common cause. If anything argues for Homer's preference for the Argive side, it is this confusion of the wills of Zeus and Hera.

> But Zeus spoke to Hera, who was his wife and his sister:
> 'So you have acted, then, lady Hera of the ox eyes.
> You have roused up Achilleus of the swift feet. It must be then
> that the flowing-haired Achaians are born of your own generation.'
>   Then the goddess the ox-eyed lady Hera answered him:
> 'Majesty, son of Kronos, what sort of thing have you spoken?
> Even one who is mortal will try to accomplish his purpose
> for another, though he be a man and knows not such wisdom as we do.
> As for me then, who claim I am highest of all the goddesses,
> both ways, since I am eldest born and am called your consort,
> yours, and you in turn are lord over all the immortals,
> how could I not weave sorrows for the men of Troy, when I hate them?'
>
> (18. 356–67)

The new-found intimacy between the king and queen of gods is proved by Zeus' attributing the rousing of Achilles to Hera (18. 357–58). But the meaning of his implication, that the Achaians are of her generation, remains hidden (unless it is a formal acknowledgment of the priority of her cult). And the meaning of Hera's reply is equally elusive; what Zeus terms her favor for the Argives, Hera herself refers to as her enmity toward Troy (18. 367) (the source of the invading followers of the sky-god?). She characteristically thinks in terms of antagonisms and negatives, even though her explanation of her actions implicitly compares Achilles' commitment to Patroklos with hers to Argos—both involvements somehow too essential to be alterable (18. 362–63).

The exchange between Zeus and Hera sounds so strange because it takes place outside the familiar contexts within which the two normally appear together (arguing) or appear among other gods (merely pretending harmony). Here they are isolated on the cosmic stage, and have no reason to feign a concord they do not feel. In view of their past appearances in the epic, we are surprised at the sincerity and courtesy with which they address each other here. It may be precisely because they appear out of familiar context that the meaning of their conversation eludes us. We must be satisfied with speculating about what the tone of their speeches suggests. Zeus' deduction of Hera's intimate relationship with the Achaians, on one hand, seems to imply that the fall of Troy has been determined by the almost accidental fact that Paris was Priam's son, that Priam's city is the one which happens to have threatened the stability of Argos—just as Achilles' hatred for Hektor stems from the coincidence that Hektor killed Patroklos. So it is fatefully convenient that Hektor happens to be the one individual crucial to Troy's survival. But the tone of Hera's speech, on the other hand, hints that her enmity toward Troy, although apparently personal, is really the divine force behind an historical necessity in the depth of human nature. It suggests a fatality inherent in Troy itself—the Troy that would support the ig-nominious deed of Paris, the Troy that would reach beyond its proper boundaries.

At any rate, the plan of Zeus is now indistinguishable from that of Hera. Hera and Thetis, too, are of one mind finally; Thetis will go for Achilles' armor (18. 369 ff.) to enable him to fight effectively once again, for his own glory and for the vengeance of Argos. Now the personal ambition of Thetis and the political aim of Hera are directed toward the same end. With the gods in agreement, Aphrodite significantly absent, the destinies of Achaians and Trojans spin to their conclusions as the poem rises to its ending.

Agamemnon Arms

The relationship between Agamemnon and Achilles, from the per-spective of Homer's theme of order and disorder, resembles that be-tween Zeus and Hera in its complications and repercussions. Agamem-non's mercenary selfishness from the beginning of the poem makes him the antitype of Achilles, whose alienation from the army is caused by sincere love for Briseis as well as pride; Achilles, his pride transformed into avenging fury out of love, becomes, in Books 23 and 24, the orderly ruler that Agamemnon should have been had he not been subject to Delusion. Homer makes the titular head of the Achaians the embodi-ment of that society's fragility as an unstable mixture of the heroic and the familial systems. Agamemnon is an heroic king, who does not share or even understand the familial motivations that lead Achilles to his isolation and tragedy; but Agamemnon is not even a good example of the heroic system he represents. Homer represents this fatal disorder in

Agamemnon's character by focusing on the king's sceptre. Agamemnon's sceptre, created by Hephaistos in the fictional past, is in brilliant contrast with the great shield of Achilles which the smith-god creates before our very eyes. When Achilles goes into battle carrying that shield, the emergence of a new social order is assured, one that combines the ferocity of the heroic with the transcendent order of the familial.

When, however, in the absence of Achilles, Agamemnon behaves in an orderly fashion, leading the Argives into the fight himself, his splendid shield identifies the prowess of the heroic order. Homer's description of this shield is second in elaboration only to that of Achilles', providing us with the depth of detail only hinted at in the earlier portrait of Agamemnon mustering his army: "Atreus' son, with whom followed far the best and bravest / people; and among them he himself stood armoured in shining / bronze, glorying, conspicuous among the great fighters, / since he was greatest among them all, and led the most people" (2. 577–80). Here the narrator adds his own poetic authority to Nestor's explanation of Agamemnon's power-base (1. 281). Homer's use of the superlative for Agamemnon, as well as for Achilles, is only the apparent contradiction which, upon examination, reveals the distinction between the two orders they represent. The magnificent ecphrasis with which Homer presents Agamemnon's arming is meant to affirm the interpolitical primacy of the Mycenaean-Argive king:

> First he placed along his legs the beautiful greaves linked
> with silver fastenings to hold the greaves at the ankles.
> Afterwards he girt on about his chest the corselet
> that Kinyras had given him once, to be a guest present.
> For the great fame and rumour of war had carried to Kypros
> how the Achaians were to sail against Troy in their vessels.
> Therefore he gave the king as a gift of grace this corselet.
> Now there were ten circles of deep cobalt upon it,
> and twelve of gold and twenty of tin. And toward the opening
> at the throat there were rearing up three serpents of cobalt
> on either side, like rainbows, which the son of Kronos
> has marked upon the clouds, to be a portent to mortals.
> Across his shoulders he slung the sword, and the nails upon it
> were golden and glittered, and closing about it the scabbard
> was silver, and gold was upon the swordstraps that held it.
> And he took up the man-enclosing elaborate stark shield,
> a thing of splendour. There were ten circles of bronze upon it,
> and set about it were twenty knobs of tin, pale-shining,
> and in the very centre another knob of dark cobalt.
> And circled in the midst of all was the blank-eyed face of the Gorgon
> with her stare of horror, and Fear was inscribed upon it, and Terror.

The strap of the shield had silver upon it, and there also on it
was coiled a cobalt snake, and there were three heads upon him
twisted to look backward and grown from a single neck, all three.
Upon his head he set the helmet, two-horned, four-sheeted,
with the horse-hair crest, and the plumes nodded terribly above it.
Then he caught up two strong spears edged with sharp bronze
and the brazen heads flashed far from him deep into heaven.
And Hera and Athene caused a crash of thunder about him,
doing honour to the lord of deep-golden Mykenai.

(11. 17–46)

The splendid arming of the king symbolizes the arming of the entire army which he is about to lead in person (11. 15–16). Here Agamemnon begins to play the orderly role, suggested by the thunderous honor of the goddesses and the strange Zeus-related rainbow image (11. 27–28), elsewhere associated with the armor of Diomedes, Nestor, Odysseus, and Aias.

The pervasive sense of majesty and awesome authority, eminently suitable to a king who is ready at last to lead his society in the fighting, is communicated by the fact that the description is, in the words of Joseph Russo

fantastically ornate and pompous and teems with suggestive images. . . . All the rich details . . . serve to underline the magnificence and power of the king of men . . . and leader of the Greek coalition. Even the detail concerning the source of the breastplate contributes to Agamemnon's stature. . . . The fame of the expedition . . . had reached . . . that island. There is also great latent dramatic power in the covert references to war in the form of the personifications of Fear, Terror, and the Gorgon, and the repeated use of snakes among the ornamental designs. ("Homer Against His Tradition," pp. 282–84).

Agamemnon is as close here to his properly ordained status as he will ever be in the *Iliad* and his shield is an epiphany of the glory resulting from the perfect attunement between a pivotal individual and the communal motivation. The personifications recall those on the aegis; they symbolize the force of a righteous war aiming to restore social stability. Elsewhere the poet speaks of "strong Hatred, defender of peoples" (20. 48) and it is to him that these figures, like those on Achilles' shield, too, are related. Note the repetition of the word δεινὸν *deinòn* ("terrible") used regularly to characterize the aegis when it leads the fight for order.

Like the metaphoric rainbows upon it, the armor is a portent to men that its bearer acts under the auspices of Zeus. The trigonal attitude of the snakes (11. 40) implies that Agamemnon's present position of leadership is his heritage from the past (as the sceptre signifies explicitly); their triune configuration implies that he is the kingliest among kings, the capital of social diversity, and, as a living king, the one who must preserve the cyclical continuity of time—acting on the example of the past to provide a model for the future, uniting the dead with men unborn, leading all to the restoration of continuous order emblazoned in the triple-headed image on his shield. Finally Hera and Athene appear miraculously to support the orderly impression, as if beckoned from heaven by the flash of his spears (11.44). They come not to interfere but to cooperate with the will of Agamemnon, now harmonized with the will of Zeus.

In all of this, Agamemnon resembles Achilles, his appearance here foreshadowing the hero's radiant appearance at the ditch in Book 18. Russo's remarks on the epithet with which Homer terminates his picture, however, reveal how the description distinguishes Agamemnon from Achilles:

"Deep-golden" . . . sums up nicely one important aspect of the elaborate description. The rich gold of Mycenae remained in the epic tradition, and Mycenae's king is presented as an opulent figure. We are forcibly reminded here in Book 11, with Achilles out of the picture and Agamemnon offering himself as champion and leader of the Greek host, of just what those qualities are that give Agamemnon ascendancy over Achilles in Books 1 and 9. Agamemnon has admitted that Achilles is "stronger"—*karteros*—but affirms that he, Agamemnon, is "greater" and "kinglier"—*pherteros* and *basileuteros*. The meaning of these distinctions is illustrated in this great arming description of the "king of men." The range of meaning of *pherteros,* as with so many Greek words, is not the same as the range of any English equivalent we might choose to translate it. *Pherteros* can mean "better" or "braver" when put in the context of physical prowess. But its basic meaning . . . is "more powerful" in the nonspecific sense of "more able to achieve," "more influential," which would follow from its root *pher-.* . . . Agamemnon *has more* than Achilles; he is wealthier, and that is the chief source of the authority and respect he commands. ("Homer Against His Tradition," p. 284).

Agamemnon represents the heroic society, whereas Achilles, allowing familial values equal consideration, insists upon the new synthesized social system whose divine orderliness is the point of Homer's poem. Other descriptions of Agamemnon's artifacts also stress their purely material splendor (for example, 2. 45).

Considered in this light, then, the glory of the scene in Book 11 is qualified, though not to the extent of Hera's robing. It is noteworthy that Agamemnon's shield is not shown in action, as is the shield of Aias. The king's armor expresses the self-interested basis of the heroic, as opposed to the familial, system. It is the kind of materialism Achilles rebels against in Book 1, as he accuses Agamemnon of being too petty, that is, too self-centered to serve the common good in a way appropriate to the head of a stable society: " 'O wrapped in shamelessness, with your mind forever on profit, / how shall any one of the Achaians readily obey you?' " (1. 149–50). Achilles' question is one of those unanswerable ones that distinguish his speech from that of others in the *Iliad*, as Adam Parry has noted. Materialism leads Agamemnon to appropriate Briseis for himself; perhaps it was even the impetus for the war, once Paris had provided a convenient excuse by violating the guest-host bond. This mercenary mentality, when it is allowed unchecked expression in action, is the fatal weakness of the heroic system. Agamemnon and Achilles act under the influence of two quite different social value-systems; and the reconciliation of those two value-systems, in Argive society, is less than perfect (another reflection of the uneasy alliance between Zeus and Hera). Homer's "message" is the necessity of repressing the worst elements of each system in order to form a new synthesized system that is stronger than either for enjoying the best of both. We are given a vision of that new society in the orderly games of Book 23.

For both Achilles and Agamemnon, after all, are in agreement on the necessity for collective action. But they are furious with each other because each has a totally different motivation. Agamemnon, expressing the heroic standard, pursues a communal course as a matter of material convenience—a centripetal attitude which values cooperation as the most effective means to individual aggrandizement. That is why there must be one king on the battlefield, as Nestor and Odysseus both know. But Achilles is moved by feelings which are both more and less concrete, the loyalty of blood bonds and the spiritual love between guest-friends, which honors collective action because it alone allows the fulfillment of the individual and the security of the family. Agamemnon, depending upon sworn oaths for his authority, is a prototype of the ethical hero; Achilles, who rules with his heart, of the moral hero. Both are egomaniac, however, and because each is the primary representative of his value-system, their conflict is explosive and disastrous. Among lesser men, the conflict might be borne without catastrophe for all; but, between these two mightiest, the repercussions can only be felt by the entire fabric of Achaian society. Homer focuses on every action of Agamemnon and of Achilles as an expression of the deepest disturbances in human nature and human history; as we examine those actions ourselves, we understand the connection between that nature and that history.

When, in the opening quarrel, Agamemnon asserts his brand of selfish individualism, Achilles moves instinctually to counterbalance the king's excess. He makes it clear in his speeches that the selfhood based on familial and personal bonds of love is one he considers to be more essentially human, or, because his own nature is still unreconciled, more divine. We understand, in his attitude toward his shield-wife Briseis, his mother, and Patroklos, that Achilles' familial emotions are outraged and violated by the heroic code as that code is enforced, arbitrarily and unevenly, by Agamemnon. Achilles tried to play Agamemnon's game and is doubly furious when Agamemnon changes the rules. That is why his counterattack is as excessive as the king's initial aggravation; Achilles is determined to prove that blood is thicker than greed. The difference between the two, then, is complicated by their exaggerations. Achilles, as we learn from Andromache later, had been, before the quarrel which opens Homer's story, well on his way toward becoming the kind of ruler who effectively combined the best qualities of the heroic and kinship systems (his treatment of King Eëtion, so unlike his angry words to Agamemnon or his furious treatment of Hektor's body). But Agamemnon's disrespect throws Achilles off track, leading him to defend the familial side of the synthesized social system he later restores in Book 23. The restoration of a peaceful, and stronger, Argos, based on the renewed equilibrium between the two systems, is brought about with the help of Achilles' divine shield, specially made for the occasion. Seeing the shield of Hephaistos, we understand the difference between Agamemnon and Achilles; for the images forged onto their shields describe their different characters. Agamemnon's shield is not only one-sided, illustrating the heroic eagerness for war and its resulting booty, but also it shows more of the individual preoccupations of its bearer. The material splendor of Achilles' shield is a very different matter; there the richness of the elements from which it is forged is subordinated to the universal nature of the figures and events it depicts. Although the heroic, or the familial, system may be suitable for some, the new society symbolized by Achilles' new shield is appropriate for all men. Agamemnon's shield tells of the inhumanity of war (no man is present upon its surface); Achilles' of its humanity, but as only one facet of human experience. No singular image like the Gorgon's impersonal, staring countenance dominates Achilles' shield; its hallmark is vibrant multiplicity, unified only by the limits of the Homeric cosmos, the circling Ocean. Agamemnon's shield emphatically symbolizes the limited heroic norm which identifies the Argive king.

The Sceptres of Argos

It will be useful to turn from this analysis of the disorderly implications of Agamemnon's shield to analysis of his most characteristic artifact, the sceptre. Throughout the *Iliad* the epithet σκηπτοῦχος *skēptoûkhos* ("sceptre-holding") defines the orderly function of kings. As Book 2 opens Agamemnon calls an assembly, inspired by the Dream sent from Zeus:

> The people
> took their seats in sober fashion and were marshalled in their places
> and gave over their clamouring. Powerful Agamemnon
> stood up holding the sceptre Hephaistos had wrought him carefully.
> Hephaistos gave it to Zeus the king, the son of Kronos,
> and Zeus in turn gave it to the courier Argeïphontes,
> and lord Hermes gave it to Pelops, driver of horses,
> and Pelops again gave it to Atreus, the shepherd of the people.
> Atreus dying left it to Thyestes of the rich flocks,
> and Thyestes left it in turn to Agamemnon to carry
> and to be lord of many islands and over all Argos.
> Leaning upon this sceptre he spoke and addressed the Argives.
>
> (2. 98–109)

Agamemnon is their lord because he lawfully possesses the sceptre which designates lordship, inherited through former kings from Zeus himself. The description of the artifact is strikingly without physical detail: "Instead of a copy, [Homer] gives us the history," says Gotthold Lessing (p. 96). Nothing here, moreover, distinguishes the individuality of Agamemnon from that of Thyestes or of Atreus; insofar as the artifact identifies him, it identifies him as one whose role in life is emphatically a communal one.

The sceptre's orderly function is to define the nature of Agamemnon's special power, the primacy of his social position. Subordinate to the sceptre is the herald's staff, passed to a man who wishes to speak out in the assembly; consequently, the possession of the sceptre marks the king's constant permission to speak. Bowra points out that Agamemnon's power has two sources: the extent of his sovereignty and his divine right (*Tradition and Design in the "Iliad,"* p. 173). The sceptre represents the latter, just as the richness of his armor implies the former. The sceptre brings him honor and makes him different from the other chieftains (1.

38, 99). Its divine power is confirmed by the other instances in which the sceptre appears, with Chryses (1. 15), with the heralds who serve as arbitrators for the duel between Aias and Hektor (7. 277), and with the judges who appear in the trial depicted on Achilles' shield (18. 505). It is interesting that Hermes, the messenger god (and bringer of hidden knowledge), appears associated with the sceptre not only here but also in his appearance in Book 24. 340.

The proper social influence of the sceptre is outlined in Nestor's arbitration:

> 'You, great man that you are, yet do not take the girl away
> but let her be, a prize as the sons of the Achaians gave her
> first. Nor, son of Peleus, think to match your strength with
> the king, since never equal with the rest is the portion of honour
> of the sceptred king to whom Zeus gives magnificence. Even
> though you are the stronger man, and the mother who bore you was
>   immortal,
> yet is this man greater who is lord over more than you rule.'
>
> (1. 275–81)

In Nestor's straightforward analysis of power, quality becomes a matter of quantity. Yet what he advises is the perfect social balance in which the king respects the individual and the individual honors the king because he represents the community. Precisely because they express these complementary dimensions of human experience Achilles and Agamemnon jeopardize the stability of their society when they oppose each other. The king is φέρτερος *phérteros* ("stronger") because he performs a Zeus-derived, Zeus-like function for the good of the commonwealth. But Agamemnon must be regularly reminded of his proper role. Achilles' semidivinity is a kind of foil to Agamemnon's inherited authority. Martin P. Nilsson notes that only Achilles receives a gift directly from a god, the shield: "Elsewhere gifts of the gods are heirlooms from past generations" (*The Myceneaen Origins of Greek Mythology*, p. 216). Achilles is more immediately in touch with the spirit of order than is Agamemnon. Agamemnon has not the personal strength of character to bear the collective responsibilities of the new social synthesis; he lacks the perfect balance between heroic and familial motivations which characterizes Achilles before the quarrel and after their complete reconciliation. Agamemnon's heroic bias is implied in the description of the sceptre's genealogical transmission—the ominous break in the succession (Agamemnon inherits the artifact not from his father, but from his uncle). Achilles' spear is given to him by Peleus, his mortal father—and complements the divine shield Thetis brings him from Olympos.

The orderliness of the sceptre relates Agamemnon to Zeus. The governing force of Zeus' own sceptre is mentioned in Glaukos' tale of Bellerophontes (6. 159). While others sacrifice to various minor gods, Agamemnon's offering and prayer is to Zeus (2. 400–403). The affinity between the king of men and the king of gods and men is explicit in Homer's description of Agamemnon's mighty presence at the opening of the catalogue of ships in Book 2.

> among them powerful Agamemnon,
> with eyes and head like Zeus who delights in thunder,
> like Ares for girth, and with the chest of Poseidon;
> like some ox of the herd pre-eminent among the others,
> a bull, who stands conspicuous in the huddling cattle;
> such was the son of Atreus as Zeus made him that day,
> conspicuous among men, and foremost among the fighters.
>
> (2. 477–83)

Agamemnon's relationship to his people is that of Zeus toward gods and men, goatherds to their flocks, the stud-animal to his herd. Zeus himself arranges the epiphany which the poet reports to us, Homer's choice of similes reflecting his own involvement in the ordering process (since the poet, through the Muses, is also directly tied to Zeus).

The head of society is identified, both by themselves and by the gods, with all its members (as in 9. 69, 73, 96–102; 1. 10, 42, 509). Bowra comments that the "heroic king is the type of all his subjects" and Whitman detects the same implication in the poet's description of Agamemnon's wound as being like the pains of childbirth. Agamemnon himself declares: " 'the cares of the Achaians perplex me. / Terribly I am in dread for the Danaans' " (10. 92–93). When he curses, the terminology is not at all personal, but strictly collective (6. 55–60). In this sense, Agamemnon and Argos are synonymous insofar as the individuals who comprise the latter act unanimously and thereby insure social survival. Odysseus clearly recognizes that social order depends on granting respect to the king: " 'Lordship for many is no good thing. Let there be one ruler, / one king, to whom the son of devious-devising Kronos / gives the sceptre and right of judgment, to watch over his people' " (2. 204–6). That order, like the sceptre which symbolizes it, derives from Zeus. The potential of the artifact as an influence upon harmonious action is vast indeed.

Ironically Agamemnon's fall from order is also associated with Zeus. As Book 2 opens, the contrast between them is striking. Zeus, troubled by his promise to Thetis, cannot sleep. Agamemnon, responsible for the troubles of the Achaians, should not be able to sleep either (2. 23–25). The

king of the gods, then, deceitfully awakens the king of men, sending
Dream to move him to battle. Agamemnon, deluded by Zeus as he has
been deluded in Book 1 by his own blindness, takes up the sceptre of his
fathers, immortal forever (2. 46). The sceptre may be immortal but
Agamemnon himself is characterized by the fallibility of mortality. Book
1 has portrayed his personal weakness; Book 2 reveals its impact on the
social level. Now as he leans upon the symbol of his royal function,
Agamemnon's own words express the disorder dominating his actions
and emotions. He uses the sceptre in the way Zeus has used the Dream,
deceiving his people as Zeus had deceived him. So the sceptre-speech
exemplifies the thematic importance of the particular context in which an
artifact appears in the poem. Like Aphrodite's girdle, intrinsically orderly, it can be used to advance the opposite of order.

Irony abounds from the king's very first statement that Zeus has
caught him in futility (2. 110 ff.). Agamemnon is right about this, but for
the wrong reasons. He tells the army that Zeus bids them return to Argos
in dishonor and that the will of Zeus cannot be resisted (2. 115–16 ff.).
Zeus, of course, has ordered no such thing. Hoping to inspire the
warriors to insist on doing what he has told them cannot be done—that
is, to go against Zeus' will in returning to the fight—Agamemnon
predicts the mnemonic outcome of their returning home at this point: for
men to come their reputation will be shameful, since they so clearly
outnumber the Trojans (2. 119 ff.). The didactic content of his message is
identical to that of Nestor's. But all else is different. Agamemnon's
reference to the rotting timbers of the decaying ships is interesting. The
ships are an image of Argive society, of which the army is the fighting
arm. The aging process, nine years spent before Troy and away from the
fatherland, has affected Argos as a whole no less than it has the army; like
the ships, their society needs patching. The Achaians must be eager to
return to insure the physical survival of their social system; that is, they
must go back to bed with their proper wives, to replant the Argive seed,
to take stock of their women and children, " 'for whose sake we came
hither' " (2. 136–38). Since Troy cannot be taken anyway, the army
should turn back to restore what remains of order at home (2. 140–41).
The response to this speech is unanimously wholehearted; the men rush
to the ships, eager to obey Agamemnon's casuistic reasoning. The
devious device has backfired.

The final reference to the ships suggests the wrongness of that reasoning and of their obedience. As the men prepare to embark, the ships are
patched hastily, with less than the careful attention their decay requires
(2. 153–54). The poet's meaning is clearly that these ships are not fit tools
of survival in the present circumstances. The attention that should be

given their disrepair is possible only when the pressure of Troy's resistance has been removed—when, that is, the city has been taken and Helen restored to Argos. The attempt to leave now is misguided because it would prove fatal to society, and to the army as well—since it would go down with the ships. In short, there is no benefit to be gained by restoring order among the remnant left at home unless Menelaos has his proper wife and queen with him when that process is initiated. Troy was not, after all, a military threat to Argos. Its threat was familial. Purely heroic norms are therefore insufficient to remove the threat to society. So it is a "homecoming beyond fate" (2. 155) which Athene's orderly intervention prevents. She embodies Agamemnon's proper intention, which his words are incapable of communicating.

Agamemnon's equation of Helen with all Argive women helps us understand the nature of Agamemnon's disorderliness (2. 138 ff.). As the spokesman for a society which synthesizes heroic and familial values he gives due recognition to the importance of maintaining bloodlines. Agamemnon seems to realize the implications of the association: that Helen's restoration is necessary for the salvation of all Achaian wives. But he himself fails to act on them. He professes familial values but does not practice them. This brings us to the sceptre of Chryses, which Agamemnon does not respect.

As the *Iliad* opens Chryses appears bearing symbols of his Apollonian priesthood "on a staff of gold" (1. 15). The sceptre takes on a more symbolic character in the way Agamemnon phrases his rebuff of the proffered ransom; he bids Chryses depart, "lest the god's staff may not protect you" (1. 28—translation mine). The insult is specifically directed to the symbol of Chryses' priestly authority—a symbol which thereby becomes active. When Achilles dashes the sceptre of Argos to the ground, poetic justice is fulfilled; his violent action, while emphasizing the sincerity of his own familial values, compensates for Agamemnon's sacrilegious treatment of Chryses, which had revealed the king's heroic bent. Moreover as Agamemnon sins against both the bond of guest-friendship (in this case, host-suppliant) and that of familial integrity, he is a parallel to Paris, and a contrast to Achilles' treatment of Priam in Book 24. Both Paris—by Hera's jealousy—and Agamemnon—by his materialistic self-interest—are blinded (cf. 24. 25–28). The emotion expressed by the king in Book 1 suggests the feelings Paris must have had in Sparta: " 'indeed I wish greatly to have her / in my own house; since I like her better than Klytaimestra / my own wife, for in truth she is no way inferior, / neither in build nor stature nor wit, not in accomplishment' " (1. 112–15). Agamemnon's personal passion for Chryseis blinds him to its repercussions on Argive society, just as Paris' passion for Helen blinds him to its evil effects on Troy. Agamemnon's inadequacy as the head of stabilized society is expressed in his purely heroic attitude toward his own wife and queen. No public-minded concern here: his interest is only selfish. Only the heroic viewpoint judges women strictly in these terms (1. 115). To Achilles, too, Briseis is a prize; but he will be quick to claim that she is also his beloved wife, and his words for her are not, like Agamemnon's, always metaphors of wealth, or badges of his personal honor. The sincerity of Achilles' love is very different from Agamemnon's feeling for Chryseis: " 'The girl I will not give back; sooner will old age come upon her / in my own house, in Argos, far from her own land, going / up and down by the loom and being in my bed as my companion' " (1. 29–31). If Agamemnon had his way, Chryseis would usurp Klytaimestra's rightful position. Chryseis is wrong for the king because he has already a royal wife. That is the significance of Homer's juxtaposing the images of the loom and bed (1.31): Klytaimestra's use of these artifacts is orderly; Chryseis' would not be. But Chryseis cannot be a substitute queen and wife for another reason: she is not an Argive. Her alien presence in Argos therefore would be no less detrimental to that society's stability than Helen's is to Troy's (1.30). Finally the superficiality of Agamemnon's feeling is proved by his suddenly expressed arbitrary willingness to take another prize woman in place of her (1. 116 ff.). Later Achilles will refuse to accept even a daughter of Agamamnon as compensation for his spear-wife (9. 141 ff.). Agamemnon's arbitrary philandering recalls that for which Hera punishes Zeus in Book 14.

The blindness that compels Agamemnon to reject Chryseis' suppliant offering dramatically expresses the disjunction in the genealogical transmission of the sceptre. Somewhere in transit from Zeus to the present Argive king the sceptre has ceased automatically to inspire orderly behavior on the part of its possessor; such behavior is now dependent on the king's individual will, on whether or not it is attuned to Zeus' transcendent governing principle. So in specifically blaspheming the sceptre of Apollo, Agamemnon offers the first evidence that his individuality is not properly aligned with the requirements of society (1. 29). His failure to heed the advice of Kalchas, who speaks on behalf of the community, is further witness to Agamemnon's blindness (1. 102 ff.). Because of this weakness his royal power is insecure; he is quick to be angry, to be jealous, to be resentful of the influence of Achilles because he himself recognizes that his functional primacy is uncertain (1. 134 ff.).

The meaning of Agamemnon's crime against Chryses has a wider importance, one which goes beyond the present circumstances to invoke by imagistic means the human purpose of epic song itself. To dishonor

Apollo's staff of gold (1. 28) is to reject the orderly presence of art in the human world, to contradict the symbolic consistency of the artifact— since it is the chief *sceptred* king who commits the act of disrespect, thereby jeopardizing the value of his own sceptre. The divine spirit of order is contradicted by the very human being whose orderly function should be most in imitation of the governing aspect of Zeus, protector of kings and suppliants. Apollo's association with Zeus' order is expressed in the scene where he holds Zeus' aegis over the body of Hektor; it is implied, even in Book 1, by Apollo's appearance in two artistic contexts: that of the Achaians' propitiatory singing (1. 472–74), and that of the lyre which he plays himself during the Olympian feast which parallels the Achaian banquet (1. 465 ff.). The baneful arrows from Apollo's silver bow dramatize the divine appropriateness of making all the Achaians suffer for the disorder of their king. Simultaneously the Apollonian arrows affirm the superiority of a sceptre that is employed, as Chryses uses it, in an orderly fashion. One artifact supports the other.

As Chryses' orderly role is opposed to Agamemnon's, so Odysseus' function in the poem is in contrast to that of the king. With Agamemnon's sceptre speech and its effect upon the Achaians, Homer distinguishes between the sceptre's communal usefulness (symbolized in his particular method of describing it) and the individual's, Agamemnon's, inability to wield it properly. Pursuing his own well-balanced technique, Homer now presents a positive dramatization of the distinction so negatively illustrated. Odysseus' assumption of the sceptre sharpens our appreciation of Agamemnon's weakness. The Achaians are rushing to embark when Athene inspires Odysseus to intervene: "He came face to face with Agamemnon, son of Atreus, / and took from him the sceptre of his fathers, immortal forever. / With this he went beside the ships of the bronze-armoured Achaians" (2. 185–87). Agamemnon's silence as he relinquishes his royal emblem to one who can use it well subtly marks the rebuff to the king's stature. As Odysseus uses the sceptre to rally the warriors, the poet carefully makes another distinction: Odysseus condemns not Agamemnon but Agamemnon's mistake. He tells the army that they have not understood the purpose of the king; he was only testing their determination (2. 192 ff.). Their disorderly reaction will anger Agamemnon, with disastrous results for them all: " 'for the anger of god-supported kings is a big matter, / to whom honour and love are given from Zeus of the counsels' " (2. 196–97). Only later will Odysseus fully understand that the fault for the present debacle is more Agamemnon's than the army's, that the king's own attitude has deprived him of the support of the divine principle of government. The understanding comes, significantly, in Book 14 where Zeus himself is deluded by Hera, when Agamemnon counsels retreat in earnest. Odysseus' reply to him on that occasion again associates Agamemnon's power with Zeus, and with the sceptre:

> 'Ruinous! I wish you directed some other unworthy
> army, and were not lord over us, over us to whom Zeus
> has appointed the accomplishing of wars, from our youth
> even into our old age until we are dead, each of us.
> . . . .
> Do not say it; for fear some other Achaian might hear this
> word, which could never at all get past the lips of any man
> who understood inside his heart how to speak soundly,
> who was a sceptred king, and all the people obeyed him
> in numbers like those of the Argives, whose lord you are.
> . . . .
> There, o leader of the people, your plan will be ruin.'
>
> (14. 84–87, 90–94, 102)

Understanding the art of speech and, like Nestor, practicing it superbly throughout the poem, Odysseus is allowed by Homer to see beyond the uncertainties of the moment to the providential plan of Zeus for an Achaian victory (14. 85–86). He knows that Agamemnon's behavior delays the fulfillment of that plan. Homer lets Odysseus, because of his orderliness, exemplify the proper use of the sceptre, embodying its symbolic significance in its literal function as he beats the wayward Argives into a semblance of organization with the staff itself as his weapon and simultaneously instructs them in its meaning, for the benefit of Homer's audience as well as Agamemnon (14. 199 ff., 203–6).

The army now reassembled away from the ships, Thersites makes his single appearance in the *Iliad* (14. 208–11 ff.). In one sense, he is a figure of disorder. Noting that the sceptre marks both the authority of the king and signifies orderly procedure (as in 2. 206), M. I. Finley comments that "Thersites . . . harangued the assembly without *themis*; he had been given no sceptre by the herald; therefore it was proper for him to receive it across his back" (*The World of Odysseus*, p. 120). The poet's characterization is explicit enough: "but one man, Thersites of the endless speech, still scolded, / who knew within his head many words, but disorderly; / vain, and without decency, to quarrel with the princes / with any word he thought might be amusing to the Argives. / This was the ugliest man who came beneath Ilion" (2. 212–16). Thersites' craft, like Nestor's and Odysseus' and Hephaistos' (in Book 1), is the poet's craft of words, but Thersites' are not words which are, in Alkinoös terms, κατά κόσμον *katà kósmon* ("according to order"). He is the individual who jeopardizes social stability by speaking against its chief governors and defenders, with kind intention toward none. His expression of individuality is parallel with Achilles' only superficially, since Thersites' motives are neither serious nor constructive. Achilles' assertion of familial values does not imply his lack of heroic qualities but only serves to complement Agamemnon's excessive emphasis on the heroic (2. 217–20). What Thersites proposes is that society desert its king completely (2. 235–38), an unthinkably chaotic course of action, equivalent to regicide, and therefore to social suicide.

Yet Thersites' words are true. His anomalous position in the assembly lends him access to the truth. Thersites' explanation of Agamemnon's selfishness strikes at the heart of the matter, more explicitly than did Achilles' general condemnation: " 'Is it some young woman to lie with in love and keep her / all to yourself apart from the others? It is not right for / you, their leader, to lead in sorrow the sons of the Achaians' " (2. 232–34). Here Agamemnon's crime is recognized as lust—as is that of Paris (24. 30). For once in his life Thersites, as the common victim of the disorder among princes who recognizes, as others apparently do not, the full implications and dangers of the quarrel, defends Achilles. But Thersites is reviled by the army as Achilles had not been (2. 270 ff.). Iliadic society is not democratic. In one sense, then, the laughter of the Achaians, as well as suggesting their sharing of their leaders' disorder, proclaims their collective shame that a base man dares to accuse princes of base motives. Achilles disdains to mention the ignominious sexual aspect of Agamemnon's folly, preferring to condemn his materialism in general. But Thersites being no princely man himself is not so nice about condemning Agamemnon's heroic values. It is therefore as much because of his lowly status as because of his intention, that Odysseus criticizes Thersites for doing exactly what Agamemnon appears to have done (that is, sustaining the homecoming)—for standing up alone, as Achilles has done with impunity, against princes (2. 250). Thersites' actions are simply not appropriate to his social station.

When Odysseus beats the ungainly man with the sceptre, it is as if Homer, at this early point in his poem, is purging his listeners of what might be their natural first reaction to punish Achilles or Agamemnon for having caused the disorganization of the Danaan army (2. 265 ff.). Odysseus' dismissal of Thersites expresses the narrator's own attitude: " 'Never again will his proud heart stir him / up, to wrangle with the princes in words of revilement' " (2. 276–77)—and Thersites doesn't appear again in the poem. Clearly Homer is declaring here the maintenance of the social system despite Achilles' alienation. His audience is not to focus on the wrongness of the secession, but rather upon the explicit reason that has caused it, the abduction of Briseis; Achilles is angry because, in effect, Agamemnon has done to him exactly what Paris had done to Menelaos. The repercussions, in each case, are similar; but Argive harmony will be restored, when Briseis is given back. The poet's audience is hereby cautioned not to be, as Thersites is, too ready to discard the social system now in the process of dissolution until it has heard the rest of Homer's poem and seen whether that process will be reversed. The disorder of Agamemnon and the alienation of Achilles are not as final and fatal as is the unruliness of Thersites. They test, he destroys. As long as it can repress Thersites effectively, the sceptre must not be dispensed with.

The resolution of the quarrel, of the war, of the poem itself, will bring order out of the opening chaos. Then the dominating image will be Achilles' shield, which controls the symbolism of the last books of the epic as the sceptre has the first three. This is no imagistic conflict, however. For the Achilles-principle does not replace the Agamemnon-principle entirely, as Achilles' courtesy toward the king in Book 23 proves. Instead they are harmonized. It is striking, then, to find the image of the sceptre, as it functions in an orderly fashion, included upon the shield itself (18. 416, 505, 557). Until then, the sceptre has regularly differentiated the two leaders. Whitman concludes: "[Agamemnon's] traditional kingly attributes, his primacy among peers, his position as marshaler of the spearmen, his personal exploits, and even his sceptre, have all been used, but used with a difference, to establish him as the opposite of Achilles—the nadir, as Achilles is the zenith, of the heroic assumption" (p. 162).

Agamemnon's weakness, as his sceptre allows us to define it, is manifested in two ways. In the first, he displays an imbalanced orientation toward the two components which comprise the new society. He is more heroic than he should be, and less familial, as his attitude toward Chryseis, Briseis, and Klytaimestra indicates. His weakness as a family man is also evident in his willingness to give Achilles any one of his daughters, without distinction among them, "without bride price" (9. 146). Perhaps this weakness is what Diomedes means when he scolds the king: " 'Son of Atreus: I will be first to fight with your folly, / . . . The son of devious-devising Kronos has given you / gifts in two ways: with the sceptre he gave you honour beyond all, / but he did not give you a heart, and of all power this is the greatest" (9. 32, 37–39). Agamemnon employs social motivations only as the expedient means of fulfilling his feudalistic individualism, whereas Achilles sincerely believes in their essential value. But the second manifestation of Agamemnon's blindness is that he betrays even the heroic code. This point is made by Achilles himself, when he tells Patroklos that Agamemnon's crime is, in purely heroic terms even, heinous, since it jeopardizes the structure upon which the heroic system relies for its continuing force: the basic equivalence of a warrior's honor with the prizes he is given as a reward for his valor (16. 52–59). Agamemnon has taken Achilles' rightful prize of honor in a dastardly misuse of his greater authority. The king's actions are misguided from any point of view. Similarly he contradicts the commonsensical arrangement by which the individual princes, in order that their joint efforts may be more effective, debate important problems in assembly to support the decision of their chief. Agamemnon upsets even this basic heroic pattern of behavior. Acting selfishly when his role is to function collectively, Agamemnon has attacked the individual honor of the one warrior who matters most to the Achaian war effort. He is indeed as Christopher Logue calls him, "the Royal thief / Who robs the man on whom his commonwealth depends."

Agamemnon's sceptre serves to individualize his behavior at the same time that it distinguishes it from Achilles'. The king's disorderly attitude in Book 1, like his sceptre speech in Book 2, has indicated to Achilles that Agamemnon is no longer in tune with the spirit of orderly government. It is fitting that Achilles' first oath is by Apollo (1. 86), since Agamemnon has specifically countermanded the orderly power of that god's sceptre—just as he will speak in anger against the other priest of Apollo, Kalchas (1. 105 ff.). The symbolism is perfectly symmetrical. Because Achilles has sworn to protect the priest of Apollo, who represents proper divine government and whose emblem has been rejected, the Achaian hero is led directly to reject the corresponding emblem—which normally signifies proper Argive order, the order now disrupted by Agamemnon's double sacrilege (toward Kalchas and Chryses). This, then, is Achilles' second oath:

> 'But I will tell you this and swear a great oath upon it:
> in the name of this sceptre, which never again will bear leaf nor
> branch, now that it has left behind the cut stump in the mountains,
> nor shall it ever blossom again, since the bronze blade stripped
> bark and leafage, and now at last the sons of the Achaians
> carry it in their hands in state when they administer
> the justice of Zeus. And this shall be a great oath before you:
> some day longing for Achilleus will come to the sons of the Achaians,
> all of them. Then stricken at heart though you be, you will be able
> to do nothing, when in their numbers before man-slaughtering Hektor
> they drop and die. And then you will eat out the heart within you
> in sorrow, that you did no honour to the best of the Achaians.'
>   Thus spoke Peleus' son and dashed to the ground the sceptre
> studded with golden nails, and sat down again.

(1. 233–46)

Nestor's intervention which follows immediately upon this speech comes too late; the basis of his arbitration no longer exists, since the harmony of Argive society can no longer be maintained. The speaker's staff is out of commission; therefore no spokesman speaks with communal authority. Before the communication is drastically interrupted by Achilles' gesture, Homer has fashioned Achilles' speech—its prophetic import like that of Zeus in Book 15—as a vehicle for conveying the sceptre's orderly significance. Havelock remarks: "The sweep of [his] anger is interrupted by an excursus on the staff as a symbol of authority . . . the essential function of the holder is then briefly memorialized. His pronouncements conserve the legal precedents" (*Preface to Plato*, p. 68). This is the way in which the didactic function of Homeric song is allied with its artistic technique. For, as Achilles dashes the sceptre to the ground (1. 245), θέμις *thémis* ("law") no longer prevails among the Argives—literally, as well as symbolically. That is the dramatic impact of the sceptre image.

Just as the staff cut from its roots is no longer green and living, so is the king no longer functional who removes himself from the respect that must be paid to the familial dimension of human life. And this is sadly ironic since the dead branch becomes, through the inspired orderliness of the art which now decorates it, eternal—as the king's image should also be (and is on the shield of Achilles). It is only poetic justice that Hektor, so dedicated to familial concerns, will be the chief instrument of Achilles' revenge on Agamemnon and the Achaians. As it falls to the ground, the sceptre reflects Agamemnon's fall from an orderly communal position—and is even a primary phallic image.

Agamemnon's staff asserts the king's right to speak at any time; but because he speaks in a disorderly fashion, Achilles' Argive sceptre, cast aside, symbolizes the new condition, that no Achaian has that right any longer. Nothing, then, could better dramatize his alienation from a society controlled by an unruly "folk-devouring king" (1. 231) than concretizing the oath sworn by dashing the symbol of order to the ground. Achilles respects order, but not this particular order which he alone clearly recognizes to be illusory. Agamemnon's devious use of his own staff has destroyed the authority of the Argive sceptre. Achilles dishonors the common sceptre of Argos, moreover, because Agamemnon has dishonored the sceptre of Apollo. Achilles thereby accomplishes intrinsically or spiritually what Agamemnon's deed caused extrinsically or physically: the disorder of the army—by plague or by the secession of its key warrior. Achilles revolts against the king because the king himself rebels against divine law, Zeus' demand for proper familial and guest-friend relations, in slighting Chryses; and against the chief support of that divine law—priestly, Apollonian order. To follow Agamemnon in his blindness would be to become οὐτιδανός *outidanós* ("good for nothing"—1. 231), an individual who has indeed been devoured by the wrongheaded attitude of his ruler. Achilles will not, like the other Achaians, be so victimized. Instead he predicts that Agamemnon's cannibalistic behavior will turn against the king himself, perhaps to eat away the weakness of his heart (1. 243).

For all the righteousness of its motivation, however, Achilles' act is an unnatural one. The sceptre, after all, is the symbol of social justice (1. 239), representing the orderly spirit of poetry itself. Achilles overtly dissociates himself from the only kind of environment in which individuality achieves fulfillment—a social one—and by doing so endangers the continuity of that environment. One sceptre identifies the community with an individual, Agamemnon; the other gives communal significance to the individual who holds it, Achilles. Individualistically employed by both men, the sceptre loses its proper function in each case. In this sense, Achilles and Agamemnon are complementary and neither man is right.

And yet, of course, it was Agamemnon's wrongheadedness that caused Achilles'. Achilles takes a familial stand only because Agamemnon proposes to act in strictly heroic terms. Homer makes it clear that Agamemnon is the more to blame by making him apologize, with eventual success, to Achilles. But before his action becomes orderly once more, Agamemnon falters several times. Even in Book 2 he confesses that he was "first to be angry" (2. 378); yet his confession has the air of expediency about it, concluding in a reassertion of his own superiority. Similarly his oath, in Book 9, that he has not slept with Briseis, though giving due acknowledgment to the familial values Achilles holds so dear, is deflated by his persistent demand for unqualified respect (9. 132–34, 160–61): a respect for his materialistic primacy. So it is fitting that Achilles rejects the embassy, with its gifts from Agamemnon, just as Agamemnon had rejected the suppliant offering of Chryses. Had they been given with a good heart, as Priam's gifts are in Book 24, Achilles might have accepted them. But Agamemnon is no more a worthy suppliant that he was a worthy host.

Ironically Agamemnon's sincere apology and confession come only when they are no longer needed. The death of Patroklos has moved Achilles to rejoin his comrades. Its very superfluity proves that Agamemnon's apology is sincere after all. It is notable (since Homer makes a point of noting it) that, as he replies to Achilles' pacification speech in Book 19, Agamemnon does not stand. This can be explained by the fact that he has been wounded; but his remaining seated also signifies the arbitrary or tenuous nature of his kingship, which he should have realized long before. His opening remarks are a plea for order, a petition to be heard (19. 78–84). This is a new attitude on the part of Agamemnon, one of courtesy and propriety. He shows a sense of his equality among princes, as if he is now thinking of himself as a kind of *servus servorum* of society. He blames his actions and emotions in the quarrel on Delusion (Ἄτη *Atē*—19. 85–91).

In fact, some credit must be given to Agamemnon's relative innocence. His loss of attunement with the principle of order was not entirely of his own doing, especially in the case of the sceptre speech which follows the appearance of the false Dream. At that point Homer had called him "Fool, who knew nothing of all the things Zeus had planned" (2. 38). Zeus has simply chosen not to reveal his foresight to Agamemnon, but rather to use the king as a means toward its fulfillment. As Agamemnon's confession in Book 19 continues, he further reveals his new-found introspection by relating the genealogy of Delusion, and recording for Achilles the tale of Zeus being deluded by Hera (19. 91 ff.), aided by Delusion himself. The tale, of course, parallels the scene in Book 14 and cannot fail to recall that present evidence of Zeus' fallibility to Homer's audience. The remembered story, moreover, proves that Agamemnon is at last fully responsive to the values sanctioned by the older, familial system; it is full of news about childbirth, generation, and royal bloodlines. The parallels between his own situation and that of Zeus are numerous. Zeus' casting down of Delusion, like his hurling Hephaistos from Olympos related in Book 1, is the historical coefficient of Agamemnon's momentous rejection of his own blindness (of his purely heroic bent) in this very scene. Both he and Zeus, furthermore, have been drawn away from order because of women, Chryseis and Hera. Now Agamemnon has no doubt that his royal role requires that he respect the individuality of Argos' most important warrior. His words communicate the king's sincerity to Achilles here as his gifts had emphasized only heroic standards; now Agamemnon's speech becomes orderly and effective. He still offers the gifts (19. 140 ff.)—strikingly, without mention of a daughter—but Achilles' response to his offer proves that the gifts are practically irrelevant (19. 145 ff.). He will accept them as tokens of the emotion he now knows Agamemnon really feels.

Having cast the beam from his own eye, Agamemnon will now turn to join with Achilles in bringing the war to a successful conclusion. The two thematic patterns are spliced together smoothly as the wrath dissolves into the war, the termination of the latter having been suspended until the quarrel was resolved. But the suspension of the war has great artistic usefulness. The poet's audience will understand its meaning better now that he has revealed to them the social implications of Achilles' wrath; for Achilles' enmity toward Agamemnon exactly parallels Agamemnon's antagonism toward Troy. By concentrating on the controversy between the two Achaian leaders Homer has provided a view of macrocosmic human experience in miniature. The difference between the war, as a threat to human survival, and the quarrel, as a threat to national survival, is shown to be a matter not of quality, but only of quantity. In both cases it is the social system which is jeopardized.

Something should be said of the precision with which Homer unravels this scheme of parallelism; the poem, introducing the wrath and the war at one and the same time, illustrates this characteristic of the poet's art superbly. From the opening lines he has affirmed the reciprocal relationship between the individual and society, by the juxtaposition of proper names with patronymics and by the poet's Zeus-like predictions of the consequences that occur when one crucial individual is pitted against another. The wrath-story reveals in miniature the elemental concerns of the legend of the Trojan war. The sexual turmoil of the quarrel, like that of the war itself, then, must reflect the general historical turmoil recorded in the *Iliad,* that is, the yet unstable alliance of the old and new—familial and heroic—social systems.

ᴧ 6 ᴩ

Hephaistos and the Galaxy
of Achilles:1

The Extraordinary God

Hephaistos, more than any other figure in the *Iliad*, embodies Homer's poetic consciousness of the governing order of Zeus. Smith-god and poet are closely allied because each, in his own technical way, serves that transcendent ordering principle—the god on Olympos, the poet on earth. Both are agents of order, bringing the potential of Zeus' will into realization through their craftsmanship. In later Greek literature, Apollo and Athene become more important artist-gods (their role foreshadowed, in the *Iliad*, by images of Apollo's lyre and Athene's weaving); but in the *Iliad* it is the ungainly smith who steadfastly pursues the spirit of harmony and reconciliation, understanding the necessity and benefit of orderly words as the basis for orderly living, among both men and gods. Hephaistos serves Hera only when she acts in an orderly fashion; he doesn't make the throne she promises to Sleep as a bribe, nor is it in the bedroom he made for her that she seduces Zeus. In Hephaistos we come closest to seeing the image of the artist, the maker, as Homer conceived of it; Homer appreciates the god's works and words in the same way he means for us to appreciate his epic (just as Dante's descriptions of the divine artistry of the *Purgatorio* are readily transposed into definitive criticism of his own divine poem).

No other ancient poet reserved such central interest for Hephaistos, and it is interesting to speculate why Homer did. No doubt part of the answer is that Hephaistos was a stranger among the Olympians, and must have been so regarded in Homer's time. Mythographers point to his foreign, Asiatic prototypical derivations, suggesting that he may have been closer to Homer's own Ionic homeland than Hera (whose mainland Greek cult preceded Zeus'). Hephaistos has been compared to the Ugaritic Kothar-and-Hasis, the Hebrew Lucifer, the Babylonian Ea,

134

and the Egyptian Ptah and Chnum. His being hurled from heaven is a typically eastern motif; there are early indications that he was worshipped at Gnossos. Hephaistos' traditionally alien nature is reflected in the various non-Homeric tales of his birth. Lucian, who gave him credit for the creation of mankind, called him a "wind child"; and one legend makes him the son of Gaia, suggesting his peculiarly chthonic character developed in other ancient stories as well as in the *Iliad*. But Homer must have subscribed to the near-contemporary version of Hesiod's *Theogony* (931) which tells of Hephaistos' parthenogenetic birth from Hera, parallel to that of Athene from Zeus; he therefore has matriarchal associations, as the story of Erichthonios also implies.

Besides Zeus, Hephaistos is the only god presented as being married in Homer. His wife, in Book 18 of the *Iliad*, is called Charis, obviously a generic name (meaning "grace"). She is one of the three Graces named by Hesiod, and we know from other sources that she is probably Aglaia. But Greek folklore, consistently connecting Hephaistos with a wife, is inconsistent in the choice of his mate's identity. In the primitive tale of Erichthonios, Hephaistos is sexually allied with Athene. George Thomson explains the myth:

According to an Attic tradition, Erichthonios, the ancestor of the royal clan of the Erechthedidai, was born from the seed which Athena brushed from her person to the ground after Hephaistos had attempted to ravish her . . . What this means is that Athena was originally regarded as the mother of Erichthonios, who was naturally fatherless, because his clan was matrilineal, and that the intervention of Hephaistos (assisted by the popular etymology of Erichthonios from *eris*, "strife," and *chthon*, "ground") is a derivative element introduced after the adoption of patrilineal descent had rendered the lack of paternity unintelligible. (P. 277)

Hephaistos' role as progenitor, then, is no less mysterious than his own manner of birth; moreover it seems to be connected with the kind of cultural and historical upheavals that must have influenced the thematic content of the *Iliad* itself. His sexual association with Athene in this legend reflects his artistic parallel to her in other versions. And we have a third account of Hephaistos' marriage. In the *Odyssey*, he is the husband of Aphrodite (8. 266–366), whom he married through the matchmaking of Hera.

The three marriage stories are confused in legend. To begin with, in the *Odyssey*, Hephaistos' artistry is related to Athene's; the πολύφρονος *polúphronos* ("ingenious") nature of the golden snare he fashions for Ares and Aphrodite is equivalent to the δόλος *dólos* ("crafty") character of the Trojan horse, built by Athene-inspired Odysseus. All three versions of Hephaistos' marriage are related in the speculative theory of Fernand Robert, who points out that the artful (Athenian) chaining of Ares by Hephaistos is a type of the legendary chaining of the goddess Eurynome. Ares and Aphrodite were worshipped together in joint temples. And Eurynome is the mother of the Graces (*Theogony*, 907–8), one of whom is married to Hephaistos in the *Iliad*. Now all of these elements form a pattern, as Robert concludes: "One may say that if the goddess of love becomes the wife of the smith, it is because the god of war, her companion in many sanctuaries, was also customarily chained" (p. 147). The confusion among the three accounts is neither resolved nor alluded to in the *Iliad*. If Homer was in a position to choose the wife he found most appropriate to his theme, it is significant that he selected the most nondescript, the most neutral, of the three; for Charis has no connotations likely to compromise Hephaistos' extraordinary position in the Iliadic world, whereas Aphrodite is firmly aligned with the Trojans (and therefore with disorder), Athene as surely with the Achaians (but for disorderly, selfish reasons).

Besides his marriages, other mythical materials reveal that Hephaistos is connected with the most elemental aspects of divinity. Just as Ares, in the *Iliad*, often seems to represent the very instinct for war, Hephaistos is regularly identified with fire itself, especially volcanic fire. Because of the jets of natural gas on the Lykian Mount Olympos and Mount Lemnos, and the frequency of lightning of Mounts Hymettus and Parnes, Hephaistos was worshipped in those places with shrines and festivals, as the fire-god; in other legends his workshop is Aetna. It was natural that he should be associated with Prometheus, his own relationship with mankind reflecting that of the hero who stole fire from his forge. Through his gift of fire, Prometheus is credited with creating mankind; it is Hephaistos who made woman (Pandora). And it was Hephaistos who first spiked Prometheus to his rock, then had compassion for him and released him.

Through his command of fire Hephaistos became known as the ideal artisan. His craftsmanship distinguishes him from the other, aristocratic gods, to whom physical work of any kind is demeaning. The catalogue of the creations of Hephaistos that can be gleaned from various traditions is evocative in its scope and connotations: with Athene he made the greaves of Herakles; and, by himself, the Herakleian shield. Athene was present when Hephaistos made for Peleus the marvelous spear carried by Achilles in the *Iliad*. He made wonderful jewelry for Thetis, provoking Hera's jealousy; a necklace for Harmonia; arrows for Artemis; and thunderbolts for Zeus. Then, of course, he made Pandora with the advice of Aphrodite and Athene. Hephaistos is also credited with Ixion's flaming wheel, serpentine in design like Agamemnon's armor in the *Iliad*; with the iron man Talos, given by him to Minos or by Zeus to Europa; and with the golden crown that glowed in the dark, smuggled to Theseus by Ariadne to enable him to escape from the labyrinth and then placed among the stars. Hephaistos was related to Athene primarily through his artistry—as the teachers of all human crafts addressed in the *Hymn to Hephaistos* (447); the two were worshipped in one temple in Athens. All these elements combine to identify Hephaistos with the powers of magic, as a sorcerer, or divine magus.

Hephaistos' special art, moreover, seems to be related to another characteristic—his lameness—which sets him apart from the other gods and goddesses. The lameness of smith-gods is a common Indo-European motif. According to the *Hymn to Pythian Apollo* (3. 315 ff.), Hephaistos was born lame and cast into the sea by Hera, who was ashamed of her child. Rescued by Thetis and Eurynome, Hephaistos set up his first smithy in a submarine grotto and fashioned wonderful jewels for his benefactors. Seeing one of these artifacts worn by Thetis, Hera became jealous and returned her son to Olympos, where he helped her rebel against Zeus. Zeus, consequently, hurled him again from heaven. This time he landed in Lemnos and set up shop there until his permanent restoration, which brought him to the position he holds in the narrative of Homer. Although Hephaistos seems to harbor no grudge against his mother, certainly his reference to her original unkind treatment of him may be taken as a qualification of his subservience to Hera; he will serve her faithfully only so long as her wishes do not contradict those of Zeus, whom Hephaistos fears and respects since the failure of the rebellion. His mind is wholly commanded by Zeus' new Olympian order.

Several unrelated stories told of Hephaistos are of interest. He was said to have killed Adonis on Mount Lebanon, perhaps explaining Aphrodite's willing infidelity to him. Because his first forge was underground, Hephaistos was associated with Rhadamanthys, the judge of the dead—as his making of Talos connects him to Minos. The appearance of Orion on the great shield in Book 18 may recall the Hesiodic legend that Hephaistos aided this hero, before his stellification, by giving him Cedalion as a helper.

Although Homer stations Hephaistos firmly on Olympos, many of these archaic chthonic elements are reflected in the *Iliad*. Homer has subordinated them all, however, to his own special symbolic purpose for the smith-god, directing their somewhat helter-skelter connotations toward the general impression of orderliness; Hephaistos represents Homer's ambition to present a model for orderly behavior. For if the god's appearance in Book 1 can be called comic, it is the satirical mode of comedy later developed by Aristophanes. Chastised by her husband, Hera

> went and sat down in silence wrenching her heart to obedience,
> and all the Uranian gods in the house of Zeus were troubled.
> Hephaistos the renowned smith rose up to speak among them,
> to bring comfort to his beloved mother, Hera of the white arms:
> 'This will be a disastrous matter and not endurable
> if you two are to quarrel thus for the sake of mortals
> and bring brawling among the gods. There will be no pleasure
> in the stately feast at all, since vile things will be uppermost.
> And I entreat my mother, though she herself understands it,
> to be ingratiating toward our father Zeus, that no longer
> our father may scold her and break up the quiet of our feasting.
> For if the Olympian who handles the lightning should be minded
> to hurl us out of our places, he is far too strong for any.
> Do you therefore approach him again with words made gentle,
> and at once the Olympian will be gracious again to us.'
>   He spoke, and springing to his feet put a two-handled goblet
> into his mother's hands and spoke again to her once more:
> 'Have patience, my mother, and endure it, though you be saddened,
> for fear that, dear as you are, I see you before my own eyes
> struck down, and then sorry though I be I shall not be able
> to do anything. It is too hard to fight against the Olympian.
> There was a time once before now I was minded to help you,
> and he caught me by the foot and threw me from the magic threshold,
> and all day long I dropped helpless, and about sunset
> I landed in Lemnos, and there was not much life left in me.
> After that fall it was the Sintian men who took care of me.'
>   He spoke, and the goddess of the white arms Hera smiled at him,
> and smiling she accepted the goblet out of her son's hand.
> Thereafter beginning from the left he poured drinks for the other
> gods, dipping up from the mixing bowl the sweet nectar.
> But among the blessed immortals uncontrollable laughter
> went up as they saw Hephaistos bustling about the palace.
>   Thus thereafter the whole day long until the sun went under
> they feasted, nor was anyone's hunger denied a fair portion,
> nor denied the beautifully wrought lyre in the hands of Apollo
> nor the antiphonal sweet sound of the Muses singing.
>   Afterwards when the light of the flaming sun went under
> they went away each one to sleep in his home where
> for each one the far-renowned strong-handed Hephaistos
> had built a house by means of his craftsmanship and cunning.
> Zeus the Olympian and lord of the lightning went to
> his own bed, where always he lay when sweet sleep came on him.
> Going up to the bed he slept and Hera of the gold throne beside him.
>
>   (1. 569–611)

The epithet "famous for his art"(1. 571—translation mine) not only identifies Hephaistos, but also justifies his right to address the assembled divinities. The orderly role Hephaistos plays in this episode makes it a microcosmic presentation of both the outcome of the epic itself and of Homer's concept of the social function of the art of words. Hephaistos' appearance here is in fact archetypal. We can appreciate his role more fully if we compare it with the roles of Nestor and Achilles in Book 23 and the role of Thersites in Book 2.

The motivation behind Hephaistos' address to the gods is both familial and widely social (1. 572–73) ff.). His first words express his consciousness of the social repercussions of marital disharmony, of antagonism between two individuals whose concord is the necessary basis for social order. The whole of the *Iliad* does the same. Hephaistos next points out the impropriety of gods allowing themselves to be affected personally by mortal affairs, succinctly stating the essential cause of the loss of equilibrium as a matter of unnatural orientation (1. 574). The symbol of that loss, for him, is the disruption of the feast—the image is emphasized by repetition (1. 575–76, 579). Generally in Homer the feast, representing the singular pleasure of peaceful harmony, is characteristically ἐσθλός *esthlós* ("good"); opposed to it are all "vile, unpeaceful things." For Homeric man the communal taking of food, because it testifies to the stability of the community, is a virtue in itself, making cause and effect reciprocal. Before the Achaians follow Achilles into battle, Odysseus will insist upon a communal repast; and Achilles will later advise Priam of the necessity for ritual eating. Furthermore, his insistence on the virtue of the feast associates Hephaistos with court poets (in this case Apollo) and by analogy, Homer himself. Alkinoös and Odysseus, in the *Odyssey* (8. 240 ff.; 21. 430 ff.), will proclaim that nothing is better than for men to enjoy themselves over food, accompanied by the lyre and song of the bard.

Just as Nestor advised Achilles to humor Agamemnon lest the army be disrupted (1. 277 ff.), Hephaistos advises his mother to placate Zeus. Authority, the bulwark of peace, requires the exercise of the art of peace; courtesy and authority must be accepted lest all the gods suffer (1. 577 ff.). Hephaistos himself not only counsels, but also exemplifies in his own speech, courteous propriety; he couches his suggestion to Hera in a diplomatic nicety (1. 577). His reason for the necessity of her acceptance of Zeus' authority also recalls Nestor's argument: Zeus cannot be resisted because he is φέρτατος *phértatos* ("strongest"), the same adjective used to describe Agamemnon's special status. The parallel is between the king of most men and the king of most gods. Each member of the community over which Zeus holds sway must act in a decorous fashion to insure that his will remains well disposed toward him. If one member breaks with decorum, the result will be ruin for them all (1. 580–81).

Now Hephaistos repeats his counsel to Hera, with more specific detail (1. 582–83). Repetition, with elaboration, is the familiar pedagogic technique of Nestor's speeches; it is the hallmark of the poet's didactic art as well. This time Hephaistos celebrates explicitly the effectiveness of ἐπέεσσι . . . μαλακοῖσιν *epéessi . . . malakoîsin* ("gentle words"—1. 582); the same kind of words he directs toward her, she must direct toward Zeus. If his speech, so courteously fashioned, influences Hera, then hers, modeled upon it, will not fail to move Zeus. So Hephaistos provides here not only a beneficial social lesson, but also personally exemplifies its effectiveness. Speaking well himself, he inspires others to speak well. The verb ἀναΐξας *anaîzas* ("he sprang up"—1. 584) connotes his characteristic application of unbounded energy to the will for order. In his unqualified eagerness, his readiness to serve the principle of harmony, Hephaistos leaps to take the cup—an artifact which will be associated later on with Nestor, too. The two-handled cup, in the hands of Hephaistos, becomes the concrete image of the feast, itself symbolic of communal harmony. Like the sceptre, it is passed from hand to hand, a tangible witness to collective concord.

Hephaistos, placing the cup in Hera's hands, addresses her a third time (1. 586). He appears, perhaps, as garrulous as Nestor is often considered. Once again he emphasizes the necessity of recognizing authority, this time by citing the consequences of Hera's potential secession: she would be struck down, before his eyes. He would be helpless to assist her (1. 587–89). The image of Hephaistos' eyes recalls the frequency with which vision is associated with the senescent passivity of Priam; perhaps it reflects the bard's traditional blindness. Like the poet in society, Hephaistos' present role is to influence the action of others, not to act himself.

Hephaistos proceeds to explain the basis of his present inactive role, by a recollected tale which provides the authority for the advice he has given Hera (1. 590 ff.). Experience—knowledge formed through memory—tells him that he will be unable to save her from Zeus' wrath and that she herself cannot hope to cope with it successfully. The story he tells of his fall from heaven at the hands of Zeus is a tale within Homer's tale of the *Iliad*, and typical of the many recollected tales Nestor calls upon from time to time to illustrate and convey his arguments. It is interesting to note that Hephaistos uses the adjective θεσπεσίοιο *thespesíoio* ("divinely wondrous") to describe the threshold of Olympos (his handiwork); Homer himself will use this word to characterize the song of Thamyris (2. 600). Hephaistos' vivid account of his somersaulting descent from the sky has something of a pathetically comic quality about it (1. 592–93), but his serious readiness to serve order is demonstrated anew in his willingness to present himself as an anti-exemplum that may help others avoid his former fate. Hephaistos' tale possesses, in fact, a potential very like that of Helen's weaving. His concluding sentence is delightfully superfluous (1. 594); the mention of the Sintians has no real relevance to Hephaistos' didactic purpose, but it does suggest his affinity to Homer himself, whose similes often go beyond their immediate purpose in exactly the same way. The total effect of the story is to present the government of Zeus as an article of faith, an unquestionable fact, in approximately the same way that Nestor's much more doubtfully logical analysis makes the primacy of Agamemnon an article of faith.

Hera is mollified by her son's earnest and reasonable presentation. She accepts the cup from him with a smile that will be described verbatim in her acceptance of Aphrodite's girdle (cf. 1. 595–96 with 14. 222–23). But there is nothing sinister about *this* smile. Unlike Helen's robe, Hephaistos' cup is effective and works in an orderly way; the artifact's potential has been realized. Homer's narrative technique here suggests that he may be remembering this cup when he describes the loom; for we see the same suspension of linear time in each image. Hephaistos' speech, including his tale, occupies the same narrative time-period in which he is placing the cup in Hera's hand and she is accepting it; just as his recollected tale is included in Homer's poem, it is included within the gesture of offering the goblet. As she takes the cup, Hera's acceptance of her son's orderly influence leads immediately to the relaxation of all the other gods, as Hephaistos moves around the banquet table meticulously (1. 597–98); he will later move just as meticulously around the shield he fashions for Achilles. When the gods partake of the nectar, itself another symbol of their immortal nature, the ritual communion of the feast is restored.

Hephaistos' success in reestablishing communal order contrasts with Nestor's failure in Book 1. Although he will eventually be successful in reintegrating Argos—when he convinces Patroklos of the necessity for social involvement by recounting past experience to him—Nestor has been sadly ineffective up to this point. More comparable to Hephaistos' role in this scene is that of Achilles in Book 23 when, with extreme courtesy and respect for social values, he brings to the Argives a feeling of unity never experienced under Agamemnon's rule.

The emotional expression of the ritual communion of the gods is their unquenchable laughter (1. 599), corresponding to the smile of Hera which signaled her personal satisfaction. Karl Reinhardt's comparison of Hephaistos to Thersites has some value. The other Achaians laugh at this

ungainly, crippled fellow, but the words he speaks are true; he recognizes the nature of Agamemnon's deed and the consequences of a king's
blindness for the people (2. 225 ff.). But the comparison can be carried no
further than this. The Argives revile Thersites because he has spoken out
of turn, and was himself the frequent object of ridicule for this characteristically disorderly attitude and comments. Nothing of the sort is
implied in the case of Hephaistos. The laughter of the gods must be
interpreted not as a pejorative in any sense, but as an expression of their
positive joy in concord, the contagion of Hephaistos' eager love for
order—as ἄσβεστος *ásbestos* ("inextinguishable") as his fire. And this
joy is enhanced by their appreciation of the fact that his lameness can
have such a wholesome influence upon the general well-being of the
community (1. 600). Even the calendar reflects the totality of the order he
has accomplished; their feast lasts a whole day (1. 601).

The formula which describes the divine feast is the familiar one
consistently applied to the banquets of men (cf. 1. 601 and 1. 468). The
recurrence suggests the exemplary nature of Hephaistos' function in this
episode; harmony, whether divine or human, has the same origins, as
well as the same outward signs. The parallel syntax extending from this
line into the next two serves to equate imagistically the feast with the lyre
of Apollo and the singing of the Muses (1. 603–4), and the only
appearance of the Muses in the *Iliad* occurs in Hephaistos' presence. The
participatory, reciprocal mode in which they sing, "responding to one
another with the sweet voice" (1. 604), is an orderly vision of divine
peace, of things as they should be when the wills of individuals are
attuned to a common natural purpose—proleptic to the peaceful scenes
portrayed upon the shield.

The feast and the day end at the same time, as the setting of the sun
closes both (1. 605); Hephaistos' successful domestication of Olympos
seems to restore the natural rhythm of the cosmos itself. The gods follow
the example of Olympian Zeus, going each to his own place of rest (1.
609). The poet notes that the individual palaces were custom-built by
Hephaistos—whom he now describes with a double epithet, as if to
congratulate the smith on his present success, adding a certain primal
quality to Hephaistos' power with this descriptive touch (1. 606–7). The
reconciliation the god has just accomplished is made to seem perfectly in
character by Homer's report of Hephaistos' previous architectural role in
the citification of Olympos. Zeus' epithet, as he goes to his own bed, may
be Homer's recognition of Hephaistos' function as analogous to the
poet's earthly role as the agent of Olympian order; for it is the same as
that applied to Zeus by the smith himself (1. 609 = 1. 580). Homer
emphasizes that this bed is Zeus' customary one (1. 601), therefore an

image of domestic harmony—reenforced here by Hera's joining her lord in sleep, the final syntactical element of the episode (1. 611). With this final stroke the scene is perfected as a prediction of the ultimate harmony of Olympos (in Book 15), and of Argos (which comes when Achilles reenters the battle); of the orderliness of humanity itself, in the concluding scene of the epic. And it will be Hephaistos' forging of the great shield, and Achilles' use of it, that will reorder both men and gods. Like the goblet here on Olympos, the shield will realize its orderly potential on earth.

The harmony with which Book 1 ends is of course temporary and therefore illusory. From his restful bed, Zeus will arise, as Book 2 opens, to cause havoc among the Achaians as he fulfills his promise to Thetis—temporarily forgotten throughout this episode. It will be because he sleeps with Hera in a very unorthodox bed in Book 14 that Zeus momentarily loses his control of the Olympians, the control symbolized by his customary bedding-down here. The scene with Hephaistos, then, is another kind of suspension of narrative logic; it is strikingly impressive, however, not despite its artificiality, but because of it. By dramatizing the successful function of Hephaistos at this early point in his poem, Homer indicates and predicts the orderly influence of art. Hephaistos becomes the model agency upon which all other orderly forces will be based throughout the poem; their meaning, so to speak, must be derived from consideration of this common denominator.

Hephaistos' function here serves as a figure for the order-promoting world of the poem itself. His character is a vivid realization of the reciprocal, hierarchical, nature of life in Homer's world, from its widest collective dimension to its most individual, sexual, manifestation. Hephaistos is the type of the singer-poet. The song of the ancient court poet serves a restorative function which parallels that of the goblet, of Hephaistos' tale, of Apollo's lyre and of the Muses' singing. After all, the singer automatically compels his audience to maintain at least the semblance of harmony demanded by their concerted attention to his recitation. Like the drinking of the nectar, here, the unanimity of the listeners is a temporary thing. As the individual gods and goddesses will awaken to pursue their various and variously selfish purposes, at odds with one another again, Hephaistos' talent will have no rest. Ultimately he will forge the shield, settling things once and for all. From the contrast between the transitory impact of the goblet and the implicitly permanent influence of the shield, we understand the didactic ambition of Homer's great poem: to be not a passing pleasure, but a continuing joy with constant effectiveness. Until the time comes for the forging of the shield, Hephaistos will be associated with the other orderly artifacts like this goblet. His creation of the sceptre, the aegis, his archetypal association with armor in general, and his building of Zeus' palace (20. 35), consistently relate Hephaistos to the principle of Olympian order. His masterly flame is as inextinguishable (17.90) as the divine laughter he inspires in the banquet of the gods.

The Galaxy of Order

Hephaistos' ordering flame illuminates the galaxy of order whose primary character is, of course, Achilles. But to understand Achilles' central relationship to Zeus' Olympian order and Homer's major theme, it is best to begin by comparing him to the other characters of his galaxy: Nestor, Diomedes, Aias, and the goddess Athene. Each of the three men participates in the ultimate resolution of disorder in the Iliadic world, as does Athene; and Homer expresses their orderliness in his description of their individualized artifacts. These Achaians don't have to be content, as Hektor must be, with the *promise* of glory; they experience glory directly, as their just reward.

The goddess who allies herself with Hera to wage war against the city of Priam introduces the galaxy of characters and images surrounding Achilles. In her regular association with the Achaians, she stands opposed to the patroness of Helen's galaxy, Aphrodite—just as the war and wisdom and community which she represents contradict the love and folly and selfishness with which Aphrodite herself is inspired and inspires Paris and Helen. And Athene—an ancient Mycenaean tutelary deity—is particularly close to Achilles (as she is to Odysseus in the *Odyssey*); in Book 1 she restrains him from drawing his sword against Agamemnon, his sudden repossession of common sense preventing his alienation from being irrevocable (1. 207 ff.). Although the *Iliad* doesn't mention Athene's birth, this scene in Book 1 suggests that Homer would have no quarrel with Hesiod, who made her the daughter of Metis ("good counsel"); yet her other birth-story, that Hephaistos split Zeus' skull with an axe to free her, full-grown and yelling, fits her warlike behavior in Homer's poem, too. Already in the *Iliad*, then, we can see a convergence of her various roles in later Greek mythology; as a goddess of the community, thereby connected with fertility and with war; as a goddess of wisdom, connected with self-defense and medicine; and as a goddess of art, especially connected with weaving, but also sexually connected (in the story of Ericthonios) with Hephaistos. Her descent from heaven in Book 19. 348–51 with nectar to nourish Achilles before the battle is a striking parallel, verbally as well as symbolically, with Thetis' descent bearing the armor from Hephaistos (cf. 18. 615–16). Like the shield, the nectar she brings is a preservative whose nature properly matches that of the hero: because he is half man, Achilles must eat, as Odysseus insists; as half god, he may partake of immortal food. In the same way, Achilles' mortality is protected by a divinely invulnerable shield.

Finally, Athene helps Achilles defeat Hektor by appearing to help the Trojan hero in the guise of Deïphobos (22.232–37). The irony of Hektor's address to the goddess is perhaps the sharpest to be found in the *Iliad*: "Then tall Hektor of the shining helm answered her: 'Deïphobos, / before now you were dearest to me by far of my brothers, / of all those who were sons of Priam and Hekabe, and now / I am minded all the more within my heart to honour you, / you who dared for my sake, when your eyes saw me, to come forth / from the fortifications, while the others stand fast inside them' " (22. 232–37). Because he thinks a brother is willing to risk his individuality for his sake, Hektor will now be ready to risk his individuality on behalf of all others in Troy. In fact, however, no Trojan has risked himself to assist Hektor. He stands alone, and his isolation and impotence against Achilles argue for the criminal selfishness of his fellow citizens. The indifferent principle of order, which Athene here represents, dictates that the sincerity of one man is not enough to save his disorderly people. So Athene fulfills her consistently warlike role in the poem, yet ennobles Helen in the process.

The nature of Athene's role is symbolized succinctly by the helmet she dons after arming herself with the aegis: "Upon her head she set the golden helm with its four sheets / and two horns, wrought with the fighting men of a hundred cities" (5. 743–44). The image of the helmet suggests the spirit of human strife itself. It is indeed universal, with its reference to a hundred cities; but the universality of the helmet is not that of the shield: it is neither objective nor realistic. Depicting only war, its restriction is evident. And indeed, for now at least, Athene is concerned only with war. She turns her head from Hekabe's robe, and takes off her own in order to don the aegis. The artifact perfectly identifies her role.

The aegis, on the other hand, is a different kind of image. Its function goes beyond the immediate, beyond the victory of the Achaians; its significance, like that of the great shield, is that of a wider human reality that transcends the national distinctions of the present. On the wider symbolic level, it is associated not with Athene only, who bears it on behalf of Argos, nor with Apollo alone, who brings it to Hektor's aid, but also with its proper owner, Zeus himself, as the principle of order. The Danaan victory, of course, is required by Olympian order. So it is quite

consistent that Athene, whose most frequent epithet associates her with
the aegis of her father, is the one who first provides Homer with an
occasion for describing the artifact in detail:

> Now in turn Athene, daughter of Zeus of the aegis,
> beside the threshold of her father slipped off her elaborate
> dress which she herself had wrought with her hands' patience,
> and now assuming the war tunic of Zeus who gathers
> the clouds, she armed in her gear for the dismal fighting.
> And across her shoulders she threw the betasselled, terrible
> aegis, all about which Terror hangs like a garland,
> and Hatred is there, and Battle Strength, and heart-freezing Onslaught
> and thereon is set the head of the grim gigantic Gorgon,
> a thing of fear and horror, portent of Zeus of the aegis.
>
> (5. 733–42)

Putting aside the art with which she is associated in times of peace,
Athene becomes the agent of order, to work the purpose of her father in
the unhappy toil of battle. It is part of the symbolic inversion that
Aphrodite, instead of Athene, is connected with the loom in the *Iliad*.
The image of Athene's spear has the same connotations; it is "heavy,
huge, thick, wherewith she beats down the battalions of fighting / men
against whom she of the mighty father is angered" (5. 746–47 = 8.
390–91). The personified forces depicted on the aegis are equivalent to
the Gorgon on the shield of Agamemnon (11. 36). There is no vision of
peace which follows war, indeed there is nothing human at all, in the
content of the aegis. It is the means only, not the end. As such, the aegis,
when Athene bears it, represents the attunement of the Argive cause
with the governmental purpose of Zeus. With that purpose Achilles, too,
will be aligned, when he decides to reenter the conflict. Although the
Achaians are routed, he must wait until his armor is finished by
Hephaistos before he can rally the army and lead them against Hektor.
Zeus will not risk the possible consequences of delay and so sends Iris to
him, who instructs Achilles to show himself to the armies at the ditch.
Following her orders, "Achilleus, the beloved of Zeus, rose up, and
Athene / swept about his powerful shoulders the fluttering aegis; / and
she, the divine among goddesses, about his head circled / a golden
cloud, and kindled from it a flame far-shining" (18. 203–6). The epiphany
of Achilles, clothed in the symbol of divine approval and bathed in the
brilliant light of eternity, heartens the stricken Argives and terrifies the
astonished Trojans, who retreat in panic. So the aegis identifies Achilles
with the cause of order.

But Zeus, after all, sees beyond the immediate necessity of destroying
Troy. As the god and principle of order, he seeks to insure man's access to

glory and to a glorious memory, regardless of national distinctions. The purely human function of the aegis is portrayed in its association with Hektor, the most noble of the Trojans: "The Trojans came down on them in a pack, and Hektor led them / in long strides, and in front of him went Phoibos Apollo / wearing a mist about his shoulders, and held the tempestuous / terrible aegis, shaggy, conspicuous, that the bronze-smith / Hephaistos had given Zeus to wear to the terror of mortals. / Gripping this in both hands he led on the Trojan people" (15. 306–11). As long as Apollo holds up the aegis the Trojans have the upper hand (15. 318–22). And it is necessary for them to prevail, in the long-range plan of Zeus, until Achilles is convinced that his involvement is the only hope for saving his nation, his own country, and—avenging Patroklos—his own honor. Zeus knows that Achilles' conviction is the necessary basis for making him an example of orderly social behavior. So, to insure the effectiveness of his stratagem, Zeus lends the aegis to Apollo. The archer-god, opposed to the Achaians from the beginning, employs it eagerly, his misty appearance recalling his night-like presence in Book 1. Moreover, it is significant that Hephaistos is identified with the aegis as its creator at this point, in its association with the Trojans; his service to order is bipartisan because, like Zeus, his perspective transcends the present international strife to comprehend the permanent meaningful-ness of Hektor's social deeds.

The final appearance of the aegis is a testimony to its symbolic function on the most universal level, one which goes beyond the present to encompass the glorious future of man—both fictive and actual. It is the aegis, in fact, which makes Achilles' gesture toward Priam, the return of Hektor's body, poetically valid. Despite Achilles' brutal treatment of the Trojan hero's body—made all the more awful by its reflection of Hektor's misuse of Achilles' old armor—and his callous threat to let Hektor's body become the prey of dogs and birds, Hektor's remains receive the honor they deserve even before Priam has arranged the funeral: "But Apollo / had pity on him, though he was only a dead man, and guarded / the body from all ugliness, and hid all of it under the golden / aegis, so that it might not be torn when Achilleus dragged it" (24. 18–21). Zeus' granting the aegis to Hektor becomes the imagistic model for Achilles' return of the robes to Priam with the body. For it shows that Achilles, too, recognizes, and asserts with his gesture, that a dead man is still a man worthy of proper treatment. In its final appearance the aegis is no longer associated with war; here alone the artifact is not called δεινός deinós ("terrible"). Hephaistos' creation serves the memory of Hektor which now does not disintegrate inhumanly with his body, but gloriously—divinely—lives on.

$$\mathcal{A}\ 7\ \mathcal{L}$$

Hephaistos and the Galaxy
of Achilles: 2

Nestor's Sidonian Cup

No other human figure in the *Iliad* is a greater storyteller than Nestor. There is an element of the comic to his love for rambling tales, voluminous arguments. But this relatively minor failing, if it really is a failing, does not detract from his characteristic nobility. Nestor is old age at its finest. His eagerness to serve, "with kind intent toward all," is very like that of Hephaistos. Nestor plays the role of the old shepherd of the people, the spokesman for the community. In contrast with Priam, his social orientation, though it may falter, never fails him. Nestor is able to represent order because the ultimate harmony of Argos is assured by the orderly foresight of Zeus. Nestor's shield is one of Homer's images of the old man's orderliness. Hard upon the heels of the fleeing Achaians, Hektor shouts encouragement to his men: " 'Follow close now and be rapid, so we may capture / the shield of Nestor, whose high fame goes up to the sky now, / how it is all of gold, the shield itself and the cross-rods' " (8. 191–93). Although Nestor's shield is presented in less detail than those of Aias, Agamemnon, and Achilles, still its symbolic significance corresponds to theirs—as Hektor asserts its fame and calculates the results of its being captured (18. 196–97). The shield is special because of its material splendor, but even more importantly, because it is Nestor's. The predicted impact of its capture defines the crucial role Nestor plays among the Danaans: he epitomizes the stability of the army; if his characteristic artifact is taken, that stability is destroyed.

Nestor represents the *total* social structure of Argos; every level of society is his concern. The image of the shield has familial associations: "So he spoke, and took up the wrought shield of his son / Thrasymedes, breaker of horses. It lay in the shelter / all shining in bronze. Thrasymedes carried the shield of his father" (14. 9–11). The continuity of human life, in the relationship between father and son, is symbolized

148

by this exchange of shields. As the younger man, Thrasymedes carries the famous shield of his noble father in battle, since Nestor rarely fights himself. The symbiosis between youth and old age is perfected in a stable society; the reciprocal integrity of the family, in turn, insures that stability. Nestor regularly speaks out for the cooperation of all in the national, collective effort; he knows that individuals, working alone, are ineffective in the business of warfare (4. 303–5). The narrator himself, in first introducing Nestor, proclaims his authority to speak on behalf of the entire society: "between them Nestor / the fair-spoken rose up, the lucid speaker of Pylos, / from whose lips the streams of words ran sweeter than honey. / In his time two generations of mortal men had perished, / those who had grown up with him and they who had been born to / these in sacred Pylos, and he was king in the third age. / He in kind intention toward both stood forth and addressed them" (1. 247–53). Nestor has endured "their going hence, even as their coming hither," and his ripeness is expressed in the equanimity with which he stands up to arbitrate, like Hephaistos, between the two men whom he regards with equal affection—but also with equal objectivity. The tale which he relates is meant to communicate to Agamemnon and Achilles the knowledge derived from memory, that international strife can bring nothing but grief to Argos, and joy to the enemy (1. 259–73), like Hektor's words to Paris in Book 3. Nestor's credo is that internal social order must be maintained at all costs.

Homer focuses Nestor's status in the images associated with him in Book 11, as introduction to Nestor's crucial convincing of Patroklos that the Myrmidons must support their Argive comrades. The description of the accouterments of Nestor's battlefield household is as rich as that of the royal palace of Alkinoös, or of Menelaos, in the *Odyssey*. The centerpiece is the famous goblet, which Schliemann thought he found at Troy.

> And lovely-haired Hekamede made them a potion, she whom
> the old man won from Tenedos, when Achilleus stormed it.
> She was the daughter of great-hearted Arsinoös. The Achaians
> chose her out for Nestor, because he was best of them all in counsel.
> First she pushed up the table in front of them, a lovely
> table, polished and with feet of cobalt, and on it
> she laid a bronze basket, with onion to go with the drinking,
> and pale honey, and beside it bread, blessed pride of the barley,
> and beside it a beautifully wrought cup which the old man brought with
>   him
> from home. It was set with golden nails, the eared handles upon it
> were four, and on either side there were fashioned two doves
> of gold, feeding, and there were double bases beneath it.

Another man with great effort could lift it full from the table,
but Nestor, aged as he was, lifted it without strain.
In this the woman like the immortals mixed them a potion
with Pramneian wine, and grated goat's-milk cheese into it
with a bronze grater, and scattered with her hand white barley into it.

(11. 623–39)

The symbolic meaning of Nestor's goblet here is connected with Hephaistos' cup ritual in Book 1. Considering it from this perspective, we understand why the poet portrays Nestor's cup and the context which surrounds it with such magnificence. For the communion between Nestor and Patroklos leads directly to what must be recognized as the most important communication in the *Iliad* (11. 640–41). Nestor's counsel to Patroklos, achieved through his lengthy narrative recollection, sets the events in motion which Zeus will outline: Patroklos' own death, and the consequent reemergence of Achilles from his unnatural isolation.

The reference to Hekamede and Tenedos associates Nestor with the orderly role destined to be played by Achilles in the immediate future, just as Achilles had performed an orderly collective role in the past when he stormed that city. The juxtaposition of Hekamede—Nestor's prize in the present war (who is herself a striking parallel to Chryseis, Briseis, and Andromache)—with the cup—his booty from days of old—contrasts the communal position Nestor now holds with the one he held in his younger days as a fighter. He is no less crucial to Argos now as an instructor than he was once as a warrior. His strength is somehow undiminished; he still lifts the goblet easily. The special mixture poured into it by Hekamede—its special quality reemphasized by the quality of the tools she uses—represents the mnemonic conviction of the tale of Neleus and the Epeian war, the pragmatic lesson of which is not lost on Patroklos. The glory of the past is married to the ensuing glorious deeds of the present in the image of the cup from which Nestor and Patroklos, old man and young, counselor and warrior, drink together. The one has made his mark on the world and the other now will make his.

The cup, moreover, suggests that Nestor's authority derives not only from his *memory* of past deeds, but also from his personal participation in them. At the same time it represents the character development of Nestor in the poem. The members of the orderly galaxy are not dissociated entirely from disorder. Yet, if they are touched by disorder, they are distinguished from members of the disorderly galaxy by the fact that the disorderliness does not finally define them. Hektor finds order beyond the present, but Nestor moves from disorder to order within the present. For Nestor errs very seriously at the opening of Homer's story. Unlike the members of Helen's galaxy, he is allowed to recover from his error, to become actively successful.

Nestor's failing at the outset of the poem can be studied as an example of the relationship between imagery and characterization. His fault in Book 1 is that he is too preoccupied with the whole, insufficiently concerned with the part. He is, in other words, so interested in the welfare of the nation that he neglects the equally important autonomy of the individual. Throughout the *Iliad*, until Achilles restores his faith, Nestor gives too little credit to the men of the present (for example, 4. 405). In his attempt to negotiate the quarrel between Agamemnon and Achilles, Nestor stresses only the authority of kings; their responsibility is not emphasized in his speech. His emphasis on the honor due to sceptred kings (1. 278–79) suggests that Nestor has not perceived, or admitted, the magnitude of Agamemnon's crime both against Apollo and against the individuality of Achilles. Nor does he fully appreciate the crucial importance of that individuality—that is, Achilles is the essential bulwark of the army, its necessary warrior, the epitome of its fighting strength. Nestor's rhetoric is right enough; but it is irrelevant. His accuracy is limited because it takes too little account of the king's responsibility toward hs subjects. Nestor is at this point the antitype of Hephaistos, of the arbitrator on the shield in Book 18, and of Achilles himself in Book 23.

Displaying his social consciousness, Nestor advises his king to assemble the army clan by clan and tribe by tribe, as the catalogue of ships is introduced (2. 362). His neglect of the individual element is all too evident: " 'Let them go perish, these one or two, who think apart from / the rest of the Achaians, since there will be no use in them' " (2. 346–47). Nestor does not consider the justification of Achilles' bitterness; instead, he dismisses it as mere rashness. Persisting in his love for order, he counsels Agamemnon to attempt to reestablish in his army the harmony disrupted by the quarrel (2. 367 ff.). He says, as it were, "Let us look at all the Achaians and see whether, even without Achilles, they are strong enough, united enough to be victorious." So he rightly reasserts the systematic basis for national effectiveness. But he, and the other Achaians, are deluded in thinking that they are sufficient against Troy without the necessary individual; their delusion serves the disorderly ambition of Hera.

Observant as he is, Nestor soon recognizes the disastrous fortunes of the Argives at the hands of Hektor as a reflection on his counseling ability. He has been wrong in encouraging Agamemnon to fight without Achilles, just as he was wrong in favoring the king unequivocally in the quarrel. His interest in order unabated, Nestor is now ready to make amends for his excessive loyalty. He tells Diomedes that Zeus himself must be against the Achaians (8. 140 ff.), using the same terms to describe the god's irresistible authority as he'd used to describe Agamemnon's to Achilles in Book 1. On Nestor's advice the finally repentant Agamemnon sends the embassy to offer gifts and the return of Briseis to Achilles in Book 9. 120 ff.

Although, through Nestor's arbitration, the king has now played his proper role, Achilles remains unconvinced of Agamemnon's sincerity. He obstinately refuses to make peace with the Danaans. Meanwhile Nestor himself exemplifies his new-found awareness of the responsibility of rulers. In Book 10 he goes in person to awaken the sleeping warriors and stir them to battle. Diomedes is amazed at being roused from slumber by the scolding words of Nestor, and replies: " 'Aged sir, / you are a hard man. You are never finished with working. / Now are there not other sons of the Achaians younger than you are / who could be going about everywhere to each of the princes / and waking them up? But you, aged sir, are too much for us' " (10. 163–67). Nestor takes Diomedes' half-serious commendation of his unelderly vigor quite seriously. He retorts that, when the people are on the brink of catastrophe, it is proper for the kings themselves to rouse the chieftains (10. 169–74). Rank, like age, is no excuse; the royal role requires vigorous action.

Convinced that all that is humanly possible has been done to placate Achilles' wrath, Nestor, his duty in the matter fulfilled, no longer sympathizes with the sulking which he must regard as excessively egocentric. Who is one man, after all, to judge the sincerity of another? The token offerings, and the solemn pledge that Agamemnon had not slept with Briseis, surely should have sufficed. As far as Nestor is concerned, Agamemnon is behaving properly once again; it is Achilles who is unnatural, for his persistent alienation is more drastic than ever since all the princes, including Agamemnon himself, have been wounded. And so Nestor concludes his tale of Neleus, which emphasizes the necessity of social reciprocity, with a clear damnation of Achilles' present position: " 'That was I, among men, if it ever happened. But Achilleus / will enjoy his own valour in loneliness, though I think / he will weep much, too late, when his people are perished from him' " (11. 761–63). The lesson he imparts to Patroklos is that the autonomy of the individual, in human life, is a qualified value. The achievement of glory demands a collective context for its recognition, for its perpetuation in memory. The individual is simply meaningless unless he acts for others. Now is the time to act, if that context is to be preserved: " 'And let him give you his splendid armor to wear to the fighting, / if perhaps the Trojans might think you are he, and give way' "

(11. 797–98). The chain of events has now been initiated which will lead to the death of Patroklos, to the forging of the shield to replace the one Hektor captures, to the reentry of Achilles, and to the death of Hektor. In his fateful assumption that Patroklos may be a substitute for Achilles, Nestor shows his desperate resolve for order, for the salvation of Argos. He is still compromising, still hesitating to admit that Achilles is uniquely important. But there is no other course of action open to Nestor, confronted with Achilles' obstinate behavior, than to trust in the hero's love for his best friend. His trust is proven valid in a way Nestor may not have foreseen: Patroklos' death motivates Achilles as nothing else had done.

The funeral games for Patroklos, the final link in the chain of events that began with Nestor's counsel, over which Achilles presides, represent the accomplishment of Nestor's steadfast ambition: the reunification of Argos. It is highly fitting that Achilles himself should recognize Nestor's role in this development, and the courtesy with which he recognizes Nestor shows he has realigned himself with the collective values the old man professes throughout the story. After prizes have been distributed to the four drivers in the horse race,

> the fifth prize, the two-handled
> jar, was left. Achilleus carried it through the assembly
> of the Argives, and gave it to Nestor, and stood by and spoke to him:
> 'This, aged sir, is yours to lay away as a treasure
> in memory of the burial of Patroklos; since never
> again will you see him among the Argives. I give you this prize
> for the giving; since never again will you fight with your fists nor wrestle,
> nor enter again the field for the spear-throwing, nor race
> on your feet; since now the hardship of old age is upon you.'

> (23. 615–23)

The fact that Achilles harbors no resentment against Nestor for the causal role he played in the death of Patroklos is tantamount to an admission of his own culpability. He must know that Nestor's counsel represented the true spirit of human order, the necessity inherent in the condition of man. If anyone is to blame, it's Achilles himself, and the rash Patroklos, who failed to obey his strictures. On the other hand, Achilles has given Nestor what he deserves. The presentation of the urn complements the image of the goblet. One prize Nestor won as warrior in the past; this he wins as observer and spokesman for order in the present. The urn's symbolic function will be to remind Nestor of his success in the Trojan campaign, one fraught with tragedy, but nonetheless the material for glorious identification in the memory of men to come. The gesture also marks the restoration of Achilles' social orderliness; the gratuitous gift is the token of the young warrior's recognition that his valor is of the same quality as that of the old counselor, that both kinds are necessary for a harmonious nation. Like Cordelia, Nestor is accepted only after it is too late. Now Achilles must surely die, as Patroklos has already. But the acceptance itself is enough. Nestor's role is fulfilled when his fellow countrymen accord him honor. His name, like Hektor's, will be remembered in song; but he himself is fortunate enough to observe its present memorialization, as he accepts the urn.

Diomedes' Shield

Hephaistos makes no armor for the Trojans in Homer's poem. The inclusion of Diomedes in the galaxy of order is marked by the fact that the corselet worn by the Achaian warrior is made by the smith-god; moreover, in the passage quoted in connection with Hektor's description of Nestor's shield, Diomedes' corselet is described as δαιδάλεον *daidáleon* ("skillfully decorated"—8. 194–95). As Book 5 opens, Athene sees to it that Diomedes' appearance will be appropriate to his ἀριστεία *aristeía* ("heroic moment"):

> There to Tydeus' son Diomedes Pallas Athene
> granted strength and daring, that he might be conspicuous
> among all the Argives and win the glory of valour.
> She made weariless fire blaze from his shield and helmet
> like that star of the waning summer who beyond all stars
> rises bathed in the ocean stream to glitter in brilliance.
> Such was the fire she made blaze from his head and his shoulders
> and urged him into the middle fighting, where most were struggling.
>
> (5. 1–8)

Just as Aias is presented in the last-ditch defense of the ships, here Diomedes is portrayed as the bulwark of the Argives, in the absence of Achilles. Diomedes' orderly association with Achilles is evident in the way this passage foreshadows Athene's transfiguration of the great Myrmidon for his terrifying epiphany to the Trojans (18. 204 ff.). In both episodes the dominant image is that of celestial fire. The star Diomedes is compared with, in fact, is one which will appear on Achilles' great shield (18. 489), made by the "weariless fire" of Hephaistos.

We recall, too, that in a similar context Homer compares Hektor's armor with a star (11. 62–63); the poet, then, employs this artifact-image with very specialized identifying force. When its wearer is to be singled out as the rallying-point for his people, his armor is presented as a celestial beacon, a focal point for their glorious engagement. In this instance, the armor so identifies Diomedes as the epitome of the Argive spirit, protector and inspiration of his nation. The special treatment given Diomedes' armor is all the more striking when we remember that, in the exchange with Glaukos, his armor will be portrayed as not only undistinguished, but also as inferior. Dramatic effect is the dominant factor in this context; for if Diomedes' armor possesses a significance which transcends the episode at hand it possesses it in a typical fashion, without specific reference to the individuality of Diomedes. On this transcendent level the fiery armor symbolizes the effectiveness of the individual hero as a bulwark to his people—a role which Diomedes happens to be playing at this point, but which others may also play.

The Huge Shield of Aias

The image of Aias' shield is remarkable not only for including something of the process of its fabrication, but also for identifying its human creator by name. With Nestor's encouragement, Aias has volunteered to meet Hektor in single combat. Now the duel begins:

> Now Aias came near him, carrying like a wall his shield
> of bronze and sevenfold ox-hide which Tychios wrought him with much toil;
> Tychios, at home in Hyle, far the best of all workers in leather
> who had made him the great gleaming shield of sevenfold ox-hide
> from strong bulls, and hammered an eighth fold of bronze upon it.
>
> (7. 219–23)

Appropriately the shield of the man who is bravest after Achilles—by his own unchallenged claim (7. 228)—is made by the best of all mortal artisans. The artifact perfectly identifies Aias. His solid mortality is contrasted with the semidivinity of Achilles in the qualitative distinction between their shields, for Achilles' is bronze throughout. And the individualizing function of Aias' shield works within the Iliadic world; as the Achaians come against them, Kebriones tells Hektor: " 'The Telamonian Aias drives them; I know him surely / for he carries the broad shield on his shoulders' " (11. 526–27). More perhaps than any other artifact in the poem the shield by its very nature combines literal with symbolic significance.

The poet's dramatic description of Aias' shield in action gives us a terminology for discussing the symbolic import of Achilles' shield (7. 245

ff.). Emphasizing his peculiarly close relationship with Aias, Homer introduces Teukros in his list of the Achaians led into battle by the son of Telamon:

> and ninth came Teukros, bending into position the curved bow,
> and took his place in the shelter of Telamonian Aias'
> shield, as Aias lifted the shield to take him. The hero
> would watch, whenever in the throng he had struck some man with an
>   arrow,
> and as the man dropped and died where he was stricken, the archer
> would run back again, like a child to the arms of his mother,
> to Aias, who would hide him in the glittering shield's protection.
>   (8. 266–72)

Teukros' somewhat ambiguous appearance here provides us with a critical language for the shield's presentation of social reciprocity. On the one hand, his actions suggest the way in which the individual's effectiveness depends upon his reliance on and support by the community. A people, an army, an individual, align themselves behind the shield; its protection provides Teukros with the necessary immunity in which he may restring his bow. The simile of the mother and child, moreover, presents Teukros as an antitype of Patroklos, whose relationship with Achilles Homer portrays in the same terms (16. 7 ff.). Teukros is safe for the moment because his filial relationship is orderly; he respects the maternal, salutary, presence. Patroklos dies precisely because he fails to heed Achilles' warnings about overextending himself. Teukros is also a contrast to Pandaros, whose bowmanship has such disastrous consequences because it is not oriented toward the general good and because its point of origin is selfishness.

Aias' special affinity to Achilles is marked in the scene describing his shield's protection of Patroklos' body; the resemblance to the Teukros episode extends even to the simile. Against Hektor's attack, "Aias covering the son of Menoitios under his broad shield / stood fast, like a lion over his young, when the lion / is leading his little ones along, and men who are hunting / come upon them in the forest. He stands in the pride of his great strength / hooding his eyes under the cover of down-drawn eyelids. / Such was Aias as he bestrode the hero Patroklos" (17. 132–37). In its immediate relevance, the simile honors Aias for his involvement with others (17. 133–34) and, in its superfluity, for his own glorious personality (17. 134–35). This time the shield is entirely successful in redeeming the fallen hero, a success which makes more poignant Achilles' failure to protect the living Patroklos.

Aias, in fact, plays an Achilles-like role throughout that hero's period of isolation. When Aias steps forward to accept the responsibility of confronting Hektor in the duel, the army, formerly divided in desire, unites immediately behind its stalwart defender (7. 178–83). It is Aias who maintains the semblance of unity which, because of his own warlike efforts and Nestor's counsel, will become eventually a reality. And Aias recognizes his subordination to Achilles' might (7. 228); he does not condemn the man whose role he has been forced, by events, to perform. But there is an element of pride in his awareness of his present destiny—of being the primary active representative of Argos. So he refers directly to the absent Achilles, when he exchanges challenges with Hektor: " 'He lies now apart among his own beaked seafaring / ships, in anger at Agamemnon, the shepherd of the people. / But here we are; and we are such men as can stand up against you; / there are plenty of us; so now begin your fight and your combat' " (7. 229–32). The balance represented by their exchange of armor is between the strength of these two leaders, between their charismatic personalities by which their peoples, each weakened by internal contention, still can recognize the need for cooperation.

The maintenance of that harmony depends upon the unanimous exercise of the virtue of αἰδώς aidōs ("respect"), the virtue Aias epitomizes throughout the *Iliad*. Because he is so characterized, Aias is the foil to Achilles, as well as being his prototype. When Achilles' αἰδώς aidōs is restored, as he makes peace with Agamemnon and all the Argives because of Patroklos' death—the peace expressed in the funeral games made possible, after all, by Aias' defense of Patroklos' body—Aias will be eclipsed by the greatest of the Danaans. Like Nestor, however, he is given due credit by Achilles—and the tribute is made specifically to his shield, when Achilles explains to Iris that he himself can't fight until he receives new armor from Hephaistos: " 'Nor do I know of another whose glorious armour I could wear / unless it were the great shield of Telamonian Aias. / But he himself wears it, I think, and goes in the foremost / of the spear-fight over the body of fallen Patroklos' " (18. 192–95). Aias' glory is recognized and proclaimed by the man who best understands its nature: this is his highest tribute, the greatest expression of respect. The parallel between the two heroes is evident: Aias makes possible the honorable funeral; Achilles will avenge the spirit of his comrade. Achilles' shield will lead to the total reunification of all Argos, when the fall of Troy brings Helen back to Menelaos. Aias' shield has made the unity of the Argive army realizable by his steadfast valor, and now realized by his service to Achilles' friend.

◁ 8 ▷

The Great Shield

Achilles is the epitome of Iliadic man. The two artifacts which uniquely belong to him, Hephaistos' shield and Peleus' spear, define not only the identity of Achilles, but also the essence of human nature as Homer conceives of it. But Homer expresses his universal significance by associating Achilles, in one place or another, with nearly every other kind of artifact in the Iliadic world. Like Priam and Hekabe, Achilles stores his treasures in a splendid chest; like Nestor, he possesses a remarkable goblet. These two artifacts are described when Patroklos, having armed himself in the old armor of his friend, prepares to lead the Myrmidons into battle:

> But meanwhile Achilleus
> went off into his shelter, and lifted the lid from a lovely
> elaborately wrought chest, which Thetis the silver-footed
> had put in his ship to carry, and filled it fairly with tunics
> and mantles to hold the wind from a man, and with fleecy blankets.
> Inside this lay a wrought goblet, nor did any other
> man drink the shining wine from it nor did Achilleus
> pour from it to any other god, but only Zeus father.
>
> (16. 220–27)

The chest, a memento of his divine mother, is a worthy receptacle for the robes which protect her son from the ravages of the temporal elements, and for the cup with which he addresses divinity.

Homer emphasizes that the goblet is to be identified with Achilles insofar as he is attuned to the order of Zeus—making it all the more significant that he should use it here in praying for Patroklos, his alter ego. The goblet imagistically complements the cup used in the ritual communion by which Nestor convinces Patroklos of the necessity for social commitment. Nestor was misguided in thinking that Patroklos could play the role of Achilles; here we see that Achilles, in a sense, shares the delusion. His alignment with the principle of order is there-

158

fore less than perfect. For Zeus knows that, if order is to be reestablished among the Argives and the army saved, Achilles himself must fight. Achilles' goblet is also a contrast to the cup used so effectively by Hephaistos in Book 1. Achilles' prayer is granted, but only in part: the Achaians will be saved; but Patroklos will lose his life in the effort (16. 250). Like Nestor's, this goblet has the potential of order; as Achilles uses it, the potential is yet unrealized. The goblet's influence will be harmonious only when, after Patroklos' death, Achilles himself has rejoined the army. Then he will use it again, this time with perfect symbolic orderliness, in his ritual opening of the funeral games: with it he offers a sacrifice to the memory of Patroklos (23. 220 ff.).

The image of the goblet is an excellent example of the way in which artifacts serve as mnemonic devices. As one unit of vision is related by the listener's memory to another like it, the unity of the poem's effect is assured. A meaningful pattern is formed by the dramas in which the cup is involved: a god uses it effectively (Book 1); a man uses it effectively (Nestor in Book 16); one who is half god and half man uses it half effectively because he has not yet come to terms with the duality of his nature; finally the hero, realizing the eternal dimension of his humanity, uses the cup effectively (Book 23, as he sacrifices with it for Patroklos) and then rewards the man upon whose use of it his own orderly use is modeled (the gift to Nestor).

Similarly, when the ghost of Patroklos appears, it is to instruct Achilles that, when he too dies, he is to have his bones laid beside those of Patroklos in the urn given by Thetis for this purpose (23. 91–92). Like the goblet, the funeral urn—which, according to the *Odyssey* (24. 74 ff.), Thetis received from Dionysos, who received it from Hephaistos, its maker—symbolizes the unanimity of the two friends. It will secure their friendship from the pain of separation only when both are dead. But the urn will remind living men who see it of the eternal aspect of such friendship. Furthermore, just as the image of this artifact evokes the intimate relationship between Achilles and Patroklos, transcending time, it also connects Achilles with Hektor, transcending space. The fact that they both play primary roles in their societies is marked by Homer's careful assignment of imagery: Hektor's is the only other funeral urn mentioned in the *Iliad* (24. 795).

Such unifying and clarifying devices inform the whole poem. Another example is the elaborate description of Achilles' battlefield house which introduces Priam's arrival for their momentous meeting (24. 447–59). The image provides the familial and hospitable context which will issue in Achilles' gracious consideration of his guest's petition. It also embodies his superlative individuality, as the strongest of the Achaians in the present warfare—but simultaneously suggests that the warrior must be complemented by the counselor and ruler, in the implied contrast with Nestor (24. 455–56). And it is not as a warrior that Achilles reacts to Priam.

Achilles' explanation of the two urns of Zeus relates the agony of Priam with that of Peleus, both made poignant by the memory of former happiness (24. 525 ff.). The image, once again, underlines Achilles' now perfect alignment with the divine principle of order. The imagery of Book 24 is indeed that of death and finality, juxtaposed with a certainty that the memory of man survives. That is the meaning of returning the robes with Hektor's body. Even the bed his comrades prepare for Priam reflects the mood of the scene perfectly. Their elaborate care in making it comfortable, on the one hand, reflects the generosity and sympathy of Achilles for his fellow sufferer; on the other hand, its covers are purple—Priam, after all, must die soon, as must Achilles himself (24. 645 ff.). Images of peace and domesticity—house, bed, robes—dominate the close of the *Iliad*. Yet, as the urns suggest, it is a peace shadowed by death—shadowed, but not overshadowed.

The shield of Achilles, described as Hephaistos makes it (in Book 18), eclipses all other artifacts through its complex and comprehensive inter-relationship with the orderly theme of Homer's poem.

The Shield's Position in the Poem

Before approaching the shield itself, we must appreciate the dramatic effect of its position in Homer's narrative. Samuel E. Bassett calls the shield "an epic *hyporcheme*, intervening between two of the most poignant moments of emotion in [the] poem" (p. 98). Before we see the shield, Homer has portrayed Achilles' grief at hearing of Patroklos' death. Then, when Thetis brings the divine armor to her son at the opening of Book 19, she finds him lying with his arms around the body of his friend. In a larger sense, the shield of Achilles is a suspension of the narrative momentum, a respite from the brutal reality of the battle (between Hektor's slaying of Patroklos and Achilles' of Hektor). In this sense the shield's appearance is comparable to that of Helen's loom in Book 3: each is a kind of respite, a time of re-creative detachment, from the pressures of reality. Furthermore, because the pictures on the shield include peace as well as war, the image plays a role like that of the simile, reminding the audience that war is only one aspect of human experience. The image of the shield widens the perspective of the poem, universalizing its visionary scope. The shield is a prephilosophical conceptual statement whose cognitive mode is intuitive rather than rational.

The immediate context within which Homer presents the shield is, of course, Book 18; but the artifact image is heralded by the events which make the forging of new arms for Achilles necessary in the first place. The wider context, then, begins when Achilles takes the first step toward the death of Patroklos, sending his friend Nestor for news of the wounded Machaon (11. 610 ff.). In his counsel to Patroklos of the necessity for the reenlistment of the Myrmidons, Nestor specifically suggests that Patroklos borrow Achilles' armor (11. 797); convinced of the propriety of Nestor's advice, Patroklos requests the use of Achilles' glorious arms (16. 40 ff.). There is something paradoxical about Patroklos' petition. Although he recognizes Achilles' indispensable role as Argive defender, his hope that the Trojans will be deceived into thinking that he is Achilles practically contradicts the recognition. Achilles is deluded also. His great love for Patroklos leads him to think his friend is capable of successfully using his armor (16. 64 ff.).

Patroklos' insufficiency as a substitute for Achilles is implied in Homer's description of his arming. Patroklos dons, in familiar formulaic order, Achilles' greaves (16. 131), corselet (16. 134–35), sword (16. 135), shield (16. 136), and helmet (16. 137): "only he did not take the spear of blameless Aiakides, / huge, heavy, thick, which no one else of all the Achaians / could handle, but Achilleus alone knew how to wield it; / the Pelian ash spear which Cheiron had brought to his father / from high on Pelion to be death for fighters" (16. 140–44). Russo interprets the exception to the general pattern: "Since it is Achilles' armor that Patroklos is putting on, we are being told quite unmistakably that Patroklos *cannot* in fact fill Achilles' shoes, cannot successfully take his place, because he lacks the special greatness and strength of his friend ("Homer Against His Tradition," p. 286)." The greatness of Achilles which the spear represents is that associated with his father, the mortal side of his lineage; so that it may be juxtaposed with his invulnerable shield, given to him by his divine mother (in a juxtaposition symbolizing Achilles' dual nature), the spear is saved from Hektor's defilement of Achilles' old armor (16. 793 ff.). As Patroklos loses the helmet, shield (16. 803), and corselet of Achilles (16. 804), as well as his own spear (16. 801), he is stripped of the protection of his real and substitute identity at one and the same time. No longer able to function effectively (16. 805 ff.), Patroklos is slain by Hektor (16. 812 ff.). The main personal consequence of the wrath of Achilles, the death of his dearest friend, has now been realized. Patroklos is one of those strong souls sent to Hades, spoken of in the proem; the necessity for Achilles' new shield is predicted at the very beginning of the epic.

As the fight over Patroklos' body continues (18. 1), Antilochos comes to

Achilles with the news of Patroklos' death (18. 2). Antilochos is appropriate for this mission because he is the son of Nestor (18. 16), at whose
behest Patroklos proposed the ill-fated substitution. The poet's attention
is directed to Achilles' state of mind before he receives the news. Like
Andromache, he expects what that news will be. Achilles' soliloquy
suggests that already the delusion which led him to allow his friend to act
in his stead is beginning to dissolve (18. 3–14). He knows that if Patroklos
is now dead it is because he disobeyed his general's strict orders to
remain in a defensive position (18. 13–14). The relative weakness of
Patroklos' individuality is defined: he has gone beyond propriety in
taking the fight away from the ships. Antilochos announces the fateful
news by equating Hektor's slaying of Patroklos with the capture of
Achilles' armor (18. 21). With the loss of friend and armor, Achilles' own
individual worth has been jeopardized. Achilles' first acts of mourning
heighten the implication of his lost identity (18. 22–27). Achilles' sudden
anonymity is figured in the dirtying of his countenance (18. 23), representing his mortal nature, and then of his immortal tunic (18. 24). His
gestures parallel Andromache's treatment of her bridal headdress. Achilles' total identity has been affected. While the mourning is taken up by all
the Myrmidons (18. 28–34), Antilochos holds Achilles' hands from their
suicidal intent (18. 33–35)—a strange flashback to Athene's identical
gesture in Book 1. Nowhere else in the *Iliad* is the possibility of suicide
mentioned. So great is Achilles' loss! He calls now upon his mother, as he
did in Book 1 (18. 34–35).

Homer's description of Thetis' reaction to the bad news parallels
Achilles' reception of the message from Antilochos (18. 37–64). Her grief,
too, is generalized, when all the daughters of Nereus take up the
lamentation; the divine family, like the Myrmidon army, is united in
grief. Their mourning takes the form of a threnody, led by Thetis (18.
51)—like the funeral singing for Hektor in Book 24. As Thetis expresses
her sorrow verbally, she speaks first of her own misfortune as a mother
(18. 56–64). Although this was the best of childbearing (18. 54), and
Achilles was perfect in his development to manhood (18. 55–58), all has
gone for nought since she will never see him return safely to the house of
his father (18. 59–60). His familial context, in its mortal dimension at
least, will be disrupted. Thinking herself unable to help him, Thetis
nevertheless determines to accompany his grief in person (18. 61–64).
She does not know yet that Achilles is ready to exchange his temporal for
his eternal identity—his unrealistic mortal pretensions to divinity, for a
divinely inspired ideal humanity—a process which she can indeed
influence. She and the other nymphs go to Troy (18. 65–69), where the
mother first comforts her son physically in an embrace (18. 70–71). The

gesture reminds us that, although Achilles' contact with Peleus is lost forever in time, he still is supported by his one divine parent; and she, in one of the poem's greatest ironies, will help him become the epitome of Iliadic man. Giving him occasion to define his anguish more specifically, Thetis asks Achilles why he is sorrowing (18. 72–77).

Achilles replies that he has received from Zeus more than he bargained for, that the joy of revenge against Agamemnon has been devalued (18. 78–93). Love is defined once more in terms of self-love. I loved Patroklos, Achilles says, " 'as well as my own life' " (18. 82). And again the armor's loss is associated with that of Patroklos, this time by Achilles himself (18. 82–85). His former identity destroyed, Achilles must find a new one, or perish anonymously. The significance of the old armor, in addition to its paternal connection (18. 84), is that it represented the disorderly potential of Achilles' birth. The arms had been given to Peleus by the gods, " 'on that day they drove you to the marriage bed of a mortal. / I wish you had gone on living then with the other goddesses / of the sea, and that Peleus had married some mortal woman' " (18. 85–87). Achilles recognizes the inherent disorder of the unnatural mixture of the two realms of being, human and divine. Achilles' own nature is divided against itself by its ambivalent origins. The violence of his wrath, he now knows, was divine, therefore in man, excessive—predictable consequences in a character formed by the union of two radically diverse natures.

Because he has indulged in that excess, because of its consequences, Achilles no longer wishes to live among men—*except as the slayer of Hektor*, that is, as avenger of Patroklos (18. 90–93). Weeping, Thetis reminds her son of the significance of that exception (18. 94): " 'Then I must lose you soon, my child, by what you are saying, / since it is decreed your death must come soon after Hektor's' " (18. 95–96). Achilles admits that his culpability, although explicable in divine terms, deserves human punishment because it resulted in the unnecessary death of the man whom most of all he should have protected (18. 98–100). His reply warrants close study:

> 'Now, since I am not going back to the beloved land of my fathers,
> since I was no light of safety to Patroklos, nor to my other °
> companions, who in their numbers went down before glorious Hektor,
> but sit here beside my ships, a useless weight on the good land,
> I, who am such as no other of the bronze-armoured Achaians
> in battle, though there are others also better in council—
> why, I wish that strife would vanish away from among gods and mortals,
> and gall, which makes a man grow angry for all his great mind,
> that gall of anger that swarms like smoke inside of a man's heart
> and becomes a thing sweeter to him by far than the dripping of honey.

So it was here that the lord of men Agamemnon angered me.
Still, we will let all this be a thing of the past, and for all our
sorrow beat down by force the anger deeply within us.
Now I shall go, to overtake that killer of a dear life,
Hektor; then I will accept my own death, at whatever
time Zeus wishes to bring it about, and the other immortals.
For not even the strength of Herakles fled away from destruction,
although he was dearest of all to lord Zeus, son of Kronos,
but his fate beat him under, and the wearisome anger of Hera.
So I likewise, if such is the fate which has been wrought for me,
shall lie still, when I am dead. Now I must win excellent glory,
and drive some one of the women of Troy, or some deep-girdled
Dardanian woman, lifting up to her soft cheeks both hands
to wipe away the close bursts of tears in her lamentation,
and learn that I stayed too long out of the fighting. Do not
hold me back from the fight, though you love me. You will not persuade
    me.'

                                                              (18. 101–26)

The syntactical disjunctions of the speech show that Homer's preabstract language is well able to express the introspective anguish of his hero. The thought begun by Achilles in line 101 is not completed until line 114; other thoughts, each in turn interrupting the one before, intervene: 102, 105, 107, 111, 112. This inward-turning quality makes the language of Achilles extraordinary, as Adam Parry suggested. Homer's expression of his character's decision to act is delayed, syntactically, in order to reveal the self-awareness from which so momentous a decision arises.

Achilles realizes, finally, the reciprocal relationship between the individual and the community demanded by social existence. There can be no quantitative restriction to love. The turn outward from selfhood to recognize the value of another self must embrace all human selves (so that personal love becomes, when generalized, "civilized respect" or "brotherhood"). To love Patroklos *only* is impossibly inhuman, a callous denial of the stature to others that he would accord to Patroklos. Not only Patroklos, but numerous good companions have fallen to Hektor (18. 102–4). The qualified love Achilles has attempted to express has no valid place in the world of men; he has been truly useless (18. 104). And this is all the more reprehensible because of the singular role, as the supreme warrior, that has been ordained for him by his inheritance of divine strength.

Now Achilles emphasizes his extraordinary individuality in order to admit that his neglect of its orderly potential is the more deeply culpable: because he is the critical individual in the Argive war his alienation was most unnatural. Like Hektor's to Troy, Achilles' commitment to Argos is the determining factor in social survival. Only an individual, after all, can bring death to an unhealthy society; for societies die individual by individual. It is significant, too, that Achilles here recognizes the limitation of his central role; he is, for now, the warrior but not the counselor (18. 106). Until the issue of the war is resolved by his action, Achilles must concentrate his social involvement on playing the role immediately required of him—the impetuous, irresistible warrior. By doing so first, however, Achilles will prepare a stable social situation in which he may then fulfill the complementary potential of his individuality. In Book 23 he is the spokesman of a society at peace with itself; with Priam, even the international conflict is suspended by his manner. But he must be the doer of deeds before he becomes the speaker of words.

The tenor of Achilles' words on the subject of strife is poignant (18. 106–10). He wishes that the world were idyllic, free from the evil which so often determines its reality. But it is not; and he himself has been affected by the evil (18. 111). The strife Achilles speaks of here is depicted by Hephaistos in the second city on the shield (18. 509–40). Condemning the evil strife that caused his excessive anger toward Agamemnon, Achilles simultaneously admits that he, paradoxically, must now follow the influence of strife in another, more orderly, direction (suggesting the distinction between the two Strifes made by Hesiod). The overwhelming force that inspired his socially destructive anger against Agamemnon, by blinding him to its possession of him, will motivate him now, in a willful possession, to stand against Hektor (18. 114). As the epitome of the warrior he knows full well how to act under its compulsion. But there is a difference. He is no longer blinded to the real nature of that sinister force, no longer personally subsumed under its power to deprive an individual of his will (18. 112–13). His enmity toward Hektor may appear to be a kind of disorder; but this time he serves force knowingly and in command of his own will, so that *he* may use *it* to reestablish the order originally displaced by his blind anger. Achilles will reunite the army of Argos, disintegrated by his wrath, and therefore will make it possible for that army to destroy the source of Argos' *general* disruption, Troy, at the same time that Hektor, the cause of Achilles' individual grief, is slain. The choice between his two fates has been made, and made in a way which redefines glory. In defense of friendship (18. 114), and of his own nation as an extension of that personal bond, Achilles is prepared to sacrifice his life (18. 116). He cites the example of Herakles; another hero who fared no better, or worse, in the business of living (18. 117–19). The "excellent glory" (18. 121) Achilles now seeks is no longer an individual virtue only, insofar as the individual is transitory and doomed to die; it is, rather, a collective value. Because he can see his former error, Achilles is attuned once again to order, sure that he is right (18. 125–26).

Even though her maternal instincts might hesitate, Thetis admits the natural orderliness of her son's determination. Her words recall Hektor's patriotic counsel to his men (15. 496 ff.): " 'Yes, it is true, my child, this is no cowardly action, / to beat aside sudden death from your afflicted companions' " (18. 128–29). To confirm her approval, its compliance with Zeus' cosmic order that Hephaistos represents (18. 136), Thetis promises Achilles new armor worthy of his great ambition, symbolic of his ability to command events (18. 136–37). Set aside by Achilles to mark the disruption of the Argive confederacy, the old armor is now worn by Hektor, becoming an omen of the dissolution of the Trojan's identity and the identity of Trojan society (18. 130–33). His own mother promises to dress Achilles for a combat which she knows will be the first step toward the destruction of his temporal selfhood (18. 134–35). But, in doing so, she brings him to a more intimate relationship with herself; the glory he will win, the individuality he will now define for himself, will be, like her, eternal: a divine humanity. Thetis' consistent familial propriety is marked subtly in her command to the nymphs who accompany her that they should tell their father Neleus where she is going (18. 138–44); her sisters, then, descend to Ocean, as Thetis mounts upward to Olympos (18. 145–47). Homer easily carries his story forward on several levels at once.

Meanwhile the Achaians are embattled still against Hektor (18. 148–65). As Homer advances toward opposing the one primary social individual to the other, Trojan to Achaian, he is careful to make Hektor a worthy antagonist by employing two comparisons that will be used later for Achilles when he finally reenters the battle. Hektor's fury is likened to a flame (18. 154), he himself to a lion (18. 161–62) in a simile that becomes an actuality on the great shield. Like Achilles, Hektor operates here under the auspices of warlike strife, his domestic, peaceful role relinquished forever. But he operates blindly at this point, as Achilles had during the quarrel; Hektor has gone beyond the limits set for him in attacking the ships—he is possessed, as Achilles was in the quarrel, with a disorderly force. So strong is this ambitious force against him that even the two Aiantes are unable to rescue Patroklos (18. 163–65). Since their combined strength is unequal to Hektor's infuriated recklessness, something must be done if Achilles is to be given the opportunity of insuring full honor to his dead friend. At this point Homer has Iris arrive on her very strange mission; even her mode of coming is singularly odd: "secretly from Zeus and the other gods, since it was Hera who sent her"

(18. 168). Achilles himself notes the strangeness by asking her what god has sent her to him (18. 182). Zeus, Iris tells Achilles, does not know of her mission (18. 185). And Hera, we might suppose, does not know of her husband's sovereign plan with which Thetis is presently involved.

Iris gives occasion for Achilles to mention Aias' shield (18. 192–95), to imply that it plays, with respect to Achilles' new one, both a comparable and a contrasting role in the story. Both shields symbolize orderly action. But, while Aias' protects the fallen individual (Patroklos), Achilles' will save society itself, in danger of falling because of the loss of Helen; simultaneously his shield perfectly reunites the army as Aias' shield alone could not. In a much larger sense, Iris' appearance defines with greater precision than ever the significance of Hephaistos' forthcoming gift. The symbolic definition of the great shield, its individualization of Achilles, is advanced by contrasting it with the aegis. Nor is the discrepancy between line 197 and lines 170–180 more than an apparent one. Note that Iris, in her first speech, remains vague about *how* Achilles is to "assist" (not "fight for"—18. 171) Patroklos. Her intention is expressed specifically for the first time *after* Achilles' puzzlement: he is simply to show himself to the Trojans (18. 201). Hera, after all, must know of Thetis' mission. In fact, it is to insure that mission's ultimate effectiveness that she has sent Iris now; the connection between Hera's and Thetis' operations, though only implicit here, prepares us for their explicit cooperation and friendship (that otherwise might seem surprising) in Book 24.

The narrative has reached a momentous turning point. In Achilles' speech (18. 112–15) the wrath- and the war-story finally are brought together: the foresight of Zeus has been realized. Hera therefore— notably in the proximity of Hephaistos—draws closer to Thetis, as she does to Zeus himself. Limited, transitory order and transcendent order now work in one direction. That Zeus does not know of Hera's mission for Iris consequently must be taken as a comment not on his, but on her, omniscience. It means that Hera does not know that her husband approves of her plan. But since his purpose is to exalt Achilles, and since that demands the rescue of Patroklos, Zeus indeed must approve. It is Achilles, "beloved of Zeus" (18. 203), mantled with the aegis held by Athene, Zeus' daughter (18. 203–4), who rises to obey Iris. The first step toward his new and final identity is taken as Hera and Athene, though they do not yet realize it themselves, are shown to be in accord with Zeus, Thetis, and Hephaistos. Whitman explains:

At Iris' instruction [Achilles] goes to the top of the trench, and as he goes, miracles gather round him. With the aegis . . . across his shoulders and Olympian fire shooting in an aura from his head, he shouts at the Trojans and sends them reeling back, while the Achaians pull . . . Patroklos to safety. The whole scene is a singular triumph of Homer's method of externalizing states into images and actions. Here Achilles, helpless and deprived of his very identity, slowly rediscovers himself, in anxiety for the corpse of his friend, and does what any helpless man would do—he shouts. But the shout is a prophecy and a self-declaration, in token of which Athena, the image of his irresistible power, shouts also. (P. 204)

The aegis figuratively outlines the identity of Achilles which will be embodied completely in the shield.

But at the same time that it rescues Patroklos and holds the Trojans at bay long enough to allow Hephaistos time for the forging, the epiphany scene also allows the necessity of that forging to be revealed—by contrasting Achilles' borrowing of the aegis with his proper possession of the shield. The aegis marks the potential orderliness of Achilles' personality in its new realignment with the Olympian principle of order; the shield signifies the actualization of that potential. But the transformation of potential to actual takes place within a continuum, which is the developing character of Achilles. The continuity of his developing character is signified by Homer's comparison of both artifacts, aegis and shield, to fire. The simile of the beacon fire is particularly apt because the beacon is the sign of hope, informing its beholders (as in the opening scene of the *Agamemnon*) that some have survived the day to fight onward to victory. The mere sight of Achilles indicates to the Argives that all is not lost, though many have been slain, now that the primary individual is ready to rescue them; he is to them all equally, as he lamented he had not been especially to Patroklos, a "light of safety" (18. 102). To the Trojans, his appearance reveals that their truly mortal enemy has now to be confronted.

The juxtaposition of the two artifacts also defines Achilles' uniquely dual nature; in his character the universal and the particular are joined, now harmoniously. One image, the aegis, is of the continuing, transcendent order of Zeus; the other is of that eternal force made incarnate in the action of Achilles with his shield. Homer knows well that, in human experience, only the living individual can act. So his action is identical with his personality and demands its own characteristic symbol. The shield must be made especially for Achilles, whose eternal life in the glorious memory of men to come will be assured only after he has employed this artifact properly in time. Before he can exist generically (in communal memory) Achilles must act as a communal individual; the shield, individually fashioned for him, both predicts and makes possible his ultimate sublimely human identity.

Achilles' cry alone is enough to drive "unspeakable confusion" among the Trojans (18. 218). Recognizing the shout as an omen, the Trojans retreat (18. 222) as the "unwearied fire" (18. 225), the signature of Hephaistos (its logical result: "unspeakable confusion"), is kindled by Athene round his head (18. 227). The disintegration of the Trojan army by the fire is proven when twelve men are trampled to death by their own companions in the rout (18. 230), predicting the twelve men Achilles will slay as Patroklos' fiery funeral cortege. The body of Patroklos is saved (18. 231); he is mourned by the Achaians, honored by them as a hero (18. 237–38). Serving Achilles again as she did in Book 1, Hera miraculously insures that he will have the leisure to wait for his new arms without worry for the Trojan attack: "Now the lady Hera of the ox eyes drove the unwilling / weariless sun god to sink in the depth of the Ocean" (18. 239–40). The order of the cosmos is upset in order that Achilles, through the agency of Hephaistos, may set it right once and for all. Among men, the battle ceases (18. 241–42).

Terrified still, the Trojans hold an assembly (18. 243); that equilibrium no longer prevails among them is marked by the fact that they do not sit down (18. 246). Poulydamas, "who alone of them looked before and behind him" (18. 250) first addresses the army. The chaotic state of the Trojan hierarchy is symbolized by their refusal to heed his, as well as Kassandra's, warnings. Poulydamas, moreover, is like Nestor among the Achaians, the perfect complement to the warrior, Hektor (18. 251–52). Unlike Achilles at this point in the story, however, Hektor does not recognize the limitations of his own role. The counselor's speech is appropriate to the situation (18. 253–83). He bids them to return behind the walls (18. 255), to resume, in other words, their orderly stance as *defenders*. Troy will not capture the ships after all (which would be to destroy Argos). Achilles' reentry is fateful (18. 260–65), like Patroklos', but also fatal. It will be no mere matter of individual warriors falling before him: " 'With him, the fight will be for the sake of our city, and women' " (18. 265). Homer has seen to it that at least one witness of Achilles' epiphany is capable of understanding and communicating the full import of his return to the fighting. Poulydamas distinguishes Achilles as the one individual who above all others makes the vital difference to all Trojans, as well as to all Argives. He proceeds to delineate the defensive positions they must take on the coming day, at the gateways and along the walls (18. 265 ff.). In a sense, the final confrontation will be between two circles: that of the shield of Achilles, representing the orderliness of human life; and that of the Trojan walls, symbolizing, because of the disorder they contain, a threat to the social mode of existence.

Hektor's reply shows that, still deluded by self-confidence, he lives in the past, faded order (18. 284–309). Not having admitted yet that his nation is dying, Hektor lives as if Troy were as great and orderly as it once had been (18. 288–89). For him at this point, life is made meaningful only by the hope that the golden age can be restored to Troy (18. 290 ff.). If he thinks himself capable of playing the savior's role, it is because Zeus has blinded him (18. 293). As Hektor works to construct a semblance of harmony he convinces the Trojans to stay and fight by offering himself as an example (18. 298–303). Trusting in the impartiality of the gods—a trust which proves his delusion—he himself will stand against Achilles (18. 309). The acclaim of the army is unanimous (18. 310). The community, like its chief individual, is itself blinded by the gods who work for order; because they are innocent of their blindess, Homer calls the Trojans νήπιοι *népioi* ("fools"—18. 311): "They gave their applause to Hektor in his counsel of evil, / but none to Poulydamas, who had spoken good sense before them" (18. 312–13). Their religion, magic, politics no longer avail the Trojans. The basic structure of their society no longer holds.

While the Trojans prepare themselves for the slaughter, the Achaians mourn Patroklos through the night (18. 314), their chant led by Achilles (18. 316) who is now compared to a lion (18. 318–22) in a simile that again prefigures the lions on the shield and is an early warning of his other-than-human status to come. His address to the Myrmidons recapitulates what he has expressed before: his equation of Patroklos with himself, his parents' grief that Achilles will have no homecoming, his vow for revenge, his knowledge that he will follow his friend underground (18. 323–42). But he will not bury Patroklos, he promises, " 'till I bring to this place the armour / and the head of Hektor' " (18. 334–35). If this threat is not to receive fulfillment, it is because Achilles cannot, in Zeus' scheme for ordering human affairs, return to his former, disorderly, identity which the armor Hektor now wears symbolizes. Achilles' vow to sacrifice twelve Trojan men on the pyre of his friend suggests that his individuality is so great that no less than a collective vengeance will satisfy him (18. 336–37). To Achilles, Patroklos is worth Troy; and that equation is the formula which insures the prevalence, the survival, of Argos. Then Trojan women will weep for Patroklos, their sorrow sincere because they lament the effect an individual can have upon the whole nation (18. 339–42); their mourning will be, in fact, for Troy, whose death Patroklos' death signifies. The body of Patroklos is anointed, placed upon a bed, and covered with a white mantle (18. 343–45); it will remain upon this bed until Hektor has been brought to his deathbed, when the lament for the Trojan replaces the sorrow for the Danaan. Witnessing all these events, Zeus and Hera confer in the remarkable exchange discussed earlier.

Finally Thetis arrives on Olympos (18. 368). Those who argue that Homer is incapable of presenting actions which are contemporaneous with one another have neglected the poet's careful way of marking her arrival. Contemporaneity is unmistakable: "Now as these two were saying things like this to each other, / Thetis of the silver feet came to the house of Hephaistos" (18. 368–69). What we witness here is the technical conclusion of another suspension of narrative progress—like that in Book 3—intended, in this case, to provide the audience with a more meaningful context by which to evaluate the great shield. Since Thetis departed for Olympos (18. 145) a great deal indeed has happened on earth. The artificiality of the device is obvious, a striking contrast to her hawklike descent from heaven with which the book abruptly ends (18. 615–16).

A domestic, familial aura surrounds Hephaistos in the wondrous house built by his own hands (18. 369–71). Hephaistos' wife, Charis, appears to offer hospitality to Thetis (18. 382–87), presenting her husband as the ideal host whose guests will receive whatever they rightfully desire. Hephaistos himself expresses his respect for his visitor in terms of the familial gratitude he owes her (18. 394 ff.). Saving him from the disorderly maternal attitude of Hera, Thetis and Eurynome became, in fact, substitutes for his proper, but unnatural, mother (18. 398). His relationship with Thetis, then, is a filial-parental one. As if to obviate the possibility that Hephaistos might refuse Thetis' forthcoming request, Homer makes the god admittedly indebted to the goddess for his very existence (18. 408), as Hephaistos tells Thetis directly (18. 424–27). The shield will be the repayment of his debt, giving in exchange for his own perpetual life, received from Thetis, not temporal "survival" to Achilles—significantly, Thetis, as an orderly agent, does not request that her son's life be spared—but the eternal perpetuation of his name through the continuing human memory of his great deeds—made possible by the shield.

To preface her request, Thetis repeats, but with added detail, her first soliloquy: her life has been singularly sorrowful because of her involuntary marriage to a mortal (18. 429–35; cf. 18. 54–65). The unnatural alliance has caused her, a divinity, to experience, because of her natural attachment to husband and son, old age (18. 435) and mortality (18. 458). As if Hephaistos were a bard ready to carry forward the momentum of song as he receives it from a breathless predecessor whose task is finished, Thetis reviews for him the story of the wrath (18. 444–46), of the war itself

(18. 447–56), and of the relationship between the two stories which may—if Hephaistos will grant her the favor she asks, thereby assuming her role as an orderly agent—come together for a tragic but nonetheless orderly conclusion (18. 457–61). Hephaistos quickly agrees to create armor for Achilles that will befit his orderly purpose and that will symbolize his new social identity (18. 462–67). The stage is set for the crucial appearance of Homer's major actor who will bear its major image; that image will be a wonder to see (18. 480).

The Informing Image

Homer's incredible elaboration of the shield of Achilles (Book 18) makes it the most singular, central image of the *Iliad*. An outline of the pictorial elements of the shield will help us appreciate its extraordinary distinction from other artifact images in the *Iliad*.

483–89	*the cosmic framework*	
	483	earth, sky, sea
	484	sun, moon
	485	constellations
	486	Orion
	487	the Bear, a fixed star
	488–89	which never sinks into Ocean
450–540	*two model cities*	
	491–508	the city of peace
	492–96	a marriage festival
	497–508	an orderly quarrel
	509–540	the city of war
	510–12	dissension among the attackers
	513–15	unanimity among the defenders
	515–20	city commissions an excursion
	521–29	the ambush; shepherds killed
	530–40	alerted, the attackers join battle
541–49	*spring*	
	541–44	orderly ploughing by community
	545–47	enhanced by offer of drink
	548–49	earth responds to plough
550–60	*summer*	
	550–55	hierarchical, communal harvest
	555–57	directed by silent king
	558–60	followed by feast
561–72	*fall*	
	561–68	vineyard harvest
	569–70	accompanied by the Linos song and lyre
	571–72	in which they join, and dance

573–89	*winter*	
	573–78	peaceful herding
	579–86	two lions attack bull, dogs and men watch helplessly
	587–89	sheep meadow
590–604	*the choros*	
	590–92	the Daidalaean dance floor
	593–98	male and female dancers
	599–602	two kinds of dance, circular and linear
	603–5	audience watches acrobats
606–7	the cosmic circumference	
	Ocean, around the rim	

The shield's comprehensive subject material immediately impresses us. In this it is like and unlike the epic itself. For the overt subject of the *Iliad* is war and contention; its realistic quality, therefore, derives from the balance provided by the poet's frequent use of similes which complement the warlike action with visions of peace. Similarly, on the shield the actions of peace complement those of war. As does no other artifact, it reflects the all-encompassing scope of Homer's poetic perspective.

Hephaistos depicts the entirety of human experience partly by contrast. As Charles R. Beye comments, "most of the basic antitheses in the human situation: permanent and fleeting, beautiful and ugly, serene and excited, ideal and real, war and peace, finite world and infinite heaven" are included, in one way or another, upon its surface (p. 143). William Watkiss Lloyd is more specific:

The formula that is introductory to the city at war and city of peace, comprises them in fact, as relatively complementary; and the parallel treatment of each in three scenes gives emphasis to the intention . . . the ambuscade of the warriors by the riverside is opposed to a lively altercation in the marketplace—a war-like incident of silence, stealth, and treachery, to a loud, clamourous, vehement incident of peace. On one side we see, in the careless piping swains approaching the fatal covert, the deceitful semblance of peace in war; and, on the other, the origin of a dispute in a manslaughter, as well as the violence of the dispute itself, betrays the seeds of contest and strife in the heart of peace. (Pp. 23, 31)

Through the juxtaposition of peaceful and warlike, political and pastoral pictures, the human world is framed. The shield is a vision of all that happens in Homer's cosmos. Though the center of vision of Hephaistos' handiwork is human life, the mundane activities of man are surrounded and put into perspective by the peripheral Ocean and the fixed stars at the center. The national diversity of mankind that Homer portrays in the antagonism between Argos and Troy is the reason why Hephaistos has created two cities on his shield. On a tool of warfare, all human scenes—from every level of the hierarchy of relations, in every possible degree of social stability—are shown. And every art known to Homeric man is also represented.

The single simile on the shield is one which likens the dance to the potter at his wheel. Art is represented on Hephaistos' artifact in both a linear and a circular mode. Each of the several scenes includes artistry, in one form or another, as an integral part of a social activity—for example, the marriage songs in the city at peace. But the dance with which the smith concludes his creation must be imagined to form the penultimate ring of pictures, surrounding all the others as does the final circle of Ocean. The question of the pictures' relationship to Iliadic reality is thereby identified with the question of art's relationship with real life—by the problem posed of the *choros'* relationship to the other scenes in the doubly fictive world of the shield. Here there is movement back and forth between peace and war, just as in the poem the similes give the sense of the wider reality of which the Trojan War is but one facet. There is, after all, no qualitative temporal distinction between peace and wartime. On the shield there is no artistic distinction between the two: the world is the same; only man's behavior is different. This is what Hubert Schrade calls the "universal intention" of the shield: "To the Poet the life of the work of art and the life of the world are one and the same, and so the boundaries between the one and the other disappear" (p. 79). In speaking of the composer's concept of poetry as an integral part of everyday life, Schrade emphasizes a crucial element of the Iliadic aesthetic: that is, not its realistic nature, but its reality.

But at the same time that poetry is practically identified with life, it is also essentially different from other human activities—no less real, but enjoying an extraordinary mode of reality all its own. The reality of poetry is the one which allows the poet to communicate to his audience an objective view of reality in general—the sense in which Aristotle considered it to be an imitation more scientific than history is. This complementary aspect of Homeric art is suggested by Karl Reinhardt's statement that the shield presents a "timeless, nameless, glance at the continuity of life" (p. 405). Like the shield, poetry encapsulates and focuses experience. The shield removes its audience momentarily, as Hephaistos' creation removes the poet who observes it, from a linear involvement with chronological concerns to a circular perspective—the visionary circumference and the intuitive center—of detachment. How, then, are the pictures of Hephaistos different from the fictive reality of the epic?

To begin with, there is neither myth nor history explicit on the shield.

There are no familiar individuals whether heroes or men, no personal genealogies. The impression is one of *presence;* there is but one reference to the past, the mention of Daidalos, and this is no more than an epic superlative. All scenes, in striking contrast with the character of early Greek art in general, are from actual, uncertain life (premythological, therefore nameless). Unlike the poem's attention to the heroic past, moreover, here the concentration is on the common people. Yet the consistent use of the imperfect tense throughout the description serves to qualify the impression of contemporaneity. The effect of the verbs is supported by the anonymous character of the men fashioned by Hephaistos. The result of this technical combination is that time is conflated—presented in an idealized manner by which past, present, and future become indistinguishable. The man is any man, the city any city; it is man as he *might* be. In another sense, if the city at war is man as he *is*, in Iliadic reality, the other city is man as he *should* be—in a reality which goes beyond and behind the fictive present. The emphasis clearly is on the ideal.

Because on the shield we know none of the figures, we have no interest except in the action going forward. On it we are shown in detail the human world entire; but, in keeping with the artifact's didactic intention, that detail is generalized. The generalization shows that Homer is interested "philosophically" in the essentials of human nature. Unlike Virgil's shield of Aeneas, Homer's goes beyond the world of his hero, insofar as that world is national or political, to represent all that is life, to portray the essentially human in isolation. Achilles' shield includes no mention of Achilles' deeds and fate. Nor does Hephaistos represent himself upon its surface, as he does in Hesiod's *Shield of Herakles.* So by the peculiar nature of the artifact, the individuality of its bearer, as well as of its maker, is emphasized precisely in the fact that individuality is eclipsed. We are to judge the meaning of Achilles' particular status by studying the generally human, doubly fictional social situations depicted on his shield.

What gives Hephaistos the ability to present contemporaneous events is his transcendent, divine viewpoint. The Olympian's detachment, like the Muse-inspired poet's, allows him to re-create an objective and universal vision because he stands outside it in the concentration of his technique (the relationship between the possession and the ecstasy of the artist). The emphatic position given to the dance, then, suggests it is Homer's way of communicating that the human artist shares in the god's aloofness precisely when he creates the images of art and artifacts. Lloyd remarks: "The last circlet of the chorus contrasts with all the rest in being continuous all round . . . absolved from all reference to the hopes and fears, the labours and dangers, the emulation and the contests of busy existence. Here all . . . blend away in the delirium of social sympathy and festive art" (pp. 40–41). The pictures, the shield itself, are invulnerable; they will be unaffected by the spears hurled against Achilles by his enemies. And because the shield is invulnerable, it is able to perform its communal function in the story, to reintegrate Argive society, as, upon it, the dance unifies the depicted events—gives them orderly meaning and direction. The artifact provides the rarest of glimpses into the poet's concept of the role of poetry.

Homer creates the impression of universality on the shield also by refraining from specifying the exact arrangement of the scenes. Their physical relationship to one another is not defined. The observation allows us to see the contrast between this artifact and the shields of Agamemnon and of Aias. In the case of the latter, the poet's elaboration is limited almost to the delineation of the actual configuration of the materials. Aias' shield is tied to the concrete, just as Aias himself is related firmly to the present Achaian crisis. No other artifact is granted the universal appearance of Achilles' shield. On it myth and history, past, present, and future, war and peace are present simultaneously. This magnificent artifact presents us with virtual access to the mind and matter of the *Iliad*.

Creating and Created

The shield of Achilles expresses a thematic tension between the process of creation and the static character of the created product. Homer does not save his description of Achilles' shield for the moment 1) when Thetis presents it to Achilles and he sees it for the first time (as in the case of the Sidonian bowl given to Nestor); 2) when the Achaians first see it in the narrative (as in the case of Agamemnon's sceptre or of Nestor's cup); 3) when Achilles arms himself with it (as with Agamemnon's and Hektor's shields, Athene's helmet and aegis, or as Virgil presents Vulcan's shield to Aeneas in *Aeneid* 8. 617 ff.); or 4) when he carries it into action against the Trojans (as with Aias' shield, Diomede's armor, the aegis). Instead Homer's audience sees the shield even before Achilles himself does, over the shoulder of its creator. While Virgil's narration stops as Aeneas looks at the god's gift, in Homer the moving eye of the observer—both poet and reader—follows the movement of creation in progress. Lessing has noted the significance of this departure from familiar psychological narrative patterns:

Homer does not paint the shield finished, but in the process of creation [using the] device of substituting progression for coexistence, and [has] thus converted the tiresome description of an object into a graphic picture of an action. We see not the shield, but the divine master-workman employed upon it . . . Not till the whole is finished do we lose sight of him; we wonder at the work, but with the believing wonder of an eye-witness who has seen it a-making. (P. 114)

The context emphasizes the process of creation; Homer's description of the shield gives to his audience a privileged revelation of art in action.

The significance of this technical innovation, the description of process, cannot be underestimated. It has to do with the nature of orally delivered or "sung" poetry as Homer inherited it. If his poem is to have proper didactic effect, his audience must be made to follow in their own lives the example set by the poet's characters. The listener must model his behavior on that of Achilles in his new identity. To enable him to do so, the poet must establish a sympathetic relationship between character and listener. That is exactly what Homer does by presenting the description at this point in the narrative. The audience's wonder at the splendor of the shield is like the amazement displayed by the Achaians and Trojans when they are allowed finally to see it, too. But because we see the shield directly through the eyes of the poet as he imagines himself watching it being fashioned, we can appreciate it better than can the two armies. So bright is its divine magnificence, they cannot look at it directly (19. 14–15). But like Achilles, we can; the audience is thereby identified with him. The points of the triangle—author, character, audience—are joined. Our appreciation is, of course, different from Achilles'. His is intuitive; he takes in its meaning, its identification of his special character, at a glance (19. 16). We must read it, or hear it, line by line, and therefore our understanding of the shield's significance must be derived from reflection and study; we gain a discursive kind of knowledge from being allowed to see the parts and process through which the shield is created. However, the dominant image of the shield's cognitive motion is not the line but the circle. First depicted are the earth, the sun, and the moon in her fullness (18. 485). Then we are shown stars that turn about a fixed place, thereby describing a circle (18. 483–88). Young men follow maidens in the circles of a dance (18. 494) while two armies surround a city (18. 509). Death personified holds a live man, a wounded man, and a dead man, the three parts to a wartime life cycle. In a more idyllic setting a ploughman wheels his team about a turn (18. 543–44). A fence surrounds a field in which youths dance. On another dancing floor men and women hold hands, forming another type of circle. The girls' heads are encircled with garlands and men's waists with belts (18. 597–98). There is a simile of a potter's wheel (18. 600) as two acrobats watch the dance revolving around them (18. 605). And the Ocean River encircles all (18. 606). Linear imagery is given, less abundantly, in the lines of a battle, of plowing, of reaping, and of dancing. The round shield is symbol as statement, whose meaning is simultaneous and complete; and, as such, it reflects the cyclical nature of the poem itself.

Homer emphasizes Hephaistos' ability to make artificial signs seem alive; the smith-god creates live dogs (in the *Odyssey*, 7. 91) and robots "like living maidens" (*Iliad*, 18. 418 ff.). The poet insists on the sensual vibrancy of the lion scene: "But among the foremost of the cattle two formidable lions / had caught hold of a bellowing bull, and he with loud lowings / was dragged away, as the dogs and the young men went in pursuit of him. / But the two lions, breaking open the hide of the great ox, / gulped the black blood and the inward guts, as meanwhile the herdsmen / were in the act of setting and urging the quick dogs on them" (18. 579–84). Except for the blackness of the blood, the vitality of the imagery here is based upon sounds: the anguish of the stricken bull (cummings' "scarlet bellowings"); the very silence of the lions, their mouths occupied with eating; the shouts of the men; the baying of the dogs (18. 586). But it is the imagery of a verbal art form—the poet's own—rather than of a plastic visual one (Hephaistos') which predominates.

What do we learn from the extraordinary point of view we are allowed during the forging of the shield? We witness the artist's absolute command over the tools and materials of his art. The bellows, for example, are a direct extension of the smith's inspired, instinctual talent: "He turned these toward the fire and gave them their orders for working. / And the bellows, all twenty of them, blew on the crucibles, / from all directions blasting forth wind to blow the flames high / now as he hurried to be at this place and now at another, / wherever Hephaistos might wish them to blow, and the work went forward" (8. 469–73). They obey him as automatically as words do the poet. With little more preliminary the work itself begins. Hephaistos creates surely, rapidly, unerringly, without revision; ideas and materials alike are at his fingertips, well under his control. There is no hint of belabored fantasy; only the imitation of reality could provide such an unbroken stream of inspiration. Hephaistos creates in this manner because he is a god. With equal sureness the poet composes his epic because he possesses, or is possessed by, the Olympian perspective—from the tradition of memory guarded by the Muses—which alone makes such universal creation possible. The result of Hephaistos' efforts, the glorious shield, is frankly incredible; we're to accept it as a vision of the whole world, full of life in all its sensuality, a moving, talking picture. But when it comes to evaluating the art of the poet, incredulousness recedes. Language can do what pictorial art can only suggest; it is Homer's language, after all, that enlivens Hephaistos' pictures—that makes them audible as well as imaginatively visible (as Dante's poetry enlivens the bas-reliefs in the *Purgatorio*). In the time it takes to recite his poem, Homer indeed presents his listeners with a world entire in its multiple dimensions.

The individual quality and existence which Hephaistos gives to his metals, moreover, are those perfectly appropriate to their potential and intended material function. The shield is to protect human life, in its collective transcendent dimension (since it will not save Achilles' temporal individuality); it is this human life that the shield's ornamentation presents. The technique employed in the shield's description, then, is directly comparable to the larger technical character of the poem itself. For it is evident that the effectiveness of the *Iliad* proceeds from the consistent impression it gives us of things clearly visualized, of life vividly rendered in its own terms—an impression achieved by the metaphoric nature of the Homeric language and by the poet's strategic deployment of imagery. The result, in the poem as on the shield, is a transformation of real time into an idealized temporality, a peculiarly poetic time within, but suspended from, everyday reality. Temporal discrimination is ignored by the audience hearing the poem, as by the observer watching the shield being formed. No thought is given, for example, to wondering whether the similes represent experience from the same historical era as do the battlefield action scenes. Time is made uniform, appearing as an essential quality of human life; the poem's impression of presenting that life in all its breadth is not limited by tying a particular portion of the presentation to an accidental aspect.

The element of circularity needs reemphasis. The shield itself is called round as the moon (19. 374); indeed the full moon appears upon its surface (18. 485). Circularity, the hallmark of perfection, is referred to both at the beginning and at the end of the description, where the dance is likened to a potter's wheel and the Ocean stream circles around the rim. The presence of the circle on the shield as the sign of perfection, of continuity (compare the many circles on Agamemnon's shield), of cyclical reciprocity, of fertility, crystallizes an important structural aspect of the poem itself. First, as for the shield, Lloyd notes:

the arrangement of the scenes in concentric rings . . . is far the most effective as a symbol for the imaginative content. For by this means we are shown in one sweep the varied life of man, dominated by the heavens, encompassed by the great waters, spreading out in widening circles from the concentrated interest and turmoil of the city to the calmer work of the fields and the dancing ring of the youth whose working-time has hardly yet begun. And perhaps the poet meant us to remember that the river of Ocean which touches the ring of youth and surrounds the whole is also the river of Death. (P. 11)

With the cosmos in the center and the Ocean on the circumference, the god has framed human life between mortality and immortality. But the focus is the eternal potential, the human access to continuing life made possible by the perpetuation of a man's honor—of his name. So the role of epic song is also figured in the arrangement. Its inspiration and focal point are identical: the continuum between man and god, between the transitory and the transcendent dimensions of human nature. The center is both the source—Socrates' internal δαίμων *daîmon* ("god")—and the goal—eternally unchanging life. The immortality of poetic aspiration— and this is the most important characteristic of the Homeric aesthetic—is based on the practical force of the communal memory preserved by the Muse-possessed poet. The preservation of that force is what the poet means to share with his audience. Homer's art is centripetal. In the Iliadic world no man goes beyond the circumference; no one becomes a star or a god. Ganymede is not mentioned; and, though the death of Helen's brothers is referred to in Book 3, their stellar fate is not. The circling Ocean limits real and poetic action at one and the same time. Yet glory, no less enduring for being natural, can be found within—found by tapping the communal treasury of memory, by attuning individual action to Zeus' principle of social order as embodied in the poet's record.

Individuality, however, is no less important than the communal dimension. Rather, the two are indistinguishable—ideally when individuals act in keeping with their intrinsic, common nature. For it is in the memory of the individual that the human community, eternal and infinite and divinely protected, resides. The fullness of personality is expressed in deeds that are worthy of being remembered by men to come because those deeds themselves serve the common human interest. The interaction between the individual and this higher community is what dancers on the shield symbolize.

> And there were young men on it and young girls, sought for their beauty
> with gifts of oxen, dancing, and holding hands at the wrist. These
> wore, the maidens long light robes, but the men wore tunics
> of finespun work and shining softly, touched with olive oil.
> And the girls wore fair garlands on their heads, while the young men
> carried golden knives that hung from sword-belts of silver.
> At whiles on their understanding feet they would run very lightly,
> as when a potter crouching makes trial of his wheel, holding
> it close in his hands, to see if it will run smooth. At another

time they would form rows, and run, rows crossing each other.
And around the lovely chorus of dancers stood a great multitude
happily watching, while among the dancers two acrobats
led the measures of song and dance revolving among them.

(18. 593–605)

Lloyd explicates the choreography: "It seems imperative on the artist to represent a double dance, a dance in a circle, of youths and maidens holding hands, and a dance in ranks—of youths opposite . . . maidens" (pp. 21–22). If this is indeed what Hephaistos has portrayed, the linear has been set against the circular and the diverse arrangement of the genders suggests the opposition is biological as well as geometrical: sterility (male + male, female + female) versus fertility (male + female), the latter recalling the marriage scene in the first city, that of peace and order. The creative potential of the circle, moreover, whether artistic or reproductive, is suggested by the simile. Lloyd notes that Kneph, "the ram-headed god of the Thebaid and Ethiopia, appears as creator in the figure of the potter with the wheel. He is said to make mankind on his wheel" (p. 35). What the poet, representing his audience as fictional spectator and thereby defining their cyclical relationship with him, sees on the circular shield—a circling dance—he communicates by means of a circular simile. It is also a circular medium—the traditional language—that enables the poet, in a larger sense, to convey to his audience what he understands of reality.

Lloyd's interpretation goes somewhat beyond what can be justified by Homer's text. It may be better to regard the double dance as giving equal value to each element, linear as well as circular, individual as well as the alliance of individuals. The intermingling of the two elements, then, has much the same symbolic purport as the juxtaposition of Achilles' straight spear with his round shield. Upon the surface of the circular shield, the central artifact-image of the poem, Homer depicts another circular art form surrounding the doubly fictional world and simultaneously lying in the center of the Iliadic world. But as in the Iliadic world the spear signifies the necessity of the individual as the basic formative element of the community (through his unique ability to act), so the dance in ranks in the world of the shield represents the reciprocity between part and whole. There is a suggestion, moreover, that all arts are equivalent in this scene: weaving (18. 595), cosmetics (18. 596), floral arrangement (18. 597), metal-work (18. 598), dancing, pottery, acrobatics (18. 604), and song (18. 605). What they have in common is *ordering toward harmonious relations*. The dancers' "understanding feet" (18. 599) are tuned naturally to the antiphonal rhythm of the cosmos, of the Muses themselves (recall 1. 604), just as the epic audience submits naturally to a kind of hypnopaideutic spell in which the poem becomes, for the moment of communication, the only reality (a communal reality like that experienced by the audience in Greek tragedy for whom the myth "comes alive" during the performance because the "critical faculties" of the individual are suspended as he allows himself to be caught up in the powerful sound of the words projected from the stage). The dance scene surrounds the two cities but is itself surrounded by the joyful audience (18. 603–4); art is in the center of the healthy society, as well as serving to define its limits. The cooperation of the individual dancers, themselves idealized (as their beauty and possession of rich artifacts proves, 18. 593–94), is that of the ideal society. All parts of this doubly fictional world are aligned harmoniously with one another, as the shield is an integral part of the Iliadic world—and as its image reflects the structure of the poem.

Some of the circular elements of the poem's structure have been mentioned already. In addition to its traditional language, and to the cyclical or geometric recurrence of key images, there is the technique of hysteron proteron by which a balance of antitheses forms a circumference that frames a focal center. Whitman's analysis is widely applicable:

One may indeed find . . . circularity penetrating all Homeric poetry . . . The root of the principle lies in a practical need . . . Homer's habit of returning to things previously mentioned in reverse order, [a] device, doubtless, of mnemonic purpose to assist the singer to keep in mind what he had said before, is also pregnant with stylistic possibilities. Like ring composition, it returns to its point of origin and effects circularity of design, while the inverted elements may also be spread out to include as a centerpiece a whole scene or scenes, as in a frame. Thus hysteron proteron and ring composition . . . suggest not only circularity, but also framing and balance. (P. 97)

Whitman's perception of the circular structural principle in the *Iliad* may remind us that circularity, in the opposition of disparate elements across a common center, is a characteristic pattern of human thought, an essential pattern. Homer need not have consciously imitated geometric pottery in order to capitalize on the potential usefulness of this structural approach, although my recent studies of the fully reciprocal structural relationship among the ancient arts (of poetry, ceramics, and textiles) suggest that he may well have done so. But as Whitman's reference to the mnemonic value of the circular principle implies, the poet need not even have been conscious of the approach. The mark of genius is the ability, whether instinctual or trained, to perceive, and then to communicate, essential patterns of experience. Homer's art is perception accurately expressed.

2

While the shield's first appearance in the narrative is indicative of change and process, its function in the Iliadic world—and symbolically in the poem—derives from its inherently static aspect. T. B. L. Webster notes how the stability of the shield, in a physical sense, complements the mobility characteristic of πόδας ὠκύς Ἀχιλλεύς *pódas ōkhòs Akhilleús* ("swift-footed Achilles"). The shield is invulnerable by nature; that is its intrinsic quality. When Achilles, once, forgets his shield's invulnerability, Homer is displeased with his hero and calls him νήπιος *népios* ("fool"—20. 262–66). The shield symbolically embodies the single transcendent element of human life: memory. The artifact's stasis, then, is derived from its imagistic representation of the function of the poem of memory as the source of cognition which alone issues in practical action. That its major role is this general didactic one is the meaning of Hephaistos' explicit statement of purpose: " 'And I wish that I could hide him away from death and its sorrow / at that time when his hard fate comes upon him, as surely / as there shall be fine armour for him, such as another / man out of many men shall wonder at, when he looks on it' " (18. 464–67). The usual function of armor doesn't hold in the case of Achilles' shield, the most impressive armor in the poem! The shield will not save its bearer from death. Achilles' newly accepted role, rather, is one which transcends his temporal individuality. He seeks glory, not in transitory life, but in the eternal life which is the communal memory, divinely presented in the poet's record, of his deeds. For his death will come gloriously, in the process of saving the Argive social system, preserving the very principle of social existence. It is Achilles' final communal role that his new shield symbolizes. Hephaistos' words could be applied as well to the poem as to the shield; he seems here to be speaking of all art. The universal effectiveness of his orderly artistry is implied by his emphatically generic reference to men (18. 466–67): not Trojans and Achaians as such, but any men will wonder at the shield. The wonder it causes, like that caused by the epic, will be a source of pleasure; but it is a very special pleasure, that which comes from the recognition of right action and from the accompanying knowledge that such action is possible for the observer, and for the listener, too—possible, and necessary.

The shield, then, is didactic. All that man, fictional or real, needs to know is presented on its surface. The image asserts the continuity between art and life. As Tom T. Tashiro comments: "The poet inhabits a world within which he has created the world of the *Iliad*, and within the world of the *Iliad* there is another world depicted on the shield . . . the world of man in two scenes—marriage for the physical continuance of

the race, a court of law for the preservation of society" (p. 66). There is
also war, as the sometimes necessary means for eradicating irreversibly
disorderly societies; and art, as the expression of social unanimity.
Carrying such a shield, Achilles covers, literally, and eclipses, symbolically, his selfhood, in order to serve others. The understanding which
leads to contemporary order comes from the memory of orderly action of
men in the past. The *Iliad* is the poem of memory which shields its
audience from a purely mortal fate. The necessity for realism is clear;
realism alone brings conviction. The audience cannot follow the example
of Perseus, on the shield of Herakles, flying through the air. But the
actions depicted on Achilles' shield are imitable. Insofar as the scenes are
more popular than they are aristocratic, furthermore, they are calculated
to show Homer's audience a contemporary mode of action which corresponds to the heroic deeds of Achilles. Deeds themselves may be various;
but the orientation which motivates them, which makes them humanly
proper, is as continuous as human nature. Achilles is orderly—and the
audience will be—by being conscious of the social order.

The shield presents exemplary social action very specifically. By portraying orderly examples, Hephaistos defines all the roles played by
individuals within a healthy society—whether he be young or old (18.494,
515), man (18. 494–95) or woman (18. 496), bride (18. 492) or groom (18.
494), prosecutor or defendant (18. 498–500), judge (18. 501) or jury (18.
503–4), combatant (18. 509 ff.) or noncombatant (18. 514), warrior or
counselor, citizen (18. 497, 502) or pastor (18. 525), laborer (18. 550 ff.) or
manager (18. 556), binder (18. 554) or reaper (18. 555), herdsman (18. 577)
or shepherd (18. 594), performer (18. 593 ff.) or audience (18. 603 ff.),
herald or cook (18. 557), commoner (18. 550 ff., 567 ff.) or king: "by them
the king in silence / and holding his staff stood near the line of the
reapers, happily" (18. 556–57). Kingship, as it is depicted here, is all it
should be. The propriety of the king's performance of his role is proven
by the orderliness of the social environment over which he presides. He
is the provider, his function associated with the fertility of sowing and
harvest. Sceptre in hand, he is a silent symbol of the governmental basis
of social equilibrium. When harmony prevails—and it is a socially
systematic harmony which obtains here, as the work is carefully divided
among various kinds of laborers (18. 550 ff.)—nothing need be said by
rulers. The contrast with Agamemnon in Book 2 is unmistakable; and the
king's behavior here foreshadows Achilles' judgment of the games in
Book 23.

Homer's special interest in the widest of communal contexts may
explain why Hephaistos begins the pictures with the two cities. The
god's initial choice of human subject material recalls Homer's own story,

the epic of an international struggle. In the two cities Hephaistos presents typical relationships, both orderly (in the first) and disorderly (in the second). Poetry does not invent the norm; it establishes it by expressing it. The shield portrays in microcosmic fashion a system of relationships. The relations in the shield's world can be catalogued; those in the song itself are no less numerous, and no more enumerable, than those in everyday life. But the shield's comprehensiveness shows us that the Homeric epic is on the verge of systematic Law. The next step is Hesiod.

To introduce one ethical perspective provided by the city scenes on the shield it is helpful to turn to Hesiod's *Works and Days*. Addressing his brother Perses, the overtly didactic Boeotian poet distinguishes between two kinds of Strife (11–12): one praiseworthy, the other blameworthy (12–13). "One stirs up cruel war and fighting, being cruel" (13–14). No one loves her (14). But the other, the second Strife, is kinder to men (19): "She stirs up even the laggard to work" (20). The second Strife is really the spirit of competition (21–23), and "This Strife is good for men" (24). Hesiod cautions his brother about the danger of confusing the two forces (27 ff.). They may appear, deceptively, to be the same; but they are as opposed to one another as good is opposed to evil. Havelock argues that Homer must have been familiar with this conceptual distinction. So the first city is a model of the benefits to be derived from living justly, under the auspices of the good Strife. It includes, indeed, the seeds of disorder, qualifying its peacefulness, in the quarrel; "but," to quote Lloyd, "only to give stronger expression to the influences by which they are controlled. The humane principle of fine and ransom supersedes the . . . barbarous rule of unappeasable vindictiveness" (p. 31). The proximity of the quarrel to the marriage festival, moreover, suggests that Strife is as natural to the human condition as is sexual attraction between individuals—and no less essentially necessary. Strife cannot be avoided; indeed it should not be. Man must only make sure that it is the good Strife which influences his words and acts. But Aphrodite knows that, because the two forces so often work together, it is relatively easy to replace the influence of the good Strife with that of the evil one. That is what happened in the quarrel in Book 1. Yet even intranational strife can be beneficial, as long as it is expressed within a *customary*, social framework; it may even be a progressive factor, since peaceful settlement automatically becomes a precedent, an example for others to follow. The confrontation of the individuals concerned is not lethal because they are separated by a representative of the community: the arbitrator, who plays the role of a Nestor or of a Poulydamas. For the unstated sources of the orator's prize is nevertheless implicitly recognizable: the ideal, orderly society itself (18. 508). Disorder therefore is dissolved by the prevalence of social regularity. Achilles, in his intuitive appreciation of the shield's meaning, learns this lesson well. He had appeared, in Book 1, as the would-be arbitrator; he failed to bring harmony to Argos because he could not remove self-interest from his arbitration. But in Book 23 he succeeds in negotiating the arguments of the various contestants to a peaceful conclusion because he himself has remained aloof from the contest.

The second city, on the other hand, presents the disastrous consequences of evil Strife. The unanimity of its citizens insufficiently counterbalances the sinister strength of the besieging army (18. 513). The strength of evil Strife is both intra- and international. There is dissension among the attackers (18. 510), who suffer a defeat because of it (18. 525 ff.); and there is the discord of the war itself, threatening both societies involved in it. So evil Strife issues in war between communities (18. 509–12), each fighting, not individually, but possessed by a general blindness. Whether it is internal (like the quarrel between Agamemnon and Achilles) or external (Achaians versus Trojans), such unruly Strife threatens the very social system. The good Strife would have brought about Nestor's successful arbitration of the dispute in Book 1 or the orderly completion of the duel between Paris and Menelaos in Book 3—reaffirming, in each case, Olympian social values. But evil Strife has only two alternatives: society will be extinguished, either by annihilation (Troy's destruction) or by alienation (Achilles' secession); or it will be weakened seriously, by the assimilation of alien individuals (Agamemnon's desire to keep Chryseis, his appropriation of Kassandra which leads to the downfall of Atreus' house, or Paris' abduction of Helen), or by the subjugation of men who are deprived by force of their individual wills (had Achilles, somehow, been forced to rejoin the army).

The contrast, of course, is between the peaceful settlement of differences and violence. The quarrel is reflected perfectly in the failure of the duel (another example of the correspondence between the wrath- and the war-story), a failure which, as Pandaros' truce-breaking indicates, will lead to collective disaster for Troy and a serious weakening, through the loss of warriors like Patroklos, for Argos. War, then, does more harm than good to both parties, regardless of the orderliness of one or of the other. The good Strife, however, whether it be the competition among the harvesters, the dancers, or the litigants, or that of the Achaian games in Book 23, contributes to the survival and progress of society. Rejecting one Strife for the other, Achilles, in his new identity, proves the effectiveness of the didactic distinction set forth upon his shield. Whitman explains that "the static symbolism engraved on the cosmic shield is now answered in the dynamic terms of action with universal import" (p. 207), as Achilles bears it into battle against the Trojans. The mobility of the primary living individual actualizes the potential of communal human life to influence orderly socially preserving action. We can now turn to examination of the central didactic element of the *Iliad*: the developing character of Achilles.

ᒪ 9 ᒧ

The Identity of Achilles

The central image of the great shield radiates outward symbolically, to focus in itself and in Achilles the main theme of Homer's epic. If we are fully to understand the thematic significance of Homer's arch-image we must study closely the step-by-step development of Achilles, for whom the artifact is made. The various attitudes Achilles displays form a pattern which is both cyclical and progressive: at the beginning and at the end of the story, Achilles is oriented toward the communal dimension of human life. Yet in each case the orientation is different. At first Achilles' communal outlook is limited to the Argive society; and it is more or less unquestioning; but at the conclusion of the poem, Achilles is attuned to the human community in its most divine, transcendent sense; and his ultimate commitment is emphatically introspective. The development of Achilles' personality indicates beyond a doubt Homer's awareness of the "self" as a center of forces that motivate action. To detect the various changes in Achilles' outlook between the first and last books of the *Iliad*, we must rely upon the evidence provided by his own actions and words. Homer's characterization of Achilles is much more complicated and subtle than most critics—because they isolate no more than a few of his several attitudes—have taken into account. Roughly in the order of their narrative occurrence (although some are simultaneous with others and all are causally interrelated) the attitudes Achilles displays are, in simplified form, as follows:

1. For Argos
   2. Against Agamemnon
3. For Briseis
   4. Against Argos
5. For the Myrmidons
6. For Patroklos
7. Transformation of attitude, through Nestor and Patroklos
8. For Argos

9. Against Hektor
10. Against Troy
11. For Agamemnon
12. For Priam
13. For Mankind

It is not only a full circle (from 1 to 8) that Achilles' development suggests, but also a widening of the circumference (from 11 to 13) to define the total humanization of the poem's major figure. The replacement of Achilles' old identity (1 through 6) with his new, transcendent, personality (7 through 10, then 11 through 12) corresponds perfectly with the loss of his old armor and his acceptance of the shield of Hephaistos.

1. For Argos

As the *Iliad* begins, Achilles is committed to the national well-being of the Achaians. His initial attitude finds its parallel on the shield in the warriors who set out impetuously from the besieged city to defend it against its attackers (18. 513 ff.). Apollo's plague has beset the army for nine days; but Agamemnon has made no attempt to resolve the disorder of his Danaans. Achilles instead calls the assembly to investigate what may be the weakness in their society which has caused its present dissolution (1. 54 ff.).

Achilles—not, as we might expect, Nestor or Odysseus—is the one who takes the first step toward the reestablishment of the army's well-being. Achilles is attuned, at this point, to the principle of order. Homer marks him as a contrast to Agamemnon by having Achilles open his petition to Kalchas—whom he treats with perfect courtesy and political acumen—with an oath to Apollo (1. 86), the very god whom Agamemnon has dishonored. Agamemnon himself, like the king depicted on the shield (18. 556), is silent; yet Agamemnon should not be silent, since order does not prevail within his society, as it does in the shield-king's.

As Homer first presents him, Achilles seems to be aware of the role each individual must play to insure the continued stability of society. He calls upon the all-knowing prophet (1. 70) who, in turn, instructs the king in his proper mode of action (1. 94 ff.). The poet defines Achilles' attitude before the quarrel in this way so that its subsequent alteration will be all the more poignant: Achilles will move toward disorder, not from potential orderliness, but from an *actual* commitment to the social principle. His initiative—however disastrous its personal consequences since his emotion goes beyond necessity—does, in fact, lead to the termination of the plague.

Another interpretation may be equally appropriate. There is potential disorder in Achilles' attitude as well as, for the present, actual order. Hera's association with him is suspiciously expedient; she abruptly deserts Achilles, and opposes Thetis, when he no longer serves her purpose of reharmonizing Argos. Agamemnon's remarks make it plain that, whether rightly or not, the king regards Achilles' characteristic attitude as a threat to social harmony. Forever, Agamemnon claims, Achilles is too ready to speak against kings, too eager for quarreling always (1. 174 ff.)—like Thersites. Although Achilles seems to be allied with the good Strife in the quarrel, it is clear that his characteristic flaw is that he all too easily, in the past, confused orderly fighting with disorderly arguing, the good Strife with the evil (1. 177)—and may indeed be under the influence of the latter even now. His social role is that of the defender in war; with the war unfinished, here he would perform the function of the counselor. Achilles seems overly confident in the scope of his effectiveness.

2. Against Agamemnon

Achilles turns against the ruler of the Argive confederacy because he recognizes that Agamemnon, through his selfish blindness, has caused the present physical disintegration of the army. Castigating the suppliant and slighting the authority of Apollo, Agamemnon has broken the laws of men and gods at the same time. And the king compounds his error, making its consequences affect the internal customary structure of society, by demanding the rightful prize of Achilles as payment for his sacrifice of Chryseis on behalf of social well-being. Doing so, he proves that he has no respect for the individual's right to a degree of autonomous value, blindly asserting his own individuality. Agamemnon has confounded all distinction—upon which social stability depends. Achilles' enmity toward Agamemnon, then, is based on the primary warrior's determination that he will no longer willingly be a part of an unnatural system of government. His behavior is not so much revolutionary as it is secessionist.

3. For Briseis

But terming Achilles' secession from the Argive nation "individualistic" causes more critical problems than it resolves. If his behavior is purely selfish, no matter how understandable selfishness may be under the circumstances, what are we to think of his relationships with Briseis and Patroklos? Rather than allow those relationships to be clouded by a suspicion of insincerity or superficiality, we must find a different interpretation. Achilles' individualism is a qualified one. If we recognize Argive society as a tenuous new system attempting to synthesize the familial mode of life with the heroic, we can begin to understand the qualification. In this light, Achilles' reaction may be considered as a reassertion of one element of the synthesis—the familial—which has been threatened by Agamemnon's attitude and behavior. That is, Achilles opposes the possibility, implicit in Agamemnon's overbearing egocentricity, of returning to a purely heroic social existence. Agamemnon's familial orientation is relatively weak since the king does not love his proper wife, Klytaimestra, as much as Achilles loves Briseis (1. 112 ff.; 9. 338–43; 21. 272–83). Agamemnon evaluates Chryseis as if she were a commodity, betraying his heroic bent; and his attitude is even more fatefully ironic if we assume that Klytaimestra is Helen's sister, as she is in many legends, making Agamemnon's desertion of her a perverse counterbalance to Menelaos, and the war's motivational pattern. In contrast Achilles regards Briseis as being much more than a prize—as being, in fact, his wife (19. 295–99).

That Briseis is the reason for Achilles' isolation from national concerns is certain; he himself says so (1. 429–30)—and he always says exactly what he means. The fantastic solemnity with which Agamemnon later swears to have preserved the girl's chastity (19. 261–65) proves that Achilles' explanation must be taken at face value. He considers himself to have been placed in a position analogous to that of Menelaos, whose familial disruption led to the war. Agamemnon's action, then, corresponds to Paris'; and Briseis is a parallel to Helen. In Achilles' mind the quarrel is founded on as righteous a basis as the war.

But Achilles' individualism is qualified by his consistent orientation toward familial values. He will not subordinate his selfhood to a petty king who is, because of his own selfishness, unable to maintain the new social synthesis (1. 292–96). For Agamemnon's attitude is self-contradictory; he values himself, but not the selfhood of others. Because of his refusal to compromise his love, Achilles becomes one of the loneliest figures in literature. Separated from his father and son, now from his promised wife and Achaian friends, his isolation is nearly total (1. 488–92). As Charles R. Beye remarks, "He withdraws from the world that has created him, because he can no longer find identity in it" (p. 137).

The inherent weakness of the new poetic society causes it to lose its identifying force for Achilles; he becomes socially anomalous. Because Agamemnon does not measure his behavior by the necessity of balancing the potentially conflicting components, he has reactivated the former opposition between the familial and the heroic systems. That is what Achilles alone, at this point, recognizes and tries to express. The new social system has proven too weak to prevent its ruler from returning, of his own accord, to heroic norms and dishonoring the familial attachment not only between himself and his queen, but also between his society's primary warrior and his rightful bedmate. Achilles has learned, perhaps through his loves, that the heroic standard alone is not enough to satisfy his heroic needs. On the surface he is indeed a fighter; but inside, Achilles' instincts are communal. Whitman comments: "Agamemnon, demanding a substitute of 'equal value' to the girl he is losing, illustrates the common [heroic] attitude. Achilles clearly feels differently about Briseis, who is commensurate with, and can symbolize, his inner convictions about his own honor; the other possessions are commensurate with force and fighting, the mode of self-assertion which in Achilles has been supreme above all others, and now is inadequate to his need" (p. 186). Achilles has accepted the more comprehensive values of the synthetic social system; because he is satisfied by the new, he will not allow Agamemnon to return to the old system.

Achilles' sociological stance, moreover, is effective; Owen implies this distinction between Achilles and Helen: Helen is unable to act effectively, whether individually or socially, because she has been deprived of her personal will by Aphrodite. But "there is no character . . . that is more of a self-willed individual, a person in his own right, than Achilles. He always speaks and acts of his own will, ἀπηλεγέως *apēlegéōs* ('without scruple') as he says his intention is to speak now (9. 308), i.e., without regard for consequences or persons" (p. 96). Homer portrays a dynamic awareness of selfhood in Achilles' animosity toward Agamemnon.

4. *Against Argos*

Achilles' secession results in the weakening of the army—an effect he fully intends. There is no doubt that he desires death for all the Danaans (16. 237); like Apollo, he would punish the whole society for the crime of its leader. He is not merely *indifferent* to Argos, as he is to Troy in the first three categories of his development; he is a self-declared enemy of Argive society. Yet even in Achilles' absence the remnant of the army manages to retain its aspirations toward unity (4. 429–32). They allow the king, as Achilles would not, to direct their individualities toward a collective purpose which on the surface seems opposed to their familial or individual ambitions. They are ready still to carry on the fight (2. 442–53). The role played by Aias, Odysseus, and Nestor, is to see to it that Achilles will have a still, if barely, intact social structure to which he may return whenever he is finally minded to. But without Achilles, their primary defender (1. 284), despite their aspiration, the Achaians are on the verge of social collapse; that is just what Achilles intended, what he requested of his mother (1. 450 ff.).

5. For the Myrmidons

Achilles' eventual return to his initial social commitment is easier because his alienation is never total. Achilles cuts himself off from the generic dimension of human life (Argos), but, as Owen notes, "his urge to protect the species is still strong" (p. 105); he never denies that he will reenter the fight to preserve his political community, the Myrmidons, should it be endangered—even if that will result automatically in the preservation of the entire Argive confederacy (9. 650–53). Achilles' secession reasserts his tribal association more strongly than ever: just as his anger identifies all the Achaians with their king, Agamemnon's personal affront to Achilles is considered a slight to all the Myrmidons (16. 269).

So while the Achaian army is being wrecked by the Myrmidon's nonparticipation, the internal order of Phthia is maintained. That is the significance of Homer's reference to the Myrmidon games, inserted in the catalogue which accompanies Agamemnon's mustering of the remnant of his forces (2. 771–79). Their wholesome competition is reflected in the dances on the shield. Discarding his new social identity, Achilles is identified still with the collective integrity of the tribe. By having him remain dedicated to this lesser communal system (level 5 on the hierarchical grid, see Appendix 1), Homer will enable Achilles to rebuild upon the model of the Myrmidon community more durable than it was before, the wider social structure that his secession has successfully demolished. What the Myrmidon games in Book 2 express on the political level, the Achaian games directed by Achilles in Book 23 will signify on the national level: the unanimous cooperation upon which a stable society depends.

6. For Patroklos

Achilles, of course, is still capable of relating to others on the most basic personal level, independent of any formal collective (family, tribe, or nation). The hero's deep love for Patroklos is the source from which his purely human love for Priam in Book 24 derives. Here selfishness and selflessness come together to form the most essential model for the widest communal spirit. Achilles' recognition of the selfhood of his

comrade is ultimately allied with his assertion of the value of his own
individuality, as Bespaloff observes: "It is not through action that Homer
reveals man's profoundest nature but rather through man's ways of
loving and choosing his love. For Hector, love is the forgetfulness of self.
For Achilles, self is at the center of love. What he adores in Patroclus is his
own reflection, purified" (p. 56). Self-love and love for another, as the
two are expressed simultaneously in the character of Achilles, underlie
the Homeric perspective by which Argos may be distinguished from
Troy as being, in the end, one a living, and the other a dying, society. In
Achilles' loving Patroklos as he loves himself (18. 80–82, 324–35), Homer
represents the perfect reciprocity between the individual and the community. The latter is made coherent through the cumulative love between individuals, although, for now, Achilles does not recognize the
wider social significance of his attachment.

The love between two men is special, but not extraordinary, not
without precedent within the Iliadic world which knows the synthesized
hierarchical system. Beye's statement that "in denying the system [Achil-
les] denies at the same time the world and his fellow men" (p. 137) is
excessive simply because it is based upon a faulty premise. Achilles, as
far as his nationalistic identity is concerned, denies not the social system
as such, but the particular, unnatural manifestation of that system which
is Agamemnon's Argos in its present state. Nor does he refute the
systems of familial, conjugal (Briseis) and parental (Thetis), or tribal
relationships. His love for Patroklos, moreover, makes his respect for
another basic communal system, that of guest-friendship, unmistakable.

Achilles' reverence for the guest-suppliant, also represented in his
intervention on behalf of Chryseis and in his hospitality to the ambassadors and courtesy toward Phoinix in Book 9, complements his familial
loyalty. In this sense, Achilles represents a new human social development: the synthesis between blood kinship and the individualistic
heroic relationship. In the new society, only if there is a *personal*
sympathy between them will the host provide his guest indefinitely with
a substitute family; only then will the guest love his host in the same way
as he loved his alienated parents. In the purely familial system, the
outsider would be feared because he is of a foreign bloodline; just as, in
the purely heroic, he would be more welcome if he brings desirable gifts.
The concept of the universal brotherhood of humanity is born with the
new synthetic society that Homer represents in Achilles' concept of a
harmonious Argos (fully realized only in Book 23).

Discussing the ambiguity of the word ξείνος *zeínos* ("guest, stranger,
friend, suppliant") M. T. Finley explains it as "a confusion symbolic of
the ambivalence which characterized all dealings with the stranger in

that archaic world" (p. 105). That the same word is applied to a guest, to a suppliant, and to a stranger, however, is perfectly understandable since, in this world of social readjustment, one man often plays the three roles simultaneously. Patroklos, in fact, does this when he comes to Achilles on Nestor's initiative in Book 16. 85. This is the first time in the *Iliad* that Homer portrays Achilles as sympathetic with his fellowmen and, as Owen points out, "it is the most telling place for making us think of their close friendship, because, in the first place, it now becomes the vital factor in the story, and also because we know it is the last time they ever talk together" (p. 146). Achilles here describes his personal, heroic, relationship with Patroklos in filial terms (16. 7–10), as he does again during the funeral of his friend (23. 222–24). There is even an implication—which must be judged in the light of Achilles' overwhelming grief—that he loved Patroklos more than he does his father Peleus (19. 321–24). That the love between the two men can be expressed in filial and parental terminology proves Patroklos' full assimilation into Achilles' own familial context. The heroic and the familial, in their love, have been successfully synthesized; Briseis' explanation of Patroklos' role in her espousal by Achilles has the same implication (19. 295).

But, in keeping with the synthesized social system, the extension of Achilles' familial feeling to Patroklos, a "stranger," is made possible only because, as Walter Leaf explains, "the bond of comradeship," an heroic ideal, "though with an exile from a distant land, is no less strong than the bond of blood" (*Homer and History*, p. 255). Leaf also explains the way in which the self-contained familial hierarchy had been opened outward to a less restricted pattern of relations by the pseudofeudalism of the individualistic, heroic system:

> The Achaian king . . . is surrounded by a body of . . . ἑταῖροι *hetaîroi* ("companions"), who are bound to him only by the tie of personal loyalty. When Patroclus leads the Myrmidons . . . it is not with words of patriotism; his appeal to them begins, "Myrmidons, companions of Achilles," and the motive of the onslaught is to do honour to Peleides (16. 269). But the Patroclus who utters his challenge to the Myrmidons is himself no Myrmidon. He is the chief ἑταῖρος *hetaîros* ("companion") because he is most closely bound to Achilles by purely personal affection. (P. 252)

The bond between them, the heroic code of guest-friendship, is not what is "purely personal"; rather the beautiful personality and familiarity of their friendship is expressed in their wholehearted subscription to the spirit of the bond, instead of merely to its letter. That mutual subscription to the spirit of love is characteristic of the new society. No such adherence to the spirit characterizes Agamemnon's relationship with

Chryseis. So Agamemnon had sinned in not living up to the potential of the heroic code, as well as in slighting familial values. He confiscates Achilles' rightful prize because he does not respect the selfhood of another, unnaturally dissociating its value from that of his own; Achilles notes explicitly that such behavior is antiheroic (16. 52–59).

For the new society to be an effective mode of social cohesiveness, relations on its most basic level (1 on the grid) must provide a substantial model for the more collective levels to imitate (5 and 6). The relationship between Achilles and Patroklos is precisely such an example. Only this kind of love can enforce voluntary cooperation on the political and national levels to enduring effect. Love's extension, from one object to many, explains the loyalty of the Myrmidons who are all, like Patroklos, companions of Achilles. But Achilles, fully satisfied with his friend and tribe, unnaturally restricts the extension of his love: "The suffering of the Achaians does not matter to [him], the distress of Patroklos does" (Pearl C. Wilson, p. 567). He has been guilty of identifying all Achaian individuals with the one he opposes, Agamemnon. But his love for Patroklos will prove to be sufficient, once delusion is dissolved, to make Achilles recognize that it cannot be distinguished from the expression of a more general communal spirit.

7. Transformation of attitude, through Nestor and Patroklos

Until now I have emphasized the positive side of Achilles' alienation from Argos—inasmuch as his secession can be justified and explained in psychological terms. His attitude has an equally momentous negative quality. Despite the divine portentousness of his relentless wrath, Achilles can't be more than human; and to fulfill his human nature, Achilles must commit his forceful individuality to the widest collective structure available to him. His denial of Argos, regardless of that society's tenuous nature, is essentially inhuman, Homer shows, because separation from temporal society denies Achilles access to the continuing dimension of humanity—immortal memory.

The kind of love he expresses for Patroklos has the potential of extending from the center of selfhood to the very circumference of the human circle which embraces all mankind. Had Achilles allowed the operation of that love to carry him to such a universal perspective, he might have been able to understand, and forgive, the characteristically human fallibility of Agamemnon long before he actually does. Achilles' anger against the king ceases only after Patroklos' death and his own self-effacing grief have conveyed to him a view of human life from the limit of mortality. He might have realized that his secession had the same disastrous effect on Argos as Patroklos' death has on him: the loss of identity, whether social or individual. In actual fact, however, Achilles' attitude indicates that he is, in a different way, as blind to true order as Agamemnon is. Nor does Achilles realize that his dearest friend does not share his own delusion. When Patroklos arrives with the news of the army's dire predicament, Achilles, having dismissed Argos from his thoughts, assumes that Patroklos has done likewise. Seeing his companion's sorrowful countenance, Achilles assumes that such anguish must be caused by the death of one of their fathers (16. 15–16). All involvements except the national one, which Patroklos now represents, have been allowed expression in Achilles' attempt to withhold his love from its widest possible social context.

Love's highest human potential is activated when Patroklos' death moves Achilles to desire revenge so strongly that he no longer cares that its accomplishment must save the Argive society as well as Patroklos' and his own personal honor. Once again, in presenting Patroklos' death, Homer has underlined the singularity of Achilles. His sorrow is great enough to make Achilles accept, at last, his own mortality. At the same time it leads him to relinquish his inhumanly excessive animosity toward his proper society.

The expression of that wrongheaded, relentless wrath had been supported by Achilles' misguided use of his divine resources. Both Thetis and Zeus hesitated to promise that his request, in Book 1, would be fulfilled. But the will of Achilles seems to prevail upon Thetis, through their blood-relationship, and upon Zeus through his political gratitude to Thetis. Yet the momentary hesitation before the compliant nod is sufficient indication that Achilles' attunement with transcendent order is less than perfect. It is ironic, then, that in resigning himself to his inescapable humanity, Achilles simultaneously becomes perfectly attuned with the divine potential inherent in his nature. His self-effacement and collective deeds provide him with an access to the divine aspect of humanity itself: the eternal continuity of the communal memory, protected by the daughters of Zeus. Yet in his pursuit of "excellent glory" (18. 121), Achilles retains a dependency on the cyclical temporality of memory in the minds of individual men to come. But since he insists that his memorialization be identified with that of Patroklos, and of Argos, Achilles' freedom is indeed as nearly total as humanly possible. So through characterization Homer explicates the meaning of the imagistic juxtaposition of Achilles' mortal spear and the immortal shield. All transient values are sublimated, by Achilles' change of attitude, to a perpetual valuation: he will sacrifice homecoming for the pleasure of avenging Patroklos. The sacrifice, however, will also make his homeland more secure, his father more honorable; it will provide a glorious example for his son; and it will save Argive society by destroying the unnatural system which has jeopardized that society's very existence, thereby ensuring the continuity of his exemplary action in memory.

A closer look at the elements which influence the transition from one attitude to another on the part of Achilles reveals the subtlety of Homer's art. Agamemnon, in the quarrel, accuses Achilles of wanting to displace the king himself (1. 287–91). The accusation may seem unwarranted by Achilles' actions at this point. But Agamemnon appears to know already what the wrath of Achilles will make evident to Homer's audience: that Achilles' overweening individuality and independent spirit, supported by the divine half of his nature, has the potential of becoming a considerable threat to Agamemnon's lordship. Achilles does not say that he wishes to be sovereign; but his words imply anarchical tendencies. Relying too unfairly upon his divine resources as he swears to protect Kalchas even from Agamemnon, Achilles is not one to be assimilated easily into a purely human social system. His eternal nature chafes at its mortal bonds. Agamemnon rightly points out to him that his proper social role is that of the defender, not that of the king of kings. Achilles is too headstrong, too ready to proclaim his superiority over his fellowmen.

In a way Achilles' detachment from his nation and from Troy, his dissociation of himself from nationalistic interests, resembles the characteristic position of Helen. Separated from the international struggle, Helen weaves and Achilles sings (9. 185 ff.). But his singing does not make Achilles a model of the poet in the same way as her weaving makes Helen an analogue to the epic composer. Her separation from action is involuntary; her art, therefore, represents her only constructive mode of behavior. Achilles' proper role is not to sing but to fight—to provide the material for song. The song he sings has no specific content (9. 187). His art is comparable to that of Hera in Book 14; if it ultimately signifies order, it does so in a disorderly manner despite his will. Right in itself, Achilles' singing is wrong in context; it is not practical, has no social use.

The warrior is no less important to social well-being than the artist. Both are healers, preservers, protectors of an established way of life—one physically, the other spiritually (16. 28 ff.). But the medicinal function of the warrior logically precedes that of the poet; physical well-being provides the basis for psychic equilibrium. When Achilles, the crucial fighter, refuses to involve himself with the society he alone *can* defend, he acts unnaturally. Patroklos' role is to make Achilles aware of the inhumanity of his behavior; that is the commission he receives from Nestor. Patroklos recites to Achilles the list of the wounded Achaians (16. 23–27):

'And over these the healers skilled in medicine are working
to cure their wounds. But you, Achilleus; who can do anything
with you? May no such anger take me as this that you cherish!
Cursed courage. What other man born hereafter shall be advantaged
unless you beat aside from the Argives this shameful destruction?
Pitiless: the rider Peleus was never your father
nor Thetis was your mother, but it was the grey sea that bore you
and the towering rocks, so sheer the heart in you is turned from us.'

(16. 28–35)

Patroklos' description of the skillful Achaian doctors (16. 28–29) is
psychologically calculated to induce Achilles to compare their own
personal relationship with the relationship between the surgeons and
the wounded that is in process, he reports, at this very moment.
Patroklos' question places him in a position analogous to that of the
physicians (16. 29–30); can he effectively heal Achilles' spiritual wound
as they can heal the physical ills of the fallen warriors? He can and
does—by suggesting that the analogy should be reversed. Achilles is the
one who must apply the preventive medicine of the supremely skilled
warrior to save the wounded and not yet wounded Achaians from utter
destruction (16. 31). Patroklos, moreover, explicitly marks the unnaturalness of Achilles' anger (16. 30); it is a blindness, like Agamemnon's,
that bespeaks the operation of evil Strife. He reminds Achilles of his
primary role, both in the present social context and in the future as well
(16. 31–32). He calls Achilles' wrathful courage accursed (16. 31) and
defines his attitude as a pitiless one (16. 33), thereby proving his ultimate
relationship with Achilles as a reflection of himself—since Patroklos here
is as outspoken and blunt as his friend characteristically is. The attitude
Achilles has displayed, Patroklos concludes, is neither human (16. 33),
nor divine (16. 34); neither familial (16. 33–34), nor heroic (16. 31–32); it is
as inanimate as the sea and the rocks (16. 34–35). Achilles' self-defined
position is totally contrary to the living, human world (16. 35). Patroklos
is unable to justify, by any valid standard, Achilles' restriction of love
from the national sphere.

Achilles is, as Patroklos describes him, the man who "refused and
would accept nothing" (18. 500), thereby jeopardizing the security of all
his fellowmen. The quarrel between the two Achaian leaders should
have been settled within the social structure, as it is implied that the
shield-quarrel will be resolved (18. 501–8). Then Patroklos' death would
have been prevented; his return to battle without Achilles would have
been unnecessary. As it is, Patroklos' advice leads to the rescue of Argos
only at the cost of his own life; his words are convincing enough for

Achilles to agree to allow him to lead the Myrmidons, but not enough for Achilles himself to cooperate.

Patroklos' Nestorian counsel, moreover, is not Achilles' first exposure to the reality of human life, else he might be excused for breaking laws of which he had no knowledge. Patroklos' speech also reflects the warning given to his headstrong son by Peleus—recalled to Achilles by Odysseus in the embassy in Book 9. Presumably because Peleus, like Agamemnon, recognized the potential weakness of Achilles, he had cautioned his son against pride of heart and quarreling—that is, against the pursuit of evil Strife; Achilles, he warns, must maintain respect for all (9. 247–51). The importance of the filial relationship makes Achilles' forgetfulness of his father's instructions a most serious flaw in his familial orientation. Patroklos now reasserts Peleus' code of behavior, that Achilles must align himself with society and move away from egocentrism.

The sense in which Achilles' behavior during and after the quarrel can be considered selfish is now clear: he thought himself capable of restricting human love to a select company of men only. Like Agamemnon's delusion, Achilles' brings physical as well as moral disintegration on the Argives, proving the absolute necessity for the primary individual to be oriented consistently toward each level of society. Achilles' disorderly position is parallel in that of Nireus as well; this, no doubt, explains the conjunction of their names in the narrative. Though personally beautiful, as Achilles is semidivine, Nireus' individuality is cursorily dismissed by the poet because it is not an integral part of a sufficiently healthy community (2. 672–75).

Beye explains the way in which the two results of the quarrel, the "major dislocation of the Greek forces" which leads to their defeat and "the inner workings of Achilles' isolated soul," are related:

What he drives himself to do (in refusing the embassy in Book 9) shows that as a hero, as a young man, as a human being, he has in every way defied the natural order of things. When Achilles opposes the very rhythm of existence he is a puny opponent for a great cosmic force. He is like Thersites and as Thersites is struck . . . by Odysseus and made to understand his place, so Achilles will inevitably suffer the effects of the natural order reasserting itself in the face of his disavowal. Achilles will be hurt. (P. 137)

National order punishes Thersites. But in Achilles' case, Zeus' transcendent principle of order will cause the hero's reattunement with it upon the widest human level, by operating internationally to bring about the one event by which Achilles can be moved: the death of Patroklos, counterbalanced by Achilles' expression of love for Priam in Book 24, when his punishment is transformed into his most glorious, most memorable orderly gesture.

Achilles finally recognizes that his unnatural self-assertion has caused the death of his dearest friend as well as the weakening of the Argive society (19. 61–64). At the same time his confession of culpability is evidence of the transcendent foresight, associated with Zeus, which Achilles now shares: " 'the Achaians will too long remember this quarrel between us' " (19. 64), he prophesies to Agamemnon. Achilles realizes, that is, that even his erring attitude has communal mnemonic value, as an anti-exemplum by which men to come may be able to avoid a repetition of it in their own lives. Herein lies his affinity to Helen; as each acts for memory, they provide the juncture between the two Iliadic galaxies.

Temporal society is, after all, Achilles' only contact with the eternal society of human nature: "Achilles' tragedy," says Adam Parry, "his final isolation, is that he can in no sense, including that of language . . . leave the society which has become alien to him" ("The Language of Achilles," p. 7). But Achilles will learn that the common language is not itself inadequate to express the fullness of his individuality. He will become a speaker of words, in Books 23 and 24, after he has fulfilled his role as a doer of deeds; and his words achieve a harmony which is both internal and external, personal and social. From Achilles' personal tragedy arises the happy termination of the communal tragedy. For from the first moment of grief (18. 102–3), Achilles understands the suffering which he has caused others. Now the perspective of the chief warrior has been widened forcibly, his delusion dissolved by grief, his isolation ended by the workings of destiny. The outcome of the change is more comic than tragic, both for Argos and for Achilles himself.

His reentry into the war assures the ultimate cohesiveness and victory of Agamemnon's army and the consequent restoration of total social order. The primary warrior, whose individuality Homer emphasizes above all others, bears a shield lacking all marks of specific personality. Upon it, the only individuals remain silent—both judge and king. So Achilles becomes self-effacing, on behalf of the needs of his living nation and of his dead friend, precisely when he assumes the shield. He hides himself not only behind it actually but also upon it poetically. And the benefit of his self-abnegation is to all Argos.

8. For Argos

In his first grief for Patroklos Achilles simultaneously grieves for the other Argives who have fallen because of his abstention from the war (18.

105 ff.). He is aligned with Achaian society. The sudden extension of
Achilles' love to encompass all the Achaians, Agamemnon included (18.
112–13), fulfills the potential from which he had previously restrained it,
but it needs explanation. The social context surrounding Achilles' self-
incriminating outburst may provide the clue to the explanation. As his
mourning for Patroklos begins, Achilles is comforted by Antilochos (18.
32 ff.), by the Myrmidon handmaidens (18. 28 ff.), by the Nereids (18. 36
ff.), by his mother (18. 70 ff.), and by the Argives fighting valiantly to
save the body of Patroklos from Hektor (18. 148 ff.). The voluntary
comfort so readily granted him by his political, familial, parental, and
national relations manifests the benefits of the social mode of existence;
that comfort expresses a love which, in his concentration on Patroklos,
Achilles has not reciprocated. The consolation, both by word and deed,
is offered to him in his moment of need gratuitously, automatically.
None of his comforters are indebted to Achilles; he becomes indebted to
them.

It is also significant that Achilles' grief is unprecedented in his personal experience. The ritual pattern followed by his comforters (18. 31,
32, 51, 71) suggests that Achilles' own ritualistic gesture of mourning (18.
23 ff.; compare Andromache's for Hektor), like his language, are his
heritage from the community which has hitherto defined his existence.
His personal anguish can be expressed at all only because the social
context provides each individual, from its store of accumulated experiences, with the means of expression. Indeed his gratitude to the stalwart
warriors who fight on to save Patroklos' body is evident in his words to
Iris (18. 194–95). The community serves the individual when he is
stricken, Patroklos in death and Achilles in mortal grief; therefore the
individual must respond in kind.

Achilles' realignment with society is further implied in his determination to preserve the honor of Patroklos. If Patroklos' memory is to be
respected by living men, Argos must be preserved; Hektor must be
beaten back so that a proper funeral may be held in peace. For temporal
society is not only itself made coherent by the concept of honor; it also
provides the material framework in which honor may find the historical
expression which becomes the basis for perpetuation in memory. Memory cannot retain an individual's glory in a vacuum; its impression will
stand out only within a social context. Men to come will remember
Patroklos in association with his funeral, with the honor accorded to him
by his contemporaries. The concept of honor prevalent in Agamemnon's
Argos, Achilles knows, may be imperfect. But he also knows now that he
must resubscribe to that concept because it is the only means by which
perpetual honor—glory in its continuing dimension—is made accessi-

ble. That had been the point of Patroklos' mission and of Phoinix's counsel in the embassy which then Achilles refused to recognize (9. 605 ff.). Now however he will win glory for his friend by reestablishing the security of Argos, the context in which glory may be recognized— through the destruction of Troy (18. 121 ff.). That is why the funeral must be delayed until Hektor is slain. Since Hektor is the essential bulwark of Troy, personal vengeance will be simultaneous with social restoration. The honor of Patroklos becomes identified, by Achilles' new orientation, with that of Menelaos.

The very concept of revenge, both as an ambition and as an accomplishment, is, after all, socially motivated. To conclude, as Owen does, that Achilles' "overmastering motive is not patriotism but the gratification of a private revenge" (p. 215) is to define the major hero of the *Iliad* as being entirely idiosyncratic in a way that dissociates him completely from Homer's didactic purpose of portraying a world attempting to stabilize a new concept of society. Achilles is not so entirely isolated; "private revenge" has no meaning—neither to Iliadic man in general nor to Achilles. It is his explicit intention to serve the honor of his friend specifically by restoring that of Argos. Anna L. Motto and John R. Clark are more accurate:

Achilles might be misunderstood by his companions, and to this extent "isolated" from them, but . . . his goals and his ideals are *never* divorced from those of his society. Just as Patroclus dies seeking to restore Menelaus' honor, so Achilles wishes to restore his own honor (before *all* the Achaians, 16. 84) and Menelaus' honor as well. This double purpose is present in his every action. Hence, his response to Patroclus' death includes concern for the other Achaians slain (21. 234). Achilles must revenge his own defilement (the loss of shield and friend), but he also consciously continues to avenge the dishonor suffered by Menelaus. Even at the heated moment when Hector is slain, Achilles is well aware of the glory "we" (all the Achaians) have won (22. 393). (P. 123)

The dual concern characterizes Achilles as the new social individual. This human model Homer presents in the action of his hero, in the double activation of the dual intention. The Homeric perspective which insists upon the reciprocity between the individual and the community finds its fullest poetic embodiment in the deeds performed by the new Achilles. The kind of love which united him with Patroklos is, for Homer, the basic formative element of the poetically synthesized society. Achilles' reassimilation into Argos is brought about by his love for another individual. So the new society, previously threatened by the quarrel between Achilles and Agamemnon, is now reformed by Achilles' reintegration. And it is made more durable.

The reformation occurs when Achilles renounces evil Strife (the Strife he wishes to kill, 18. 107). His renunciation dramatically expresses a moral revolution. Achilles' role in the Iliadic world becomes one with his poetic role both within and beyond that world—as an exemplum. The new moral stature of Achilles provides Homer with the occasion for the most extraordinary imagistic presentation, corresponding perfectly to the poem's dramatic movement: the central image associated with Achilles' new identity, the armor of Hephaistos.

The arming of Achilles is delayed from the moment of Achilles' announcement of its intention (19. 23). The prelude serves as a dramatic explication of the symbolic function of the arms as emblems of their bearer's new collective identity. Even Achilles' acceptance of the arms from the hands of his mother predicts their significance; his reaction is compared to the flare of the sun, the cosmic fire that marks his transcendent role (19. 17). Once again Achilles calls the Achaians to assemble. Homer emphasizes that the army's response to his cry is unanimous, including even the laggards (19.40 ff., 54). All individuals are reassimilated into a harmonious chain of community in which each link is not only important but also necessary. Once the primary individual is reattuned to society, reunification occurs rapidly and surely. This assembly is different from the one in Book 1. Achilles and Agamemnon are able to concur in a mutual, national commitment because each man, this time, suppresses his own, and respects the other's individuality (cf. 19. 56 ff., 19. 77 ff.).

The unity of Argos is symbolized in the communal feast arranged by Odysseus in preparation for the battle (19. 266 ff.). The sacrifice which precedes the feast is described in a way that emphasizes the restored equilibrium of the nation with the king-priest at its head (19. 266–75). But Homer never allows us to lose sight of Achilles' singular role in the orderly development; while the Danaans banquet, Athene descends from Olympos with nectar for Achilles (19. 350 ff.). The divine nourishment distinguishes the extraordinary humanity of the hero. Achilles, as his semidivinity represents, possesses special access to the transcendent dimension of order. Athene's appearance here reminds us that the potential forcefulness of Achilles, prefigured in her former appearance with Zeus' aegis, is about to be realized in action.

Now the arming will make it clear that Achilles' indispensability and charisma are the cause and effect of his realignment with his communal responsibilities, arranged by the foresight of Zeus. The arming defines Achilles' new identity as, paradoxically, a generic individuality; he becomes possessed, as he arms, by Zeus' governing principle of communal order. As he dons his divine armor, Achilles activates the individual's potential for socially beneficial action:

> The shining swept to the sky and all earth was laughing about them
> under the glitter of bronze and beneath their feet stirred the thunder
> of men, within whose midst brilliant Achilleus helmed him.
> A clash went from the grinding of his teeth, and his eyes glowed
> as if they were the stare of a fire, and the heart inside him
> was entered with sorrow beyond endurance. Raging at the Trojans
> he put on the gifts of the god, that Hephaistos wrought him with much
>   toil.
>   First he placed along his legs the fair greaves linked with
> silver fastenings to hold the greaves at the ankles.
> Afterward he girt on about his chest the corselet,
> and across his shoulders slung the sword with the nails of silver,
> a bronze sword, and caught up the great shield, huge and heavy
> next, and from it the light glimmered far, as from the moon.
> And as when from across water a light shines to mariners
> from a blazing fire, when the fire is burning high in the mountains
> in a desolate steading, as the mariners are carried unwilling
> by storm winds over the fish-swarming sea, far away from their loved
>   ones;
> so the light from the fair elaborate shield of Achilleus
> shot into the high air. And lifting the helm he set it
> massive upon his head, and the helmet crested with horse-hair
> shone like a star, the golden fringes were shaken about it
> which Hephaistos had driven close along the horn of the helmet,
> And brilliant Achilleus tried himself in his armour, to see
> if it fitted close, and how his glorious limbs ran within it,
> and the armour became as wings and upheld the shepherd of the people.
> Next he pulled out from its standing place the spear of his father,
> huge, heavy, thick, which no one else of all the Achaians
> could handle, but Achilleus alone knew how to wield it,
> the Pelian ash spear which Cheiron had brought to his father
> from high on Pelion, to be death for fighters in battle.
>
> (19. 362–91)

Perhaps the most astonishing thing about this miraculous arming is that, as Russo notes, for all its singular elements, it is yet "duly built upon the standard core of stock formulaic verses common to all arming scenes" ("Homer Against His Tradition," p. 286). Yet the special far outweighs the typical, as the arming motif is calculated to individualize the new role of Achilles. The armor, on the outside, perfectly reflects both the sorrow and rage within Achilles and the irresistible force of the Olympian order he will now serve.

The description of the arming is organized to emphasize the identification of the individual with the community, through the use of the familiar circular techniques of ring composition and hysteron proteron. The description begins and ends with reference to the communal dimension of human life, to the Achaians (19. 362–64) identified generically with the cosmos, and to the enemies of Achilles in general who, at this moment, are the Trojans (19. 391). The second and penultimate elements stress the individuality of Achilles, one in a transcendent (19. 364–67), the other in a temporal sense (19. 389–90). The third and antepenultimate are, again, communal; they refer to the Trojans (19. 367) and to the Achaians (19. 388–89) specifically, each time relating to their definitive influence upon Achilles. Then the divine armor (19. 367–74) is juxtaposed with the mortal spear (19. 387–88), one associated with Achilles' mother, the other with his father. In the center is the simile that defines the relationship between the individual (beacon fire) and the community (mariners) in the idealistic manner characteristic of the shield's own pictorial art (19. 375–80).

The total effect of the description is to identify Achilles with Argos. Details accumulate to contribute to this presentational meaning. The Achaians are regularly associated with bronze, as they are here (19. 363); and Homer departs from the usual sword formula to remark that Achilles' sword is also bronze (19. 373). So Achilles' psychological realignment with his nation is confirmed, and even extended, by the imagery. The scene presents the individual and society as, indeed, not only identified with one another but also identical. Thomas M. Greene notes that, in epics generally, "the hero must be acting for the community, the City; he may incarnate the City" (p. 15). That is what happens here. Achilles' change of attitude has allowed him, because of his semidivinity, to become Argos incarnate. Achilles is, for now, a daemon, possessed by the continuity of Argos. The description presents a double sublimation. Argos rises from disorder into effective order as the Achaians become the collective epitome of warlike unanimity because Achilles is there among them (19. 362–64). Then as we watch him arm, Achilles himself is transfigured before our eyes. He becomes larger than life—an elemental entity like fire, as his anguish is transformed into action (19. 365–67). And his transcendent potential is realized in time precisely when his personal sorrow turns to hatred against the common enemy of his society; not Hektor, but all Trojans (19. 367–68). Achilles rises above the limitations of his individuality to become the embodiment of his nation, which, as his personal charismatic power expands, itself becomes imbued with his character; the Danaans, too, are firelike (19. 362). The daemon which is Argos incarnate possesses all the Argives.

The transfiguration of Argos depends upon the extension of Achilles' love, upon his own exaltation—that is the import of the similes. The gleam of the shield is likened first to the moon (19. 374), the cosmic light which, in its fullness, actually appears on the surface of the shield (18. 484). Homer declares that art and reality form a continuum. The wondrous artistry of the shield is what causes the artifact to have such an awesome effect upon its beholders. Next, the shield, like the aegis in Book 18, becomes a beacon of hope, a moral rallying point, a focus for the community as it observes its chief defender arming himself for the national battle (19. 375–80). As the shield replaces the aegis, active involvement fulfills Achilles' intention; and the order of Zeus takes human form.

The simile of the mariners reasserts the present idealized state of the Achaians, for they are identified with the sailors. Like them, the Argives are separated by the sea from their loved ones (19. 376). Achilles' reenlistment is the signal that their return is imminent. In their state of exaltation, of unanimity epitomized, the Achaians themselves are raised to the transcendent level from which Achilles derives the force of his own transfiguration. Previous to the restoration of national harmony, they were unable to look upon the shield (19. 14–15). Now, however, it is precisely by looking upon it that they, like Achilles, are magnified; such is the pragmatic, didactic effectiveness of Hephaistos' art. Clive Bell's aesthetic analysis fits: "The contemplation of pure form leads to a state of extraordinary exaltation and complete detachment from the concerns of life . . . The emotion which exalts has been transmitted through the forms contemplated, by the artist who created them" (p. 68). Through the agency of Hephaistos the divine ordering fire is humanized, both in Achilles and in the other Argives; all are ready to subordinate individual ambitions to the common good.

Yet another simile compares Achilles' helmet to a star (19. 382). Many stars appear upon the surface of the shield, and we have already seen how Achilles' armor is described from Priam's point of view as the warrior goes forth to meet Hektor. The celestial simile Homer employs recalls that used to signify the armor's communal role in Book 19; for the image in Book 22 reveals the ominous nature of the coming duel:

> he swept across the flat land in full shining, like that star
> which comes on in the autumn and whose conspicuous brightness
> far outshines the stars that are numbered in the night's darkening,
> the star they give the name of Orion's Dog, which is brightest
> among the stars, and yet is wrought as a sign of evil
> and brings on the great fever for unfortunate mortals.
> Such was the flare of the bronze that girt his chest in his running.
>
> (22. 26–32)

Well might Priam groan aloud at this epiphany! (22. 33). Homer twice asserts the paradoxical nature of the Dog Star, splendidly beautiful but malign. And this particular heavenly body—which appears *upon* the shield as well—is highly appropriate to the context in which it is presented, in juxtaposition with the old age of Priam and of Hekabe on the wall, and with the declining moments of Troy itself. This is not the summer star of Diomedes (as in 5. 1–8), but one which shines in autumn, the harbinger of winter. To liken Achilles to that star which is a glory to itself but a herald of great ill for those whom it influences is Homer's way of giving his hero poetic license to act freely as he must at this point, without concern for anything but his radical purpose of reordering the world by rooting out disorder.

But the description of Achilles' arming in Book 19 implies that the armor's potential is barely tapped by the national stature it has allowed Achilles to assume. The fire of Hephaistos which forged the armor is eternal; and the man who enjoys its support may himself rise to its transcendent level. So the shield shines, not only for the contemporary Achaians who follow it, but also "into the high air" (19. 380). When Homer says that the armor, like wings, lifts Achilles he means that his hero has at last realized his supernatural potential—immortal, beyond time and space—as "shepherd of his people" (19. 386). As the arming ends, Argos becomes, for the momentous engagement with its mortal national enemy, Achilles; and Achilles, Argos. From now on he will use the generic "we" (as in 21. 393).

The suspension of natural law, the breach of its separation among the various realms of living and nonliving things, continues from the arming, to expand throughout the orderly warfare Achilles now initiates. Critics have marked, in Books 20–22, a change of tone from the otherwise consistent realism of the *Iliad*. Bowra explains that in these books we seem to be witnessing a more "primitive stage of heroic poetry," although Homer has, in the *Iliad*, carefully "confined [it] to a special sphere" (*Heroic Poetry*, p. 565). But Achilles' behavior at this crucial point in the war- and wrath-stories must be examined more carefully; the "change of tone" is more than just a suspension of narrative realism to dramatize the importance of Achilles' reentry. Instead, it is another example of Homer finding a way to express an extraordinary situation: Achilles is out of his mind. The warfare he now initiates is orderly from Zeus' farsighted viewpoint, because it results in the final destruction of disorderly Troy; but viewed from the narrative ground-level, his present way of fighting is unnatural and inhuman. To explain it one way, Zeus has possessed Achilles, though with Achilles' full acquiescence, to make of him a finely tuned instrument of order. Achilles himself, however, is as crazy as a dog; the divine excess in him has consumed the man, so that he breaks all the civilized rules of war that he once, in the campaign against Thebes, was the first to institute and uphold. To restore order, disorder must be destroyed by a force that transcends all orderly categories; Achilles, once he dons the armor, is that elemental force. Like Hera in Book 14, Achilles here no longer has the slightest respect for order; accidentally he may be serving the right cause but in himself he contains only mad violence. As a result, his behavior is bizarre, at the least; his perceptions are as exaggerated as his actions and his words. Mounting his chariot, Achilles addresses his horses—and they reply! (19. 403). As the fight progresses, rivers and fire engage in elemental conflict: transcendent, superhuman (21. 342) against transitory, subhuman, force; being versus change (21. 320 ff.). Achilles himself is likened to an inhuman fire which destroys a forest tree by tree, just as he demolishes Troy warrior by warrior (20. 490–93). He now appears exactly as Patroklos had described him in his antisocial state of mind in Book 16: as an inanimate being—but fire, instead of water (which may reflect Zeus' superiority over Poseidon, since Hephaistos serves the Olympian sky-god). Ultimately, however, Achilles' present inhumanity has a positive sense, as it didn't in Book 16; for he is now applying it against his enemies instead of against his friends. But he is terribly inhuman nonetheless, "gigantic" (22. 92) as the towering rock which threatens to fall upon his foes.

He is like the terrible lion who cares not for his own life but desires only to massacre Aineias (20. 165–73)—though not even a lion is so foolhardy. Or he is the young man who leads the proud bull to the slaughter exactly as the lions do on the shield (20. 403–5). Or, in another metaphor, he reduces his enemies to the intimidated state of fawns (21. 29). The animal imagery is significantly generic; individually they are anonymous. And it is sheer brute force that Achilles represents, too essential to be identified with a name. (Beowulf, who confronts Grendel with his bare hands, exercises the same animal force derived from the heart of life itself.) He directs his horses to trample down living men as oxen grind barley beneath their hooves (20. 495–502). He is immortal in behavior as well as in origin (21. 18). He is an insatiable dolphin, devouring all unwary fish (21. 22–26). And to the fish he consigns Lykaon (21. 122–27) and Asteropaios (21. 203–4). In his swift, unerring, relentless pursuit, Achilles is like the marauding black eagle, the dread of all (22. 252–54).

Throughout his furious exaltation Achilles is nonetheless aware that his extraordinary individuality is being possessed by an overarching force to achieve the destruction of an unnatural society. War is always inhumane, but inhuman only in a restricted sense; its inhumanity is sometimes justified in history by the necessity for one society to extinguish another that has committed crimes against the social system itself. That is why the Olympian art of the smith and of the poet, too, has transhumanized the epic's major man to the status of an ideal, generic agent of human order reasserting itself through the expulsion of disorder. When Achilles confronts Hektor and refuses his request for an honorable death, they meet not as individuals capable of personal love (as Hektor met with Aias, or Glaukos with Diomedes) but as avatars of their respective nations. "Achilles at this moment," says Bespaloff, "is aware of not being a man, and admits it" (p. 43): " 'As there are no trustworthy oaths between men and lions, / nor wolves and lambs have spirit that can be brought to agreement / but forever these hold feelings of hate for each other, / so there can be no love between you and me, nor shall there be' " (22. 262–65). So he accomplishes Zeus' purpose, clearing the way, by killing Hektor, for the restoration of social order in the human world. Only after that has been accomplished can Achilles be human once again, can he be himself. Then he will treat the suppliant Priam as befits a man who knows what it is to love another—and as Zeus demands.

Now, however, Achilles must immortalize his new identity by performing the deed which will insure the temporal survival of his people. He speaks to Hektor as Argos would to Troy. They cannot swear a common oath because Hektor's contractual powers are unequal to Achilles' (22. 266). Hektor's city is destined for extinction, because it has been an unnatural threat to the social system and to Agamemnon's Argos. The Trojan has no communal authority to support his oath, no bond of common background with Achilles. Not their similarity as individual heroes, but their distinction as Troy and Argos, determines Achilles' attitude. Because the communal role each man plays is the primary one now, concord (like that between Glaukos and Diomedes) is impossible for them. Achilles' unforgiving attitude here reasserts the transformation of personal into generic revenge; he demands payment from Hektor for " 'all those / sorrows of my companions you killed' " (22. 271–72). Those who would call Achilles' motivation purely personal must explain why he does not invoke the name of Patroklos at this significant point.

The force of his love for Patroklos led to Achilles' change of attitude that made possible his willing possession by Zeus' ordered rage. Love for one man is now extended maniacally to embrace all the Argives. Achilles' self-love, too, is transformed and shared among his fellowmen, as the Achaians themselves are possessed, for the duration, by a previously unknown military effectiveness. Only through such an energetic outpouring of love and self, the *Iliad* implies, can the individual find access to perpetuation in memory. We may call Achilles' *initial* motive personal. But Hephaistos has given him the shield. And its strength is so vast that as he carries it into battle all the Danaans are protected behind it, behind Achilles. Achilles, the human god and divine man, becomes identical with Argos, becomes the blind power of Argos' righteousness, an object of grief and rage; and the transcendent spirit of order enters the transitory world of living men, embodied in both an individual and in a nation. As Helen was, involuntarily, an object of disorder, Achilles has allowed himself to be made an object of order—at the expense of his own sanity.

9. Against Hektor

Until Patroklos is avenged Achilles will maintain his dedication to Strife. But this time it is the good Strife (for whom disorder is just one of the faces of order) that compels him to direct the full force of his enmity against Hektor when, before, the evil Strife had directed it against Agamemnon. Like the army in the besieged city, Achilles goes out to bring the threatened destruction upon the threatening antagonist. Homer has prepared Hektor to be a proper victim of Achilles' new wrath in two significant ways: Hektor must, like Achilles, embody his society and he must, like Troy, be disorderly. And, in fact, Hektor is, at this point, deluded by what he considers to be his irresistible strength. His single breach of order was in carrying the rightfully defensive combat against the Achaians and, subsequently, slaying Patroklos with unnaturally self-righteous brutality. But the single crime committed by Hektor is sufficient to condemn him to death at the same time that it firmly identifies him with his ill-fated nation.

Hektor's temporarily erratic behavior, moreover, makes him appear very like the old Achilles in the quarrel—whose armor he is now wearing. Or, like Pandaros, Hektor follows the direction of evil Strife. The imagery is perfectly appropriate to the characterization: Hektor removes his old armor, which had identified him properly, to don the arms of Achilles (17. 192 ff.). Hektor, at this moment, is deeply in error; Zeus himself intervenes to interpret the earthly scene from his orderly transcendent perspective (17. 199–206). But Hektor, perhaps too fully under the control of his delusion, is not allowed to hear the words of Zeus. Zeus speaks, instead, directly to Homer's audience, revealing to us the orderly nature of Homeric poetry. Hektor must be allowed to fall into this fatal error so that the plan of Zeus may be fulfilled and order reestablished among men. The plan of Zeus and the didactic purpose of the poet are here virtually indistinguishable.

Zeus equates Hektor's donning of the armor with suicide. The armor covers his identity as the dust will cover the face of Achilles in his ritual mourning; both maskings of identity are temporary, but Hektor's is fatally temporary. The arms of Achilles will not protect the life of their improper bearer, but will destroy him (17. 199–201). Hektor's behavior is now doubly reprehensible—in taking the offensive and killing the closest friend of the one Achaian whose reengagement can lead to Troy's destruction, and in compounding the crime by assuming that primary individual's very identity, equating his own merely human prowess with the semidivine might of Achilles (17. 202–4). We now understand that Patroklos' error was the same, the assumption of another man's identity (and incomplete at that, since he didn't take Achilles' spear) for the most important confrontation of his life. Homer asserts the elemental aspect, the *typicality* of the duel between Hektor and Achilles, by noting that the two heroes chase each other around the city of Priam, "while all the gods were looking upon them" (22. 166). The circular pursuit, likened to the patterns of a game, recalls the peaceful circularity of the dance upon the shield (22. 162–65). In a sense, the duel is poetic—since each combatant, in his own way, is personally detached from his own acts. Here the poet underlines the importance of the circular pattern by employing a strikingly effective narrative technique, an unusually precise and calculated simile. He compares the pursuit to a Sisyphian kind of dream, reducing the film, so to speak, first to slow motion; and then projecting it frame by frame until, at last, he presents the chase as a vivid still picture: "As in a dream a man is not able to follow one who runs / from him, nor can the runner escape, nor the other pursue him, / so he could not run him down in his speed, nor the other get clear" (22. 199–201). As the poet suggests the suspension of his usual narrative momentum, his art becomes an imitation of the pictorial art of the smith-god. He presents the two men locked in mortal combat eternally, like figures on a Grecian urn. Homer emphasizes the pattern of their duel so forcefully so that we will retain the pattern itself—an essential pattern—in our memory, and ponder its significance.

The kind of individuality stressed throughout the duel is that primary individuality, possessed by both men, since each man has been identified with all his people. That is the emphasis in the common oath requested by Hektor and refused by Achilles (22. 260 ff.). And Hektor finally realizes that his temporal individuality is doomed because Troy is destined for destruction. The forces of order—governmental and poetic—have treated him well, or as well as possible under the circumstances: Hektor must die, but he is granted a reprieve from total oblivion. His blindness is removed just before the final engagement begins: he resigns his temporal selfhood to death, but, in determining to die struggling, he consigns his eternal identity to memory (22. 304–5).

The dream sequence is now broken; the pursuit, which allowed both Hektor and Homer's audience a time for reflection, has ended. As the fateful action begins, the imagery is once again dramatic; Achilles' new shield protects him in this cosmically orderly endeavor (22. 313–14; cf. 22. 290). But Hektor's shield is no defense to him—because Achilles knows the weak spots in his old armor. Through the flaw in his old identity, Achilles slays Hektor with his flawless spear (22. 325); while Hektor's spear hits but is stopped by Achilles' divine shield (22. 290). The contrast between the spears, and between the shields, suggests again the difference between the societies represented by the two heroes. Consider, first, the shields which stand for the communal dimension. It is appropriate that Hektor should bear Achilles' old shield because Troy *is* as Argos *was* during the quarrel, when Achilles' old, erratic, identity prevailed. The nation should protect the individual, as Achilles' new shield does; but Troy does not support Hektor. So Hektor's individuality, like his power to make common oaths, is undefined; it loses its essential value. That is why his spear, which is *not* that of Achilles, cannot pierce the great shield. But Achilles' spear is effective because his nation does support him; their relationship is perfectly reciprocal: society protects the individual by defending him from aggressors (the shield); the individual protects the nation by attacking its enemies (the spear). Finally, Achilles' spear is the one he's always used because it represents the human part of his nature; Achilles' basic humanity, its potential for order (expressed in his love for Patroklos), in the end, extends to all Argos. It is interesting that Achilles' old armor, moreover, had been associated, in the description of it that Homer gives at the time of Hektor's unnatural arming, with the Uranian gods (17. 195). As the new shield, then, made by the Olympian Hephaistos, overcomes the old, so does Achilles' defeat of Hektor signify the victory of Zeus' providential order over the arcane forces of chaos generally symbolized by the Uranians. In other words, the human potential for order overcomes the human potential for disorder, represented by Hektor and the armor he wears to his death.

Achilles' humanity is both his own glory and his downfall. More than any other figure in the *Iliad*, he seems prone to death. In taking up the war, he condemns himself to death, after all; yet in so doing Achilles realizes the divine depth of his humanity—since only by accepting death does man learn of the immortality of continuing memory. This moribund quality of Homer's hero is the result of the enormous tension in which his dual nature must exist; in short, Achilles' humanity is not capable of supporting the excesses of emotion and self-confidence to which his divinity sometimes leads him. The oath he swears over the dying Hektor is a case in point. Achilles disdains Hektor's suppliant posture and calls him a dog, unwilling to admit his humanity (22. 345). He wishes, like Hekabe and Hera, to eat the flesh of his defeated enemy raw (22. 346–48); at any rate, the dogs will eat it (22. 348, 354), and no ransom, not even if Priam should give him Hektor's weight in gold, will redeem his body (22. 349–52). He will not allow Hektor, in death, to be restored to his family (22. 352–53); in his madness, he means to deprive Hektor of this final nobility, this last remnant of honorable humanity.

In the light of Achilles' generic role at this point, the oath can be explained easily enough: it is made for the ears of all those who would threaten Argos, now or in time to come—a brutally primitive warning of superior strength, but serving a basic orderly purpose. Yet with respect to Achilles the man it is patently excessive, recalling the equal rashness of Achilles' oath in Book 1 not to fight unless the fire came to his own ships. Hektor himself recognizes the oath as an indication of Achilles' fatal weakness: " 'I know you well as I look upon you, I know that I could not / persuade you, since indeed in your breast is a heart of iron. / Be careful now; for I might be made into the gods' curse / upon you, on that day when Paris and Phoibos Apollo / destroy you in the Skaian gates, for all your valour' " (22. 356–60). Achilles' oath represents an individual's fall from order not from insufficiency but from superfluity. Achilles, in his unnecessary speech, goes beyond the limits of his assigned orderly role; his behavior, therefore, parallels Patroklos' and Hektor's, in their moments of blindness. Achilles has achieved Zeus' orderly purpose in dealing Hektor a mortal wound; and was chosen by his fate to be the agent of order because of his supernatural potential. That potential, in his reengagement with Troy, was directed by the good Strife. Now, however, the evil Strife has taken possession of him, since her sister's work is finished. The pattern of the quarrel is repeated. It is not the communal, but the egocentric Achilles who displays this subhuman attitude so different from his superhuman effectiveness. If Achilles is to be rehumanized he must somehow contradict this sacrilegious oath; he must atone for the whole mad business. That is what he does in Book 24 where Hektor's request, now made by Priam, is granted almost as if it were a programmatic eventuality.

Homer's characterization of Achilles is subtle, his development of the hero's personality never ceasing for a moment. So the oath not only represents a lapse of Achilles' communal stature, but also indicates the continual tension between the new identity and the old, between the quarrel-wrath and the revenge-wrath. Achilles' words and acts immediately after the oath and Hektor's death suggest the ambivalence of outlook which distinguishes him as being the most introspective of all Homer's characters. Following the customary procedure over the fallen victim, Achilles reclaims his old armor (22. 368–69). But that this is indeed a reclamation of what had formerly been his own is not marked, either by him or by the narrator. It would seem, from the silent deed, that whatever ambiguity remained in Achilles' attitude has been resolved; that the new has completely overshadowed the old Achilles. But his proclamation to the Achaians reveals that the ambivalence is stronger now than ever:

> 'Friends, who are leaders of the Argives and keep their counsel:
> since the gods have granted me the killing of this man
> who has done us much damage, such as not all the others together
> have done, come, let us go in armour about the city
> to see if we can find out what purpose is in the Trojans,
> whether they will abandon their high city, now that this man
> has fallen, or are minded to stay, though Hektor lives no longer.
> Yet still, why does the heart within me debate on these things?
> There is a dead man who lies by the ships, unwept, unburied:
> Patroklos: and I will not forget him, never so long as
> I remain among the living and my knees have their spring beneath me.
> And though the dead forget the dead in the house of Hades,
> even there I shall still remember my beloved companion.
> But now, you young men of the Achaians, let us go back, singing
> a victory song, to our hollow ships; and take this with us.
> We have won ourselves enormous fame; we have killed the great Hektor
> whom the Trojans glorified as if he were a god in their city.'
>
> (22. 378–94)

The psychological complexity of this speech makes it as hard to analyze as are the subtleties of an actual personality. Once Achilles had decided to reenter the conflict, the death of Hektor was inevitable, the doom of Troy irrevocable, the restoration of Argos assured. For Hektor epitomized both the social threat and the personal source of Achilles' anguish (22. 380–81). At first Achilles asserts the interrelationship between his potent individuality and the principle of order as the source of this victory over the common enemy (22. 378–80). He also recognizes Hektor's pivotal role in the Trojan system, and knows that that system is now ripe for the fall (22. 381–84). He seems eager to have it done with, to fulfill the potential of his national stature in the final definitive action. His concern is all with the communal interest, as the good Strife would dictate.

Abruptly, however, his mind turns to Patroklos (22. 385). Perhaps his dwelling upon the results of his deeds leads Achilles to recall their original motivation; or perhaps it is at this moment that evil Strife usurps her sister's possession of Achilles' mind. At any rate, the fall of Troy, although it is now certainly imminent, is postponed. Of all the suspensions of narrative development in the *Iliad* this one is certainly the most momentous, the one most essential to the ultimate character of Homer's epic. It places the satisfaction of Patroklos' honor before that of Argos. Menelaos must wait until Achilles' personal responsibility to his friend has been fulfilled before receiving his reward, the return of Helen. The conjugal relationship is one which has prevailed, more or less strongly, in both the familial and the heroic society. But Homer considers the kind of personal love that Achilles has for Patroklos as the necessary basis of the new, synthetic social system; even marital love should be as personally strong as this love (suggested by Achilles' reaction to Briseis' abduction). That is why Achilles' love is given priority here. Homer makes the funeral, with its taste of peace and concord, the experiential basis for the return of Hektor's body to the suppliant Priam. Priam, in effect, will take the place of Patroklos to share Achilles' deep affection for a living individual. The result of the transference will be a model for general, purely human, community.

Yet Homer builds this final order out of Achilles' present disorder. Consider the rashness of his vow to remember Patroklos even in death, which he himself admits to be unnatural (22. 389–90); he holds on to the dead, because he has no human object for his still burning emotion. Or consider how Agamemnon must regard the returning army, singing its song of victory (22. 392); it brings back with it, not Helen, but the body of Hektor (22. 392). That is certainly cause for gratitude and pride. But, until Helen is returned and Troy destroyed and looted, the ships, after all, will remain hollow (22. 392). Would he not consider Achilles' demand to hold the funeral first as being somewhat whimsical and headstrong? If so, Agamemnon would no doubt be advised to remain silent, as indeed he does. Achilles has assured for himself the unanimous support of the army in his plan. If it is a compromise he counsels, the army is blind to that. For Achilles proves an expert propagandist; his speech ends with the extension of his glory to his companions. He employs, in contrast to the opening of the speech (22. 379), the collective "we" (22. 393–94). In order to accomplish his personal desire, Achilles enlists the entire army in his cause by sharing his renown with all the Achaians. He suggests that every one of his companions was necessary in the killing of a man who was worshipped like a god. Do the Argives forget that, when the time for killing arrived, Achilles refused their cooperation? (22. 394). Yet they will be rewarded for their forgetfulness when, in the games, Achilles will remain passive as they participate. In this sense Homer provides a model by which the effect of the individual upon a culture is communicable. Achilles' idiosyncratic insistence upon the funeral changes Argos from a tenuous to a stable new society, affirming its synthetic values.

Quite a different conclusion has equal validity. Achilles may be thought to counsel the return because he senses that Argos is not, after all, as unified as it must be before going against Troy definitively. With his help it has destroyed Troy's primary defender. But the very fact that Hektor's death makes the death of Troy necessary tells Achilles that a society which depends upon a single individual is always on the brink of destruction. So Argos' remaining weakness concerns him above all others: for Patroklos' name to survive, Argos must survive. He must reconcile himself with Agamemnon more completely by returning the gesture the king had made in offering him the fine gifts. Achilles had set them aside in his impatience to begin the battle; now, during the funeral games, the gesture will be reciprocated. Nor would Achilles join the Achaian feast before his engagement with Hektor; he will do so in Book 23. The exaltation of the Danaans that accompanied the arming of Achilles was no less significant for being a momentary phenomenon like the fire to which it was compared. But the unanimity of the funeral games shows signs of a social integrity which has every promise of survival for a long time. Finally there is a positive consideration that may have influenced Achilles' sudden change of mind. His new plan conforms to the didactic purpose of the poet, to the governmental order of Zeus; for it will result in the communication of an exemplary pattern of relations, in making a matter of public recognition, in a religious ritual witnessed by the gods, the strong personal love between Achilles and Patroklos. The games become the dramatic equivalent of the shield of Hephaistos—just as they imitate the symbolic action upon its surface. The prizes distributed by Achilles, like the cup he gives to Nestor, will remind all beholders that this special friendship is the basic model for social formation. The funeral prizes, then, were foreshadowed imagistically by the prize the judge gives to the best speaker, on the shield. So intricately enmeshed are the thematic patterns in this poem that both interpretations are valid.

10. Against Troy

Achilles' animosity toward Troy is, of course, simultaneous with his hatred for Hektor. He has identified the individual with his society from the start, when he vowed to slay twelve Trojan youths on Patroklos' bier so that the Trojan women would mourn for his friend (18. 336–42).

Lykaon's suppliant posture prefigures Hektor's, symbolizing Achilles'
equal treatment of all Trojans (21. 64–97). As he will say to Hektor also,
Achilles tells Lykaon that he will accept no ransom (21. 99)—just as he
will make no common oaths. He speaks of his former individuality, of his
mercy in the heroic mode (21. 100–02); but declares that his new determination is that all Trojans must, in keeping with the plan of the gods, die
(21. 103–5). Even Lykaon must die; Achilles scolds him for thinking that
his selfhood is in some way immune from the common fate of all mortals,
Patroklos and Achilles himself included (21. 106–13). Slaying him without mercy (21. 114–19), Achilles slings Lykaon's body into the river,
boasting derisively (21. 120–27). His terrible actions have an emblematic
nature, strongly emphasizing Achilles' generic stature and crazed state
of mind. And his words are those of nationalistic fervor and insanity:

> 'Die on, all; till we come to the city of sacred Ilion,
> you in flight and I killing you from behind; and there will not
> be any rescue for you from your silvery-whirled strong-running
> river, for all the numbers of bulls you dedicate to it
> and drown single-foot horses alive in its eddies. And yet
> even so, die all an evil death, till all of you
> pay for the death of Patroklos and the slaughter of the Achaians
> whom you killed beside the running ships, when I was not with them.'
>
> (21. 128–35)

Achilles is more the maniacal reformer than the rebel. His new function
is to re-create the synthetic society upon a firmer foundation than it has
had both in Argos and in the Troad. Here Homer emphasizes the
destructive element of reformation. Achilles' rhetoric makes it clear,
however, that even in his madness he still honors his relationships with
Patroklos and with the other Argives. He hates Troy, then, not because
he detests the social system itself, but because he respects it now more
than ever. It has supported him in his grief, it has forgiven his wrath; the
Achaians cooperate willingly in his revenge. Troy, on the other hand,
must be destroyed entirely so that it won't become the model—inferior to
the exemplary status Argos expresses under Achilles' new regime—for
future social existence. Weak in itself, through the selfishness of pivotal
individuals and the attempted assimilation of a foreign royal wife, Troy
is also a threat to the stability of the Argive system—both conjugal and
interpersonal (with respect to Helen and Patroklos).

Achilles' speech expresses, in its general condemnation of all Trojans,
an orderly attitude, as the elemental conflict which follows it signifies.
The river rises against him. His mad lust for blood is unnatural; yet it is

not for personal revenge, but for national revenge that he is possessed. Zeus has so used Patroklos to destroy Troy and initiate a new order among men. So Hephaistos, against whom no god can stand, comes to the rescue of Achilles and, in a reverse of the natural order, defeats the water with his unquenchable flame (21. 357 ff.). The transcendent spirit of order is made incarnate to signify the rightness of Achilles' words and deeds. The gods must support a necessary apocalypse, even if the bearer of the apocalypse is temporarily outrageous. Poseidon's speech to Apollo gives a similar impression. He recalls the history of Troy, showing that it has ever been as characteristically disorderly as it is in the present (21. 442–47). But Troy's doom is sealed when its disorder affects another society—just as Zeus threatens Hera and Poseidon when they would jeopardize the harmony of Olympos. The Troadic system must be destroyed due to the crime of the contemporary individual, Paris, against Argos and against Zeus' law. The destruction coincidentally will avenge the ignominy suffered by the gods at the hands of Laomedon. Note that both men are royal; their erring behavior has collective repercussions. Destruction, Poseidon concludes, must include the Trojan wives and children as well as their warriors (21. 458–60). For the moment, Apollo is convinced; even his sister Artemis cannot restore his willingness to take arms on behalf of the Trojans (21. 467–77); he stands impassively by as Hera beats her (21. 489 ff.). So Homer prepares Apollo for the more properly objective role he will play in Book 24, protecting Hektor with his aegis because the Trojan is a worthy man, not because he is a Trojan.

There is one anomaly in the pattern of Achilles' destruction of the individuals who confront him. That is his meeting with Aineias. This Trojan's confrontation with Achilles is qualified from its very inception by the fact that it is forced upon him unwillingly by Apollo disguised as Lykaon (20. 79–90). Yet there is nobility even in Aineias' hesitation. His objection to the proposal that he should combat Achilles does not derive from an inferior, fatally flawed, society. Rather it comes from Aineias' positive recognition of the temporary natural superiority of Achilles and, by implication, of Argos (20. 90 ff.). He tells Apollo that no man now can fight Achilles rightfully because Achilles is supported by the force of order itself (20. 97–99). The Trojans can win this war, he concludes, only if Achilles again removes himself from it (20. 100–102). Nevertheless Apollo's rebuttal is cogent enough to convince Aineias that he is capable of meeting Achilles in battle because, like Achilles, he shares the resources of divinity (20. 104–9). Aineias, then, is a singular individual in his own right. The difference between his special quality among men and that of Achilles is accidental—simply that Aineias' time for exaltation to social stature has not yet come, whereas Achilles is destined to prove supreme at this moment in history.

As the two heroes approach each other on the plain, the poet presents them as being equally extraordinary, each among his respective companions (20. 158–59). Achilles' address to Aineias suggests that he is puzzled by the Trojan's courage and purpose (20. 177 ff.); he does not, after all, know that Apollo influenced Aineias to stand against him. Achilles deduces from his incomplete evidence that Aineais desires sovereignty in Troy and tells him that his desire can't be fulfilled, even if Aineias were to kill him, since Priam will honor his own sons first (20. 179–83). In any event, Achilles warns, Aineias will not be able to kill him (20. 186–94); therefore he should return to the protection of the Trojan ranks, lest he be the victim instead (20. 196–98). For some reason Achilles seems unwilling to slay this man, an attitude in striking contrast with his general enmity toward the Trojans.

Aineias' social temperament is explicit in his proud but courteous reply. He scolds Achilles for treating him like a child; they must not act like children or squabbling women (20. 201, 211, 245, 251–56), controlled by unmanly emotion. He knows the proper manners of wars and hatred (20. 202); for he, too, is descended from the gods. Aineias compares Achilles' divine genealogy with his own, more glorious, one (20. 206–41); and concludes that Zeus himself, to whose will Aineias is attuned perfectly, will determine the issue of their conflict. Perhaps because Aineias' redoubtable heritage and association with the order of Olympian Zeus warns him that this engagement is somehow disorderly—suspended from his assigned opposition to Troy, transcending the historical events of the Iliadic world—Achilles' unwillingness turns to fear. For once, he is terrified by the attack of an enemy (20. 261–62). Even Achilles, in his new generic identity, recognizes the power of another primary individual, one perhaps more orderly than he is, who can also stand for community; and because Aineias' social stature is not, like Hektor's, associated primarily with the city of Troy, recognition turns to fear. In fact, Aineias' spear strikes the great shield, which moans from the impact (20. 260). This is when Achilles holds it away, afraid that it will prove insufficient to protect him (20. 261).

Achilles' sudden encouragement almost seems to be the result of the narrator's scolding words (20. 265–66); there is no other explicit explanation of his reversal. Presumably Achilles has recalled to mind the purpose he now pursues under the auspices of the transcendent spirit of order. If Aineias insists on acting like a Trojan, Achilles will treat him like one. So his spear pierces Aineias' shield straight through, nearly killing him (20. 273–80). The poet has arrived at a thematic nexus. He has presented both men as being on the side of order; but now one endangers the life of the other. That is why at this point Poseidon declares it proper for him to intervene. Aineias' close escape but apparently forthcoming death proves to the gods allied with Hera that an inimical deity, Apollo, must have inspired Aineias' recklessness. Poseidon declares it is not orderly for Aineias, guiltless himself, to suffer for the sorrows of others (20. 293–98). Therefore they must prevent what would be a most disorderly occurrence; Zeus himself would be angry if Achilles kills Aineias (20. 301–2). Here again Homer reveals the universal foresight of Zeus, recalling his willingness to allow the death of his own son Sarpedon, because the historical order of human life demanded it. Poseidon suggests that Zeus' previous love for Troy is destined to bear fruit in the future creation of a new society, more durable than Troy, from the same seed as that from which Priam's nation issued:

'It is destined that he shall be the survivor,
that the generation of Dardanos shall not die, without seed
obliterated, since Dardanos was dearest to Kronides
of all his sons that have been born to him from mortal women.
For Kronos' son has cursed the generation of Priam,
and now the might of Aineias shall be lord over the Trojans,
and his sons' sons, and those who are born of their seed hereafter.'
(20. 302–8)

The future of Troy is made to parallel that of Argos itself; its destruction, after all, will not be total. One individual, an orderly one with divine potential, will survive to re-create a new society—precisely as Achilles, the Achaian counterpart of Aineias, will reform the Argive coalition. The continuity of human life, its progressive aspect by which the present builds upon the past (in the case of Argos) and the future upon the present (Troy), is asserted at the same time that the necessity for the annihilation of disorderly elements is affirmed. Aineias is saved from Achilles' righteous wrath by the gods, the very ones who favor Argos (20. 310–45); and Achilles, momentarily sane, recognizes the orderliness of their intervention and concurs with it (20. 347–48). His brotherhood with Aineias is implicit in Achilles' compliance with the purpose of the gods; it foreshadows his explicit affinity with Priam, just as it recalls his love for Patroklos.

In the altogether special case of Aineias, then, Homer tempers the destructiveness of war by allowing his audience a glimpse of its constructive purpose; from Homer's vision of universality and continuity, expressed in this unique battlefield confrontation between heroes, the

Aeneid will be born. But, after all, Aineias is presented as being, in this sense, no more a professed Trojan than Priam will be when he abdicates his royal role to become stranger-suppliant in the camp of Achilles. Aineias will found a new Troy, as Achilles in Book 23 founds a new Argos—or as Odysseus founds a new Ithaca in the *Odyssey*.

Those who are unqualifiedly Trojans, however, are uniformly victims of Achilles' wrath—like brush burnt out by an amoral fire. Homer portrays the death throes of Troadic society in the cumulative anguish of its component individuals. Agenor's introspective deliberation is an example; he ponders the dilemma in his mind, whether he should stand against Achilles and consequently die defending his nation; or run, defending himself, and let his nation die. But the latter alternative, Agenor recognizes, is only an illusion. There is no place for him to run to, no valid or stable structure in which he could survive by himself. The isolated individual is nothing at all; therefore he determines, in much the same manner as Hektor, to die (21. 550–70). Before the righteous might of Achilles, the Trojan army literally disintegrates. The whole dissolves as the parts disperse, each in his own way. The collective is reduced to an ineffective, amorphous mass of self-concerned individuals: "all this time the rest of the Trojans fled in a body / gladly into the town, and the city was filled with their swarming. / They dared no longer outside the wall and outside the city / to wait for each other and find out which one had got away / and who had died in the battle, so hastily were they streaming / into the city, each man as his knees and feet could rescue him" (21. 606–11). Their headlong retreat vividly presents the effect of an orderly society upon a disorderly one. The protective shell surrounding Troy is shattered. Only one individual remains outside, Hektor, who must maintain the integrity of his proper orbit as best he can alone. But the orbit is decaying.

11. For Agamemnon

Before Argos can begin its reformed existence as a durable new society, external stability must be supported by internal solidarity. Two things are necessary. One is the defeat of its national enemy and the restoration of Helen; the other is the formation of strong personal love, on the model of Achilles' friendship with Patroklos, between its primary individuals. Both requirements are fulfilled by the funeral games in Book 23. The burial of Patroklos, of course, is only made possible at all by Hektor's death—which, in turn, insures the imminent destruction of Troy. And during the funeral games Achilles and Agamemnon, providing the examples which many other important individuals will follow, demonstrate by their words and actions a mutual respect previously only implied by their complementary confessions. Achilles' acceptance of Agamemnon's propitiatory gifts symbolizes his acceptance of the framework of society. As the result of Achilles' renewed loyalty to the social system, he and the king cooperate in every way: Agamemnon himself directs the preparation of the funeral pyre (23. 110 ff.). In the morning they officiate together in the business of the pyre and burial mound (23. 235 ff.).

The gathering of the horsemen is described dramatically by recalling the genealogy of each man as well as his glorious involvement in the present war (23. 287 ff.). This, the final presentation of the Achaians in the *Iliad*, demonstrates Argos' achievement of harmony; in contrast with the presentation through the eyes of Helen on the wall, this one is given from an Achaian viewpoint. It also recalls the catalogue of ships in Book 2. There the imperfect integrity of Argos is signified by the poet's reference to the Myrmidons' absence from the assembly of forces. Because they are the greatest warriors their refusal to participate in the war undermines the effectiveness of the entire Argive confederacy (2. 686 ff.). But the internal stability of Phthia itself, as the Myrmidon games imply, remains intact as the good Strife operates among the unarmed fighters to insure the cohesiveness that comes with vigorous competition (2. 771–75). That minor integrity becomes in Book 23 the model for the major social harmony which results from the funeral games. The list of participants serves as a kind of remustering, a completed catalogue of all the individual parts of society now unanimously involved in a common purpose. Showing us who has survived the war, the list is at the same time a kind of review of the Trojan saga and a proof that Argos, the body politic, is still strong. There are no funeral games in Troy. But the Achaian games are sponsored by the leader of the Myrmidons. The species has returned to the generic fold.

Under the auspices of a social entity composed of the kind of strong personal bonds expressed in the model friendship of its leader, the games transfer the quality of the Myrmidons' harmony to the entire society. Here the individual and communal dimensions of human life are perfectly aligned with one another. Achilles holds the games to memorialize his personal friendship—fulfilling his responsibility to the honor of Patroklos, as well as marking his own honor (23. 247–48), by submitting Patroklos and his deeds to the judgment of the Danaan public. His love for the dead man is extended to embrace all the living. The cyclical continuity of the living and the dead is symbolized by the turning-post for the horse race which Nestor explicates for Antilochos: " 'Either it is the grave-mark of someone who died long ago, / or was set as a racing goal by men who lived before our time' " (23. 331–32). The mnemonic function of the artifact, as Nestor interprets it for his son, is to provide authoritative significance to the present games by revealing them to be based upon an orderly precedent. Simultaneously the stone represents a progress from past to present; formerly, Nestor suggests, it served one purpose or another. Now, in a sense, the marker serves both at once, being both a goal for the living and a memorial to the dead man whom their contest honors.

In proposing and refereeing the games, Achilles performs an orderly role like that of Odysseus carrying the sceptre in Book 2 or arranging the feast before battle in Book 19. He is the source of the prizes which simultaneously memorialize the honor of the winning contestants, of Argos, of Patroklos, and of himself. His new identity is symbolically conveyed to the recipients of the gifts through those gifts themselves. Receiver and giver become together the ideal orderly society, one epitomizing the collective, the other the individual, as they exist under the best of circumstances.

The emotion Achilles expressed in his epiphany at the trench is refined and generalized here. He does not shout during the contests but speaks with quiet force, like the silent king on the shield, neither participating nor interfering with his people; or like the perfect arbitrator in the marketplace of the shield's first city, maintaining his neutrality in the face of emotional outbursts from the various contenders. He performs a socially restorative role like that of the court poet, or of Helen with her drugs in the *Odyssey*. It is permissible now that he be the healer, with words, in peace, just as before it was proper for him to be the physician, with deeds, in war. No longer is he the self-assertive individual Agamemnon described in Book 1. 176–79. Achilles' previous willingness to serve society only insofar as he judged it served him has been recognized to be an excessive attitude, proven to be inhuman, just as Patroklos defined it. He has learned, after all, that society may provide the individual with essential services that he neither expected nor could manage without.

Achilles' new-found harmony with Agamemnon is revealed most dramatically in the contest for the spear-throwing. The king comes forward to try his hand against the others, but Achilles, respectfully, will not allow him to compete. He explains that he has two reasons for his hesitation (23. 885–97): the king is superior, by his position, to the others and should not compete with them as if he were among peers. And Achilles has no right to judge Agamemnon in such a contest; the king's power is inherited, and cannot be weighed by temporary or individualistic standards. Instead Achilles praises Agamemnon for his humility and valor and courteously offers him a prize. The happy new bond between the two primary individuals is marked by the fact that neither participates in the games. Achilles refrains from the engagement because of his de facto jurisdiction and superiority, Agamemnon since he is detached ex officio. But Homer implies a certain equivalence between them in their mutual suspension from the action.

In a sense Achilles is providing a model for the mode of kingship that Agamemnon must imitate if he is to remain the head of a new synthetic society. Books 23 and 24 can be regarded as a unit exemplifying ideal human behavior, one in a public, the other in a private, sense. The lesson for Agamemnon, in Book 23, is that he must learn to love as Achilles has loved. Although Agamemnon's courteous reaction to Achilles' diplomacy suggests that he takes the lesson to heart, Homer doesn't develop the character of the king further. It will be Achilles in Book 24 who receives a suppliant, as Agamemnon had in Book 1; but Priam will be treated very differently from Chryses. Given the king's terrible condemnation of all things Trojan, as spoken to Menelaos (6. 55–60), it must be assumed that he would neither understand nor approve of Achilles' generosity toward the Trojan ruler. Achilles consequently warns Priam (24. 653–55). Homer has not selected Agamemnon to be an exemplary individual under the new society. Achilles—and Priam—suffice for the poet's didactic purpose. But the reconciliation here suggests that we are no longer to despise Agamemnon for his former errors even though he can't replace Patroklos in Achilles' affections—a role only Priam can play. The poet's audience must accept Agamemnon, as Achilles does, for the virtues that he has, rather than demand of him behavior beyond his capabilities.

The games in themselves play an important symbolic function in the structure of the *Iliad*: they represent the accomplishment of the shield's role in the transitory action of the poem's world. Now that Hektor's death and Patroklos' funeral have insured the destruction of the old and inferior (Argos as well as Troy), and the establishment of the new social system, the potential orderliness of the arbitration in the first city can be realized. The games, then, are analogous to the dance on the shield's circumference. The contrast is between the good and evil competition, the peaceful and warlike resolution of opposition. J. J. Sheppard notes how consistently Homer emphasizes the necessity for vanquishing evil Strife from among men. That was the import of Peleus' advice (9. 254 ff.), Phoinix's exemplum (9. 479 ff.), and Achilles' final recognition of the justice of his father's counsel (18. 108). Internal animosity and quarreling destroys the γένος *génos* ("race"); to be beneficial, strife must be directed outward toward the common enemy. Within the social structure, a calmer form of contention must prevail.

Homer's ambition is not to replace war with games. War, at one historical juncture or another, is clearly necessary to insure the maintenance of a stable international structure in which the new society can exist securely. When a society is threatened, as the Myrmidon tribe is in Book 2, games can enhance its ability to fight with its enemies by providing an opportunity for practical cooperation. Or when social survival is not at stake the games can provide an outlet for natural human tensions which otherwise might result in internal dissension. Conducted properly, as they are by Achilles, the games heighten the individuals' sense of the unity of their society. Justice, in the established rules of athletic competition, heals all wounds, because it is of the ideal kind which can exist only in a controlled situation, tempered with mercy and with the recognition of the role of chance in victory and defeat. Achilles reestablishes the propriety of each individual's role.

The outcome of the horse race is a case in point (23. 566 ff.), a striking contrast with the quarrel between Agamemnon and Achilles in Book 1. The argument between Menelaos and Antilochos has every potential of issuing in disastrous, irrevocable social consequences. But instead of allowing it to do so (allowing evil Strife to step in), Menelaos acts reasonably (as Agamemnon should have acted) and Antilochos responds with humility (as Achilles should have). The result is not only the restoration of internal concord but also its enhancement. The two men part better friends than they were before; and all who observe their amicable agreement, arbitrated by Achilles, are heartened. Menelaos' generosity toward Antilochos makes us wonder how Achilles might have acted had Agamemnon conceded to him at the start by returning Chryseis without his selfish bargain. Homer shows that Strife between individuals becomes evil, not naturally, but only when one blindly sets himself against the other.

Finally the narrative position of the games recalls that of the shield's description at the same time that the games provide a kind of balance to the shield, inasmuch as one precedes and the other follows Achilles' furious revenge for Patroklos. They provide a welcome respite from the high tragedy of Hektor's death and the brutal pathos of Patroklos' funeral; they also serve to renew the audience's powers of attention and emotional response for the continuation of Achilles' callous treatment of Hektor's body at the opening of Book 24—and its transformation, through the intervention of the gods, into the very different, sublimely noble, pathos of Achilles' meeting with Priam. Imagistically the games resemble the shield because they emphasize the reciprocity upon which the new society depends. Their orderly structure, like the pictorial contents of the shield, prepares the individual to assume a communal personality, to accept an orientation toward a common social purpose.

Also like the shield, the games are a kind of microcosmic recapitulation of the Iliadic world, and of the war. The gods play their familiar roles here, intervening on behalf of their favorites. Eumelos, as in the war itself, is wounded in the games. The events of the Trojan conflict pass before the mind of the listener as the singer tells of Menelaos' caution, Antilochos' boldness and ambition, Nestor's sagacity, Aias' stolid combat, Diomedes' bravado, and Odysseus' wily stratagems. The action of Achilles reconciles, before and during the games, the antitheses of the shield's world. There are two cities on the shield. Now Achilles' deeds in war (Books 20–22) and words in peace (Book 23) prove that both aspects of Strife can be united in the behavior of a single personality. Action can be so various, and yet consistent, only when it is the expression of developing character. And characterization, like imagery, distinguishes Homer's art.

12. For Priam

Achilles' new identity has been defined so far purely in terms of his reformation of Argive society in peace and in war. But, while it raises the individual to national stature, the potential of Achilles' semidivine and therefore singular love has not been exhausted. Even the old Achilles, in his indifference toward Troy, was capable of merciful and dignified relations with his enemies. In this sense the "old" and "new" Achilles are continuous. As the restorer of Argos and the avenger of Patroklos, Achilles retains a kind of detached perspective, evident in his acceptance of Aineias' escape, which comes, unlike his former indifference, from an attitude of selflessness. His speech over Hektor's body with its puzzling ambivalence represents the tension between his generic, living, hatred and his love for the dead Patroklos. One is a source of destructive action, the other linked with the reconstructive tendency; just as one is merely· transitory, the other transcendent. The second tendency culminates in Achilles' feeling for Priam.

As the funeral concludes, Achilles has effectively defined his new identity as one which will be associated in the minds of men to come with his national stature. His cruel treatment of Hektor's body after the funeral suggests at least two interpretations (24. 5 ff.). If, on the one hand, Books 23 and 24 are to be regarded as parallel, rather than progressive, facets of Achilles' development, then the opening of Book 24

is a repetition of Achilles' attitudes before the funeral—a repetition
meant to prepare for his private reconciliation, as Book 23 presented his
public resolution. On the other hand, the scene may suggest that Achilles
is yet dissatisifed with his selfhood. The foresight of Zeus has been
realized by turning Achilles' divine resources to the service of society,
making him assume a social identity. Achilles, for the historical moment
in which the fate of Troy is decided, was, so to speak, deprived of his
natural individuality and thereby dehumanized. Now that Achilles'
sacrifice has accomplished Zeus' orderly plan, the gods are less than fair
to their agent. They have, it is true, insured the memorialization of his
living social function and of his dead personal relationship with Patroklos. But they have left Achilles to live a while longer without allowing his
individuality an outlet for the expression of a vital love like his old one;
for a while it found controlled outlet in the ritual games. His divine
potential, which transformed his personal sorrow into effective social
wrath and then into social unification, is still in him, however. Because
of this the transformation is reversed, in a retrogressive sense. Righteous
wrath becomes disorderly, unnatural sorrow, as he vents his still violent
emotions against the helpless body of Hektor, the only object for his
mania. So the circle is completed, since his anger was first expressed
against himself (Book 18), then against the living Hektor (Books 20–22),
now against the dead Hektor stripped of the old armor of the old Achilles!
Because his humanity hasn't been restored to its natural balance, no
constructive recourse for action is open to the reformed Achilles; he is
still possessed but not of himself. In his love for Priam, Achilles' new
individuality will be associated with the transcendent dimension of
glory already assured to his communally effective deeds.

Nowhere is the complexity of the *Iliad*'s thematic interrelationships
more evident than it is in Book 24. Here the role played by Achilles
reflects that of Agamemnon (as the receiver of a suppliant), of Priam (as a
mourner), of Hektor (as the murderer of a precious life), even of Paris (as
one possessing what belongs to another); while Priam's position reflects
that of Chryses (as suppliant), Achilles himself, Peleus (as father),
Patroklos (as guest-friend), and of Menelaos. So are Hektor and Patroklos
associated with each other here; and Hektor with Chryseis, Briseis, and
Helen. The exchange of gifts between Achilles and Priam, moreover,
resembles the exchanges between Aias and Hektor and between Glaukos
and Diomedes. Nearly every relationship possible in the social system is
touched upon; but the emphasis is upon those more private levels at the
base of the scale: the personal bond of guest-friendship and the filial-
parental relationship.

Each set of relations—so intricate is the presentational pattern of this scene—necessarily involves all the others, making analytical explication difficult. In his grief for Hektor, Priam plays the part that Peleus will soon play. Achilles' return of the body of the old man's son becomes a tacit plea for his enemies, when he himself has been slain, to do likewise lest Peleus be deprived of the final comfort of giving Achilles an honorable burial. The association between Hektor and Patroklos follows from this one, since Achilles cannot help recalling the consolation he himself experienced in providing his friend with glorious memorialization. He well understands Priam's wish to do the same for Hektor. Achilles and Priam form a kinship of suffering, both living on, beyond the death of their dearest beloved. Achilles realizes that the satisfaction derived from the funeral rites is a great and necessary human one that should be granted to every man. He relents because he knows that the loss of Patroklos can't be remedied by persisting in a totally nationalistic orientation that would prohibit the return of Hektor's body. His dear friend has been slain unnaturally and rather than perpetuate the inversion of the natural order by retaining and further defiling Hektor's body, he returns it, mindful of his own father; and the gods, as the projection of the bard's consciousness of human orderliness, advise and support the decision.

Achilles sees in Priam, as he had in Patroklos, a reflection of himself. The old man's sorrow once again achieves the transformation of wrath to anguish. But this time the sorrow of Achilles is expressed without regard for national consideration: it is simply human. So Achilles, whose consistent respect for guests led to the formation of his friendship with the stranger Patroklos, extends to Priam a love as sincere as that he held for the young man killed by Priam's son. Perhaps youth drew Achilles and Patroklos together. Now it is old age—since both men stand close to death—which becomes the basis for Achilles' new purely personal love. Whitman notes the irony in the fact that "only after abandoning all human hope does [Achilles] at last . . . achieve his greatest communion with humanity" (p. 205).

It is Priam's example, of course, that enables Achilles to act in this purely human manner; to relinquish, that is, his formerly nationalistic orientation—and also to relinquish all claim to superficial honor, as Priam does in kissing the hands of his own son's murderer. For Hektor's death has brought Priam to lay aside his royal role in order to behave only as an individual father. Imitating Priam's suspension of his nationalistic orientation, Achilles is relieved of his communal responsibility. He becomes human once again at the same time that he finds an outlet for the expression of his selfhood—an expression that is ironically generic and personal at once. It is the gods themselves, in Book 24, whose appeal leads to this realization (371, 465–67, 485 ff.). Achilles' divine potential is realized at last in the fullest possible sense as he comes to act in an *absolute* way. Love moved Achilles first from the center of individuality only outward to the ring in which the second city appears on the shield; it made him sufficiently committed to others to save his nation. As such, his love has no redeeming effect on all humanity. The games establish Argos as a society firmly unified and harmonious. But Achilles' potential aspires to a selflessness that goes beyond the centripetal existence of a particular, temporal society. Achilles' recognition of the resemblance between Priam and his own father, indeed any father or suppliant or guest or mourner, moves him farther outward—to the circumference of the dancers and the Ocean—into attunement with the collective structure of human nature and of the orderly cosmos itself, which is now seen to be the transcendent model upon which every transitory society must be based.

Troy, even Argos, will fall, now or later. But humanity will survive these national catastrophes. Achilles' return of Hektor's body is the optimistic gesture which redeems humanity in the largest sense by offering it as an example to be preserved in memory, through which the transcendent model of human life is made accessible and imitable. This is what is signified by the aura of sublimity which surrounds their meeting, its impression of poignant nobility and austerity—so very different from the petty and mundane effect of Agamemnon's treatment of Chryses in Book 1. In their mutual determination in the face of imminent death to live with honor as long as life yet remains to them, Priam and Achilles share a detachment from everyday reality like the dancers' separation from the fictional world of the shield. Whitman explains:

When Priam appears . . . the immovable is moved. Since he has renounced his own life, Achilles can look, as it were, from a distance upon the living and their emotions, including his own. And the very detachment of his vision brings him closer than he has ever been before to real communion with his fellow humans. In a sense, Achilles has attained the truly classical ideal . . . that mysterious union of detachment and immediacy, of passion and order. (P. 218)

Sharing the physical position of the dancers on the verge of the Ocean boundary, or the perspective of the poet, "Priam and Achilles," as Whitman says, "see life whole, and with the freedom of men on the last verge of time, they forget present circumstances, and admire each other's beauty" (p. 219).

In Achilles' progress to a human viewpoint equivalent to the poet's, the social structure of man's life, outlined in the hierarchical grid, has been carefully delineated. Homer has portrayed him first as he is related to Patroklos on the purely interpersonal level (1). He has shown him, with Briseis, in the personal familial context (2); and with Thetis and Peleus in the parental familial context (3). The sincerity and depth of his affection for Patroklos makes Achilles' friend appear almost as if he were Achilles' natural brother (4). Then we have seen him associated with the unanimity of the Myrmidons, all of whom are his close companions (5). In his transfiguration Achilles was identified with Argos, his love extended to all his nation (6). In his hero's character Homer has recapitulated the progress of social development in human history. Yet the vision of the *Iliad* is cyclical as well as progressive. That is the significance of Achilles' meeting with Priam, the return to the interpersonal level (1) by which the temporal perfection of the social circle is opened to the assurance of continuity—at the same time that it is an expression of a collective orientation which is essential, transcending the temporal and the national (beyond 6).

13. For Mankind

Although Homer has prepared us for it through the consistency of his characterization, imagery, and dramatization, the meeting between Priam and Achilles nevertheless comes as a surprise. The scene is a flash of illumination in which the meaning of all that has preceded it in the *Iliad* is revealed at once and immediately.

A closer look at the process by which the total humanizing of Achilles has come about will reveal the incisiveness of Owen's statement that Homer has created "a character too big for the simple revenge story. We have seen too much of the terrific intensity of his feeling to be ready to imagine that his grief could be allayed by revenge" (p. 237). Achilles is distinguished from all other figures in the poem. Wilson explains:

As the plot unfolds, [Achilles] shows no concern for any suffering but his own. Such a feeling [as the love expressed by Hektor] is still unknown to Achilles, not because he is incapable of it, but because it has not yet been awakened by his experience. When this awakening comes, Achilles goes beyond his opponent. Hektor's sympathy embraces everyone in his family, and in his city. That of Achilles reaches out to all humanity, and transmutes even hatred of an enemy into gentleness. (P. 560).

Homer does not leave Achilles and his shield to symbolize a purely nationalistic orientation, however noble such an expression of selflessness is. That role, instead, is allotted to Aias, who symbolizes Argos in the present; and to Agamemnon, who stands for the continuing dimension of the Achaian social system. But Achilles' shield, joining past and future with an ideal present, identifies its bearer as one who comes to terms with human nature itself and, in the process, finds the satisfaction that comes from the assurance of a transcendent life—of an eternal existence in the living, divinely-supported, memory of men to come. Finding that satisfaction himself, Achilles is now ready to share it with other men, to allow Priam also to fashion a token of honor that will become material for memory—and will further enhance the memory of Achilles. He will allow the king to hold a funeral, as he himself had done to preserve the glory of his friend: "The burial is made possible by Achilles, who had slain Hektor . . . but had come at last to understand that the anger that parts men is born and dies, but the bond of their common humanity is everlasting" (p. 574). Wilson defines that bond as "the understanding that grows out of suffering and needs no statement in words, because it is so profoundly felt" (p. 573). That is why Priam can take leave of Achilles without formality, slipping away by night, and yet needn't fear that his host will be offended or reverse his promise to hold back the battle.

The operation of Zeus in Book 24 significantly adds to the glory of Achilles' achievement of total, truly divine, humanity. The gods are filled with compassion as they see him in his helpless rage defiling the body of Hektor (24. 23). The Trojan party among them urges that Hermes be sent to steal the corpse and return it secretly to Troy (24. 24). But Hera and her allies, remembering their old enmity toward Troy, do not concur in this proposal (24. 25–30). It is not by accident that they leave the decisive action up to Achilles, as Homer's image of the new man (who understands that his only access to divinity lies in his acceptance of mortality). Apollo, associated now with the lyre as the symbol of harmony rather than with his bow, stands forth to begin the divine debate in an orderly fashion. He accuses the immortals of behaving in a destructive manner, as if they, too, were deluded by evil Strife (24. 33). He balances Hektor's consistent respect for them and his generally noble life against the orderly gesture they should now make toward his body (24. 33–35). Since the gods have achieved their purposes by enforcing Hektor's separation from all he loved most dearly in life, they should restore him in death to the bosom of his family (24. 36–38). Instead of doing this, Apollo says, they have prevented such an orderly conclusion by allowing Achilles to remain beyond necessity in his exalted nationalistic posture. Now he is blinded like a lion by his wrath which no longer serves the principle of order (24. 39–43). In the dehumanized state in which they have left him, " 'Achilleus has destroyed pity, and there is not in him / any shame; which does much harm to men but profits them also' " (24. 44–45). Apollo's observation of Achilles' present attitude reveals its pathetically ironic nature. For in a more human moment Achilles had expressed his wish to destroy not pity, but the very force which now again moves him. Apollo then describes the human process by which grief is transformed into action, since it is unnatural for the living to become immovable because of an unfulfillable love for the dead (24. 46–48): " 'for the Destinies put in mortal men the heart of endurance' " (24. 49). Achilles' persistent grief instead has been turned into a rage which does no good or honor to Patroklos, to Hektor, to himself, or to any man (24.50–52). The earth itself is dishonored by his fury (24. 53–54). Achilles' mode of action is no longer exemplary.

Apollo has spoken in a way that indicates he is motivated no longer by national affinities or divine jealousies but by the principle of order itself. He appears here as he did in the feast on Olympos in Book 1, urging orderliness through the music of orderly words. And Hera, as she was then, is moved not to agree with him (24. 56): her only concern is that Achilles should be granted the greater honor (24. 57–60). She points out that it was the gods themselves, and Apollo with his lyre, who presided over the marriage of his father and mother (24. 61–63).

At this point Zeus arbitrates between the two parties and reconciles them. He assures Hera that Achilles' singularity will be remembered (24. 65–66) but agrees with Apollo's evaluation of Hektor, adding that he himself loved this man (24. 66–70). Yet it would be disrespectful to Achilles' divine potential, to the possibilities of his character, if they were to steal the body from him (24. 71–72)—a course of action Zeus therefore dismisses. For once beyond question, Zeus has a worthy plan with which all the gods comply. Even the ruler of Olympos comes into the fullness of his nature in Book 24. He summons Thetis to the assembly where she is greeted by Hera herself (24. 74–100). Their enmity forgotten, Hera places a "beautiful golden goblet" in her hands, and comforts Thetis for her sorrow (24. 101–2). Once this ritual is duly completed Zeus sends Thetis to inspire in her son a change of heart (24. 103–37). As if a great burden had been lifted from his shoulders, Achilles responds to his mother's suggestion immediately and succinctly: " 'So be it. He can bring the ransom and take off the body, / if the Olympian himself so urgently bids it' " (24. 139–40). Achilles' lack of hesitation suggests the psychological process through which intuition of an idea, perception of its absolute appropriateness, and commitment, occur within the mind simultaneously; he is, in an instant, no longer possessed by evil Strife, once again in possession of his orderly *obedient* soul: he no longer defies

Zeus or ignores his fundamental laws. His rash threat to the dying Hektor is reversed instantaneously and Achilles seems relieved that a human outlet for constructive action—and love—has been reopened to him.

The change in Achilles' attitude is nonetheless momentous for being a subtle one of emphasis. He identifies glory now as primarily a generic rather than a purely individual value. Whitman's interpretation confirms my view that his new attitude is the consequence of the perspective provided by Phoinix, Peleus, Nestor, and Patroklos:

> He had said that his honor was "from Zeus," and that he would fight only when the fire reached his own ships, and this was as much to say: individual honor is strictly between the transcendent aspect of man himself and the universe; he alone knows what it is and he alone can get satisfaction from it. But Patroklos has heard the opposite from Nestor, and the fact that Achilles listens to Patroklos' appeal, the fact that he had the curiosity to send him out in the first place, shows that Achilles himself knows that the opposite is also true, that the heroic spirit, if it is to exist as a reality, must act in this world. (P. 196)

But Whitman's analysis, too, must be qualified. It is not that Achilles rejects the pursuit of the absolute, of the cosmic within himself, on behalf of the human. It is rather that he realizes the absolute is to be found, ultimately, in his common share of human nature with other men—that it is more "heroic" to strive for generic, essential humanity, to live with mortality and limitation, than to seek an escape from the limitations of humanity (the lesson Gilgamesh also learns).

In his wrath against Hektor and Troy, Achilles proves that the pursuit of glory, formerly considered false and valueless, is allied to his love for Patroklos, transcending individuality. It is a communal virtue and aspiration, the tool by which society insures invigorating competition among its members (as in the games) or directs them to fight eagerly and effectively against a common enemy (as in the revenge). So it is glory which insures social survival. And glory conceived of in this manner brings Achilles a kind of continuity inasmuch as he shared vicariously in the continuation of society itself by abnegating his selfhood and individual prowess. In the new society, accordingly, glory is defined through a dual mode of behavior. Commitment to others leads to individual death. But socially oriented death leads to life in memory, in turn a source of society's persistence. That persistence is therefore activated by the individual's past recollected glory. The alternatives, consequently, must be restated. It is not really life against honor, but transitory honor (of the purely heroic kind) against transcendent honor (of the new society) in a continuing life of remembrance. Or it is present individualistic renown versus future social renown.

The final reillumination of glory, however, comes only after the death of Hektor and the funeral games, in the meeting with Priam. There glory is realized to be both individual and generic, a value which unites the expression of selfhood and of selflessness into a single memorable act. For an eternal life of individuality, without nationalistic limitation, is possible as well, if a human being acts as a human *should* act. He must redefine his friends and enemies in a way that knows no transient association with particular historical systems: he must redefine them purely as a human being, whose essential enemy is death, whose natural love is life. But this kind of glory demands that the individual who would achieve it must accept at the same time that he disdains it: "If Homer exalts individual greatness and delights in it . . . he nevertheless does not give it immunity from death. He has not made [Achilles] invulnerable" (p. 88). As Bespaloff implies, Achilles becomes vulnerable, that is, truly human, only after he has descended from his exalted nationalistic stature to meet Priam as an individual. The tradition records that he will be wounded fatally not through his divine communal shield, but behind it.

The shield, insofar as its pictures are ideal and not connected with any particular society but with humanity itself, also symbolizes this new glory, as does the supranational character of the poem's own eclectic language. Greene argues that two "forms of continuity" in the *Iliad* are glory and fatherhood. But he rejects glory and accepts only fatherhood as a true access to a sense of transcendent life. Yet in the meeting with Priam it is evident that both are true values and are, in fact, interrelated in the same way that the two scenes in the first city on the shield are complementary: one signifies the physical perpetuation of the race (fatherhood, the marriage festival); the other its perpetuation through orderly behavior (glory, the trial in the marketplace). And orderly behavior is epitomized in Achilles' love for Patroklos. That is why the death of Patroklos leaves Achilles, until he meets Priam, with no positive recourse in action, no proper object for his affection. Until he meets Priam, Achilles has no one left to love in this life. Therefore he has sought to live in a purely transcendent dimension by supervising memorable deeds in the games. Since Patroklos has become identified with the human genus itself in death, Achilles can be reunited with his friend by acting generically. Yet such a mode of action, because it ends with the embers of the ritual pyre, can only leave his still living personality dissatisfied and unfulfilled. By recognizing the universality of fatherhood, however,

Achilles is able to extend his orderly love for Patroklos to Priam—thereby achieving his ultimate human glory as a simple individual. This glory Achilles accepts willingly; in fact, its value depends upon the commitment of his personal will. Yet, paradoxically, by expressing his love for the ruler of Trojan society Achilles has fashioned a selfhood that is indeed generic or essentially human.

In his final purely human attitude, Achilles defines enemies and friends not in terms of nationality but in the light of the cosmic determinants of human nature. Pity signifies Achilles' ultimate commitment to life, while relentlessness, like Strife itself, is seen to be the hallmark of death and destruction and therefore antithetical to glory which will be everlasting. The force which Achilles now opposes even more strongly than he had opposed Troy and Hektor is defined by Thomas Greene: "The Achaian warrior's antagonist is not so much the Trojan as it is death itself, and time, flux, oblivion, mutability, operating within the grey ironic perplexities of that dim world" (p. 41). Greene's initial perspective is perfectly accurate: "Death and oblivion can be overcome only through glory . . . valuable because it represents *a form of continuity*. Glory is a figurative expression of life beyond the pyre" (p. 41). Glory so understood is not just a symbolic value; it is as real, as pragmatically effective, as is the poem, the art of memory itself. As Achilles did in Book 23 and will again in this scene, Priam uses words, the weapons of peace, to achieve his purpose. So the dominant motif of the *Iliad* is not force, but the tempering of force with love, of war with the speaker's art of words. Homer presents his hero with eternal life from the very hands of death.

Clearly, in his final characterization, Achilles exemplifies what Homer considers to be "major man" (in Wallace Stevens' sense of the term). Beye says as much in commenting that "the distinguishing mark of Achilles . . . is his superabundant vitality. As Agamemnon said: 'This man wishes to be superior to all other men' " (1. 287). "In Achilles, this is no simple political desire. He wants all things, to surpass all men, to break through the limitations of natural man, so as to realize himself" (p. 140). It is not, of course, through the boundaries of human nature itself that Achilles seeks to break, but through those that limit man's nature in time and space. In Achilles' aspiration and its accomplishment Homer has represented the essential quality of human experience which poetry seeks to communicate and consequently make realizable by others. Achilles discovers that the eternal, the divine, resides within his own humanity—and, when he does, the Olympians are temporarily forgotten. It is man who dominates the closing scenes of Book 24, humanity joyfully pursuing the course of Olympian order now clearly recognized.

Of the two forms of continuity, fatherhood and glory, it is clear that the latter is the one most closely allied with Homer's concept of the role of the poet in human society. In the scene with Priam the glory of words overshadows that of deeds, the "prestige of force" gives way to the forcefulness of peaceful communication. Glory, the force of social cohesiveness, depends for its constant renewal in each age upon the poet's function as the guardian of history and transmitter of memory. His role is connected with fatherhood, but it is even more widely generic, inasmuch as it transcends the kinship of blood to invoke the natural community of spirit.

The technique by which Achilles comments on reality is the same as that of the poet: language itself. Samuel E. Bassett notes the implicit resemblance between the hero of the *Odyssey* and the major figure of the *Iliad*: "The nearest approach to a *raisonneur* . . . is that of Homer himself" (p. 190). Compare the subject of Achilles' singing, κλέα ἀνδρῶν *khléa andrôn* ("glorious deeds of men"—9. 189), to that of Helen's robe. Here the human material of the art form is universalized and emphatically nonspecific—much more like that of the shield. Bespaloff remarks that "friendship and music are Achilles' only deliverance" (p. 104). And the combination is strikingly appropriate to his dual nature; friendship represents the transitory, which will be made, by its extension to Priam, transcendent; while music suggests the process by which the human is made to embody the divine.

Achilles often speaks of the mnemonic potential of his acts, as if he were predicting that the *Iliad* would be born from his quarrel with Agamemnon (19. 63–64). His perspective is very like the poet's Olympian detachment. Achilles suspects that social crises are somehow beyond the vision of the individual, even of the king. Indeed Troy's doom is caused ultimately by the goddesses in their jealousy or even, by extrapolation from legend, by the marriage of Thetis and Peleus. Yet Achilles possesses such a comprehensive vision while remaining only an individual; in this way, his individuality is revealed to be extraordinary. Achilles' ability, like Helen's, to see the pattern in which he himself is involved is the objective viewpoint epitomized. Whitman relates Achilles' introspection of the art of the singer:

The quarrel with Agamemnon was merely . . . the impetus which drove Achilles from the simple assumptions of the other princely heroes onto the path where heroism means the search for the dignity and meaning of the self. Is it an over-interpretation to see a symbol of this self-search in Achilles' song of the "glories of men"? . . . Achilles is the only one who actually sings . . . perhaps for the very reason that to Homer, the practice of epic singing was profoundly involved with the roots of early self-consciousness, the estimation of one's self in the light of the future's retrospect. The deeply brooding Helen says that she . . . will be the subject of a song hereafter, and it is by no means impossible that Homer, before plunging Achilles into the first phase of the search for his true place in history, envisioned that search in terms of what poets, himself included, must sing of him, and so introduced him with a lyre in his hand, consulting and re-creating the heroic tradition to which he would add a new perspective. (Pp. 193–94)

The social relationship between the doer of deeds and the speaker of words was, in the synthesized society envisioned by Homer, a particularly close one. The ideal, as Havelock suggests, was for the two functions to be simultaneous in a single individual. The prince honored Calliope not by aesthetic inclination, but because his communal power and service to the commonwealth depended upon effective utterance. It is toward the realization of such a poetic-political equation that Homer has made Achilles aspire.

Achilles' last words in the *Iliad* are all the more significant for being understated by the narrator, for being unemphatically individualistic: " 'Then all this, aged Priam, shall be done as you ask it. / I will hold off our attack for as much time as you bid me' " (24. 669–70). By now we cannot doubt Achilles' extraordinary ability to suspend the forces of historical reality. Nor can we doubt the transcendent orderliness of his willingness to do so, that Priam—and the shade of Hektor—might savor the final taste of honor which alone defeats death. Achilles' last words suggest that the communication between him and Priam, international though it must be, will be continued somehow—if not physically, then certainly spiritually or mnemonically. Achilles will sense how much time Priam requires, so perfectly attuned to each other have they become in the explosion of love that has occurred between them.

Hephaistos and Homer

The final noteworthy aspect of the image of Achilles' shield is its close association with its artistic creator. Hephaistos' peculiar mode of existence in the Iliadic world reflects upon the significance of the artifact, just as the shield in turn defines its creator. It is remarkable that Hera considers Xanthus' watery attack upon Achilles as a personal affront to Hephaistos. Identifying Achilles, in his exalted state, with the gods and with nature itself, Homer emphasizes the close relationship between the maker and the bearer of the great shield. Achilles is supreme among men; Hera declares that no other god can match his strength against Hephaistos (21. 357). Their respective strengths and limitations form a complementary synthesis which distinguishes the extraordinary artistic import of this artifact from that of any other in the poem. Achilles, with his semidivine nature, is like Hephaistos; but, unlike the god, he is not primarily an artist. Hephaistos, in his distinctive orderliness among the gods, is like Achilles; but he is not a man, not limited by mortality.

The complementarity between Achilles and Hephaistos is suggested by the numerous thematic associations between them. Whitman has demonstrated amply their imagistic relation through the appearance of fire. From fire the shield is forged and like fire it appears as Achilles carries it into battle. In the case of both god and man, the image is transferred from the artifact to its creator and user. Hephaistos is often synonymous with fire and Achilles, too, is fire incarnate (19. 10–22). As he delights in accepting the armor from Thetis, Achilles' eyes gleam like the sun, symbolizing his intuitive recognition of the pragmatic value of the shield. Whitman remarks that when Hephaistos descends to protect Achilles from the river with his fire, "Achilles himself, in the middle of [the flame], is untouched" (pp. 270–72). Nature is turned aside as the divine fire quenches the divine, but less orderly, water. The combat between Hephaistos and Xanthus is perfectly parallel with Achilles' fight against Troy. For, as Whitman notes, the "arms of Achilles are tokens of man's own grasp of the absolute. Achilles' fire is also an absolute, hence it threatens to upset fate, or the temporal world process, even as it licks up the waters of Troy." The incongruity lies in the fact that an individual is capable of single-handedly destroying a whole people. The opposition between Achilles, in his new nationalistic identity, and the image of water is also a contrast with his former identification. Achilles was originally associated with water, not only through his mother, but also through his geographical origins and the context of his prayer to Thetis in Book 1. His ancestral seat was the river Spercheios in Hellas (23. 141–51).

Of course Achilles and Hephaistos are also related through Thetis. She saved the god in his time of need; in return, he made her wonderful jewelry. Hephaistos also gave her, through Dionysos, the golden urn for the ashes of Achilles and Patroklos, prefiguring his Iliadic gifts of the arms (6. 130; 23. 92; *Odyssey*, 24. 75). Thetis, moreover, represents Zeus' transcendent principle of order which Hephaistos invokes so effectively at the feast on Olympos in Book 1. Accordingly, rather than excusing her son's behavior toward Hektor's body, she agrees with Zeus that Achilles' anger is excessive, and subsequently transforms it into pity (24. 120–32); she is a kind of exorcist, freeing Achilles from the evil spirit that possessed him. Zeus' orderly plan is accomplished through the artistry of Hephaistos, the maker of both the shield and the aegis.

Hephaistos, then, respects and supports the authority of Zeus, while Achilles is διίφιλε *diífile* ("dear to Zeus"—1. 74). Morality and poetry are united in the figure of the divine father whose daughters include both the Muses and the Prayers (4. 502 ff.). Zeus represents the principle of government (24. 65 ff., 97 ff.) at the same time that he is the generic source of poetry itself. He is the crucible from which issue all orderly forces. Achilles' analogical role is differentiated from that of Hephaistos by the fact that the god's dual orientation toward government and art is eternally unchanging whereas the man's is shown to develop in the poem. Hephaistos consistently respects creativity and petitions because he is by nature perfectly cognizant of their equally important orderliness. But in Books 9 and 22 Achilles rejects the pleas of the ambassadors and of Hektor; his artistry with the lyre in Book 9 is that of an amateur. Only at the close of the poem does Achilles come into the perfect attunement with order that characterizes Hephaistos when he respects the urging of Thetis, the will of Zeus, and the supplication of Priam and returns the robes with Hektor's body—the robes, as his personal gesture. His abrupt capitulation to Zeus' plan as Thetis announces it recalls the moment of intuition in which Achilles recognized the full significance of his shield (24. 139–40). So Homer portrays the way in which profession becomes vocation, and vocation profession. The linear development of character is suspended as Achilles is given suddenly a perfect vision of the circular relationship between ethical and poetic purposes. And because of this vision Achilles fully actualizes the potential of his being dear to Zeus. He becomes the epitome of the man of words, as he is already the man of deeds. This alliance between the prince and the poet in a single personality is the goal toward which Achilles has been striving unwittingly throughout his anguished development. He is, in the end, a kind of avatar of Hephaistos.

But it is clearly the *governing* force of Olympian order which Achilles symbolizes most emphatically. Hephaistos, on the other hand, reflects more clearly the *artistic* character of the poet-prince. Homer describes the orderliness of his creativity as a necessary agent of social equilibrium. All the products he makes are shown to possess eternal and protective life, affirming and insuring the continuity of human nature at the same time—precisely as does the poem. The vividness of Hephaistos' creations represents Homer's insistence upon realism as the only means of convincing the audience of the authority of his vision—and of their consequent responsibility for orderly action which follows from their acceptance of the vision. So the shield and the poem share a single methodology. The two arts merge, becoming indistinguishable one from the other as the poet, through the process of narration, describes the process by which the shield is forged. The shield's structural formation becomes, in short, the key to the linguistic pattern by which the poem itself gradually reveals the widening scope of its vision until, in Book 24 as in the proem, the universal boundaries of experience have been defined.

The center which creates the circumference and defines the entire circle of experience is the poet's own transcendent (cosmic, divine, eternal) point of view. And the boundaries of the experience comprehended by his vision prove to be, finally, the limits of the human cosmos. The *Iliad* begins and ends with the name of a man; the gods, though transcendent, are enveloped by humanity in the sense that they are existentially meaningless without man. They exist but they have value because they are the perfect figurative expression of essential human orderliness, recognized in the ideal individual. The retreat from selfhood leads Achilles to find at last that the truest communion with all men is the fullest realization of the selfhood common to all.

Hephaistos' art is like Homer's own in more than its process. The subject matter, perspective, and symbolic quality of the shield are perfect internal representations of the *Iliad*. Homer turns, in the shield, to reveal the essential relevance of his story to the whole of human experience; to reveal, that is, the essential nature of his poetic vision. This conclusion that the shield is a kind of ideal microcosm which allows us to comprehend at a glance the thematic expanse of the epic is suggested by the many parallels between Hephaistos' pictures and situations and scenes throughout the *Iliad*. Hephaistos clearly intends his pictures to be imitations of Iliadic reality; he speaks of the Ocean to Thetis (18. 399) in exactly the same terms as he will depict it on the shield (18. 607). Bounded by that stream is the whole of human reality, both fictional and real, in all its various aspects.

In a sense Homer uses the description of the shield as an opportunity to instruct his audience on his own particular artistic ambition. That ambition is to complement his historical responsibilities with a philosophical perspective which transcends the particularities of past and present events to illuminate the essential patterns of human life. For this reason, time, which restricts the poet within the narrative proper, is conflated on the shield. And the shield's implied metaphysical order is a telescoped statement of the poet's "world view." Therefore, as Beye notes, the shield's "quarrel is reconciled by judgment and good speaking" (p. 144)—in the same way that the conflict between Agamemnon and Achilles is dissolved in the Iliadic world.

It follows that Homer considers his poem to be the "good speaking" by which contemporary antagonisms, among his audience, may be resolved. The epic is a vast exemplum of the benefits of social order and the disastrous consequences of disorder, showing the ways in which men have pursued both forces. So Beye recalls that the "ambush [is] led by Hate, Confusion and Death—the very antitheses of the civilized arts— music, dancing, oratory—through which in the first city order and continuity existed" (p. 144). And, in the poem, the hatred of Hera, the selfish delusion of Hektor, and Hektor's death, lead to the imminent barrenness of Troy. The ploughing scene on the shield explicitly con- nects order—in the unanimity of the workers who toil together under the direction of their king—with fertility. In the first city the joy of orderly government (the arbitration scene) is united with the joy of procreative alliances (the marriage festival). And creative joy is the final element under which all the others are subsumed and revealed to be but different facets of the same spirit of hierarchical human orderliness. In the Iliadic world all three manifestations of orderly behavior are present, among men, in Achilles alone—who plays the lyre and tells two remembered stories to Priam, organizes the games, and finally sleeps again with Briseis. And his divine counterpart is Hephaistos, who creates the shield, reconciles the gods, and maintains his marital bliss intact. The totally orderly orientation which Hephaistos always possesses toward social values, Achilles will come to enjoy at the close of Homer's story. So the exhilaration of the dance upon the shield's rim is reminiscent of the joyful feast on Olympos over which Hephaistos presides in Book 1, at the same time that it prefigures—and makes possible—the social spirit of happy brotherhood manifested in the funeral games for Patroklos.

The symbolic significance of the great shield makes it the closest analogue Homer has given us to the didactic potential of his poem. The shield's function is almost purely symbolic since the artifact doesn't function in its usual way: the shield will not save Achilles from death (18. 464–67). Instead, Lloyd says, Hephaistos "designs a work which em- bodies the spirit and moral of the occasion, and seizes and sets forth its leading motive with such scope of symbolism as befits an artist god" (p. 42) who in turn presents a work of art to a fictional recipient. Therefore, as his possession of the shield symbolizes Achilles' grasp of the absolute, so our retention of the poem in memory signifies and proves our appreciation of and commitment to the transcendent order it embodies.

Although Hephaistos' creation resembles Homer's in so many ways, the shield-world is obviously distinguished from the world of the poem. Paolo Vivante's outline of the microcosmic character of Book 1 implies that the shield's analogical quality is limited, in the first place, by the quite understandable fact that Hephaistos' world does not include as many aspects of reality as does Homer's. The first distinction, then, is a quantitative one. Dawn, night, Olympos, are absent, for example, from the inlaid surface. But in a sense the image is restricted dramatically as well: it disappears from view after Book 22, its symbolic influence in the last two books being only implicit. The shield moreover is helpless against the river (21. 317–18); Hephaistos has to supplement his art by coming himself to the rescue of Achilles.

But the most noteworthy discrepancy between the shield and the *Iliad* is a qualitative matter, having to do with Homer's extraordinary ambition for this great epic. In his poem "The Shield of Achilles," W. H. Auden speaks of,

> An unintelligible multitude
> A million eyes, a million boots in line
> Without expression, waiting for a sign.

Certainly Auden's description does not fit Homer's shield; expression is Hephaistos' forte. The modern poet is referring to the faceless mass of contemporary individuals smothered by technological society. Yet Auden's description nevertheless suggests an aesthetic distinction between the shield and the poem in which it stands. Hephaistos' handiwork represents the opposite of the historical extreme: poetry which is purely scientific or philosophical. As such, of course, it emphasizes Homer's determination to communicate not only the facts connected with a specific historical period but also the essential, unchanging nature of human existence. But Homer's overriding purpose in the *Iliad* is to go much further: to combine the historical with the scientific, adding conviction to the latter by the mnemonic authority of the former. In this sense Hephaistos might be considered to be the antithesis of Helen, whose stories are purely historical. Her art is of the present only. Unlike Helen, moreover, Hephaistos is more properly "Homeric" by the fact that he himself remains anonymous within his created world. There is no metal-worker upon the shield, a striking omission among the many arts that are represented.

Yet there is a lyre among the pictures (18. 567–72). The context in which it appears serves to define the medicinal role of singing in terms of fertility and the joy of social well-being and cohesiveness—as if Homer commissioned Hephaistos to forge his signature in his stead. That is the small luxury the composer of the *Iliad* allows himself for so conscientiously and self-effacingly illuminating the signatures of all other things in human experience. The sign for which the nameless figures on the shield are waiting is that provided by the poet himself: his words create a world in which they become definite individuals. Achilles is not Everyman, but derives his typicality from the pattern of his actions; his character is emphatically personal. Homeric creativity is truly an embodiment of the spirit, a particularization of the general, making the absolute and eternal accidental and transitory; not for the purpose of denying the reality of the abstract and ideal, but for the opposite reason: so that they may be experienced, believed in, and therefore acted upon. Homer's unfaltering vision of essential human nature enables him to share his transcendent perspective with others by objectifying it, in character, action, and artifact; it is the composer of the poem who, in J. W. Mackail's words, "fixes life, makes it imaginatively visible. Round that point, for that moment, the whole universe groups itself, takes rhythm and complete-ness" (p. 36). Only the point is not detached from the listener but becomes part of him; the moment lasts as long as memory retains the song.

Poetry in the Homeric aesthetic can be a meaningful force for construc-tive action only if it carries the conviction of true history to support the poet's insight into the requirements of humanity in its continuing dimension; in this sense, he is the first legislator. The point around which the poet aligns his contemporary world is one that communicates a vision of particularities and generalities at the same time, of ideals which have proven to be realizable; of limited individuals who have been gloriously liberated through their attunement with the collective human spirit from the gloomy limits of temporality. But the change and anguish associated with time are revealed simultaneously to be the only human access to transcendence. Such a synthesis can't be accomplished by a god; Hephaistos exists in one dimension only. He is eternally immutable; to him history means nothing. The human poet alone, composing the poem of memory, can concretize the absolute and make the incarnation credible because, in himself, he experiences the full force of time as well as of eternity and therefore he is able to communicate his vision to his fellowmen. They can tell us much about the poem's aesthetic, but the artifacts in the *Iliad*, even the great shield of Achilles made by Hephaistos, are not perfect representations. The nature of Homer's verbal shield of memory could be reflected best only in the tales of memory with which the *Iliad* abounds. Our final step in understand-ing the poem's aesthetic must be to analyze the contexts of remembering and recounting memory—moments when the present is shaped by the past.

∽ 10 ∾

The Shield of Memory

Song and Story

The most comprehensive artistic pattern in the *Iliad* is the function of memory, narratives of past deeds. The poet's own craft of words unites men and gods and, among men themselves, one galaxy with the other. More than any artifact, the tales from memory provide us with access to Homer's concept of the nature of his own creativity: its source, mode of being, and practical effectiveness. Present either explicitly or implicitly from the beginning of the *Iliad* to the end, the art of words, of the singer or the practiced speaker, comprehends the limits of human experience, asserting human life and accepting the humanness of death. So in Book 1 the Achaians' song of propitiation to Apollo marks the lifting of the plague and the restoration of vitality to Argos (1. 473–75); but death for both the individual and the nation is the theme of the Trojans' sorrowful hymn for Hektor in Book 24. 721 ff.

Determining Homer's aesthetic from the actual songs of the *Iliad* is not as easy as it is in the *Odyssey*. The poet's self-awareness is thematically explicit in the *Odyssey*, since that epic presents not only actual bards, in the persons of Phemios and Demodokos, but also authoritative aestheticians, in Alkinoös and Odysseus. Odysseus praises the perfect artistic form and historical accuracy of Demodokos' tale of the Trojan war (*Odyssey* 8. 479 ff.), thereby defining realistic song at the same time that he prefers to hear and practice an art whose character is less serious, or more fanciful (*Odyssey* 8. 492 ff.). Odysseus' criticism has implications both within and beyond the Odyssean world. Odysseus says that Demodokos' historical realism must have one of two derivations (*Odyssey* 8.491): it may be that of an eyewitness, thereby justifying Odysseus' own assumption of the singer's role in Book 9; or it may be a knowledge gained from the perfect transmission of facts through the oral tradition (suggesting the authority of Homer himself). Although the Homer of the *Odyssey* departs from historical realism, as does Odysseus, the authority

245

here attributed to Demodokos is entirely applicable to the Homer of the *Iliad*. But the nature of the Odyssean art is quite different from that of the *Iliad*. The *Odyssey* is not the perfect synthesis of history and philosophy; but a patent neglect of the first element—or allowance of full imaginative freedom in dealing with it—for the purpose of exploring the unknown dimensions of the second from a subjective perspective.

The emphatically subjective nature of the *Odyssey* is most evident when Odysseus becomes himself the storyteller. As Alice Mariani puts it, "the poet . . . makes us quite conscious of the involuted contrivance of his hero acting as his own poet" (p. 78). In Books 9 through 12, the poet's identification with his hero is so complete, since fictional and real narrator are simultaneous, that the implication is unmistakable. Homer intends the identification to be recognizably reversible: Odysseus becomes the poet. Alkinoös, in fact, calls Odysseus a bard and bestows the gifts on him appropriate to the aesthetic delight he has caused the Phaiakians (*Odyssey* 9. 363–69). Alkinoös' critical appreciation of Odysseus' art symbolizes the accomplishment by the poet of a momentous definition. Homer proves that the effectiveness of song does not depend upon its realistic or historical accuracy but issues primarily from the beauty of its form. Mariani comments: "Whether the tale is true or false, Alkinoös' praise of its singer is proved true by his people's enchanted response . . . and his own" (pp. 85–86). A remarkable transference has taken place. For Odysseus' tale, and the *Odyssey* itself, is no less didactically effective than the *Iliad* or than Hephaistos' shield. The artistic beauty of his kind of song is also an intimation of the immortality latent in transitory human experience. Alkinoös, says Mariani, "implicitly recognizes the wonder of it, that joy should come out of suffering, that the impermanence of man's condition should become, in the poet's weaving of those threads, an immortal song" (p. 86). What has happened is that individual genius has nearly replaced communal history as the source of the didactic intention. The communal influence which the Homer of the *Iliad* finds in the combination of historical fact and personal imagination, the Odyssean composer discovers to reside solely within the limits of his own mind. He detects in individuality the abiding presence of the continuing spirit of humanity. And his discovery signals the more or less imminent termination of the epic tradition, or at least defines its possibility—and opens the way for the emergence of the lyric poet. For, recognizing the presence of generic humanity in the individual (from the final character of Achilles in the *Iliad*), the Odyssean poet cannot resist the new-found impulse to investigate the nature of individuality itself, of the mind which can contain a world within it—and to make the exploration an integral part of the theme: ἔννεπε μοι *énnepe moi* ("tell me"—*Odyssey* 1.1) is his invocation to the Muse, with the implied emphasis being that he, a personality with a talent indigenous to himself and distinct from others, will relate the Muse's story in his own way.

But the Homer of the *Iliad* marks his anonymity from the very opening, strikingly different, invocation: ἄειδε, θεα *áeide, thea* ("sing, goddess"— 1. 1). The Muse is an objectified force outside the bard to whose compulsion he subordinates his personality; in a sense, he allows himself to be possessed so that he becomes only the human voice through which the divine Muse sings. The understated presence of song, however, does not extend to the doubly fictional world of Hephaistos. There Homer gives himself the license to comment upon his own creativity. The shield of Achilles and the personality of its creator are the closest approximations in the *Iliad* to Odysseus' fabrication of his own ὀδυσσέια *odusseia*. The qualified universality derived from imaginative action in the *Odyssey* is achieved, and made more convincing, in the *Iliad* by the imagery which frames realistic temporal action in a more credibly transcendent setting. In the central image, upon the surface of Achilles' shield, there are no less than four instances of singing which together occupy a fourth of the lines devoted to the delineation of Hephaistos' world. We can hope to learn something of how Homer viewed his own art form from these various shield songs.

In the first city the brides are led to meet their husbands to the accompaniment of song, dance, and the playing of lyres and flutes; while an audience of women looks on in admiration (18. 493–96). Then there are the two herdsmen happily making music on their pipes as they lead their complacent charges, until all are slaughtered by the ambushing warriors (18. 526 ff.). As young men and women labor together in the vineyard, their work is lightened by the lyrist and singer who leads the Linos song to which their voices provide the refrain (18. 569–71). Even the feet of the harvesters keep time to the music, as song merges imperceptibly with dance (18. 572). Finally Hephaistos forges the splendid dance floor upon which youths and maidens dance with grace and precision (18. 591–601) as the joyful bystanders watch and join in the singing (18. 603–5).

The structural autonomy of this final scene suggests that it serves thematically as a culmination of all the preceding scenes without bearing an explicitly logical relationship to them. In each of the four instances the occasion for song is somehow a communal one. In each case, the occasion for the artistic expression is allied with its purpose. Never an isolated activity, singing is always relevant to social situations. It is, like the marriage ritual, husbandry, and agriculture which it accompanies, a force of organization and creative order. The bride song and the watchers' response to it signifies the harmonious relationship between conjugal love and the communal joy derived from proper procreative alliances (18. 496); the watching women share in the happiness of the brides and grooms. With the herdsmen, the implication is that their music not only embodies their comradeship (in the absence of the larger community which they serve) but also assists them in the management of their animals. For the harvesters in the vineyard, physical fertility—of the grapes which they have gathered together—is transformed through the agency of song and dance into a spiritual joy shared by all. The action of their labor becomes, as they hear the song, emotion; and that emotion, in turn, is changed to artistic action as their feet respond to the music automatically. Similarly, in the *choros*, the perfect form of the dancers is not only a thing of beauty in itself, a wonder to behold, but it also causes the observers to participate in their moving patterns and experience the beauty themselves at the same time that they re-create it. As the onlookers join in the dance the parts are integrated perfectly to form a unanimous whole. Song represents the spirit of community and concord—reinforces it and creates it anew.

More generally, the songs on the shield appear in situations exemplary of orderliness in the various realms of human activity—sexual, agricultural, governmental, and artistic. Order is contrasted with disorder, peace contrasted with war. The bridal song occurs in the peaceful city; in the city at war there is no effective art. The herdsmen, of course, are citizens of the second city. But the disastrous social repercussions of war are symbolized perfectly when the peacefulness of their playing is brutally interrupted by the attackers—just as Paris' lyre (and Apollo's) is quieted by the Trojan war. The marriage song is associated with the conjugal and familial levels of the social system, and the herdsmen's piping with interpersonal bonds. So it is fitting that in the harvest scene the presence of the king marks the political aspect of communal life; the orderliness of the laborers' cooperation is defined by the silent appearance of their ruler. Finally the dance floor is an image of an altogether transcendent peace, a representation of essential, ideal society; the aura which surrounds it recalls the constructive competition of the Myrmidon games in Book 2 and presages that of the Achaian games in Book 23.

The smith does not neglect the technical aspects of song. In the city the singing is connected with the playing of flutes and lyres and with dancing; it has an antiphonal quality very like that displayed by the Muses in Book 1. The lyre and dance appear again in the vineyard song which even more explicitly suggests something about the way in which art affects its audience. As the rhythm of the singing is recapitulated physically in the steps of the dancers it is clear that the beauty of the song's form has been transmitted to the listeners' bodies directly, without the intervention of individual consciousness. This operation of the emotion produced by art is what makes the two different formal expressions perfectly synchronized. The form is the essential force which can shape whatever materials—whether verbal, corporeal, or metallic—that come into contact with it. This is the significance of the final dance which so meticulously emphasizes formal patterns. The essential primacy of form is the underlying artistic principle that leads Homer to fashion artifact-images that are analogous to his poem. What is communicated through Homeric art is the *pattern* of things—whether of practical behavior in everyday matters or of specifically artistic gestures. The audience in the *choros* participates in the dance because they have perceived the patterns themselves; the artists have become paradigms, models upon whose actions those of the observers can be based. The artistic emotion by which the form of art is transmitted to the audience and consequently realized in their recapitulation of it is precisely the human technique by which the spirit of community is made concrete in the experience of the individual. The artist's extraordinary ability to inform the emotions of his audience directly through his mimetic incantation defines his essential social role; for it is the court poet who makes the communal spirit actual in the suspension of his audience from the concerns of temporality, in the moment of their participation.

There is a definable progression on the shield from the occasional to the pure song, from the particular to the general quality of the art. This heightens the impression that Homer is making a statement here about his own creativity. Hephaistos represents songs specifically appropriate to marriage festivals, to pastoral occupations, and to the activities of harvest. These songs are like those of propitiation or of mourning in the Iliadic world itself. All such occasional songs, however, are subsumed under the generalized singing, without specific context or content, of the *choros*. The generalization is what makes it feasible for us to conclude that the epic poem, as it was originally sung, shares the nature of songs delineated on the shield (and variant texts of the *Iliad* have an inspired court bard "playing his lyre"—as in *Odyssey* 4.17—as the closing image on the shield before the circling ocean). The technical aspects of epic song are identical, including the accompaniment by dance as well as by the lyre; and, as the *Odyssey* amply demonstrates, its emotional effectiveness, for the community, is the same.

The Homeric poet's communal role is extraordinary; his position cannot be defined by reference to the coordinates by which the roles of others are normally connected with one social level or another. This is implied by Eumaios in the *Odyssey*. He defines the bard, the prophet, the healer, and the builder, as being the only kind of strangers one would deliberately send for from outside the community *(Odyssey* 17. 386). The men who share this autonomous, international identity are called δημιοεργοὶ *dēmioergoì* (*Odyssey* 17. 383; 19. 135), a word which in classical Attic refers to any creative craftsman. But in Homer's time its meaning is more specific and more revealing. As its etymology suggests a δημιοερ-γὸς *dēmioergòs* is "one who does work pertaining to the entire communi-ty, the δῆμος *dēmos*," that is, whose function is to serve the society as such. These special crafts are distinguished from those, like weaving, which pertain to a single household. Frank H. Stubbings notes that smiths and potters also were considered to be δημιοεργοὶ *dēmioergoì* (p. 537).

The practicality of the poet's art, then, is proven by the categorical name by which he is defined as belonging to that group of men who perform services of protection for all society. Even among δημιοεργοὶ *dēmioergoì* the singer is extraordinary, for the product of his art is immune from the dissolution visited by time upon all things material. The special divinity of Achilles' new shield—its Olympian invulnerability—also symbolizes Homer's belief that his artifact of words, which includes the shield as well as being included upon it, alone will survive forever. The poem, as the shield of memory, relies upon the continuity of human nature at the same time that it insures that con-tinuity.

There is, of course, an important difference between the *Iliad* itself and the songs upon the shield. The singing in Hephaistos' world has no subject matter. This is obvious in the case of the *choros* song; but even though the general nature of the bridal song and the song of Linos is clear, it is not specifically revealed. The absence of temporality from the shield world deprives these songs of a definable human content; there is no history in this metal world to sing about. The shield songs neverthe-less are effectively didactic, in a limited sense: the audience learns from the dancers and singers the patterns of their dance and song. But the patterns are ideal ones only; they are purely artistic in a way foreign to Homer's concept of the informative influence of pragmatic poetry. They do not provide the listener with convincing patterns of practical, orderly behavior.

Homer's world is much more realistic than that of Hephaistos because it accepts the full implications of time and change. Because it has a history, it is a world which, like the real one, includes the function of remembering in human experience. Memory, in which the perspective on continuity is brought to bear upon the listener's confrontation with change and uncertainty, is what allows Iliadic man to escape the concrete present to experience the ideal continuum represented on the shield. In this realistic fictional world song is the vehicle by which the memory of the individual is communicated to others and therefore made an actualization of the generic spirit. A review of explicit instances of song in the *Iliad* demonstrates its universal presence, in both galaxies. With the addition of the mnemonic element, song within the Iliadic world displays the qualities characteristic of singing on the shield. More comprehensively even than the artifacts, song symbolizes social orderliness as the necessary pattern for salutary human behavior: it invokes the example of orderly human actions in the past in order to convince men of the present that they in turn are responsible for providing an example to men of the future.

Characters in both galaxies recognize the social function of memory and singing. The central figures of Helen's galaxy, in fact, are related to one another through the imagery of song. Hektor, berating his brother for his unmanly timidity in the face of Menelaos' challenge, asserts that neither his lyre nor Aphrodite will help Paris maintain such an unnatural attitude (3. 54). The singing of Paris is ineffective, Hektor implies, because it isn't oriented toward the community; it serves only his own pleasure. From the disorderliness of Paris' lyre, both in the occasion for its use and in the purpose, order cannot be expected to arise. Because Paris' art doesn't benefit society it will not protect him individually.

Helen herself, of course, defines Hektor's poetic destiny for him by predicting that they will become characters in a song for men to come (6. 357). Hektor will be remembered and gloriously identified for his determination to fight for the life of his society, fully knowing that his efforts will be politically ineffective. But Hektor's efforts will become effective, and eternally so, when his self-effacing deed becomes an example to future men; paradoxically, by committing his individuality to a particular society, Hektor will be associated forever with the essential social nature of human life. And Troy itself, as it is served so faithfully by Hektor, will also survive in memory. He therefore must perform the glorious deed, must die struggling, in order to provide the material context for the memory and song of his name. As a mnemonic example Hektor perfectly epitomizes man as he should be, dedicated to every level of social relationships and cognizant of their relative values. In his final choice the actual becomes the ideal, the historical merges with the typical.

Two other references to song in Helen's galaxy are also connected with Hektor. Hoping to prevent Hektor from submitting to the delusion of disorderly self-confidence, Poulydamas warns him that his role is that of the warrior, not that of the counselor (13. 727–28). Each member of society is assigned by Zeus a different talent to enable him to perform a special function, whether it be the talent of the warrior, of the dancer, or of the singer (13. 730–31). Yet all social functions are interdependent. The relationship between warfare and singing is that both protect the stability of society. One, the art of words, must guide the other, the art of deeds. Hektor's warfare rightfully must be directed by Poulydamas' orderly perspective. Poulydamas knows that his fighting must, in the present circumstances, be strictly defensive; that is its orderly role. And Hektor's neglect of Poulydamas' words leads to a disorder which is fatal both for him and for the community he protects. Imagistically, his deafness to the art of words issues in the song of lamentation over Hektor's body and the imminent doom of his city (24. 721).

The song that unites the two galaxies is that of Apollo. The immortal bard is associated with Helen's galaxy throughout the poem, but in a less emphatic way than are Hera and Athene. His lyre celebrates the unanimity accomplished by Hephaistos in the communal feast on Olympos (1. 603). As the antiphonal voices of the Muses accompany Apollo's playing, the divine song is clearly sacramental in nature. It is the outward expression of the internal harmony among the gods, a striking prefigurement of the *choros* on the shield. And it is also a prediction that such perfect harmony will be experienced by men in the Iliadic world. At the same time, inasmuch as it distinguishes the Olympians by their immortality from the tragic beauty of human life, the song is, as Mackail comments, also "the implied background . . . to a foreground which gives the . . . spectacle of earth, with its war and wandering, its burden of toil and trouble and death" (p. 72). The song of Apollo represents the detachment of the artist, his extraordinary mode of existence derived from his sharing of the Olympian perspective.

The first image of song in the *Iliad* is the propitiatory hymn of the Argives which concludes their ritual sacrifice and communal feast in honor of Apollo (1. 472–75). From his aloof position Apollo hears their singing and listens in gladness. The divine poet is here the audience, just as Homer becomes the audience as he watches Hephaistos at work. The reciprocal nature of the artistic experience, the interaction of the singer's and the listener's memory and consciousness, and of men and gods, is suggested by this reversal of roles on the part of Apollo. His acceptance of the Achaian song also has a very practical relevance: it signals the end of the plague, the restoration of social order. The song is literally effective in the Iliadic world; but it is also symbolically appropriate, a fitting artistic recompense for Agamemnon's crime against another art associated with Apollo—the sceptre of the god carried by Chryses. The imagistic progression begins with the orderly sceptre, held by a guest-suppliant as the symbol of his right to respect, but dishonored through the disorderly attitude of the Argive king, his host. The disorder, consequently, is extended from the primary individual's attitude to the physical state of the community as the sceptre gives way to the silver bow as an instrument of divine justice. Its purpose achieved, the bow is put aside because the Achaian song testifies to Agamemnon's and Argos' recognition of their error and their admission of Apollo's orderliness. The song is the sign of justice fulfilled.

But Apollo is associated also with the orderly galaxy. In the past it was his lyre that led the bridal song at the fateful marriage of Peleus and Thetis (24. 60, 63), reminding us that lyres accompany the ritual festival on the shield. Achilles' special poetic destiny is symbolized by the presence of the divine bard at his parents' wedding. Hera's reminder to Apollo of his former artistic connection with Achilles is enough to make the god agree with her on the necessity of honoring Achilles' extraordinary virtue. The memory is therefore effective in enhancing Achilles' humanity by allowing him to take the definitive action of returning Hektor's body.

Apollo is one of the two fictive singers outside the shield. Among men, Achilles alone is shown actually singing with the lyre (9. 189). Achilles is also consistently conscious of the mnemonic import of song in human experience. He knows that the actions of present men will be preserved in the memory of men to come and will be evaluated on the basis of their service or disservice to the hierarchy (19. 63–64). That knowledge eventually affects his own acts. It is interesting that, in the *Odyssey*, the Muses themselves lead the lamentation for Achilles (24. 720 ff.); for his singing in the *Iliad* is strongly similar to Demodokos': like the Odyssean bard, Achilles sings heroic lays. But in Book 9 Achilles' artistry is as disorderly as is Paris', since he sings in isolation from the army. Achilles is accompanied only by Patroklos, in the company of other Myrmidons; but the proper δημιοεργὸς *dēmioergòs* is supposed to serve the community in the widest sense, not limiting himself to one subgroup.

We are reminded of the transcendent mode of being which distinguishes gods from men by the fact that Apollo plays his lyre both in the fictive present (Book 1) and in the past (Book 24). Achilles sings only in the present; his singing is complemented by that of Thamyris (2. 595 ff.), who sings only in the past. Thamyris no longer practices his art because the Muses have canceled his poetic license. The reason for their action is explained by the narrator. Thamyris' artistic ambition was egomaniacal, his delusion that of unwarranted confidence in his autonomous talent. His contest with the Muses suggests his attempt to reject tradition, asserting himself alone. Thamyris would alter the didactic nature of art to make it a value in and for itself. So its communal occasion and purpose are denied. Thamyris is in a sense the mnemonic example that should have prevented Achilles and Paris from indulging in an egocentric artistry. He is also the example overcome by Homer in the *Odyssey*.

The punishment meted out to Thamyris by the Muses is as appropriate to the nature of his art as it is revealing. They take from him his "wondrous song" and make him forgetful of the art of the lyre, thereby defining the components of the poet's vocation. The ἀοιδὴν θεσπεσίην *aoidēn thespesiēn* ("wondrous song") represents the incantatory beauty of the poem's metrical and structural consistency which produces the emotional response, the artistic and religious awe from the listener's sensual appreciation of its form. And Thamyris is deprived of his memory, from which alone the didactic meaning of the song issues—its content, the patterns of behavioral precedent which become examples to the audience. Because he himself has separated his art from the communal framework in which it is properly expressed, the Muses have arranged that it loses its generic effectiveness—both emotional and cognitive, aesthetic and practical. So it is clear that the transcendent perspective, represented by the Muses, is what makes the alliance between form and content, beauty and meaning, possible. Because Thamyris alienates the Muses, the artistic perspective is denied him.

These explicit references to singing tell us a great deal about the poet's concept of the significance of his extraordinary art and of his special social role. But there are yet other contexts which suggest the composer's self-awareness. The intimate relationship between song and memory suggests that certain narrative descriptions of remembering reveal Homer's view of poetry. Two groups of such descriptions warrant analysis. The first includes tales of past events recalled by characters specifically to affect the attitude or action of others. The second group consists of peculiar units in the narrative in which the narrator himself calls upon his own mnemonic resources and those of his contemporary audience to provide background perspective to the events he means to illustrate. In addition to less conventionalized units, the frequent use of the genealogical and catalogue motifs suggests the comprehensive scope of the tradition from which the thematic material of the *Iliad* is drawn. For the tradition includes not only the story of the Trojan war, but all of history and human experience. Yet in both groups the implications about the nature of song are the same as those suggested in the explicit instances of singing both outside and upon the shield.

We have already discussed Hephaistos' story about his fall from Olympos at the hands of Zeus (1. 592 ff.). Here the purpose as well as the occasion for the recollection is emphatically communal; Hephaistos' intention is to have his mother respect the authority of Zeus, who is her husband, the father of the gods, and their ruler. His tale is didactically effective in momentarily preventing Hera from disrupting the orderliness of the divine society under Zeus' government. Related to Hephaistos' tale is Sleep's reminder to Hera of the disastrous repercussions of his former service to her when she deceived Zeus about the birth of Herakles (14. 249 ff.). Only the protection of Night had saved Sleep from experiencing physically the wrath of the father of the gods. The story he tells is convincing enough to force Hera to offer him a more worthwhile bribe in return for his services this time.

It would seem that the adventures of Herakles comprise a body of legend which is common heritage—to all within the Iliadic world, and to Homer's audience. The story is evoked again by Agamemnon, who uses it to illustrate to Achilles the pattern of delusion to which the king, like Zeus himself, has fallen victim (19. 85 ff.). Agamemnon selects those elements of the Herakleian saga which parallel, with notable precision, the behavioral components of his own situation. His purpose, after all, is overtly didactic—to justify his behavior to Achilles by proving to him that all men and gods alike are subject to delusion and fallibility (19. 91–94). The story is both particularly relevant to Agamemnon's folly and generally applicable to life in the Iliadic world. The behavior of Zeus and Hera in the tale follows an archetypal pattern by which order is confounded by the potential of disorder inherent within it. The events in Book 14, where Hera seduces Zeus in the fictive present, are defined by reference to the same pattern—perhaps explaining why Sleep is moved to recall the Herakleian story (and Zeus to list Herakles among the sons he mentions to Hera). So are the events in the Achaian quarrel; there is a subtle reminiscence of Achilles' blindness insofar as Zeus initiates his own troubles by making a rash oath (19. 103–5). As in Hephaistos' tale, Zeus expresses his anger at being tricked by Hera by hurling her agent, Delusion, from Olympos (19. 125–28).

Agamemnon's tale serves the wider purpose of explaining the presence of Delusion among men at the same time that it explains his own victimization by the fallen force. Like Zeus, however, Agamemnon now recognizes the deceitful nature of his former attitude and is ready to redress the insult to Achilles (19. 135 ff.); like Zeus he casts out Delusion (19. 137). The tale, with the accompanying admission of guilt, is successful in restoring Argive unanimity: Achilles agrees to rededicate himself to the common cause (19. 145). The social significance of the recollected story is defined both by its effectiveness and by its own thematic content which includes uxorial deceit, illicit sexual relations, the mixture of the divine and human realms, childbirth, generation, and royal bloodlines. Sovereignty in the doubly fictional (or historical) world of the tale is seen to be an accidental quality, for only by the accident of his prior birth, Eurystheus, instead of Herakles, becomes the lord of the Argives. Agamemnon's own lordship is also a matter of heritage; it is purely generic, rather than individual, in its origin—he did not earn it himself. Agamemnon's realization of this fact explains the humility which characterizes the exercise of his royal authority from here on.

When he wishes to intimidate Hera and force her into compliance with his authority, Zeus often draws upon the resources of memory and imagination. He, too, refers to the story of Herakles, using it as an exemplum of what will happen to Hera if she pursues an antagonistic course in the present as she did in the past (15. 18 ff.). Even the gods in the Iliadic world appreciate the meaning of history and memory. But Zeus is able also to use creative imagination to fashion a metaphorical tale which serves the same didactic purpose as the story of Herakles. His story of the golden chain is not historical, but purely scientific or philosophical; yet it serves a pragmatic function, in preventing the gods from openly warring against one another (8. 5 ff.).

Achilles' storytelling is a striking counterpart to that of Zeus. In Book 24 Achilles instructs Priam in propriety by relating to him an historical tale and a philosophical, metaphorical story. His purpose in referring to the legend of Niobe (24. 600 ff.) is equivalent to Odysseus' in insisting upon the necessity for a feast before the battle. In each case, eating is recognized to be both literally and symbolically related to man's affirmation of life itself, showing his reconciliation to life's limitations. So Niobe reflects not only Priam but also Achilles himself. She grieves for the death of her children (24. 602 ff.), just as Priam mourns for Hektor, and Achilles laments Patroklos—since Homer compared their relationship to the filial-parental bond (16. 7 ff.). The recurrence here of the number "12" is interesting (24. 603). Are Niobe's twelve children thereby intended to remind us of the twelve Trojan youths sacrificed on Patroklos' pyre by Achilles?

In the tale told by Achilles Apollo's silver bow appears as the agent of order (24. 605); Achilles recognizes the significance of the principle of order whether it manifests itself in the past or in the present. Niobe's disorder follows a pattern repeated many times within the present Iliadic world. Presuming to compare herself to Leto, Niobe is a prototype of Thamyris' pride, Agamemnon's blasphemous treatment of Apollo's priest, and Achilles' overweening reliance upon his own divine connections. She is also an antitype of Agamemnon's new-found humble aspect, inasmuch as her sin is selfish pride in her familial, generative, prowess—something which is determined by powers far beyond the control of the individual. Like Hektor, Niobe's children go unburied until the gods intervene (24. 610). But the difference between the doubly fictional world of Niobe and the Iliadic universe is signified by the contrast between the divine interventions in each instance. In the case of Niobe's children, the gods bury them directly (24. 612); but Homer's vision of human nobility is marked by Zeus' decision to allow Achilles to take the definitive step toward the reestablishment of universal human order.

Following the god's suggestion, but of his own will, Achilles reaffirms the value of life derived from the acceptance of death, both for himself and for Priam. As Apollo says at the beginning of Book 24, it is unnatural for Achilles to be worn out with weeping. Now Achilles himself communicates that orderly perspective to Priam as he bids the old man to eat, following the example of Niobe (24. 613). Then, as their feast begins with due order and mutual participation, the effectiveness of Achilles' historical storytelling is proven (24. 621 ff.). The harmony between Priam and Achilles symbolizes concord among all men, the fulfillment of the image of peaceful unanimity created by Hephaistos' tale and the singing in Book 1—and wrought large upon the surface of the shield.

Achilles also seeks to form Priam's attitude, to make it a reflection of his own detachment, by telling him the philosophical story of Zeus' two jars (24. 525 ff.). In this metaphorical tale, the emphasis is upon the providential order represented by Zeus and its comprehensive effect upon all men (24. 529). Specifically, Achilles suggests the parallel between Peleus and Priam. Both men were blessed with familial strength and happiness which turned, in both cases, into deepest sorrow. There are two lessons to be learned from this pattern: first, since fate is not to be controlled by the individual whom it affects, the best attitude possible for man is one of resignation and equanimity in the face of change. Second, the only kind of love which is safe from the incursions of time is, not the familial, but the purely human personal relationship. Achilles has lost Patroklos; but he is still able to love Priam. And Priam's condemnation of his other children, his insistence that Hektor is his one son, shows that he, too, is pursuing a love which is even more essential than the bond between father and son. As Thetis had counseled him, Achilles advises Priam to end his grief (24. 549–51); there is nothing Priam can do to alter his situation, brought upon him by the operation of the gods (24. 547). Achilles' metaphor of the jars is the expression of divine order by a man who is perfectly attuned to it.

These lesser examples of internal representations of the verbal art lead us to those more extended mnemonic units which are, if only because of their greater length and scope, much more comparable to the epic itself. Recall the dramatic effect of Glaukos' story of Bellerophontes which moves Diomedes to suggest their exchange of armor. Gilbert Murray notes that the story is told by Glaukos "in a form which clearly suggests a recapitulation or allusion [implying] the existence elsewhere of a completer poetical treatment of the same subject" (p. 175). Indeed what Glaukos relates is very much like the creation of a bard (6. 156–202). What suggests that Homer is here having Glaukos invoke a distinct epic tradition familiar both to the fictive listener, Diomedes, and to the poet's contemporary audience is the insufficiency of the information provided by the narrative. As Murray puts it,

one wants more explanation all through. What "blameless guiding of the gods" led Bellerophon to Lycia (171–72)? What "signs of the gods" showed him how to slay the Chimaera (183)? Above all, how did he become "hated of all the gods," and go wandering (200–201)? . . . Is it not that the poet . . . is in the first place referring to an existing legend, and secondly, one may almost say, quoting from an existing poem? (Pp. 175–76)

Murray argues incisively that this impression is confirmed by the consideration that Diomedes' reference to Lykourgos and Dionysos, in the challenge which leads to Glaukos' genealogical tale, is derived from the same Corinthian body of legend to which Bellerophontes' adventures belong.

If this passage is evidence that Homer consciously drew material from specific, autonomously existing, epic cycles dealing with periods of history outside that of the Trojan war, as is now generally believed, it surely indicates the poet's self-awareness. Homer seems to be using the art of verbal recollection as an underlying imagistic principle to organize his own great poem of memory. The frequent appearance of such recollected tales serves as a continuously instructive critical commentary on the poem we are reading (or hearing), a direction to the listener to interpret what he hears in the light of what he has heard before and in the manner of interpretation followed by the fictive listeners. We are not surprised that all the remembered tales in the *Iliad* are replete with thematic parallels to Homer's own story. The Iliadic poet does not repeat other songs entire, but purposefully selects those portions of them by which the patterns of actions and attitudes in his own poem are illuminated.

Glaukos' story is of a hero who experiences adversity due to the blind resentment of a king who, like Agamemnon, is able to affect the hero's social status because he is φέρτερος *phérteros* ("stronger"), since he rules with the sceptre of Zeus (6. 158–59). It is a story, like Agamemnon's own story about Herakles, about unnatural royal lust, political intrigue, delusion among princes, the rite of hospitality, superhuman challenges to individual prowess, the hero's attunement with transcendent order, the ambush and slaughter of a people, a king's recognition of his erratic behavior, social propriety and the fertility which results, and the isolation of the extraordinary individual. It deals with an exile, an expatriate, who finds his true identity in an alien environment.

More specifically, Anteia's deceit is archetypal, reminiscent of the biblical account of Joseph and the pharaoh's wife or of the story of Phaedra. The mysterious, magical properties of the "murderous symbols" (6. 168) add to the esoteric aura of the story, its impression of presenting the sinister, inchoate, forces of social disruption. The mention of Xanthos, moreover, proves that the reality of the tale is historical, not imaginary (6. 172); Glaukos and Diomedes actually meet near the Trojan namesake of that Lykian river. The unnamed lord of Lykia is the historical exemplum, communicated by Glaukos, by which the chain of memories issuing in the present exchange of armor is initiated. For he is the model of the respectful host, reminding Diomedes that his own ancestor Oineus repeated this essential pattern of behavior toward Bellerophontes (6. 173–75). One memory leads to another, and the two together form the inspiration for pragmatic action—a spiritual force is given concrete form.

The resemblance between the labors of Bellerophontes and those of Herakles suggest the interpenetration of oral traditions (6. 180–90). The analogical complementarity between the recollected tale and the artifact-image in the *Iliad* is marked by the similarity between this ambush and the one on the shield (6. 188–90). Up until the ambush the story of Bellerophontes emphasizes the effects of kingly disorder upon the pivotal individual, and upon the community (the men slain by Bellerophontes) as well. But the slaughter of his best men leads the Lykian king to recognize the disorderliness of the symbols sent by Proitos and of his own response to them, and to proclaim his recognition of the obvious orderliness of Bellerophontes as one which proves, by its effect in action, that he is attuned with divinity (6. 191). The king's consequent gesture is exactly that made by Agamemnon when he is ready to admit his mistreatment of Achilles: he offers the hero his daughter (6. 192). Bellerophontes is also rewarded with a τέμενος *témenos* ("land reserve"), over which he is to preside as does the king upon the shield (6. 195). His reward, symbolizing society's recognition of his primary orderliness, has literal issue in the children who bring glory to their father and to their people alike (6. 197–99). And his progeny reflect

Bellerophontes' harmonious mode of being so perfectly that Zeus reemphasizes his approval of the hero's behavior by himself allying sexually with Laodameia to produce Sarpedon (6. 199). Glaukos' relation to Sarpedon, the son of Zeus, explains why the outcome of his confrontation with Diomedes is justified. As in the case of the meeting between Aineias and Achilles, both men are allowed to survive because both are connected with the principle of order. Yet Glaukos' story ends with uncertainty and the implications of tragedy. Bellerophontes' final unexplained isolation from the human sphere is an absolute reversal of the status of Achilles at the termination of the *Iliad*. It serves to define the historical inferiority of Troy to Argos at the same time that it heightens the impact of Achilles' superiority.

Though not a singer, Nestor by his frequent storytelling defines the social role of the experienced counselor as being practically synonymous with that of the poet of memory. But Nestor's reasoning does not stir powerful emotions and is therefore in one important respect different— that's why he is so often mistakenly linked with Shakespeare's Polonius. From Nestor's habit of justifying his advice through recollection, it becomes clear that bard and counselor are just different expressions for a function that is also performed by the prophet. Nestor, Kalchas, and Poulydamas all serve society in more or less the same way. Knowledge of the future, like the perception of the significance of present actions, is based upon a recognition of the essential patterns of human life derived from a comprehensive awareness of the past. Three instances of Nestor's bardlike function in the Iliadic world show how he is a kind of reflection of the epic poet himself.

In Book 7 Nestor plays a crucial role in arranging the duel between Aias and Hektor. Aias is motivated to perform an exemplary deed by Nestor's counsel. Nestor refers to the shame of Peleus that would be caused by his knowledge of the present cowardice of the Achaians before Hektor, so different from their past courage that Peleus remembers with pride (7. 124–31). Nestor declares that he himself would bear the responsibility of meeting Hektor if only he were as strong as he was in his youth (7. 132–33). A younger man must bear it instead. To prove that his authority in this counsel is based on his glorious deeds in his youth, Nestor recalls his performance in the Pylian war, when an event corresponding to Hektor's present challenge occurred (7. 134 ff.). The enemy champion Ereuthalion stood forth to challenge Nestor's people (7. 136). Ereuthalion's armor evokes again the Corinthian saga involving Lykourgos (7. 137–49), recalling Glaukos' tale. But there is a difference between Glaukos' and Diomedes' accounts of these events and Nestor's. For Nestor himself was involved actually in that war just as, like them, he is in the present conflict; and he is also effective in both the past and the present through his deeds and words, respectively. So Nestor resembles the poet inasmuch as he shares the poet's transcendence of time. As in the present, no one dared to answer the champion's challenge (7. 150–51). But Nestor alone came forward, fought with Ereuthalion, and vanquished him with the help of Athene (7. 152–54). Were he still in possession of the physical strength he then enjoyed Nestor himself could defeat even Hektor (7. 157–58). His willingness immediately affects his listeners, suggesting the emotional impact characteristic of Homer's art. Homer emphasizes with a succinct syntactical conjunction (7. 161) that Nestor's story is the direct cause of the eagerness displayed by the volunteers who now offer themselves for the duel. Nestor's invocation of an orderly pattern of behavior in the past inspires that pattern's repetition in the present.

Nestor's mnemonic art plays its most important role, of course, when he convinces Patroklos of the necessity of the reinvolvement of Myrmidons in the national cause. Since Nestor's strength is not what it was, Achilles alone can save the army from its present crisis (11. 669–70). Nestor tells the story of the Epeian war in which his own defeat of Itymoneus restored the equilibrium of Neleus' society by enriching it materially (11. 671–72). Nestor's victory brought internal order to Pylos (11. 684–86) at the same time that it was the basis for stabilizing Pylos' external front, since it allowed Neleus to pay off his foreign debts (11. 687–88). Nestor thereby rescued his nation from the weakened position into which it had fallen because of the coming of Herakles (11. 689–90).

Just as Hektor has now wounded the best of the Achaians, leaving only Achilles intact, so Herakles had killed all the sons of Neleus except Nestor (11. 690–92). Therefore the weakened Pylian nation became the object of disdain and exploitation since there were no individuals remaining strong enough to defend it (11. 693–94). But because of Nestor's act Neleus is able to reconstruct social order. From the spoils won by his young son, the king takes for himself the largest share (11. 702), giving the rest to his people to divide fairly among themselves (11. 703–4). The just distribution of booty among all members of Pylian society (11. 705) is in striking contrast to Agamemnon's overweening selfishness in Book 1 and also looks forward to Book 23; and the internal stability of Pylos is marked by their harmonious sacrifice to the gods (11. 706).

Seeking revenge for Itymoneus the Epeians attacked the city of Thryoessa and lay siege to it (11. 706–12), just as the Trojans have now threatened the Achaian ships. Stirred up by Athene, however, the Pylians are unanimously eager to cooperate in the defense (11. 713–16). This is the crucial point of Nestor's story: the people are ready, but lack a distinguished leader. Neleus, mindful of his other lost sons (like Priam), refuses to allow the young Nestor to take part in the battle. His attempt to hide his son must remind Homer's audience of the story of Peleus' similarly motivated effort to disguise Achilles as a girl to prevent the Danaans from taking him with them to Troy. From this point on, Nestor's didactic intention is apparent: it is the reentry of Achilles which he is portraying; that is the essential pattern Nestor means to reincarnate in the present. Nestor took part in the war despite his father's prohibition (11. 717 ff.); like Hektor he defends his parent of his own accord. The sacrifice to Zeus, the communal feast, and the night's slumber with armor near at hand (11. 726–30) are perfect parallels to the Argives' preparation for the final engagement under the leadership of Achilles. Communal unity comes with the commitment of the pivotal individual.

After another sacrifice to Zeus, marking the divine orderliness of their defensive posture, the Pylians join battle with the Epeians at dawn (11. 735). As the fight begins Nestor is outstanding among his people; he is the first to kill a man (11. 737). And the man he kills is Moulios (11. 745), the Epeian leader, whose death causes the rout of the entire army. As the Pylians follow up their advantage by pursuing the now disorderly remnant of the enemy, Zeus imbues all the Pylians with the strength of Nestor (11. 752)—as the Achaians will share Achilles' exaltation. All the Epeians are killed, their armor taken by the victorious Pylians (11. 754). At this point Nestor's narration subtly betrays its pragmatic intention; he ceases to call his people "Pylians," but now refers to them by their generic name: the joyful Ἀχαιοὶ *Akhaioì* ("Achaians"—11. 759) give proper thanks to Zeus and to Nestor, just as the same nation will thank Zeus and Achilles in the immediate future. Nestor concludes his story with a phrase that marks his social orderliness, the ultimate theme of his tale: " 'That was I, among men' " (11. 761). The reciprocity between the individual and the community is clearly defined; his recollected tale is a microcosm of the *Iliad*, the Epeian war a prototype of the Trojan. Patroklos is convinced. He leaves the tent of Nestor to employ the art of words, learned from Nestor, upon Achilles. The continuum between words and deeds, between past and present, fiction and reality, remembered action and real action, is fatefully reaffirmed.

A third example of Nestor's practical memory is his reply to Achilles' presentation of the jar in Book 23 as a mark of the national respect earned by the old man. The situation recalls to Nestor another portion of the Epeian story, before the war between Elis and Pylos. As always, Nestor's memory is perfectly appropriate to the present circumstances. He speaks of the burial of the Epeian hero Amaryngkeus and the funeral games held at Bouprasion at which the young Nestor distinguished himself (23.

630–31). He took first prize in nearly every event, defeating Klytomedes at boxing, Anglaios at wrestling, Iphiklos in the foot race, and Polydoros and Phyleus in spear-casting (23. 634–37); Nestor lost only in the chariot race (23. 638). The order in which he recounts the various games is a subtle witness to the relevance of memory to reality, for it reverses exactly the actual events at Patroklos' funeral, where the horse race is first, followed by the boxing match between Epeios and Eurylos, the wrestling bout between Odysseus and Aias, the foot race, and the spear-throw. Nestor presents himself as the epitome of Achaian prowess. He is a parallel to Achilles who refrains from participating in the games not only from respect for Patroklos, but also because he knows that he would be victorious in them all. Achilles is Nestor's successor in social action. The gift signifies the cyclical continuity of social existence—how action leads to words of counsel which in turn lead to memory—as the old Nestor receives the honor due to him from the man who plays his orderly role in the present. Nestor concludes his recollection with a most significant address to his benefactor:

'Go now, and honour the death of your companion with contests.
I accept this from you gratefully, and my heart is happy
that you have remembered me and my kindness, that I am not forgotten
for the honour that should be my honour among the Achaians.
May the gods, for what you have done for me, give you great happiness.'
(23. 646–50)

Nestor's last words in the *Iliad* distinguish the didactic import of the tale he tells here from that of all the others he has invoked throughout the poem. Before now Nestor's intention has always been related to the motivation of a specific pragmatic purpose: he sought to arbitrate in the quarrel between Achilles and Agamemnon (1. 254 ff.; cf. 9. 96 ff.), advised the building of the wall and the burial of the dead (7. 327 ff.), suggested the spy mission (10. 204 ff.), urged Agamemnon to placate Achilles with gifts (9. 111 ff.), and inspired Patroklos to intercede with Achilles. In each case his words result in action that is socially beneficial; in each case, he speaks from memory. Here, however, his speech is self-reflective, defining the essence of the art of counsel. As the counterpart of Achilles whose exercise of authority in the present is so pronounced, Nestor asserts that authority is orderly because it follows precedent. His brief narrative has outlined that precedent—the orderliness of the Epeian games. Nestor's concluding remarks symbolize the point of transmission through which past and present are united in an unbroken continuum. For his authorization, no less than Achilles', defines the orderliness of the funeral games for Patroklos (23. 646).

And Nestor accepts Achilles' gift as the token of his recognition of the fundamental social role of the transmitter of memory (23. 647–48). Nestor calls upon the divinity which inspires him to accord the same happiness to Achilles (23. 650). Old age blesses youth in a perfect closure of the generation gap, defining the very instant in which the tradition is communicated. But the vertical continuity symbolized by Nestor's words, from one generation to another, presages the horizontal continuity in Achilles' treatment of Priam. In Book 24 the young man recognizes the value of the old king, repeating the courtesy of Book 23; but the recognition also affirms Achilles' final awareness of the community of man in the present, on an essential plane that makes national or political distinctions irrelevant. In extending his love beyond space as well as beyond time, Achilles himself experiences the extraordinary poetic satisfaction that Nestor wishes for him.

The dominant artistic imagery of Book 9 is that of song and memory. Here Homer presents Achilles with his lyre. During the embassy Phoinix appears in the bardlike role that defines his status in the Iliadic world. The old man relates to Achilles first his own history and genealogy and then the story of Meleagros, the most extended memorial tale in the *Iliad*. Phoinix reminds Achilles of his own past in order to justify his influence upon the young warrior (9. 447 ff.). The patterns of the autobiographical events he recounts are essentially generic, although accidentally particular; it is a story of wrath, dislocation, compassion, hierarchical turmoil, sexual manipulation, the breaking and honoring of taboos. Like Patroklos, Phoinix is related to Achilles by the bond of guest-friendship, although in his case it is inherited rather than direct. He is an expatriate like so many others. Phoinix was compelled to leave his Helladic homeland by the wrath of his own father (9. 447–48). Amyntor, like Agamemnon, disrupted the stability of his royal household by preferring a concubine to his queenly wife (9. 449–50). Phoinix's mother, hoping to regain the loyalty of her errant husband, begged her son to lie in love with his father's mistress. But the stratagem failed; Amyntor wished death upon his son. His curses against Phoinix, though proper in form, were less than fatal because he himself was blinded by excessive disorder (9. 453–57).

Phoinix, recalling Achilles in Book 1, then determined to murder his father, ridding his family and kingdom of an unalterably disordered individual (9. 458). He, too, was prevented from this ignominious deed by the counsel of the gods and his friends. Although he had broken the law of incest, Phoinix respected the taboo against parricide and regicide, recognizing that such a crime would irrevocably cut him off from honor

(9. 459–61). Perhaps because they hoped to retain the natural heir to their kingdom, his kinsmen protected Phoinix from Amyntor's wrath and from his own folly (9. 464–74). But his iconoclastic alliance with his father's mistress had made Phoinix vulnerable to his father's curses: he would now be barren. Phoinix himself was aware then that he was in fact no longer a proper heir. No longer able to maintain a viable identity or to perform a wholesome function within such an environment, Phoinix took the only remaining orderly action: eluding the vigilance of his defenders he escaped from Hellas and sought sanctuary in Phthia (9. 475–79).

He was able to do this because Phthia was the seat of the society which included, as a political subdivision, Hellas. Phoinix's crime was a political rather than social or national one (9. 478); it did not affect the stability of Peleus' entire government. Peleus ruled many cities, of which Hellas was one (9. 395–96; 16. 594–95). It was no contradiction to order, therefore, that Peleus received Phoinix with hospitality and honor (9. 480). The old king treated the stranger as if he belonged to his own family, granting him political responsibilities as well (9. 481–84). So Phoinix was able to redefine himself in a new social context; one political environment could be substituted for the other. The assimilation then became reciprocal when Phoinix became another father to Achilles (9. 485–91), enduring a parent's suffering and displaying a father's patience and dedication in raising the youth to manhood. Disorder had indeed affected Phoinix, inasmuch as he was now deprived of producing offspring of his own blood (9. 492–93); political systems, after all, must be valued and protected. But the social system is greater, more essential. Peleus' orderliness allowed Phoinix to enjoy the paternal role by acting as if Achilles were his natural son. Phoinix's story is calculated well to move Achilles from his pitiless attitude—as Phoinix explicitly states (9. 497). He should follow the example provided by his own father. And if the tale fails to convince Achilles, the fault lies in his unresponsive posture and perhaps also because Phoinix's argument in favor of pity is weaker than the one for deserting the fight.

Sensing that he has not yet achieved the purpose of the embassy, Phoinix renews his attempt by recalling the saga of Meleagros. The events in this story are, not surprisingly, reflections both of Phoinix's autobiography and of Homer's *Iliad*. The tale of Meleagros is also distinguished by a purposeful introduction by its narrator; nowhere else is the didactic intention of memory stated so specifically. Phoinix pleads with Achilles to listen to the logic of the ambassadors and to recognize the orderliness of their mission:

>   Do not you make vain their argument
> nor their footsteps, though before this one could not blame your anger.
> Thus it was in the old days also, the deeds that we hear of
> from the great men, when the swelling anger descended upon them.
> The heroes would take gifts; they would listen, and be persuaded.
> For I remember this action of old, it is not a new thing,
> and how it went; you are all my friends, I will tell it among you.
>
>   (9. 522–28)

Even the occasion of Phoinix's recollection is analogous to a singer's
performance, immediately following the hospitable feast Achilles has
given for the ambassadors. As the rite of hospitality demands, the
thought of gifts may come only after the guest has been accorded the
honor and respect due to him. And it is about the acceptance of the gifts
that Phoinix speaks. His story is intended to explicate their symbolic
significance, to instruct the Achaians as well as Achilles in the proper
mode of behavior by which the warrior's acceptance should be recognized (9. 528). Homer emphasizes the social setting of the telling, as well
as its communal purpose. Phoinix's recitation is an altogether remarkable performance—a most important glimpse of Homeric self-awareness.
The tale of Meleagros is the perfect example of Havelock's observation
that "the epic dramatizes the educative process itself" (p. 120). The story
is a microcosmic *Iliad* and Phoinix's method of narration parallels
Homer's own.

The succinct quality of Phoinix's opening lines crystallizes the general
thematic framework in which the wrath of Meleagros is to appear as
effectively as the proem of the *Iliad*. Meleagros' social development is
portrayed against the tumultuous background of international conflict.
The offensive and the defensive parties are defined at the outset, as are
their respective emotions and the results of these emotions upon the
emotions of the enemy (9. 529–32). The situation parallels the present
moment in which the Argives, in the ironic reversal of fortunes caused
by the quarrel, are being besieged by the Trojans. Now that Phoinix has
outlined the wider framework of history in which the particular story of
Meleagros plays a formative part, he turns back in time, exactly like
Homer after the proem, to present the origins of the war.

The primary cause of this war is also a divinity (9. 532). Artemis'
position in the past has two reflections in the present: as far as the Trojan
war is concerned, she behaves like the jealous Hera; but, in the story of
the wrath of Achilles, she is the angry Apollo. Like Hera, Artemis is
associated with a golden throne (9. 533); and her arrows are related to
those of her brother (9. 538). Oineus is the precursor of both Paris and
Agamemnon; his appearance here recalls Diomedes' reference to him (9.

534–37). Oineus' delusion has separated him from the principle of order (9. 537). As in Book 1, so here, the blindness of the (Kalydonian) king has catastrophic repercussions upon an entire society (9. 538). The boar let loose as the agent of Artemis' wrath has several parallels in the Iliadic world (9. 539–40). It is an embodiment of the consequences of Agamemnon's wrath upon his people. Separating the trees from their roots (9. 542), the boar is like the force of Achilles' anger which dashes the sceptre of Argos to the ground—the gesture that symbolizes the physical weakening of the Argive nation by the isolation of its chief warrior. Or the boar is like Hektor who brings havoc among the Danaans. Finally the animal presages Achilles' supernatural charisma, in his new social identity, which allows him to fell the Trojans as an unquenchable fire destroys a forest, individual by individual and tree by tree. Meleagros' killing of the boar (9. 543) corresponds to Agamemnon's admission of his error—to which the present embassy bears witness. It is Achilles' orderliness finally conquering the disorderly elements in his nature, and the consequent slaying of Hektor who represents the social threat to Argos (as well as, wearing the old armor of Achilles, one who has not discarded his own personal disorder). Ultimately Meleagros' deed defines the pattern by which Achilles, in Book 24, replaces the destructiveness of nationalistic hatred with universal love.

The chain of causality in Phoinix's tale is less complicated and therefore more easily discernible than that of Homer's world: Oineus' error has led to the jealousy of Artemis and her commissioning of the boar. Now the death of the boar increases the goddess' anger and causes her to inspire the Kouretes to wage war upon the Kalydonians (9. 548). As long as Meleagros is involved in the defense, however, the Aitolians are immune from defeat (9. 550–52). Phoinix, in two lines, recapitulates the Achaian situation that has prevailed for nine years preceding the quarrel. The situation changes when Meleagros is angered (9. 553). Phoinix intervenes in his objective narrative to make a generalization which explicates his didactic intention. Clearly he refers to Achilles (9. 554), whose emotions have overcome his reason, whose social orderliness has been disrupted by personal disorder—just what happened in the case of Meleagros. Althaia is the counterpart of Agamemnon as the cause of the hero's wrath (9. 555).

Because of his mother's unnatural behavior, Meleagros resigns his national commitment to concentrate all his loyalty upon Kleopatra (9. 556). His wife is analogous to Patroklos, or to Briseis. Meleagros attempts to isolate conjugal love from parental love just as Achilles will attempt to limit his affection to the interpersonal level, separating himself from the national context. Of course Kleopatra's relationship with Meleagros also resembles Achilles' with Briseis. Meleagros isolates himself from the battle; he is an archetype of the sulking Achilles (9. 565). Homer may be revealing his sources.

Phoinix describes Althaia's cursing her son in much the same terms as he had related Amyntor's curses against him (9. 566). In this case, however, the consequences affect the Aitolian society as well as the individual and are therefore more sharply analogous to the repercussions of Agamemnon's treatment of Achilles (9. 571). Now it is evident that Phoinix's second tale is an improvement—and as realistic as Homer's, since the cause of the war is revealed to be human as well as divine (9. 573). Owing to Artemis' increased anger and to Althaia's curse of her son, the Aitolians are attacked by the Kouretes. Phoinix has reconstructed his remembered pattern of historical events to the point at which the past and the present are proven to be circumstantially related. For the next events in his narrative perfectly reflect the present situation, the meeting between Achilles and the envoys. The progression of petitions is carefully delineated. First the elders and the priests plead with Meleagros to reenter the engagement, offering him a τέμενος *témenos* ("land reserve") as the appropriate reward for his abnegation of individual grievances (9. 574–81): that is, just what Agamemnon now offers to Achilles. The agency of the priests proves that the offer of gifts is essentially orderly; they act on behalf of the entire society to allow Meleagros the opportunity of resuming his former harmonious human status without losing face and before his nation is damaged seriously.

After Meleagros' refusal of the elders, his father suspends the dignified protocol of his royal role to come in person as a suppliant to his son (9. 581). The social disorderliness of Meleagros' attitude is dramatically symbolized in the image of the old king pounding on the young prince's bedroom doors in vain (9. 582–83). The bedroom retreat, of course, recalls Paris' behavior; Hektor finds his brother in the bedroom (Book 6). Oineus' action here contrasts with that of both Priam and Agamemnon. Priam doesn't beg Hektor to involve himself in the battle—he does the very opposite. Nor does Agamemnon come in person to Achilles as Priam does; his delegation of the embassy suggests that his selfishness is still in effect, at least to a degree. The most telling parallel to Oineus, however, is Phoinix himself: the preceding autobiography served to frame his supplication in the context of fatherhood.

But Oineus, too, fails to move Meleagros; just as Phoinix has failed until now to move Achilles. Therefore Althaia herself arrives to plead with her son (9. 584). From this point forward, Phoinix becomes the prophet as well as the transmitter of memory. Althaia's action is stated without explanation. But the implications of her presence are nonetheless clear: she must have relented from her personal vendetta. She performs the proper function of the responsible queen; her attitude, like Hekabe's in Book 6, is no longer selfish, but humble. So the scene presages that in which Agamemnon goes in person to express his remorse and ask forgiveness of Achilles. Althaia is accompanied by Meleagros' sisters, in another familiar pattern. Paris' brother comes to denounce his egocentric behavior and demand his recommitment to the society it has endangered.

The failure of his entire personal family is followed by the unsuccessful attempt by his friends to reconcile Meleagros (9. 585–87). Meleagros remains obstinate until his chamber itself is assaulted and Kalydon set on fire (9. 588–89). Phoinix, of course, knows that Achilles has promised that he would not fight until his own ships were endangered; that knowledge explains his selection from his store of memory. But it is the foreknowledge of Homer himself that directs the analogical quality of this scene. The situation Phoinix describes is equally as critical as that which will prevail when Patroklos comes to entreat Achilles to save the wounded Achaians and the threatened ships in Book 16.

Kleopatra now intercedes with her husband on behalf of her nation (9. 590). Her general description of the social anguish which comes inevitably upon all individuals alike at the fall of a city (9. 591–94) is very like Andromache's speech and Hektor's reply in their last meeting on the wall where the envisioned sorrow is all the more painful for being applicable to the present characters. Though Kleopatra does not seem to experience the sorrow she predicts as Andromache does, she, like Andromache, speaks in tears (9. 591). Johannes Kakridis suspects that Kleopatra may indeed have been the model from which Homer derived his characterization of Andromache. Like Meleagros, Hektor too loves his wife more than anyone else—as Achilles loves Briseis. The value system in which the wife outranks all others seems to be indigenous to the new society; for the conjugal relationship connects both blood and true personal affection.

Kleopatra's counterpart in the Iliadic world is Patroklos. And before the final incentive of death it is Patroklos' speech, defining the inhumanity of Achilles' attitude, that convinces the Achaian hero to allow the Myrmidons to save the stricken Argives. Like Meleagros, Achilles' concern is only with his personal honor, as yet unclearly defined, together with the loss of Briseis, his love for Patroklos, his own ships and people. Webster suggests how Phoinix's mnemonic knowledge of the past is related to Homer's poetic foresight: "The story of Meleager is a large scale simile. It is a working model of the present situation and of the future course of action which the poet knows: Achilles will defend the ships when they are burning. . . . Everything which is irrelevant to its function is left out" (p. 249). At the same time the tale, like the great shield, is instructive in itself; it is a vast exemplum of social mores, revealing essential human order with a relevance that transcends historical events.

Meleagros' conversion is expressed in the imagery of action, as he dons his armor (9. 595–96) exactly as Achilles will in Book 19. The momentous event also recalls Paris' arming; but unlike Paris', Meleagros' reentry into battle is socially constructive. Kakridis notes that Meleagros' unnatural isolation was caused by a social insult, on the familial-parental level, but that his reinvolvement is motivated by the social persuasion of Kleopatra, on the familial-personal level. His loyalty to one social relationship serves to counteract his enmity toward another, with the result that his total communal orientation is effectively reactivated. There is a crucial difference between Meleagros and Achilles in this respect. Meleagros shows no concern about the safety of the Aetolians; by vanquishing the Kouretes at his wife's request he incidentally saves the remaining Kalydonians. But such an interpretation of Achilles' conversion is unacceptably narrow. Homer has enhanced the universality of his inherited materials, widened the scope of the tradition, by presenting Achilles as being no less concerned with Argos than he is with the honor of Patroklos. The restoration of society in the *Iliad* is far from being incidental. Achilles, like Meleagros (9. 597), saves his people from the inevitable consequences of a further prolongation of his excessive wrath.

The concluding emphasis of Phoinix's tale is also very different from the ending of the *Iliad*. Meaning to warn Achilles of the detrimental effect his continued isolation may have upon himself as well as upon his nation, Phoinix recalls that Meleagros' rescue of Kalydon was not followed by his receiving the gifts that had been promised to him formerly (9. 598–99). The implication is that, because of his excessively prolonged alienation from his society, Meleagros received no communal recognition for his eventual rescue of Kalydon. The obstinate expression of egoism results, ironically despite Meleagros' final conversion, in the loss of social identity: that is what will happen to Achilles, Phoinix implies, if he does not accept the gifts that are offered now (9. 600–605). All opportunity for experiencing the glorious honor of his fellowmen in the present will be denied him. Achilles' response is that his honor is from Zeus and does not depend upon the goodwill of men (9. 606 ff.). He considers gifts, at this point, irrelevant to honor. Achilles has rejected the purely heroic code professed by Agamemnon, and reflected in Kleopatra. He has judged Phoinix's counsel that he should accept the offerings as no less materialistic than Agamemnon's attitude in the quarrel. In this sense Phoinix is indeed culpable; his emphasis falls upon the literal value of the gifts rather than upon their symbolic significance. And, to pursue the analogy between Phoinix and the poet (as my student John B. Lima points out), perhaps his storytelling fails because it is a noticeable reversal in the host-guest relationship; Phoinix should be listening to Achilles' storytelling (or to his court poet), not doing all the talking himself. When Achilles finally accepts material presents from Agamemnon, he does so only because he recognizes that they are outward signs of the king's internal sincerity; it is what they stand for that moves Achilles. Therefore ultimately the difference between Agamemnon's present attitude—the haughtiness with which he commissions the embassy and the self-confident way in which he is sure that his gifts will be sufficient—and the one he will display after Patroklos' death explains why Phoinix's story is ineffective. Well-ordered in itself, his tale is devalued by the social framework in which it appears—like Hephaistos' tale in Book 1, which has only temporary effect. John Lima's parallel outline summarizes the relationship between Phoinix's story and the *Iliad*:

The Tale of Meleagros	*The Iliad*
The primary cause of the war is the wrath of a divinity.	The underlying cause of the war is the wrath of a divinity.
Oineus' delusion leads to disorder.	Agamemnon's blindness leads to disorder.
Artemis' wrath releases the destructive boar.	Apollo releases his plague arrows.
The boar is killed to temporarily relieve the Aitolians.	Agamemnon subdues his own obstinancy to temporarily relieve the Achaians.
The Aitolians hold off their enemy as long as Meleagros fights.	The Achaians hold off the Trojans as long as Achilles fights.
The elders send an embassy to Meleagros.	Agamemnon sends an embassy to Achilles.
Meleagros rejects the gift of land. Oineus pleads with Meleagros.	Achilles rejects the gifts of Agamemnon. Phoinix pleads with Achilles.
Meleagros fails to yield to the embassy because of personal honor.	Achilles is unyielding because of personal honor.
Meleagros holds out until Kalydon is set on fire.	Achilles holds out until the ships of the Myrmidons are threatened with fire.
Meleagros eventually fights out of love for Kleopatra.	Achilles eventually fights out of love for Patroklos.

Meleagros develops a social conscience.	Achilles substitutes a general human love for nationalistic hatred.
Meleagros and the Aitolians form a single dramatic entity.	Achilles and Argos are imagistically a unit (Book 10).
Meleagros eventually eliminates the threat to his people.	Achilles eliminates the threat to the Argives.

A comparable social inadequacy explains why Achilles' own singing in Book 9 must be considered disorderly. Memory is meaningless in isolation. But the image of Achilles with his lyre nevertheless possesses great significance in our recognition of Homer's self-awareness. When the envoys have left the camp of Agamemnon,

> Now they came beside the shelters and ships of the Myrmidons
> and they found Achilleus delighting his heart in a lyre, clear-sounding,
> splendid and carefully wrought, with a bridge of silver upon it,
> which he won out of the spoils when he ruined Eëtion's city.
> With this he was pleasuring his heart, and singing of men's fame,
> as Patroklos was sitting over against him, alone, in silence,
> watching Aikides and the time he would leave off singing.
>
> (9. 185–91)

The daedalean splendor of the artifact is appropriate to Achilles' orderly potential, just as the unspecified nature of his song nicely symbolizes the fact that his poetic potential has not yet been realized (9. 187–89). The passage also deepens our awareness of the importance of the friendship between Achilles and Patroklos by suggesting that their relationship is comparable to that of the poet and his audience (9. 190–91). The most important imagistic element here is Homer's mention of the lyre's origin (9. 188). The story of Eëtion and Achilles' sack of Thebes is the most prominent and extraordinary mnemonic image in the *Iliad*, surpassing by the frequency of its recurrence in significant situations even the much lengthier tale of Meleagros which appears only once. Even more widely than Phoinix's story references to Achilles' great foray radiate throughout the *Iliad* to define the human patterns operating in Homer's fictional world. The poet purposely uses his audience's independent knowledge of the Theban tradition as a principle of organization by which we are able to fully appreciate the intricate interrelationships among the major characters in the poem of Achilles' wrath. By noting their respective connections with the great foray of Achilles, Homer makes the conjunctions of his characters seem tangible evidence of a transcendent design for which fate is too murky a term. The design by which the destinies of

Chryseis, Briseis, Andromache, and Pedasos are meshed with those of Agamemnon, Klytaimestra, Patroklos, Hektor, and Achilles must be attributed by Homer and by his audience to the pragmatic workings of Zeus' governing principle. Achilles is the first to evoke the memory of the sack of Thebes when he explains to Thetis the cause of his grievance against Agamemnon. Among the spoils won by his prowess in that campaign was Chryseis, the prize chosen fairly by the Achaians for their king (1. 366–69). Chryseis is, of course, the primary cause of the present quarrel. She plies the Argive king's loom as an alien presence in his household (1. 31)—the exact fate Andromache predicted for herself. The victim of a forceful removal from her natural environment by a foreign prince, Chryseis is the first whose position parallels Helen's. Should Agamemnon fulfill his desire to substitute her for Klytaimestra all Argos would be disrupted; indeed because he refuses to return her to Chryses, the army is physically punished. The arrows of Apollo are equivalent to the onslaught of the Argives against Troy caused by Paris' refusal to restore Helen.

The social turmoil of Theban, as well as of Trojan, history seems to affect women especially. Homer sees them as the most basic symbols of the individual and generic fertility threatened by international conflict and internal social upheaval. That women are so generally presented as the victims of disorder makes it all the more paradoxical that Helen seems to have been involved in the process of disorder itself, although her involvement is curtailed in the fictional present. The next reference to Thebes reveals the connection between Briseis, whom John W. Zarker calls "the actual catalyst for the wrath of Achilles" (p. 112), and its first cause, Chryseis. This time it is the narrator's allusion; Homer describes Briseis' origins and present captive status in a way which "joins together the fates of Lyrnessos and Thebes, of Briseis and Chryseis" (p. 112). The poet emphasizes Achilles' perfect right to his prize by noting the great effort it took to achieve the double victory (2. 690–93). Achilles' relationship with Briseis is orderly in contrast to Agamemnon's with Chryseis. There is no one, for Briseis, from her former natural environment surviving to demand her loyalty and love. Agamemnon's appropriation of her is no less disorderly than Paris' abduction of Helen. For Achilles alone now defines Briseis' identity, provides her with a stable social framework as Hektor does for Andromache.

Briseis' lament over the body of Patroklos (19. 290–99) makes it clear that Achilles is everything to her, as Hektor is to Andromache. Because her involvement with Achilles is total, Briseis' mourning combines personal grief with generic sorrow. At the same time her speech provides the occasion for defining the loss of her past identity through Achilles' slaying of her husband and for revealing the precise nature of her present relationships with Achilles and Patroklos (19. 291–94). It was through the agency of Patroklos that Briseis became the espoused wife of Achilles, finding what she considers a reprieve from her otherwise inevitably sorrowful destiny (19. 295–99). Homer makes it evident here that Patroklos' role is also widely social: his matchmaking is calculated to insure the natural fulfillment of Achilles' familial and royal position by providing him with a proper consort, a womb from which his progeny may issue to continue his line and the integrity of Phthia. In her reference to her own past and present circumstances, then, Briseis also affirms that Achilles' wrath is far from being solely heroic, materialistic, jealousy. Were it not for this scene our conclusion might be very different. As it is, the loss of Briseis affects Achilles no less than Helen's loss does Menelaos.

Briseis is related actually to Andromache as she is symbolically to Helen. Zarker remarks that "Homer makes the equation between the fate of the captive Briseis of Lyrnessos, whose husband was slain before the city by Achilles, and of Andromache of Troy, who will lose her husband in the same way by the same hand. Homer seems to be spinning a web of foreboding and ultimate destruction over Troy by intermittent references to Achilles' former exploits" (p. 112). All four Iliadic women are involved in the same fateful pattern, marked by the poem's images of memory. The memory of Thebes is most poignant to Andromache. At her first appearance in the *Iliad*, Homer presents her as the daughter of Eëtion given in marriage to Hektor (6. 395–98). The narrator's reference to Thebes prepares his audience for Andromache's recollection of the role played by Achilles in that city's fall—and in her own consequent loss of social identity (6. 396–97):

'It was brilliant Achilleus who slew my father, Eëtion,
when he stormed the strong-founded citadel of the Kilikians,
Thebe of the towering gates. He killed Eëtion
but did not strip his armour, for his heart respected the dead man,
but burned the body in all its elaborate war gear
and piled a grave mound over it, and the nymphs of the mountains,
daughters of Zeus of the aegis, planted elm trees about it.
And they who were my seven brothers in the great house all went
upon a single day down into the house of the death god,
for swift-footed brilliant Achilleus slaughtered all of them
as they were tending their white sheep and their lumbering oxen;
and when he had led my mother, who was queen under wooded Plakos,
here, along with all his other possessions, Achilleus
released her again, accepting ransom beyond count, but Artemis
of the showering arrows struck her down in the halls of her father.

Hektor, thus you are father to me, and my honoured mother,
you are my brother, and you it is who are my young husband.'

(6. 414–30)

Andromache is related to Hektor in much the same way as Briseis and
Patroklos are to Achilles. Only the fact that she married Hektor before the
fall of Thebes distinguishes Andromache's status from Chryseis'. She is a
guest, but not a captive. Yet like Briseis, Andromache's present social
position, defined solely through Hektor, is one she has assumed because
of the dissolution of her native environment.

Andromache reminds her husband of the fate of Eëtion in order to
argue against his return to the war which promises to have similar
consequences for Hektor. Her recollection includes Achilles' generous
respect for his defeated enemies, both in the matter of the funeral and of
the ransom. Owen remarks that "the conduct of Achilles [is] the more
noticeable because we have just witnessed Agamemnon's mercilessness
to Adrestus (6. 55 ff.)" (p. 69). The proleptic contrast, with Achilles'
treatment of Hektor's body, is even more significant. For it is memory
this time which proves that Achilles, until he meets with Priam, has yet
to fully realize the orderly potential of his individuality. Picturing
Achilles as "the heroic chivalric epic ideal," Andromache's account, says
Zarker, "reveals the Achilles before the wrath and as he will be again
after receiving Priam and returning the body of Hektor" (p. 11).

Andromache's final reference to Thebes has to do with the headdress
given to her by Aphrodite on the occasion of her departure from Eëtion's
house to wed Hektor (22. 470–72). The headdress, unlike the lyre taken
from the fallen city, would seem to have escaped the influence of
Achilles, to have remained a symbol of order; now, of course, it is
precisely because of him that Andromache casts it to the ground. In her
first words of mourning, Andromache explicitly compares the fate of
Hektor and Troy to her own destiny and that of Thebes (22. 477–81). Like
the artifact Andromache has escaped captivity at Thebes only to find that
Achilles' influence over her social existence is, after all, inevitable. The
entire Troadic system must pay for his anger, city by city until the capital
itself is destroyed.

Rejecting the gifts of Agamemnon, Achilles explains to Odysseus that
he has ample material treasure of his own, including the iron he won
from Thebes (9. 366)—Homer does not lose sight of even such an
apparently mundane object. The iron is mentioned again in the funeral
games of Book 23 where it is both symbol and prize for the shot put.
Achilles describes the extraordinary value of the metal in graphic terms
which form the final testimony in the *Iliad* to the wealth of Thebes and the
physical prowess of Eëtion (23. 826–36). The dual function of the iron in

the Achaian games, as it is involved both in action and in remembrance of action accomplished, implies the continuity of human life in which a vigorous society is able to assimilate the wholesome elements of the less orderly society it has defeated. The good of Thebes will survive as it contributes to the reformed Argive society.

Zarker analyzes the role played by Pedasos, the last example of the *Iliad*'s Theban imagery:

> Among the other possessions is . . . Pedasos (16. 152–53). Pedasos becomes in one way a symbol of Achilles himself. When alive, he symbolizes the actions of Achilles at Thebes, his success in storming and taking it as well as his kindness and mercy afterward. . . . The horses lead Patroclus beyond the ditch and are accomplices in his forgetfulness of the warnings of Achilles. Sarpedon in aiming at Patroclus hits Pedasos (16. 468–69). . . .
>
> The fall of Pedasos into the dust foreshadows the fall of Achilles' crest from the head of Patroclus and the imminent death of Achilles. With the death of Pedasos the final rage and madness of Achilles caused by the death of Patroclus is also foreshadowed. No longer is Achilles to be noble, kind, and merciful. His spirit becomes hardened by the fire of his wrath transferred from Agamemnon to the Trojans and Hector; the chivalric treatment of the defeated is to become a thing of the past. Yet the theme of Eetion and Thebes suggests to the auditor that Achilles will not always be wrathful, since he was not so in the past. By the use of this theme, in the incident of Pedasos the horse, Homer prepares his audience for the changes to be wrought in the character of Achilles in Books 23 and 24, for Achilles' return to normality. (P. 111)

Pedasos, a mortal yoked with immortal partners, also perfectly symbolizes the dual nature of Achilles himself.

In his description of Hephaistos' making of the great shield, Homer seems to deemphasize the critical boundary between his actual art and the artistry he portrays. Because that boundary, between fictional artist and the poet himself, is allowed in certain contexts to be so elusive we are justified in considering artifacts as analogues to the poem. The imagery of the Theban saga is an emphatic confirmation of this interpretation. Methodically, it would seem, Homer has juxtaposed, nearly always very closely, his own narrative references to Eëtion with the recollections of fictional narrators, Achilles and Andromache.

Catalogues, Invocations, and Miniatures

In his preface to *Hesiod*, Richmond Lattimore argues that the catalogue and genealogy are the kinds of poetry characteristic of the Boeotian tradition of which Homer was not a part but with which he must have been familiar. The most important catalogue in the *Iliad*, of course, is that of the Achaian ships in Book 2. The catalogue, a suspension from the linear momentum of Homer's story, has several important functions. Thomas W. Allen notes that it is a kind of *dramatis personae* (p. 35). The catalogue of ships, says John Crossett, also functions as a microcosmic presentation of the "war in miniature, its whole history, so constructed as to prefigure the story of Achilles" (p. 244). Homer manipulates even this intrinsically undramatic traditional motif by including within it a reference to the Myrmidons who do not, strictly speaking, belong in the muster at this point in the story. The catalogue provides him with a unique opportunity for delineating the historical background within which his particular theme is to be elaborated. This catalogue, moreover, may have an even more significant, if less easily definable, role in the poet's attempt to memorialize accurately the period of social upheaval in which the heroic and the familial systems underwent the process which would lead to their eventual fusion. It may represent Homer's attempt to define the synthesization of society in a world, unlike his own, which had not yet accomplished it completely.

The opening of the catalogue, for example, illustrates Homer's regular insistence upon the subordination of individual to communal values in a time of social crisis such as the present. The series of similes by which the catalogue is introduced has an effect like that of the camera technique of panning into focus. Homer presents the massing of the Achaian host by likening it to the transcendent image of fire (2. 455–58), the generic sense being implicit in the adjective θεσπεσίοιο *thespesíoio* ("wondrous"—2. 457). He then compares the troops to the nations of birds (2. 459), subdivided into various tribes (2. 460); to the nations of flies (2. 469 ff.); and to those of goats and kine (2. 474 ff.). From the largest group to the smallest collective—as from the inanimate, to the animal, to the human world—the poet's emphasis is upon community. The only individual isolated in the imagistic introduction is the head of the community, the generic individual. And Agamemnon is likened to a stud bull (2. 475 ff.). As the catalogue proper begins, individuals are named only by way of identifying the various troops. Because he has so few men with him, Nireus is worthless (2. 672–75). And so is Achilles practically, in the *Iliad*, because, despite the many and strong men he brings with him, he refuses to engage his army in the national cause. Wartime, Homer implies, is the worst possible occasion for a display of iconoclastic personality. Only when Achilles becomes himself a generic individual, carrying the universalized shield, is he orderly once more. Then Argos itself is reordered.

The microcosmic nature of the catalogue of ships is further marked by its introduction—the most extended, most revealing invocation in the *Iliad*. This second invocation is the aesthetic complement to the first one in the proem—"Sing, goddess" (1. 1). This second invocation is a departure from Homer's usual self-abnegation, setting the catalogue apart as a peculiar and semiautonomous dramatic unit. The catalogue's relationship to the plot of the *Iliad* resembles that of the *choros* to the previous scenes upon the shield. It is no less thematically relevant for being a symbolic rather than a structural factor; like the great shield, the catalogue belongs to the pattern of symbolic action.

Homer has presented, through the progression of animal similes, the dramatic assembling of all the Argives by their king. We have seen how the description of the muster ends with the image of Agamemnon, like a bull at the head of his herd (2. 480–83). So emphatically collective have the similes been up till now, the sudden attention to the individual comes as a surprise. Even more startling and unexpected is the poet's abrupt reference to himself—so fully intent has he made us upon the massive collective presence of the army. It is almost as if Agamemnon has arranged his troops in parade formation in order that they might be reviewed by human memory itself, as the past and fictional world submits for a moment to the real and present one of the poet's audience. On one hand Homer is offering the product of his own artistry for our inspection, approval, and reaction. On the other, he is directing his listener to judge the significance of history. To prepare him for that practical and aesthetic responsibility, Homer now reveals to his listener in the invocation the relationship between his art and human experience. He knows that his traditional, divinely ordered theme is magnificent. His only concern is that his individual talent and technique will be equal to the task of communicating that theme in its perfection. By drawing attention to the role of the poet of memory, finally, Homer equates himself with Agamemnon. As the king protects and serves the community in time, the poet assures the interests of human continuity. An old man close to death, Nestor, encourages Agamemnon to assemble his troops. But the poet asks the goddesses who transcend death for the inspiration he needs to record the historical significance of that assembly, its essential meaning:

> Tell me now, you Muses who have your homes on Olympos.
> For you, who are goddesses, are there, and you know all things,
> and we have heard only the rumour of it and know nothing.
> Who then of those were the chief men and the lords of the Danaans?
> I could not tell over the multitude of them nor name them,
> not if I had ten tongues and ten mouths, not if I had
> a voice never to be broken and a heart of bronze within me,

not unless the Muses of Olympia, daughters
of Zeus of the aegis, remembered all those who came beneath Ilion.
I will tell the lords of the ships, and the ships numbers.

(2. 484–93)

The poet, after establishing the superiority of the Muses of memory over the individual memory of any individual, allows himself to become the mouthpiece of the Muses. Through an ironic extended negation (2. 489–90), Homer implies his poetic exaltation through images which predict that of Achilles. He transcends individuality, that is, having "ten tongues" and "ten mouths" (2. 489). Similarly as Achilles required the unquenchable flame of Hephaistos to accomplish his orderly social role, so the singer needs a φωνὴ δ' ἄρρηκτος *phōnè d'árrēktos* ("unwearying voice") to construct and maintain the imagery of symbolic action by which the essence of Achilles' act may be communicated to the audience. The bronze mouth is the invulnerable, enduring poem itself which, like the shield (made by Hephaistos' "unquenchable flame"), protects society at the same time that it memorializes the individual associated with it. The bronze symbolizes the ideal artistic talent demanded by the momentous nature of the historical events Homer wishes to transmit and interpret; it is the ἀοιδὴν θεσπεσίην *aoidèn thespesién* ("wondrous song") Thamyris lost, which Homer can sing because he honors the Muses.

With such a mouth and voice, Homer would be prepared to realize the service expected from one whose status is divinely ordained, religious as well as social. We are to assume that he possesses these qualities by the fact that the narrator proceeds to do exactly what he says himself incapable of doing: he recites the catalogue (2. 493). The sudden shift in direction marked in this last line of the invocation suggests the same kind of spontaneous and willful possession which occurs when Achilles reacts to Thetis' mission from Zeus in Book 24. Homer asks the Muses to possess him because he understands their orderly role in the communication of Zeus' governing principle; only if man submits himself freely to their influence can he hope for the establishment of Zeus' Olympian order on earth. And the poet is the intermediary who, by his willful submission to the daughters of Zeus and memory, makes the earthly establishment of Zeus' order possible.

It is worth pausing to consider how Homer's other invocations to his Muse provide direct evidence of his orderly theme. Each invocation is dramatically relevant in a way that enhances the immediate narrative context in which it appears. The narrator asks the goddesses for special guidance when Agamemnon, performing at last his proper royal role as the leader of Argos, goes forth to join battle with the enemies of his society (11. 218–19); when Aias, the crucial bulwark of the Achaians in the absence of Achilles, stands firmly to defend the ships (14. 508–9); and when the ships themselves are threatened by Hektor's fire (16. 112–13). In the last case the invocation serves to remind us of the immense social significance of this event.

Related to these three invocations are the narrator's occasional direct addresses to his characters. Homer calls out to Menelaos (7. 104; 13. 603), to Patroklos (16. 784), to the Trojans (18. 311), and to Achilles (20. 264)—each time in a situation which is definitive inasmuch as the action in which the character or characters addressed are engaging signifies their imminent attunement with or separation from the principle of order. The poet's address to Patroklos, for example, bestows tragic irony upon the moment by juxtaposing it with the transcendent viewpoint of the poet. The direct address, on one hand, emphasizes the distinction between the limited vision of the transitory fictive individual and the eternal and universal perspective of the poet. Moreover since that transcendent perspective is accessible to men—Achilles, Priam, Helen, and Hektor all achieve it sooner or later—the address indicates that Patroklos has not realized the potential of his humanity. The poet's vision is superior to his, then, only because Homer does not lose sight of the generic dimension of human action. But Patroklos has lost sight of it; he is acting here, like Hektor, in blind self-confidence. On the other hand, direct address also implies the contact between reality and fiction, between past and present, between time and eternity; it indicates that the narrator himself embodies in his generic perspective the continuity of humanity. Since the character does not hear it, direct address is a kind of suspension of the fiction. But it is a purposeful suspension, intended to inform us that our experience is comparable to Patroklos'. The comparison is possible because the poet conveys that common nature, his memory standing between the contemporary and the past-fictive individual to unite them under the auspices of memory. One instance of direct address is unique in the *Iliad*. Describing the crucial fighting at the Achaian gates, Homer suddenly despairs of recording factually the events at hand: "It were too much toil for me, as if I were a god, to tell all this" (12. 176). Nevertheless he proceeds to report the combat. But instead of factual details the narrator invokes the imagery of inhuman fire (12. 177 ff.) to define the momentous significance of the defense of the ships. Now fire is associated symbolically with Hephaistos. So it is as if Homer were here consciously imitating the divine artist. He turns his fictive identification with Hephaistos to account by borrowing the imagistic tools associated with the smith in order to transmit the true import of the Achaian crisis to his listener.

Corresponding to this somewhat anomalous direct address is the peculiar second invocation in the catalogue of ships. Although his mighty record of the Argive forces has proceeded smoothly and rapidly up till now, the singer finds it necessary to call again upon his Muse to insure its proper completion and perfection: "Tell me then, Muse, who of them all was the best and bravest, / of the men, and the men's horses, who went with the sons of Atreus" (2. 761–62). In itself the call to the Muse confirms the traditional aspect of his art; but the juxtaposition of the two personal pronouns (2. 761) implies that the Iliadic composer is aware of the synthetic nature of his aesthetic. The generic personality of the Muse is here intimately related syntactically to the individuality of the poet in a kind of self-possession.

Other catalogues include the Trojan one which follows the Achaian list and the catalogue of rivers in Book 21. The Myrmidon catalogue presented on the occasion of Patroklos' reentry into battle (16. 170 ff.) is not finally perfected until Achilles himself rejoins his society. That is the significance of the miniature Achaian catalogue in Book 23. Still another instance of the catalogue motif is the list of Nereids related by the narrator when he presents so dramatically Achilles' initial grief for Patroklos in Book 18. Owen calls this skeleton catalogue "a stroke of perfect poetic judgment; a list of lovely names that by almost nothing but lovely sounds conjure up a lovely scene, comes to heal the pain. It is just the relief and release of feeling that was needed: the strain of thought is for the moment completely lifted, and the mind finds rest and refreshment in sheer beauty that requires not the slightest effort to comprehend it" (p. 177).

The catalogue and the genealogy, closely related motifs, are often overlooked ("Skip the last half of Book 2!") because they are felt to be somehow extraneous or unessential to the story. Homer's social perspective suggests that these traditional motifs are no less integral to the general Iliadic vision. Their mutual interrelationship, to begin with, suggests their perfect integration into the poem's socially determined world. In a sense, the traditional catalogue is a shorthand compilation of genealogical material. This is suggested by the fact that the catalogue of ships contains extended social information about some heroes and gives merely the patronymic for others. Homer's natural way of introducing new characters is in terms of their past and present social coordinates. Here an entire army is introduced in this manner. Consider some examples of the genealogical motif within the catalogue itself—a unit suspended from the general storyline but not detached from its essential patterns.

Homer reports succinctly the story of Askalaphos and Ialmenos, sons of Ares (2. 512), "whom Astyoche bore to him in the house of Aktor / Azeus' son, a modest maiden; she went into the chamber / with strong Ares, who was laid in bed with her secretly" (2. 513–15). The heroic birth of these two men parallels that of Kleopatra in the doubly fictional world of Meleagros, and of Achilles, Helen, and Aineias in the Iliadic world itself. The reference to the secrecy of this commingling of the human and divine must recall to Homer's audience Hera's deviousness in Book 14 of the *Iliad*. Schedios and Epistrophos are identified in the catalogue only by a citation of their father and grandfather (2. 517–18); Elephenor by a reference to his father, his father's divine protector, and his political position (2. 540–41). There is mention of the familial disorder in the heritage of Meges, whose father became an expatriate for reasons which recall Phoinix's exile (2. 627 ff.). The veracity of the Meleagros story is given authority, in a stroke, by Homer's notation of the presence of Thoas, leader of the Aitolians, separated by several generations from the heroic redeemer of Kalydon (2. 638 ff.). Especially interesting is Tlepolemos of Rhodes (2. 653–54),

> he whom Astyocheia bore to the strength of Herakles.
> Herakles brought her from Ephyra and the river Selleeis
> after he sacked many cities of strong, god-supported fighters.
> Now when Tlepolemos was grown in the strong-built mansion,
> he struck to death his own father's beloved uncle,
> Likymnios, scion of Ares, a man already ageing.
> At once he put ships together and assembled a host of people
> and went fugitive over the sea, since the others threatened,
> the rest of the sons and the grandsons of the strength of Herakles.
> And he came to Rhodes a wanderer, a man of misfortune,
> and they settled there in triple division by tribes, beloved
> of Zeus himself, who is lord over all gods and all men,
> Kronos' son, who showered the wonder of wealth upon them.
>
> (2. 658–70)

Here the principle governing the poet's decision to extend his treatment of a particular figure in the Danaan muster is revealed. Homer elaborates those figures who are symbolically related to the action and theme of his epic. Tlepolemos' relevance to Homer's vision—not his minor significance in the Trojan war—explains why the poet finds it worthwhile to delve into his past. The pattern of his genealogy resembles that displayed by so many in the Iliadic world and in its memory. There is an allusion to the Herakleian tradition from which Zeus and Agamemnon derive their tales (2. 658). Herakles' prowess (2. 660) recalls that of Bellerophontes and of Achilles, as his abduction of Astyocheia reflects Paris' of Helen (2.

659). Like Phoinix's and Patroklos', Tlepolemos' crime is both familial and political, but not national or generally social—since he is still able to command a remnant of his people (2. 662–64). Like them, moreover, he becomes an expatriate (2. 665); a man of sorrows like Bellerophontes (2. 667). But his final social reformation recalls the honor received by Bellerophontes from the Lykian king, signifying his attunement with the divine principle of order by which Achilles, too, is ultimately informed (2. 668–69). His establishment of a new society corresponds to the destiny of Aineias (2. 670) and to the achievement of Achilles in Book 23.

The catalogue mentions other sons of Herakles (2. 679). The appearance in this list of Protesilaos (2. 698 ff.) proves that Homer is just as interested in developing his philosophical perspective, his symbolic pattern, as he is in accurately recording historical facts. Strictly speaking Protesilaos is an anomaly in the catalogue of the Achaians assembled by Agamemnon, since he is already dead. Homer includes him only because he is interested in portraying the essential sorrow of widowhood, expressed by his wife, and the tragedy of a marriage that must be forever without issue (2. 700–701). The parallel with Menelaos and Helen, who are also without sons because of the abduction, is evident. But Protesilaos and his wife also predict the essential pattern which recurs with Achilles and Briseis. Protesilaos is the first Achaian to have been killed at Troy (2. 702). Homer remembers every significant detail. The brief mention of Alkestis is enough to illustrate her archetypal association with Helen as a singularly beautiful woman (2. 714). The isolation of Philoktetes from his society, because of his terrible wound, contrasts with Achilles' less self-effacing separation from Argos (2. 721). Philoktetes' quarantine is beneficial to the nation that would have been threatened physically by his presence.

The catalogue of ships becomes a kind of guidebook to Homer's use of the imagery of memory as a technique of thematic continuity, at the same time that it may also be a list of the poet's available repertoire. Throughout the narrative proper, when Homer sees fit to elaborate, his elaboration of a particular hero's status becomes another miniature epic which nearly always reveals a history replete with conflicts of loyalties upon one or several social levels. The mnemonic art of the narrator merges with that of his own characters. The ghost of Patroklos, for example, reminds Achilles of the events which led to the formation of their extraordinary friendship. Menoitios had brought the young stranger to Phthia from Opous, " 'by reason of a baneful manslaying, / on that day when I killed the son of Amphidamas. I was / a child only, nor intended it, but was angered over a dice game. / There the rider Peleus took me into his own house / and brought me carefully up, and named me to be your henchman' " (23. 86–90). His brief recollection bears witness to the pathetic inexorability of social taboos that care nothing for intention or the excuse of immaturity. Patroklos is shown as analogous to Phoinix; he is an exile, a homicide, a victim of social upheaval. His assimilation by a new society, that of Peleus, makes him share the borrowed status of Briseis and Andromache; and it is a contrast with Troy's unsuccessful assimilation of Helen—suggesting that the Troadic nation falls because it honors a relationship, between Helen and Paris, which is not legitimate in the way that the friendship between Achilles and Patroklos is. And Peleus' characteristic hospitality is emphasized again, implying that such generosity is inherent to Achilles and will be expressed again when his wrath dissolves.

Patroklos' story is similar to that of Tlepolemos; it is also like the tale of Medon briefly stated by the narrator during a battle scene. The context in which Medon appears includes the presence of the Epeians about whose history Nestor is constantly speaking (13. 685); as the bastard son of Oïleus, Medon is the stepbrother of Aias (cf. 13.694 and 13.701), "yet he was living away from / the land of his fathers, in Phylake, since he had killed a man, / the brother of Eriopis, his stepmother and wife of Oïleus" (13. 695–97). As in the cases of Phoinix and Patroklos, here a familial crime has political repercussions upon the individual. There is an intriguing relationship between Medon and Lykophron. Medon, although he fights by the side of Aias at Troy, does not live in his brother's land any longer. His place has been taken, as it were, by this man from Kythera who now lives with Aias because he, too, killed a man in his homeland (15. 430–32). Epeigeus completes this minor trilogy of exiled familial homicides. The brilliant son of Agakles (16. 571), "He was one who was lord before in strong-founded Boudeion, / but now, since he had happened to kill his high-born cousin, / had come suppliant to Peleus and to Thetis the silver-footed, / and these sent him to follow Achilleus, who broke men in battle" (16. 572–75). In such a world of social turmoil it is not surprising that the familial system seems to have been constantly rearranged by the influence of the heroic code of interpersonal relations. Phoinix and Patroklos are not the only exiles who accompany Achilles and share his social definition. The strength of a leader seems to depend at least partly upon the number of such strangers who are attached to him, serve his cause, and are, in turn, protected by him. Aias and Achilles appear to be related symbolically in yet another respect. The formulaic reference to Boudeion here is poignantly effective, suggesting how tenuous even the apparently strongest government may be when the influence of evil Strife affects the behavior of its ruler.

As the poet's recollection of the histories of Medon, Lykophron, and

Epeigeus seems to form one imagistic unit, so does his treatment of
Othryoneus, Iphidamas, and Euchenor appear to form another. Despite
his serious wound, the stalwart Idomeneus manages to kill Othryoneus,

> a man who had lived in Kabesos,
> who was newly come in the wake of the rumour of war, and had asked
> Priam for the hand of the loveliest of his daughters,
> Kassandra, without bride price, but had promised a great work for her,
> to drive back the unwilling sons of the Achaians from Troy land,
> and aged Priam had bent his head in assent, and promised
> to give her, so Othryoneus fought in the faith of his promises.
>
> (13. 363–69)

Would Homer have been led to notice this victim of a somewhat
undistinguished Achaian had not Othryoneus been connected with the
extra-Iliadic story of Agamemnon and Kassandra? Here he supplements
that tradition by reporting the marital alliance Kassandra might have
made if Troy had not fallen. The alliance between Othryoneus and
Kassandra would have been a disorderly quality appropriate to the social
weakness of Troy itself. Either way, Apollo is avenged for Kassandra's
slight. For Othryoneus' character is even less admirable than is
Agamemnon's; he seems to have been too much the overeager, brash,
entrepreneur—following the rumor of war and presumptuously demanding the first daughter of the king. His presumption is ominously
like the deluded self-confidence which casts Hektor into his fatal error. It
is therefore ironic that this man who boasted that he could personally
conquer the Achaians should be slain, not by Aias or Diomedes, central
bulwarks of the Argives, but by a relatively minor character. His death
recalls Hektor's, by which a perfect marriage is disrupted; and Achilles',
by which an unformalized one will be rendered void.

Idomeneus' taunt of the dead warrior suggests the boasting of Achilles
over his Trojan victims. But Homer, as if his elaboration of Othryoneus
has inspired him to capitalize upon its symbolic potential, makes
Idomeneus' speech symbolically significant in itself:

> 'Othryoneus, I congratulate you beyond all others
> if it is here that you will bring to pass what you promised
> to Dardanian Priam, who in turn promised you his daughter.
> See now, we also would make you a promise, and we would fulfil it;
> we would give you the loveliest of Atreides' daughters,
> and bring her here from Argos to be your wife, if you joined us
> and helped us storm the strong-founded city of Ilion.
> Come then with me, so we can meet by our seafaring vessels
> about a marriage; we here are not bad matchmakers for you.'
>
> (13. 374–82)

This is one of the few occasions in the *Iliad* where Homer qualifies the general admiration with which he usually treats Priam. Idomeneus interprets the king's promise to Othryoneus in a way that makes it appear similar to Agamemnon's disorderly attitude toward Chryseis— and to the Achaian king's treatment of Iphigeneia. There is something of excessive expediency in Priam's behavior that identifies the tragic fault of Troy as being, like Argos before Agamemnon's conversion, more an heroic than a new synthesized society. Elsewhere there is a reference to Hektor's monetary relationship with the Troadic allies. Clearly the orientation of the warrior's participating in the defense of Troy is more individualistic than selflessly nationalistic. Not guilty of this disorderly focus himself, Idomeneus perceives the flaw in Othryoneus' character and sadistically exploits it by implying that the Trojan might well have been an Achaian instead, had he been offered greater material compensation by the Argives, and the hand of Agamemnon's daughter. What makes it all the more ironic is the implicit parallel with Paris who, like Othryoneus, wooed Helen solely on the basis of boasted prowess and removed her from Menelaos without bride price (3. 430). Achilles' rejection of a king's daughter proves his orientation is not the purely heroic one of Othryoneus. Idomeneus, after all, is making promises to a dead man; the matchmaking he proposes, as a result, is indeed a most horrible one. Othryoneus' bride, now joined to him forever, is Death herself: that is who will meet him by the ships. Othryoneus' marriage with Death terribly symbolizes the wages of Troy's social disorder.

The complement to Othryoneus is Iphidamas. Iphidamas is the son of Antenor (11. 221)

> who had been reared in generous Thrace, the mother of sheepflocks.
> Kisseus had raised him in his own house when he was little,
> his mother's father, whose child was Theano, the girl of the fair cheeks.
> But when he had arrived at the stature of powerful manhood
> Kisseus detained him there and gave him his daughter. Married
> he went away from the bride chamber, looking for glory
> from the Achaians, with twelve curved ships that followed with him.
> . . . .
> So Iphidamas fell there and went into the brazen slumber,
> unhappy, who came to help his own people, and left his young wife
> a bride, and had known no delight from her yet, and given much for her.
>
> (11. 222–28, 241–43)

Though their fate is nearly identical, there is yet a striking difference between Iphidamas and Othryoneus. For this man is, like Hektor, the epitome of selfless commitment to the glory which comes only from communally oriented action. He comes, unlike Othryoneus, accompanied by supporters and does not boast that victory will come by his own individual prowess. It is fitting that Agamemnon should be the one who slays him, since like the Achaian king Iphidamas is a man of redoubtable means (11. 244 ff.). The circumstances in which he is slain are also appropriate. For it is in Book 11 that Agamemnon finally assumes his collective responsibilities and goes forth to lead his army in person. Like him, Iphidamas has come to Troy in the service of his people (11. 242). His death is a truly tragic one, whereas Othryoneus' is at best pathetic.

The deathly trilogy is complete with Euchenor, whose significance was pointed out to me by my student Sharon Scull.

> There was a man, Euchenor, son of the seer Polyidos,
> a rich man and good, who lived in his house at Korinth,
> who knew well that it was his death when he went on shipboard,
> since many times the good old man Polyidos had told him
> that he must die in his own house of a painful sickness
> or go with the ships of the Achaians and be killed by the Trojans.
> He therefore chose to avoid the troublesome price the Achaians
> would ask, and the hateful sickness so his heart might not be afflicted.
>
> (13. 663–70)

When Paris dispatches this man without even a struggle (13. 671–72), we are not troubled. Euchenor, though he reflects both the fates of Philoktetes (2. 716–25) and of Achilles himself, is a worthless man because he is only choosing the easy way out—doing the right thing for the wrong reasons. Not glory, but convenience, leads him to the war—and specifically monetary and physical convenience, equal to the greed of Othryoneus or to the cowardice of the very man who kills him—and to be a lesser man than Paris is little indeed. When Achilles reenters the battle, knowing that fighting means certain death for him, his decision has nothing to do with material gain or consideration of pain.

Bassett marks the similarity between another function of these mnemonic units in the narrative and that of the similes: "The miniatures give a glimpse into the life of the past, not in its crises, but in its peace and happiness, so that the Trojan war gains perspective by a background in a real world where war is only an incident, not the main business of life. Finally, in the miniatures . . . as well as in the similes an emotion is suggested which heightens the interest in the tales of battle" (p. 94). But since the great majority of these miniature recollections deal with conflict and social disorder, we are not allowed to forget that the sorrows of war are a heritage from the past as well as the experience of the present (and

Bassett's view is exaggerated). The contrast between war and peace is ultimately unrelated to temporal distinctions: it is apparent in both the fictional present and past, as well as in the time of the poet himself. But the conclusion which Bassett proceeds to draw from his analysis is altogether accurate. He argues that the miniatures rarely include "details which help us to form a visual image of" the heroes involved, "and then only casually." And "this fact . . . seems to show that [Homer] was less interested in giving a distinct visual picture than an emotional impression; in other words, that Homer cared less for the surroundings of human life than for that life itself" (p. 94). The purpose of the imagery of memory is to define more abstractly than in the narrative proper the essential patterns of human experience which the realistic detail of the narrative makes historically convincing. Certainly this purpose is accomplished.

The continuous aspect of the Iliadic aesthetic explains why it is so hard to separate the knowledge of the characters from that of Homer himself. Knowledge, through memory, is regarded as a continuum, to which the character, the poet, and his audience have equal access through different tangents. Idomeneus' speech to Othryoneus, for example, proves that he knows the history of the Trojan warrior although his knowledge has no foundation within Homer's fiction. He knows it, in fact, in exactly the same way that the poet's audience now knows that history. The narrator himself has communicated it to us, and apparently to his character as well, in the immediately preceding lines. So the world of the remembered past, whether fictional or real, and the contemporary world in which the poet addresses his audience are accidentally distinct but essentially comparable manifestations of continuing human experience. Only because the poet and his audience are equally convinced that the generic spirit transcending time can be experienced by the individual to whom time is vitally important is it possible for the *Iliad* to be composed at all—and to be made communally effective, through the artful beauty of its language that makes it the most powerful shield of memory.

Appendixes
Annotated Bibliography
Indexes

Appendix 1

Homeric Hierarchical Structures

The social system existing in the Iliadic world, both among Trojans and Achaians, is illustrated on the following speculative hierarchical grid which may be useful in understanding the complex relations among the human beings of Homer's world.

Hierarchical Level	Characteristic Hierarchy(ies)	Examples / Comments
INDIVIDUAL	heroic	Paris' selfishness and ambivalence; Agamemnon's blindness and remorse
	heroic and familial (new synthesized hierarchy/n.s.h.)	Achilles' introspection, expressed as both pride and love
(1) Interpersonal	heroic	the two Aiantes, forming a unit in battle
(The guest-friend relationship exists in all three hierarchies)	familial	Glaukos-Diomedes, who spare each other because of ancestral ties
	n.s.h.	Achilles-Patroklos, whose love is as strong as familial love; but they are also heroic companions; Achilles-Priam

Hierarchical Level	Characteristic Hierarchy)ies)	Examples / Comments
(2) Conjugal	heroic	Agamemnon-Klytaimestra: marriage as contractual arrangement for material reasons
	familial	Hektor-Andromache: marriage with love
	n.s.h.	Achilles-Briseis: she is his prize, and he loves her
(3) Parental-Filial	heroic	Agamemnon-daughters whom he offers to Achilles as gifts
	familial	Priam-Hektor; in the end, blood is stronger than politics
	n.s.h.	Achilles-Peleus, whose love is secure enough to allow substitution and transference: to Phoinix, then to Priam
(4) Fraternal (clan)	heroic	Agamemnon-Menelaos, whose brotherhood is secondary to their material motives
	familial	Paris-Hektor, whose brotherhood causes tension between them because of Paris' disorderly behavior
	n.s.h.	Achilles-Hektor, in Book 24, where the transposition is implied by Achilles' response to Priam's comparison of himself with Peleus; in this hierarchy love is stronger than blood (brotherhood based on love)

Hierarchical Level	Characteristic Hierarchy(ies)	Examples / Comments
(5) Political (city, kingdom)	heroic	Mycenae, no indication of blood bonds holding city together; also Phthia, Pylos
	familial	Troy, where Priam's palace seems to symbolize the close kinship of all Trojans
	n.s.h.	Argos reunited under Achilles' orderly direction in Book 23
(6) National (confederation)	heroic	The Troad, which Hektor implies is held together by purely mercenary ties; Argos, insofar as it is held together by the desire for the greater spoils that come with cooperation
	familial	The Troad, inasmuch as the Dardanians (the race of Dardanos) are destined to survive the destruction of Troy through the person of Aineias; Argos, insofar as the war is based on Agamemnon's fraternal loyalty and the Tyndarean oath taken by Helen's suitors
	n.s.h.	Hellas, in Homer's own day, its unity implied in the eclectic language of the poem and the fact that both Trojans and Achians are obviously Hellenes
GENERIC HUMANITY	heroic	Doesn't exist: see Glaukos' leaf-simile—every man and every generation for itself

Hierarchical Level	Characteristic Hierarchy(ies)	Examples / Comments
	familial	Exists as far as a family's memory (genealogy) is preserved—as Glaukos' recitation proves
	n.s.h.	Achilles-Priam, here the circle turns to complete itself, as interpersonal relations can be formed that transcend national distinctions through the combined force of love and mutual recognition of courage (the basis for a "shield of memory" that is pan-Hellenic)

The disorder that exists among Homer's gods because Zeus has not yet established firmly his ideal Olympian governmental order also exists in the human social system because it is constructed from two antithetical hierarchies. *The familial hierarchy* stresses the communal orientation based upon a primary blood-relationship; the individual is subordinate to the group. In this system, the progression of values ascends from the individual to the city, from the narrowest level of relations to the widest. More specifically, the kingship system supports the central levels of Iliadic society—conjugal family (2) through political (5). The blood relationship demands that each member of society must value the integrity of each level of his relations to other men in ascending order. So the jeopardy to his city requires Hektor to subordinate his conjugal and parental concerns, invoking Paris' cooperation by appealing to their fraternal bond. Unless the stability of the city is maintained, that of the marriage, as well as of the parental and fraternal family, cannot persist.

But the first and last levels of Iliadic society, the national and the interpersonal (guest-friendship) are determined characteristically by self-interest (suggesting that the concept of the individual and the concept of the State emerged simultaneously). The concept of heroic personal prowess underlies the autonomy of the individual in *the heroic hierarchy*. So Achilles cooperates with Agamemnon on the national level (6)—while the Myrmidons imitate his cooperation by their relationship with Achilles on the levels of familial orientation (2) through (5)—because it is in his own interest to do so. Note that Hektor pays the Troadic allies for their service to Troy; the nation, unlike the city, is not united by kinship. The feudal quality of both national armies is evident in the fact that the nation, unlike the groups united by blood relations (2) through (5), is amalgamated by solemn oaths of fealty rather than by unspoken familial loyalty. International oaths must be possible, in light of Agamemnon's truce with Priam in Book 3—where it fails to bring peace, and contrasts with Achilles' unofficialized, but all the more significant, promise to Priam at the end of Book 24 to hold back the Achaians until Hektor is buried. The nation is only a very tenuous collective in its individualistically motivated structure and mode of construction; the individual may secede from it with relative impunity, although the national consequences of his secession may be tremendous.

The hierarchical value-direction in the familial society is from (1) to (6); in the heroic society, from (6) to (1). In one the individual serves the nation; in the other, the reverse is normal. Though neither system is ideal in itself, each has qualities of the Homeric ideal.

The nation (an entity that, historically, only began to exist under the heroic system which saw the advantage of linking several cities together to form a larger army) is now seeking to base its motivational force upon the central kinship system which it will eventually replace with the concept of patriotism. But in the period portrayed by the *Iliad*, the nation has not yet entirely succeeded in establishing its categorical identity. So the two hierarchical extremes, (1) and (6), not yet substantially attuned with each other, conflict with the center, (2) through (5), which still holds. And Achilles speaks of his secession from the army, now in terms of his deprivation of rightful spoils, now in terms of how it will better serve his own kingly, familial (filial, paternal, and conjugal) status.

The *Iliad*, seen as a practical, didactic poem addressed to the Homeric audience, implicitly asserts that only when a person acts on the highest communal level available to him is a human being most noble, his actions most glorious, his name most memorable. To understand itself best, that is, each station on Zeus' golden chain must imitate the station above—not the one below. An individual is most orderly—most in keeping with Zeus' ordering principle—when he expresses himself in action on the widest possible social plane, that of generic humanity. The less a community is based upon particular (like blood) affinities, and the more upon recognition of the general sharing of human nature, the closer it comes to Zeus' Olympian ideal. The aspiration toward the establishment of a thriving community that is not only national (like the harmonious state of Argos in Book 23) but also international or generically human (Achilles and Priam in Book 24) therefore must be a proleptic vision of the time in which Homer composed his great expression of world order. At least it can be said that the tradition from which the *Iliad* derived embodied—in the international linguistically eclectic yet universally understood, character of its language—the generic human spirit Homer emblazons on the shield of Achilles.

The *Iliad* seems to reflect a historical progression something like the following (purposefully avoiding specific names and dates because of the archaeological and anthropological uncertainties involved at all points):

(1) Pre-Iliadic World

A. First the familial bond was dominant, its highest expression the πόλις *pólis* ("city"). The poem's many genealogies mark an awareness of the profound influence of the kinship system. In this era, associated with the matriarchal Autochthones, M. I. Finley notes: "The coexistence of three distinct but overlapping groups, class, kin, and *oikos* (household), was what defined a man's life, materially and psychologically. The demands of each of the three did not always coincide; when they conflicted openly there were inevitable tensions and disequilibriums" (p. 79). Perhaps it was precisely because of such normal tensions (like the conflict between the patrilineal and matrilineal systems), that it became possible for

B. an individualistic element to be introduced into this environment (the coming of the patriarchal, nomadic Mycenaeans) that sought to build wider social alliances by joining together their more or less autonomous clans on a common basis of self-interest, individual prowess, and the mutual aggrandizement of each lord's material riches. The invading nomads (reflected in the character of Herakles, the wandering hero) sought forcefully to impose their own feudalistic, patriarchal way of life upon the familial, matriarchal society of the conquered subjects (the marriage of Zeus and Hera?). They may also have shown the indigenous matriarchs, in their isolated cities, how to form expedient alliances—occasional institutes serving a wider common good.

(2) Iliadic World

Here the two ways of life, the Autochthonian (familial) and the Mycenaean (heroic) jockey with each other in the effort to construct a new social system—the Achaian confederacy against Troy—which derives its vigor from the peculiar strength of each of the two orientations. But the process of mutual assimilation is unresolved in the period reflected by the poem. The peace which prevails, as far as social determination is concerned, between the Mycenaean war-lords and the conquered people is a real, but uneasy one. The turmoil in the Iliadic world is on the essential level of determining the nature of social patterns to which men will subscribe, rather than on the more superficial level of wholesale conflict which occurs in the preceding dark age (when the Mycenaeans were forcing their system upon the Autochthones). As a consequence of their conflict, both the familial and the heroic orientations were weakened, as the *Iliad* amply illustrates.

(3) Post-Iliadic World

A. Immediately before the time in which the *Iliad* was composed and the oral culture was coming to an end (between the Iliadic time and the time of Homer's audience), something like a synthesis of heroic and familial values must have been established. The Achaians, in Book 23, exemplify such a reformed society. The new system planted itself firmly in the hearts of its adherents by replacing, evenly, both the one based on the blood-relationship and the individualistic code of the warlords with a concept of federation—a nascent patriotism—that derived its motivating force from the most effective qualities of each original social system.

The new synthesis, however, seems to have been realized through the subtle reassertion of the prior familial bond as the one found to be more essentially durable than the heroic; this may explain the central importance of a woman, Helen, in a world which otherwise treats women as pawns. The warlords, that is, were finally assimilated by the indigenous (matrilineal) population; and that may be why Zeus is so worried, when he first speaks in Book 1, about incurring Hera's wrath *again*. The family became once again the basic legal unit, but became so precisely as a basis for the wider unit of the nation; in this light, Homer's likening Achilles' relationship with Patroklos to that between mother and daughter takes on more certain meaning: they are as close as two individuals can be, under any system, because their love shares the strength of both former hierarchies.

B. The new society could not survive and spread unless its members understood and put into action the qualities necessary to preserve its integrity and strength. By showing them the turmoil through which the present hierarchical society had been created by men of the past Homer's poem inspires its audience to behave in a way that will insure that society's continuation. Book 5 makes the universality of disorder manifest in the most unnatural battle between men and gods. Clearly the source of disorder within each realm of existence, mortal and immortal, has been, in one sense at least, the interference of the other. Paris, for example, is behind the sibling rivalry of the three goddesses; Thetis' marriage to Peleus, as she knows and constantly laments, can come to nothing but evil because the seed conceived in that marriage is Achilles, the Trojan War (the apple of Discord), and cosmic confusion. All this is because Thetis, Aphrodite, and Hera will not stay on their side of the horizontal line between men and gods—instead, lowering themselves (on the chain) to the level of humans. So Thetis' faction opposes Hera's in yet another departure from order, just as Aphrodite's opposes Hera's and Athene's; Poseidon remembers his former equality, threatening Zeus's dominance; and Zeus is holding onto the golden chain, trying to keep the whole world from falling apart. The heavenly disharmony has its reflection, and result, in the world of man. Because Paris crossed the vertical line between two endogamous nations, Trojans war with Achaians on the national level; intranationally, Myrmidons are at odds with the other Argives, the pro-Helen party in Troy with the anti-Helen. Politically, the city of Troy opposes Menelaos' Sparta. Hektor and Paris argue, their fraternal relationship uneasy and strained to the breaking point. In the familial situation, the interests of Paris' conjugal relationship contradict his responsibility toward his paternal family. And marital disorder is shown in the relations between Helen and Paris; Helen and Menelaos; Briseis and Achilles; Agamemnon, Chryseis, and Klytaimestra; Hektor and Andromache—the last torn apart unwillingly by the war just as the first are torn apart by the quarrel in Book 1. Even on the interpersonal level (1), relationships are broken: Achilles loses Patroklos. So it is not surprising that Homeric individuals are also torn apart internally by conflicts of love and loyalty: Hektor, Priam, Paris, and most importantly, Helen and Achilles. Zeus fully understands the individual human being's dilemma because he, too, is faced with conflicting interests. His reconciliation of the gods at the end of the epic is the simultaneous triumph of poetic, religious, and governmental order. When Homer makes the will of Achilles freely concur with the will of the Olympian, the order his great poem illustrates comes into such definitive focus that we can never forget its beautiful human consequences: the love between Achilles and Priam—an undying memory that shields all who keep it in mind from the ravages of disorder.

Appendix 2

Horses in the *Iliad*

Homer's presentation of the relationship between order and disorder includes a consistent thematic pattern in his treatment of the animal kingdom—as my brief discussion of the symbolic role of dogs in the poem indicates. Horses are at least equally important. (Much of what follows was suggested by research done by my student Sara Saxe.) Horses are considered valuable by both men, as Achilles says (1. 152), and gods (5. 355 ff.)—whose horses are always "gold-bridled." After the contested chariot race during the funeral games for Patroklos, Menelaos asks Antilochos to swear an equine oath: " 'Stand in front of your horses and chariot, and in your hand take / up the narrow whip with which you drove them before, then / lay your hand on the horses and swear by him who encircles / the earth and shakes it you used no guile to baffle my chariot' " (23. 582–85). This ritualized connection between horses and Poseidon raises once again the question of divine priority—since both Poseidon and Zeus seem to be the chief gods of horsemanship (23. 306 ff.); only these two gods have their horses described as "flying-footed" (8. 41 = 13.23). The importance of horses to the gods is evident: their horses are attended by the Hours, who unyoke them for Hera and Athene (8. 443), and by Fear and Terror, who harness them for Ares (15. 119). Poseidon's horsemanship is distinguished; he alone has golden hobbles for his horses, "not to be broken or slipped from, so they would wait there steadfast / for their lord gone" (13. 36–38). Saxe notes that no other god has to hobble his horses; nor do men. Perhaps this implies (from a mythographic point of view) the river-god's novitiate with these land animals; though, at another point in the poem, he seems to know very well what he's doing with horses when he builds a ramp for them to cross the Trojan ditch. Perhaps most significantly in the question of priority between Zeus and Poseidon, Poseidon unhitches Zeus' horses, serving as his steward when the father of gods and men returns to Olympos from Ida (8. 440). It is hard not to see this gesture as a sign of Zeus' precedence over even the famed shaker of the earth, or at least as Homer's recognition of Zeus' return to governmental priority over his brother.

Hera's characteristic potential for disorder is emphasized by Homer's detailed elaboration of her preparations to descend with Athene into earthly battle:

> Then Hebe in speed set about the chariot the curved wheels
> eight-spoked and brazen, with an axle of iron both ways.

299

Golden is the wheel's felly imperishable, and outside it
is joined, a wonder to look upon, the brazen running-rim,
and the silver naves revolve on either side of the chariot,
whereas the car itself is lashed fast with plaiting of gold
and silver, with double chariot rails that circle about it,
and the pole of the chariot is of silver, to whose extremity
Hebe made fast the golden and splendid yoke, and fastened
the harness, golden and splendid, and underneath the yoke Hera,
furious for hate and battle, led the swift-running horses.

(5. 722–32)

The ecphrasis has a dramatic effect here similar to that achieved in Homer's description of the stringing of Pandaros' bow: by dwelling on the details of the harnessing, and of the artifact itself (the chariot and its components and appurtenances), the poet gives our minds time to recognize subliminally the dire consequences of the action that this glorious chariot and these divine horses will now initiate. The powerful significance of the moment, moreover, is highlighted by the use of the term θαῦμα ἰδέσθαι *thaûma idésthai* ("a marvel to behold"), the term Hephaistos uses to describe the shield he will build for Achilles. As in the case of Aphrodite's magic girdle (which Hera borrows to seduce Zeus), here, too, with the marvelous chariot, we understand that art in itself implies neither order nor disorder when allied with functional objects; the impact depends on the will of the user.

Among men also, the possession of horses and the knowledge of horsemanship signify social value. Horses are worthy prizes (23. 259, 265), and important spoils of this war (5. 25, 162–63; 10. 480–98; 19. 281) as they were of previous wars (11. 679 ff.). Among the gifts offered to Achilles by Agamemnon—unsuccessfully in Book 9, and successfully in Book 19—were " 'twelve horses, strong, race-competitors / who have won prizes in the speed of their feet. That man would not be / poor in possessions, to whom were given all these have won me, / nor be unpossessed of dearly honoured gold, were he given / all the prizes these single-foot horses have won for me' " (9. 123–27 = 9. 265–69 = 19. 244–48). The repetition of Agamemnon's boast becomes a mnemonic unit that leads us, in Book 19, to automatically recall and compare the previous gift-offering so that we further understand the circumstantial difference of this one that leads to Achilles' acceptance of the gifts.

Because they are so valuable, horses are taken care of even when the men are worn out from fighting, as the famous scene that closes Book 8 demonstrates (8. 502 ff.; cf. 10. 564 ff.); and in the heat of battle and slaughter, men are careful not to let their horses get unduly terrified (10. 492–93). There are even times when horses seem to be considered as important as men (21. 520). It's not surprising that a person's nobility is directly connected with the possession of horses (2. 1; 24. 493). Hera expresses her indignation at Zeus' wish to end the war by saying she has worn out her horses gathering her people (4. 27–28). And the cheekpiece simile used to describe Menelaos' wound indicates the respected position of horses, since the artifact is made specifically for the horse's sake as well as for the horseman's (4. 141 ff.). Agamemnon disdains the Kadmeians who "lash their horses" (4. 391)—an apparently derogatory epithet applied to the Trojans in general by the culprit-bowman Pandaros (5. 102).

Hektor's epithetical helmet has a horsehair crest with plumes "nodding terribly" (3. 337)—although Paris, as well as Agamemnon, Patroklos, and Teukros among the Achaians also have such helmets. In addition to Hektor, Nestor (whose familial epithet is "the Gerenian horseman") and Diomedes are regularly called "breaker of horses"—an epithet used once or twice of Kisseus, Kastor, Hippasos, Nestor's son Thrasymedes, Antenor, and Hyperenor—five Trojans and four Achaians. According to Saxe's data, even though Trojans are generically called "breakers of horses" (3. 128), horses are associated twice as often with the Achaians as with the Trojans—although both sides employ the animals in identical ways (for example, 11. 47 = 12. 84). Only Argos and Trikka (and the latter only once) are called "horse-pasturing" in the *Iliad*. Eumelos, the Thessalian son of Admetos and Alkestos (the two made famous by Euripides' *Alkestos*), owns Apollo-bred, perfectly matched, bird-swift horses (2. 763–66), while the finest horses among the Trojans are those of Rhesos and Aineias—the former, described by Dolon to Odysseus and Diomedes, show no inkling of immortality (10. 433 ff.); while the latter have an immortal status tinged with disorder, as I'll discuss shortly. So it is in perfect keeping with the poem's overall thematic structure that the horses of Achilles prove superior to those of his ultimate Trojan foes, Aineias and Hektor. Achilles' horses are animal counterparts to his human excellence (2. 770). This pattern is confirmed when we notice that Pandaros, the despicable Trojan who reinitiates the conflict in Homer's story, left his "excellent horses" at home despite his father's advice; he explains that he spared his horses because they had "grown accustomed to eating all they wished" (5. 192–201) and their hunger would be insecure on the battlefield. This effete attitude not only suggests the underlying weakness of Troy—a holding back from total commitment that Paris also reflects at the opening of Book 3 when Menelaos accepts his challenge to a duel—but also corresponds to the cowardly character of the bowman, a nonheroic warrior who must hide behind others for protection while he rearms his weapon. Pandaros is only living up to his disorderly Trojan nature in leaving his fine horses out of the war to save Troy.

In general horses represent the neutral orderliness of the universe, as animals whose actions are dictated by the wills of their masters (and who are, in this respect, analogous to the artifacts in thematic function). They can be, alternately, the indifferent war-machines who pull chariots into deadly battle (3. 113), trample fallen warriors (5. 588), or drag Hektor's body behind them (22. 464); or the steadfast companions-in-arms who, like Hephaistos, are always ready to obey orderly requests: in the evening, after the battle, standing "each beside his chariot" patiently waiting to serve their masters again tomorrow (2. 775–78; 3. 326; or 8. 542–62, the last being the famous closing scene of Book 8 where the hysteron proteron contrasts the orderly patience of the horses with the disorder prevalent among men); guarding their masters tirelessly during the night (10.

471); or being generally never reluctant to do anything required of them. Accordingly horses are symbols of security on the battlefield (5. 106). In this way, the horses in the *Iliad* contrast with the more or less useless and ungrateful dogs who are hardly more civilized than wolves since, during this time of war, their ordinary frolicsome activities—and sustenance—are curtailed. Saxe points out that when anyone wants to find someone, he is likely to find him by his horses (8. 100).

Obversely, when a man's horses are missing, the situation is likely to be disorderly, as when Hippokoön awakens after the night raid of Odysseus and Diomedes (10. 519 ff.; cf. 11. 339 ff.). In a darkly comic version of this motif, Zeus suspects something is amiss when Hera appears on Mount Ida to seduce him: "He stood before her and called her by name and spoke to her: 'Hera, / what is your desire that you come down here from Olympos? / And your horses are not here, nor your chariot, which you would ride in' " (14. 297–99). The narrative impact here is all the more effective since Homer has earlier described Hera's elaborate chariot. Not the chariot's artistry, but the artistry of the concealed girdle, is being made by Hera's will to determine this particular episode. So Hera tells her husband she's left her horses in the foothills (14. 307), leaving us to imagine, if we want to, the queen of the gods in all her well-perfumed finery climbing the mountain on foot (since Zeus is too preoccupied with the aphrodisiac spell to be this rational now).

Generally, too, horses are remarkable for their intelligence (5. 218–23 = 8. 105–10); but, oddly enough, the Trojan horses of Adrestos know so little about the battlefield that they indirectly bring about their master's death at the hands of Menelaos and Agamemnon (6. 38 ff.). Even the stalwart faithful horses, therefore, can't protect their drivers from the inevitabilities of disorder—nor a weaker man from a stronger (or more orderly) man, as when Glaukos kills Iphinoös (7. 13–18; see 11. 531). The sensitivity of horses—an anthropomorphic quality no doubt derived from their great value as possessions—is shown poignantly on occasions where their masters have fallen to powers beyond the horses' prowess to affect: "and in many places the strong-necked horses / rattled their empty chariots along the causeways of battle, / and longed for their haughty charioteers, who were lying / along the ground, to delight no longer their wives, but the vultures" (11. 159–62).

As we would expect (parallel to the poetic function of the artifacts), the thematic significance of horses is focused in their conjunction with the major figures of the *Iliad*, Aineias, Patroklos, Hektor, and Achilles. In the single combat between Aineias and Achilles, the contest is also between the heroes' horses. We learn from Diomedes the origin of the famous horses of Aineias:

> 'These are of that strain which Zeus of the wide brows granted
> once to Tros, recompense for his son Ganymedes, and therefore
> are the finest of all horses beneath the sun and the daybreak;
> and the lord of men Anchises stole horses from this breed,
> without the knowledge of Laomedon putting mares under them.

From these there was bred for him a string of six in his great house.
Four of these, keeping them himself, he raised at his mangers,
but these two he gave to Aineias, two horses urgent of terror.
If we might only take these we should win ourselves excellent glory.'

(5. 265–73)

So valuable were the horses of Tros, that Laomedon, in his generations, wouldn't even give them to Herakles in proper settlement of his debt (5. 640 ff.)—as we learn from the strange story exchanged by Tlepolemos and Sarpedon before they renew the wrath of the past with present wounds and death—an anti-exemplum expressing the blasphemous (anti-Zeus and anti-*xeinia*) behavior of Laomedon that led to an earlier destruction of Ilion, implicitly justifying the present by the past. In the generation preceding Aineias, Anchises, the second cousin of the man to whom the horses now generically belong—Priam (son of Laomedon, son of Ilos)—has stolen the horses in a disorderly, ominous act that recalls the ambiguous implications of the indirect transmission of Agamemnon's sceptre. Moreover the theft is compounded by the mortal breeding: first, the divine horses are abducted from their divinely authorized owner; then they are bred to mortal mares. The crime is darkened further by the incestuous aspect. In Homer's story, Aineias' horses are captured by Sthenelos and given to Deïpylos (5. 321–25), assimilated by the Achaians, so that when Aineias faces Achilles he is missing his fantastic steeds.

Homer expands on the legend of the Trojan horses when, in the confrontation between the two heroes in Book 20, he has Aineias conclude his claim to equality with Achilles by reciting his genealogy and including an extended reference to the miraculous breeding of the North Wind with the mares of his ancestor Dardanos, the son of Zeus,

'who founded Dardania, since there was yet no sacred Ilion
made a city in the plain to be a centre of peoples,
but they lived yet in the underhills of Ida with all her waters.
Dardanos in turn had a son, the king, Erichthonios,
who became the richest of mortal men, and in his possession
were three thousand horses who pastured along the low grasslands,
mares in their pride with their young colts; and with these the
     North Wind
fell in love as they pastured there, and took on upon him
the likeness of a dark-maned stallion, and coupled with them,
and the mares conceiving of him bore to him twelve young horses.'

(20. 216–26)

Tros is the son of Erichthonios; Ganymedes, the son of Tros. Zeus gave Tros the horses described in 5. 265–72 when he took Ganymedes away from his brothers—Assarakos (father of Capys, father of Anchises, father of Aineias) and Ilos (of Laomedon-Priam-Hektor). If one assumes that Tros inherited his father's

horses, then Zeus' present of stallions confirms the immortality of the Trojan
herd. And it simultaneously confirms the blasphemy of Anchises' act in stealing
the strain without the permission of his uncle. In any case, the horses of Aineias
are immortal in their origins—as are those of Achilles. Either Homer has
remembered that Diomedes' captured them, so that Aineias faces Achilles finally
with mortal horses against Achilles' immortal ones; or, what is equally possible,
he has forgotten and pits disorderly immortal horses against orderly immortal
horses. The thematic effect, in the second possible case, confirms my discussion
of the heroes' duel: two like charges can only repel; it's impossible for their fight
to reach a natural conclusion—as the intervention of the gods to remove Aineias
implies. What proves this is another piece of evidence discovered by Saxe:
Achilles' horses are children of the West Wind (16. 151). Obviously two winds
cannot come to blows without total consequences to cosmic order; and that
ultimate confrontation is reserved, in Homer's epic, for Achilles and Hektor—so
Aineias must be spared at all costs to the theme of the *Iliad*.

Hektor is called "breaker of horses" in the closing lines of the poem, and is
generally associated epithetically with his famous horsehair crest which
frightens Astyanax in the poignant scene on the Trojan wall. When Hektor enters
battle in Book 15, Homer describes his favorite warrior's vigor in this simile: "As
when some stalled horse who has been corn-fed at the manger / breaking free of
his rope gallops over the plain in thunder / to his accustomed bathing place in a
sweet-running river / and in the pride of his strength holds high his head, and
the mane floats / over his shoulders; sure of his glorious strength, the quick
knees / carry him to the loved places and the pasture of horses" (15. 263–68). The
irony of this metaphor, in its mnemonic function, is that the precise same words
are used to describe Paris entering battle, at Hektor's coercion, in Book 6. 506–11.
What is expected and believable of Hektor is all the more unbelievable when
applied to his cowardly brother; and a reverse effect occurs: because the simile is
applied to Hektor second, it makes us recall the debility of Paris to live up to the
metaphorical promise, so that we suddenly understand the pathetic futility of
Hektor's strength in defense of a nation of men like Paris and Pandaros. We know
from his usual behavior that Hektor's horsemanship is superbly effective, based
on his technical expertise and on his loving care for his horses—Xanthos,
Podargos, Aithon, and Lampos (8. 177–86; cf. 17. 175 ff.). But this mastery
doesn't save him because, with horses as with armor, Hektor makes a tragically
fatal mistake that expresses his single but sufficient *hubris*. Hektor promises the
horses of Achilles to the spy Dolon (10. 304 ff.), swearing an empty oath by
Zeus—equivalent to his blasphemous donning of Achilles' armor that makes
Zeus thunder his disapproval for our ears (10. 329). Dolon recognizes Hektor's
deception (10.391–93), and Odysseus defines Hektor's mistake clearly: " 'Surely
now, these were mighty gifts that your heart longed after, / the horses of valiant
Aiakides. They are difficult horses / for mortal men to manage, or even to ride
behind them / for all except Achilles, who was born of an immortal mother' " (10.
401–4). Xanthos, the gods' name for the Zeus-born river that crosses the Trojan
plain (and related to Astyanax's proper name, Skamandrios), is the name of both

a horse of Hektor's and of one of Achilles' (8. 184; 16. 149). This may be merely the convenience of metrics or the coincidence of common names; or it may further underline the triumph of Achilles' immortality over Hektor's mortality, redefining in a complicated reversal of nomenclature the future of Hektor's son, who will meet his fate among Achaians rather than among Trojans. The difference between Hektor and his invincible opponent is further emphasized when Mentes says to Hektor, persuading him to give up his pride and return to his orderly defensive position against Menelaos, " 'you, Hektor, run after what can never be captured, / the horses of valiant Aiakides; they are difficult horses / for mortal man to manage, or even to ride behind them' " (17. 75–77). The futility of Hektor's role is expressed simply and beautifully in Mentes' first words (17. 75). In this case, however, Hektor gives up the pursuit of Achilles' horses (who will therefore later bring Achilles against him, fatally); by contrast, the tainted immortal horses of Aineias are captured by Diomedes (23. 287)—so that an Achaian's horsemanship succeeds where the chief Trojan's fails.

We are introduced formally to the horses of Achilles after Patroklos has armed for battle:

> For him Automedon led the fast-running horses under
> the yoke, Xanthos and Balios, who tore with the winds' speed,
> horses stormy Podarge once conceived of the west wind
> and bore, as she grazed in the meadow beside the swirl of the Ocean.
> In the traces beside these he put unfaulted Pedasos
> whom Achilleus brought back once when he stormed Eëtion's city.
> He, mortal as he was, ran beside the immortal horses.
>
> (16. 148–54)

Just as Patroklos reflects the mortal alter ego of Achilles, so too (as I've discussed previously, following Zarker's interpretation), Pedasos in yoke with Balios and Xanthos reflects Achilles' split personality. Judged in terms of his horses, Achilles is two-thirds immortal and one-third mortal—the same combination that was not enough to save Gilgamesh from death. When Pedasos is killed by Sarpedon and Automedon expediently and expeditiously cuts the horse loose, that action is a symbolic prediction of the imminent death of Patroklos— and also of Achilles, whose mortality Patroklos represents specifically by wearing Achilles' old, mortal armor (16. 467 ff.). And the immortal horses, who survive to carry Achilles later into battle, represent another striking symbolic inversion. Achilles inherited them from his father, Peleus, who received them as gifts from the gods (16. 381). We learn more about the divine horses from Achilles himself, when he explains that there would be no contest if he were to enter the horse race in honor of Patroklos: " 'You know how much my horses surpass in their speed all others; / yes, for they are immortal horses, and Poseidon gave them / to Peleus my father, who in turn gave them into my hands' " (23. 276–78). We remember that it was Poseidon who chided Aineias for fighting with Achilles, after hurling him off the battlefield where his horses are not enough to overcome the Achaian warrior (20. 331 ff.). The derivation of his horses lends further divine authority to Achilles' character, since we now see that he is supported by Poseidon as well as by Zeus—reminding us that Achilles' mother, after all, is a goddess of the sea. Moreover, there is a subtle recollection, in this little speech directed primarily to Agamemnon, of the direct nature of the transmission in Achilles' case (contrasting with the sceptre Agamemnon has inherited indirectly from Zeus). And the immortal horses from his father correspond to the immortal shield brought to him by his mother; the mortal spear of Peleus, on the other hand, is the actual instrument that will kill Hektor who deserves to die because he's killed Patroklos (whose death Pedasos' death foreshadows, and who is carrying his own, not Achilles' spear), because he's wearing Achilles' paternal armor, and because he rashly promised Dolon the horses of Achilles.

When Patroklos dies, "his horsemanship all forgotten" (16. 775), the horsehair helmet of Achilles is trampled in the dust by the same immortal horses who survive Pedasos and Patroklos, as if Achilles' divine nature inevitably must destroy his human life (16. 793–97). But when the furor abates,

> the horses of Aiakides standing apart from battle
> wept, as they had done since they heard how their charioteer
> had fallen in the dust at the hands of murderous Hektor.
> In truth Automedon, the powerful son of Diores,
> hit them over and over again with the stroke of the flying
> lash, or talked to them, sometimes entreating them, sometimes
>   threatening.
> They were unwilling to go back to the wide passage of Helle
> and the ships, or back into the fighting after the Achaians,
> but still as stands a grave monument which is set over
> the mounded tomb of a dead man or lady, they stood there
> holding motionless in its place the fair-wrought chariot,
> leaning their heads along the ground, and warm tears were running
> earthward from underneath the lids of the mourning horses
> who longed for their charioteer, while their bright manes were made
>   dirty
> as they streamed down either side of the yoke from under the yoke
>   pad.

$$\text{(17. 426–40)}$$

In a salient departure from his usual "realism," Homer brings to us in this beautifully poignant scene the shocking nature of war that has led to the death of Achilles' dearest companion. The use of the verb πυνθάνομαι *punthánomai* ("learn by inquiry; ascertain, hear tell of"—Autenrieth) marks the intelligence Homer ascribes to these horses (17. 428). Soon Achilles will hear tell of his friend's death, and his mourning will begin, already prefigured by theirs; the horses mourn first because they are both witnesses and instruments. Achilles, too, was instrumental but, in his self-enforced alienation, was not a witness to his friend's last moments; and he is consequently more culpable than the horses, even though they trampled the helmet under them (a gesture that parallels Andromache's violent discarding of her bridal headdress in Book 22). Their trampling of Achilles' paternal helmet, instead, in a symbolic reproof of their recalcitrant master. And the simile Homer uses here is most appropriate, foreshadowing the funeral games in which horses will play a central role in several ways—but not these immortal horses who, like Achilles, will remain aloof then because they have already done their mourning by way of action, have already played their fateful role in the tragedy. Here their inaction inversely reflects Achilles' inaction; they will not leave the battlefield as he will not enter it. When they leave, he will enter; they will bring him back with them. They are as firm as stone because Achilles' heart has been, as Patroklos pointed out, harder than the "towering rocks" (16. 35). Yet these are immortal horses, after all, and cannot by nature suffer long. Zeus intervenes to overcome their temporary inertia and restores their vitality:

> As he watched the mourning horses the son of Kronos pitied them,
> and stirred his head and spoke to his own spirit: 'Poor wretches,
> why then did we ever give you to the lord Peleus,
> a mortal man, and you yourselves are immortal and ageless?
> Only so that among unhappy men you also might be grieved?
> Since among all creatures that breathe on earth and crawl on it
> there is not anywhere a thing more dismal than man is.
> At least the son of Priam, Hektor, shall not mount behind you
> in the carefully wrought chariot. I will not let him. Is it not
> enough for him that he has the armour and glories in wearing it?
> But now I will put vigour into your knees and your spirits
> so that you bring back Automedon out of the fighting
> safe to the hollow ships . . .'
>
> (17. 441–53)

Even more notable because Zeus showed no such concern over Aineias' horses, his speech here about the horses of Achilles vividly recalls Thetis' frequent laments for her involvement in human, mortal affairs. It's also significant that Zeus' use of the first person plural in reference to the gift to Peleus explicitly proves his hegemony over Poseidon. His comparison of the horses to "dismal" men is telling: the horses have no unearthly ambitions; only man knows enough to think he is more than he is—and that is the human tragedy of the *Iliad*. The orderly patient horses, never testing their place on the great chain of being, stand always in contrast to the disorderly motions that dominate men's minds in this epic. So Zeus reinvigorates Xanthos and Balios (17. 458) because they are meant to play a role in the restoration of order among men. They will carry Automedon home in order to carry Achilles, later, into battle against the perpetrator of the present disorder, Hektor. Perhaps Zeus has not forgotten Hektor's previous rash threat to give Dolon Achilles' horses; in any case, we know the god is not pleased with Hektor's hubristic assumption of Achilles' armor—another case of a man not respecting his proper place on the chain. In the battle scenes that follow, the same motifs are repeated (17. 475 ff.). Hektor asks Aineias to join him in winning the horses of Achilles (17. 486 ff.) but Automedon and Alkimedon, precisely because they are mindful of their individual limitations (17. 475 ff., 501 ff.), manage to employ Achilles' horses in a successful engagement as they protect Patroklos' body, fend off proud Hektor and Aineias, and flee safely from the battlefield.

When Achilles, at last, is recommitted to the Argive cause and howls in anguished hatred from the ditch under the aegis of Zeus and Athene, even the Trojan horses are terrified "since their hearts saw the coming afflictions" (18. 224)—as if the exalted appearance of Achilles is powerful enough to elevate the nature of all he confronts, further proved when his own horse takes on speech. The normally neutral, though intelligent, horses here seem to share the prophetic insight of Kassandra. After Achilles' arming has been described in splendid detail,

> Automedon and Alkimos, in charge of the horses,
> yoked them, and put the fair breast straps about them, and forced the
>   bits home
> between their jaws, and pulled the reins back against the compacted
> chariot seat, and one, Automedon, took up the shining
> whip caught close in his hand and vaulted up to the chariot,
> while behind him Achilleus helmed for battle took his stance
> shining in all his armour like the sun when he crosses above us,
> and cried in a terrible voice on the horses of his father:
> 'Xanthos, Balios . . . famed sons of Podarge,
> take care to bring in another way your charioteer back
> to the company of the Danaans, when we give over fighting,
> not leave him to lie fallen there, as you did to Patroklos.'
>   Then from beneath the yoke the gleam-footed horse answered him,
> Xanthos, and as he spoke bowed his head, so that all the mane
> fell away from the pad and swept the ground by the cross-yoke;
> the goddess of the white arms, Hera, had put a voice in him:
> 'We shall still keep you safe for this time, o hard Achilleus.
> And yet the day of your death is near, but it is not we
> who are to blame, but a great god and powerful Destiny.
> For it was not because we were slow, because we were careless,
> that the Trojans have taken the armour from the shoulders of Patroklos,
> but it was that high god, the child of lovely-haired Leto,
> who killed him among the champions and gave the glory to Hektor.
> But for us, we two could run with the blast of the west wind
> who they say is the lightest of all things; yet still for you
> there is destiny to be killed in force by a god and a mortal.'
>   When he had spoken so the Furies stopped the voice in him,
> but deeply disturbed, Achilleus of the swift feet answered him:
> 'Xanthos, why do you prophesy my death? This is not for you.
> I myself know well it is destined for me to die here

far from my beloved father and mother. But for all that
I will not stop till the Trojans have had enough of my fighting.'
He spoke, and shouting held on in the foremost his single-foot horses.

(19. 392–425)

Homer's detailed description of the yoking parallels the emphatic *lentando* tempo of the episode of Pandaros' bow-stringing, with the result that the structural impact of the action for which this yoking is a preparation will be appreciated in advance and heightened by the suspense. Like Hephaistos' shield-work (18. 464–67), the horses' prowess cannot spare Achilles' life, though they will make it possible for him to win immortality in memory by his deeds. The passage has many ramifications besides the supernatural speech of Xanthos itself, which indicates a momentary breakage of the links on the golden chain for the purpose of cosmic explication. There is the explicit comparison of Achilles to the sun-god ready to begin a new orderly day as he stands tall in his chariot; Homer involves the very cosmos in his mnemonic art (so that the sun above us, from this point on, should remind us of Achilles at the moment of his heroic ripeness—19. 398). Achilles' "terrible" invocation to the horses suggests that he is no longer communicating with men as equals on the same link of the chain—and indeed he says this explicitly to Hektor at the moment of his revenge (22. 262–66). His implied reproof of the horses for not bringing back Patroklos safely reminds us that Pedasos, too, is dead; and Achilles goes forth into the poem's ultimate battle drawn only by his two immortal horses—another symbolic explanation for his exaltation beyond the limits of ordinary humanity: his mortality is left behind, dead with Patroklos. The description of Xanthos' manner of speaking, with his mane touching the ground, suggests that Hera's endowing the horse with speech is a form of daemonic possession (19. 405–7). The clearest statement of Achilles' destiny comes from his horse, who calls him hard—recognizing the connection between Achilles' character and his fate (19. 408–10), and once again recalling the assessment of Patroklos in Book 16, later repeated by Priam in Achilles' camp. Xanthos' reference to a "great god and powerful Destiny" who are to blame, not anyone else, including the horses themselves, is an unusually definite description of the poem's moral view, and quite distinct from the moral system described by Zeus in *Odyssey* 1.32 (where he blames all man's miseries on man, claiming that the gods are not responsible). Then Xanthos clearly equates the loss of a man's armor with the loss of his mortal life in a most essential context, since he is speaking to the very man whose armor Patroklos was wearing through the misguided judgment of both companions (19. 413–14). Odd, too, is the horse's specific prediction that a god and a mortal will kill Achilles, prefiguring the continuation of the cyclical story beyond the purposes of Homer's *Iliad* (19. 417). The sudden, unexplained and inexplicable interruption of Xanthos' speech by the Furies merges with Achilles' own retort in which the hero assumes command over his own momentarily extraordinary nature, over the impending disorder that will lead to ultimate order, and over his horses at one and the same time as he rushes them into the battlefield (19. 421–24). It is as if Achilles is directing Xanthos back to his proper position on the chain because Achilles himself is, for the time being, occupying an abnormally high link under the compulsion of Zeus' will to restore everyone along the chain to their proper positions once and for all. But the most poignant lines of the passage are those in which the horses distinguish their reality from that of all mortals, including even Achilles (19. 415–17), bringing home to us again the tragic import of Homer's poem: that the disorder of humanity leads to the death of human beings, regardless of the measure of their individual guilt—since death knows no distinctions in its finality.

As archaeologists have confirmed (noting the similarity and connection between Mycenaean and Scythian nomadic cultures in this, among other respects), horses play an equally important role in the funeral rites of noblemen—as they do in the case of Patroklos. Book 23 opens with a strangely unexplained horse-ritual initiated by Achilles:

> 'Myrmidons, you of the fast horses, my steadfast companions,
> we must not yet slip free of the chariots our single-foot horses,
> But with these very horses and chariots we must drive close up
> to Patroklos and mourn him, since such is the privilege of
>   the perished.
> Then, when we have taken full satisfaction from the sorrowful
> dirge, we shall set our horses free, and all of us eat here.'
>   He spoke, and all of them assembled moaned, and Achilleus
>   led them.
> Three times, mourning, they drove their horses with flowing
>   manes about
> the body, and among them Thetis stirred the passion for weeping
>   (23. 6–14)

When Patroklos is buried, four horses are burned on the pyre with him (23. 171–72; see 23. 238ff.), finding their mortality in the birth of their master's immortal memory (secured by the properly ritualized funeral).

Homer shows, in general, little tactical knowledge of horsemanship. Agamemnon enters battle leaving his chariot behind as if it would only get in the way, its only apparent purpose for escape (4. 226 ff.). Battle orders seem perversely given to get the horses "fouled in the multitude" between the foot soldiers (4. 297, 301; 13. 534, 682). If two chariots meet in battle, the outcome is equal; but when a chariot meets someone on foot, the person on the ground is usually victorious, striking the charioteer out of his vehicle. Captured horses are not reused immediately but are always sent back to the ships (5. 161); and the Phrygians are singled out because they "fight from horses" (10. 431). The poet's firsthand experience with horses in battle is extremely doubtful in some instances, as when Hektor claims, "I know how to storm my way into the struggle of flying horses" (7. 240), or as when the horses of Achilles leap over the ditch with his chariot following behind them (cf. 15. 352 ff.). This feat, admirable enough for the horses themselves, could only be extremely painful for the chariot and its occupants—since the horses have no way of gauging how far beyond the ditch they need to land to make sure the car also clears it. The most remarkable imaginary horsemanship is the simile used to describe Aias fighting on the decks of the ships:

> And as a man who is an expert rider of horses
> who when he has chosen and coupled four horses out of many
> makes his way over the plain galloping toward a great city
> along the travelled road, and many turn to admire him,
> men or women, while he steadily and never slipping
> jumps and shifts his stance from one to another as they gallop;
> so Aias ranged crossing from deck to deck of the fast ships.

(15. 679–85)

Saxe explains that this may be a perfect simile for ships bobbing up and down at anchor—although the ships are, in fact, beached—but it is an extremely awkward action and "one that would be impossible to do without slipping."

On the other hand, Homer does seem to know the details of horse racing (23. 318 ff.). We have seen already how the horse race in Book 23, in which Athene destroys Eumelos' chariot and Diomedes' horses are slowed by Apollo (23. 375 ff.), is a microcosm of the war: the same interference of divine and human realms, with the race as the more orderly stage, this time. The outcome of the chariot race—the easy reconciliation between Antilochos and Menelaos through the fair-minded arbitration of Achilles—is an exemplary contrast to the quarrel between Achilles and Agamemnon in Book 1. So despite Homer's inconsistent knowledge of horses as animals of war, there's no doubt about his masterly manipulation of horses as symbols of order and disorder—reminding us that Plato's Socrates, in the *Ion*, was questioning the art of the rhapsode Ion, not the art of Homer.

Annotated Bibliography

Texts

Homeri Opera. Edited by David B. Munro and Thomas W. Allen. 2 vols. 1902. 3d ed. Oxford, Eng. 1957.

The Iliad. Edited by Walter Leaf. 2 vols. London, 1886.

The Iliad. Translated by A. T. Murray. 2 vols. London, 1924.

The Iliad. Translated by Robert Fitzgerald. Garden City, N.Y., 1974.

The Iliad of Homer. Edited by Walter Leaf and M. A. Bayfield. 2 vols. 1895. 2d ed. London, 1962. This edition was used for all citations of the Greek text.

The Iliad of Homer. Translated by Richmond Lattimore. 1951. Reprint ed. Chicago, Ill., 1967. Unless otherwise indicated, Lattimore's translation is used throughout this book.

The Odyssey. Translated by A. T. Murray. 2 vols. London, 1919.

The Odyssey. Translated by Robert Fitzgerald. Garden City, N.Y. 1961.

The Odyssey of Homer. Translated by Richmond Lattimore. 1965. Reprint ed. New York, 1967. This translation of the *Odyssey* is used throughout.

Criticism

Abercrombie, Lascelles. *The Epic: An Essay*. 1914. London, 1922. Even though he wrote before Milman Parry, Abercrombie's intuition of the Homeric epics is so accurate that his work is hardly outdated. (See especially pp. 18, 52.)

Allen, Thomas W. *The Homeric Catalogue of Ships*. Oxford, Eng., 1921.

Amory, Anne. "The Gates of Horn and Ivory." *Yale Classical Studies* 20 (1966): 35–40.

Aristotle. *Poetica*. Translated by W. Hamilton Fyfe. 1927. Cambridge, Eng., 1965.

Armstrong, James I. "The Arming Motif in the *Iliad*." *American Journal of Philology* 79 (1958): 337–54. The treatment of Patroklos' arming is especially interesting.

Arnold, Matthew. "On Translating Homer." In *The Poetry and Criticism of Matthew Arnold*, edited by A. Dwight Culler, pp. 217–32. Boston, 1961.

Atchity, Kenneth John. "The Message of Idaios: Formulaic Departure?" *Classical Philology* 68, October 1973, p. 297.

———. "Achilles' Sidonian Bowl." *Classical Outlook* 51, November 1973, pp. 25–26.

———. "Iris in *Iliad* 18." *Arethusa* 7 (Fall 1974): 221–22.

———. "Teucer in the *Iliad*." *Classical Outlook* 52, February 1975, p. 62.

———. "The Power of Words in the *Iliad*." *Classical Outlook* 53, September 1975, pp. 5–6.

———. "Homer's Ultimate Vision." *Classical Outlook* 53, May 1976, p. 98.

———. "Structure in *Iliad* 3." *Classical Outlook* 54, March 1977, pp. 74–75.

———. "The Omen in *Iliad* 2." *Classical Outlook* 54, May 1977, pp. 100–101.

Auden, W. H. "The Shield of Achilles." In *Homer*, edited by George Steiner and Robert Fagles, pp. 79–80. Englewood Cliffs, N.J., 1962.

Auerbach, Erich. "Odysseus' Scar." In *Mimesis*. Translated by Willard Trask. 1946. Garden City, N.Y., 1957. Although I admire and agree with most of this brilliant essay, I cannot agree that what Homer "narrates is for the time being the only present, and fills both the stage and the reader's mind completely." This would deny the active function of the audience's memory. Nor can I agree that "the Homeric poems . . . contain no teaching and no secret second meaning." Teaching does not have to be concealed to be present—and the *Iliad* is didactic in the general sense I have described. If Homer makes his audience forget reality for a while, he does so only that they may face it again more effectively. (See pp. 3, 4, 11, 12.)

Austin, Norman. *Archery at the Dark of the Moon. Poetic Problems in Homer's Odyssey*. Berkeley and Los Angeles, 1975. Austin's introduction definitively refutes the excesses of "Parryistic" analysis, exposing the flaws in Parry's selection of data and consequent conclusions. Austin's study of the *Odyssey* heralds a new, critically more sensible and sensitive, era in Homeric studies that will allow those who love the poems to discuss their poetics without apologies for "intentionalism," and without lengthy argumentative preambles that try to straddle two antithetical views of Homeric poetry. "It should be a trusim," Austin writes, "that a poet with his eye fixed chiefly on metrical economy could never have produced either the *Iliad* or the *Odyssey*. The vast vocabulary, the richness and variety of expressions, the conjunction of rhythm, sound, and sense, are not the work of a mnemonic efficiency expert" (p. 63).

Bassett, Samuel E. *The Poetry of Homer*. Berkeley, 1938. I owe much to this work, especially in finding corroboration for my own observations: the symbiotic relationship between Priam and Hektor (p. 8); the appropriate use of the present tense to describe divine armor (pp. 90–91); the contrapuntal effect of the miniatures and the similes (p. 94); Cretan influence of the dance on the shield (p. 98); the single suggestion of suicide from grief (p. 99); the cognitive relationship between narrator and audience with respect to the characters (p. 131); the contrast between Hektor's momentary *hubris* over Patroklos and Achilles' use of the plural when he has slain Hektor (p. 188); Hektor's association with women, Achilles' with men (pp. 190–91); and Bassett's dual characterization of Homer as a realist and idealist simultaneously (p. 244).

Bell, Clive. *Art*. New York, 1914. Bell's statement applies to the shield of Achilles: "The contemplation of pure form leads to a state of extraordinary exaltation and complete detachment from the concerns of life . . . It is tempting to suppose that the emotion which exalts has been transmitted through the forms we contemplate, by the artist who created them" (p. 68). As the first sight of the shield affects Achilles in Book 19, so we are affected by the formal impact of the poem of memory.

Bespaloff, Rachel. *On the Iliad*. Translated by Mary McCarthy. New York, 1947. Especially influential were Bespaloff's remarks on Hektor's dilemma (p. 41); the suitability of the poem's warlike subject to the contemplation of glory (p. 43); the relationship between poetic memorialization and immortality (p. 45); Helen's anomalous character (11. 66 ff.); the redemption of horror by beauty and truth, especially with Helen on the wall and Priam in the camp of Achilles (pp. 103 ff.); the difference between the faith of Homer and that of Christianity (p. 119). This last has been especially provocative: "Whereas faith in the Resurrection affirms the principle of communion, joining each individual member of the chosen people, then each nation, and at last the human race to God in universal salvation, belief in immortality consecrates the principle of oneness, exalts the incomparable event—named Hector, or Achilles, or Helen—that emerges from Becoming for a single instant and forever. Man immortalizes the object of his love, and this function of his is the loftiest reason for his activity. God does just the opposite: He creates out of nothing and restores the dead to life."

Bespaloff writes so movingly of Helen, Hektor, Priam, and Achilles because she recognizes in the poetic consciousness which informs the *Iliad* the implicit association of beauty with oneness, permanence, and being. Yet she has marked also Homer's awareness of the uniqueness characterizing things subject to the flux of becoming. Even more importantly she understands that the peculiar aesthetic quality of the *Iliad* derives from the interpenetration of all these elements. That constant interpenetration is what gives the world of Homer's *Iliad* its realistic texture, explaining the generic optimism of the poem's close. Bespaloff may leave the impression of being overly deterministic primarily because of her anachronistic application of Platonic and Christian categories to the consciousness behind the poem—in her pursuit of a sociopolitical purpose. Despite these reservations I owe her work an immense debt of inspiration.

Beye, Charles Rowan. *The Iliad, the Odyssey and the Epic Tradition*. Garden City, N.Y., 1966. Beye defines "ekphrasis" as "the poetic description of material objects of art" (p. 143), providing a term for the self-reflexiveness found in the artifacts. I value his discussion of the poet's use of his Muse to enhance the objectivity of his story (p. 18); the narrative illogic of Helen on the wall (p. 20); the social significance of Achilles' withdrawal and reentry (pp. 137 ff.); Achilles' superlative vitality (p. 142); the connection between genealogies and the sense of order expressed by the poem (p. 142); the inclusion on Achilles' shield of "most of the basic antitheses in the human situation" (p. 143); the importance of the ultimate position accorded by Hephaistos to "creative joy" (p. 144); Andromache's multiple social roles (p. 150); the aptness of the washbasins seen by Hektor in his last moments (p. 154); and of Achilles' telling of the story of Niobe as evidence that he is now ready to accept fully his humanity (p. 157).

———. *Ancient Greek Literature and Society*. Garden City, N.Y., 1975. "One thing is clear: these are no primitive, inchoate attempts at poetry. They are sophisticated, fully developed narrative poems of unusual subtlety and control" (p. 31). Beye corroborates my interpretation of the cheekpiece simile (p. 43); emphasizes the questioning introspection of Achilles (p. 72); compares the didactic roles of Phoinix and Nestor (p. 73); and, in discussing Hesiod, implies that Zeus as an ordering principle comes later than Homer. I agree that Hesiod formalized the principle more explicitly but have argued that it is nonetheless intuitively present in Homer's conception of the universe.

Bolling, G. M. "*Poikilos* and *Throna*." *American Journal of Philology* (1958): 275–82. In his discussion of the root-meaning of Homeric epithets like εὔθρονος *eúthronos* and χρυσόθρονος *chrusóthronos*, Bolling concludes that the stem refers not to "thrones" but to sacred flowers that possessed magical properties to the Greeks of Homer's time. These flowers were woven into the fabric of clothes, so that χρυσόθρονος *chrusóthronos* means "golden-flowered," referring to the embroidery of a person's clothes, rather than "golden-throned." The weaving of the flowers is a kind of sacred act and, in 22.441, when Andromache weaves θρόνα *thróna* at her loom as she hears of Hektor's death, she "is weaving a charm for his protection and ordering her maids to prepare for him a hot bath that he will never enjoy. It must have been a wish to make his audience sympathize with Andromache that made the poet break for once his *tabu* on θρόνα." Bolling's linguistic analysis, therefore, confirms my interpretation of the intentional pathos of this scene. My colleague Elizabeth Barber speculates that the weaving of θρόνα as a kind of fetish to protect the wearer corresponds to the artistic intention behind armor as well—that is, the depiction of desirable actions on the surface of the object by which those actions may be accomplished. Her research into the function and form of early Greek textiles parallels my views of the consistent functionality of beautiful objects in the Homeric poems and indicates a comprehensive aesthetic that applies also to the Homeric poems themselves, in their didactic symbiosis of form and content.

Borges, Jorge Luis. "The Maker." In *Dreamtigers*. Translated from *El Hacedor* by Mildred Boyer and Harold Morland. New York, 1970. This is a moving and insightful description of the aesthetic relationship between physical and imaginative vision.

Bowra, Sir Maurice. *Tradition and Design in the Iliad*. Oxford, Eng., 1930. Bowra sees the fate of Troy in a perspective much like mine: "Troy falls because the Trojans condone the guilt of Paris . . . His crime passed all the limits allowed to the heroic age; it violated not only wedlock but hospitality" (p. 25). There is a definite disagreement, then, between theories of the disorderliness of Troy and the ultimate orderliness of Argos and interpretations which see the two sides of the conflict as equal morally. On the other hand, Bowra's insistence that Homer's was not a "useful" poetry (p. 69) is clearly based on what I have termed an overly narrow definition of "use." I have been alternately enlightened and provoked by his treatment of the dual nature of Agamemnon's sovereignty (p. 173); the absence of a sense of glory after death (p. 236); what Bowra considers Homer's primary emphasis on the individual (p. 241); the supernatural aura surrounding Achilles at the trench in Book 18 (p. 247); and whether or not death makes everything meaningless in the world of the song (p. 249).

———. *Heroic Poetry*. London, 1952. This was useful on the connection between prophets and poets (p. 19); the singer's claim to telling the truth (p. 40); the necessity for the hero to be socially oriented (p. 64). Achilles' dual motivation for reentering the fight (p. 103); Hektor's ambiguous historical position (p. 112); the realism and objectivity which characterize epic truth (p. 132); the attitude toward time in epic poetry (p. 313); the archaeology of the shield (p. 396); the completeness of Homer's vision of life (p. 566). Bowra's commonsensical suggestion about the singer's anonymity agrees with Lord's: "the audience knows who the poet is" (p. 405).

———. *Homer and His Forerunners*. Edinburgh, 1955. Most interesting is his argument that the scheme of generations in the *Iliad* is purely artistic (p. 18).

———. "The Meaning of the Heroic Age." In *The Language and Background of Homer*, edited by G. S. Kirk, pp. 22–48. Cambridge, Eng., 1964. The special relationship between the king and the gods (p. 28) and the anthropomorphism of Homer are discussed (p. 47).

Budgen, Frank. "James Joyce: An Encounter with Homer." In *Homer*, edited by George Steiner and Robert Fagles, pp. 156–57. Englewood Cliffs, N.J., 1962. Quotes Joyce's observation that we know more about a Homeric character, in terms of his social context, than we do about any other character in literature.

Burke, Kenneth. *Language as Symbolic Action*. Berkeley, 1966. Burke's general approach to the understanding of the way in which symbolism serves theme has influenced my own in more ways than I consciously recognize.

Calhoun, George M. "Homeric Repetitions." *Classical Philology* 12 (1933): 112–14. Here Calhoun defines Homer as "a supremely great poet, working with traditional material," a definition which seems undeniably accurate.

———. "The Art of Formula in Homer." *Classical Philology* 14 (1935): 187–92.

———. "Polity and Society (i) the Homeric Picture." In *A Companion to Homer*, edited by Alan J. B. Wace and Frank H. Stubbings, pp. 431–52. London, 1962.

Carpenter, Rhys. *Folk Tale, Fiction and Saga in the Homeric Epics*. Berkeley, 1946.

Chadwick, H. Munro. *The Heroic Age*. Cambridge, Eng., 1926. Various stories about Helen are included (p. 266). Most significant to my study was Chadwick's discussion of the "break-up of normal relations as characteristic of an heroic age . . . a relaxation of the bonds of kinship, which shows itself especially in fatal strife between relatives" (p. 359).

Combellack, Frederick M. "Milman Parry and Homeric Artistry." *Comparative Literature* 11 (Summer 1959): 1–15. Combellack goes further than Parry would ever have gone in asserting, "for all that any critic . . . can now show, the occasional highly appropriate word may, like the occasional highly inappropriate one, be purely coincidental—part of the law of averages . . . in the use of the formulary style." Although the statement is accurate enough when taken literally (that is, in reference to single words), extrapolation from it denies the artistry of the poems altogether. The work of Austin, Russo, and Adam Parry, among others, has shown that such pessimism is not justified.

Cook, Arthur Bernard. *Zeus, A Study in Ancient Religion*. Vol. 1. New York, 1914. Notes Hephaistos' Egyptian affinities (p. 433); his connection with Ariadne's crown (p. 492); the iron man, Talos (p. 719); Rhadamanthys, judge of the dead (p. 330); Ixion's wheel (p. 202); and Helen's connection with ball lightning (p. 733).

Creed, Robert P. "The Singer Looks at His Sources." *Comparative Literature* 14 (Winter 1962): 44–52. Creed argues for the veristic basis of Homeric song, from analogy: "If Demodocus had told inaccurately the story of the Trojan horse, the heroes who had performed the deeds recounted could themselves have corrected these first or early singers of their adventures . . . We are thus subtly assured that . . . Homer, who through Demodocus links himself with a singer contemporary with Odysseus, is telling us what really happened in those distant days."

Crossett, John. "The Art of Homer's Catalogue of Ships." *Classical Journal* 64, March 1969, pp. 241–49. Crossett discusses the panning effect of progressing from genus to species to individual at the opening of the catalogue as a way of emphasizing the social impact of war (p. 241). He notes that, for his refusal to fight, Achilles is as worthless as Nireus (p. 243); that the catalogue is a microcosm of the war (p. 244), a device by which the wrath-story and the war-tale are woven together (p. 245).

Delcourt, M. *Hephaistos ou la légende du Magicien*. Paris, 1957.

Desan, Wilfrid D. *The Planetary Man: A Noetic Prelude to a United World*. Vol. 1. Washington, D.C., 1961. I owe a great deal to Desan's metaphysical appreciation of the complex existential reciprocity between the individual and the collective dimensions of human experience.

Dietrich, B. C. *Death, Fate and the Gods: The Development of a Religious Idea in Greek Popular Belief and in Homer*. London, 1965. Dietrich discusses the twofold genealogy of Helen, her association with birds and with vegetation, her ambivalent attachment to Artemis and Aphrodite, and her generally chthonic affinities.

Dimock, George. Review of Adam Parry, *The Collected Papers of Milman Parry*. *Yale Review* 60 (Summer 1971): 585–90. Dimock's summary of Homer's relationship to the tradition is incisive: "The poet thinks not just in words but in meter . . . So we need no longer think of Homer struggling to fit prefabricated phrases into the pattern of the hexameter, but rather of the pattern of the hexameter in his mind generating the metrical utterances which express his thought. If Achilles is swift-footed, it is essentially because the poet thinks of him that way, however unemphatically, and not because of the meter. By the same token, if the *Iliad* is the greatest poem ever

composed, it is because Homer composed it that way and not because of the
stereotypes furnished by the tradition, however useful they may have been
to him. The poet uses the stereotypes to think with, and therefore the *Iliad*
does more than provide heroic mood-music; it shows us our ultimate
concerns. . . . So oral poetry is not so different from the written variety after
all" (p. 589).

Dodds, E. R. *The Greeks and the Irrational*. Boston, 1951. Dodds' seminal work
clearly demonstrates the way in which intent is subordinate to act in the oral
tradition (p. 3); the gods are used to express the poet's sense of ultimate
order, beyond the individual (p. 18); that the Homeric poems reflect "stir-
rings of individualism in a society where family solidarity was still universally taken for granted" (p. 47); and that the singer's mysterious relationship
to the past, represented by the Muses, put him in the same category as the
seers (p. 81).

Duethorn, Guenter A. *Achilles' Shield and the Structure of the Iliad*. Amherst, 1962.

Dyer, Louis. *Syllabus of Forty Lectures on Homer*. Oxford, Eng., 1898.

Finley, M. I. *The World of Odysseus*. 1954. Revised ed. New York, 1965. Finley's
discussion of the social upheavals implied in the epics is instructive, if not
fully authenticated (p. 30). He notes the number of expatriates (p. 194); the
connection between Hephaistos' art and Athene's (p. 72); the relationship
between kinship and territorial systems (pp. 79–80): the king's representation of the "community-principle" (p. 112); Thersites' impropriety (p. 120);
and the fact that "Hector's notion of social obligation is fundamentally
non-heroic. It reflects the new element, the community, at the one point at
which it was permitted to override everything else, the point of defense
against an invader" (p. 125).

———. "Homer and Mycenae: Property and Tenure." In G. S. Kirk, ed. *The
Language and Background of Homer*, pp. 191–217. Cambridge, Eng., 1964.
Finley's summary is a capsule statement of the social conflict discussed
speculatively in my appendix: "Alliance by kinship, marriage and guest-
friendship on the one hand, and allegiance to a king on the other, adequately
explain a very large proportion of the obligations of Homeric society."
Homer's visionary perspective is defined in its attempt to synthesize precisely these two systems of alliance.

Frazer, Sir James George. *The New Golden Bough*. Edited and abridged by
Theodor H. Gaster. 1959. Revised ed. with notes and foreword by T. H. G.
New York, 1964. Frazer provides background on Hephaistos (pp. 527, 704)
and on the sense in which the primitive king is "the avatar of perpetual
being . . . the god in his immediate (vs. continuous) aspect" (p. 169).

Gardner, Ernest A. *A Handbook of Greek Sculpture*. Vol. 1. London, 1896. Gardner,
in addition to providing general background on Hephaistos (pp. 66 ff.),
notes that, in contrast with early Greek art in general, the scenes upon
Achilles' shield are all from actual life—none from mythology (p. 70).

Geddes, William D. *The Problem of the Homeric Poems*. London, 1878. Geddes
notes Helen's connections with Hera (p. 109) and the fact that Homer does
not discuss Helen's guilt (p. 100).

Glotz, G. *The Greek City and Its Institutions*. Translated by N. Mallinson. New York, 1929. My anthropological / sociological constructs parallel those of Glotz in many respects. "In theory, the family remained sovereign; in fact if often had to yield to that nameless collective will which was able to place so formidable a weapon in the hands of a king" (p. 9). Glotz argues that "the 'polis' became a really 'political' institution without destroying the clans, the phratries or the tribes; indeed, it was only possible for it to become so by incorporating these groups" (p. 12). My own view of the synthesizing process is very like this. I also owe to this work a better understanding of the significance of the expatriate status: "To belong to no *genos* meant to have no place in the social structure of the city: to be without hearth (*anestos*) was to be without phratry (*aphratros*) deprived of the protection which *themis* (*athemistos*) secured for man, devoid of all social worth and consequently outside all law (*atimatos*)." Glotz refers to *Iliad* 20:63.

Gordon, Cyrus H. *Homer and the Bible*. New York, 1955.

Gray, D. H. F. "Metal-working in Homer." *Journal of Hellenic Studies* 74 (1954): 1–16.

Greene, Thomas. *The Descent from Heaven: A Study in Epic Continuity*. New Haven, 1963. Even though I cannot agree with Greene's conclusion that Achilles' reentry is only a vendetta, "without purpose or hope, a ritual suicide" (p. 42), I have been inspired continually by Greene's essay on the Homeric epics. Among his many general statements that ring true of the *Iliad*: "Any given detail, any smaller visual unit, has to be related to its place in that larger whole. The whole is what the poet is intent upon" (p. 13); "The implications expand to suggest, if not frankly to assert, a cosmic power struggle" (p. 18); of epic in general: "It must remain the expression of the ritual community, the collective City of Man" (p. 23); "The Poet stands midway between the hero and his audience. He is the amphibian, the mediator, the messenger, the guide who is inspired and inspires in turn. He is the Knower of the Names, the speaker to those who cannot speak of high things" (p. 25); "He joins his audience in a common anonymity" (p. 12); "the arch-image . . . becomes inseparable from the action it contains" (p. 12). Greene also states that the epic here "acquires an austerity that is peculiarly human" (p. 14), that the hero "must be acting for the community . . . he may incarnate the City, but he must be nonetheless an individual with a name" (p. 15). He argues that epic "draws upon sexual springs to invigorate the imagination" (p. 23); I have shown how this is certainly true of the *Iliad*.

Speaking directly on the *Iliad*, Greene remarks that "the Achaian warrior's antagonist is not so much the Trojan as it is death itself, and time, flux, oblivion, mutability, operating within the grey ironic perplexities of that dim world" (p. 41), that the poem posits "two forms of continuity set over against the flux: fatherhood, and funerals" (p. 47). Greene discounts the sociological implications of Achilles' final attitude because he is convinced that Homer's outlook on human experience is pervasively pessimistic. The

Iliad does not end in a mood of despair; nor is there anything dim about Homer's world.

Guthrie, W. C. *The Greeks and Their Gods*. London, 1950. Guthrie notes the legend that Menelaos gains immortality by marriage to Helen (p. 291); and that Hephaistos made the golden urn brought by Thetis to Achilles (p. 164).

Harriott, Rosemary. *Poetry and Criticism Before Plato*. London, 1969. Harriott explains that, to the Homeric Greek, "Mnemosyne was both Memory, the accumulated store of inherited knowledge and the Reminder, who caused *klea andron* ('the glorious deeds of men') . . . to be recalled and kept fresh" (p. 18). She interprets the dancing on Achilles' shield: when Homer said that the chorus ". . . 'danced with skilled feet' he meant that they know the steps and performed them competently" (p. 93). I would clarify that their knowledge is mnemonic and physical, not cognitive and intellectual. Harriott also emphasizes the oral process of education as a continuous one, by comparison with the literate process (p. 107). Her criticism of Havelock is interesting; she says Homer cannot have written for posterity: "if Homer was consciously didactic, his aim can only have been the broad one shared by the greatest writers, to teach by illuminating the ways of gods and men with his own particular insight" (p. 108). This kind of teaching is precisely what I refer to in my "redefinition" of Havelock's didacticism. What is strange here, however, is the distinction made by Harriott between composing for the audience and composing for posterity. In an oral culture such a distinction has no meaning: the audience and posterity are continuous in a pedagogical sense.

Havelock, Eric A. *Preface to Plato*. Cambridge, Eng., 1963. This book is one of the most influential to the present study, along with Bespaloff's and Cedric Whitman's. I subscribe to Havelock's premise that the Homeric epic is a kind of "tribal encyclopedia" which records "public usage (*nomos*) and private habit (*ethos*)" (p. 66). Where I differ is in the degree of detailed pedagogic subject matter involved; in my view, the pragmatic aesthetic of the *Iliad* is its transmission of essential patterns of orderly human behavior rather than of accidental rituals or processes.

Citation of passages to which I am indebted would be endless, but a few most important ones include: Havelock's interpretation of Nestor's admonishment of Achilles, which illustrates the way in which "relationships . . . basic to the stability of the social structure are . . . recapitulated" (p. 68) in the Homeric song; the way in which "psychological is combined with social obligation; there is no moral judgment passed. The minstrel is simply reporting and describing; and this gives to the epic idiom its consciously dispassionate quality, elevating it in the grand manner. But it is in the grand manner because the poetised speech is devoted to framing a 'pedagogic' observation in preserved and permanent form" (p. 69). Havelock emphasizes the reciprocal connection between a descriptive and a prescriptive aesthetic motivation (p. 76). He points out that Mnemosune symbolizes "not just the memory considered as a mental phenomenon, but rather the total act of remembering, recalling, memorialising, and memorising, which is achieved in epic verse" (p. 91). He calls "the Muses . . . the eponymous representatives of the poets themselves (p. 98) . . . If they teach history and prophecy, if they prescribe morality, issue orders, and give judgements, thus also betrays the poet's own function in the contemporary scene" (p. 99). He shows the genetic connection between Mnemosune and Zeus, explaining why "the province of the Muses is that political and moral order which under Zeus has come to be established" (p. 100). So the power of the prince was associated in oral cultures with effective utterance (pp. 107-8): the doer of deeds and the speaker of tales perform equivalent service to the community (p. 109).

Referring to the appearance of Phoinix in Book 9 Havelock comments that the "epic dramatizes the educational process" (p. 120). He explains the sense in which "speech, bodily reflex, rhythmic doing [were] controlled by the metrical pattern" (p. 146). Because of this biological assimilation process, "the artist identified with his story and the audience identified with the artist" (p. 159), until all become generically anonymous. "You submit to the paideutic spell. You allowed yourself to become 'musical' in the functional sense of that Greek term" (p. 159). So the purpose of the epic is to affect action on the part of the audience (p. 167).

As for technique, Havelock's observation is central that "visual resemblance [was] a method of assisting memory: acoustic echo, causal sequence" (p. 187). So the images of artifacts are themselves pedagogic techniques through which ideal standards of behavior are transmitted. "To be effectively retained in the memory, the epic had to utilise this psychological aid as far as it could. So its units of vision are highly visualized in order that vision may lead on to vision" (p. 188).

Finally Havelock's insistence upon the necessity of focusing critical attention on the nature of the Homeric aesthetic if the poem itself is ever to be understood in its own terms effectively solves the problem of reconciling the poet's individuality with the collective tradition. He has proven that the objective quality of the *Iliad* stems from the poet's unfailing concern with making the exemplary and symbolic at all times literally relevant to the particulars of action and character. His speculations about the didacticism of the *Iliad*, uniting the poem's historical, political, psychological, linguistic, and aesthetic dimensions under a single coherent principle, provide the theoretical principles by which my own approach to the poem of memory has been refined.

———. "Thoughtful Hesiod." *Yale Classical Studies* 20 (1966): 61–72. Here Havelock argues that Homer, too, must have been aware of Hesiod's discrimination of Strife into two principles.

Hesiod. Translated by Richmond Lattimore. 1959. Ann Arbor, Mich., 1968. The Lattimore translation is used throughout.

Jaeger, Werner. *Paideia: The Ideals of Greek Culture*. Vol. 1, *Archaic Greece, The Mind of Athens*. 1939. 2d ed. New York, 1965. Jaeger's seminal study of the origins of Western education corroborates the view of the Homeric epics as didactic poems. His work is especially useful in its treatment of the Greek educative ideal of excellence (p. 9); the didactic nature of *Iliad* 9 (pp. 26–27); the definition of *paradeigma*, as "examples for imitation"; the integration of ethics and aesthetics in early Greek thought (p. 35); the power of art "of converting the human soul" (p. 36 ff.); the bond between poetry and myth: "The myth . . . acts as a pattern for life—not chiefly by providing a traditional event to parallel some occurrence in daily life, but by its own nature; for the traditions of the past are made up of glory, of the reports of great men and lofty actions, not of casual incidents. The uncommon has a compelling force, even when it is merely described and acknowledged. But the bard does more than describe the uncommon; he praises what is praiseworthy in the world. Like the Homeric heroes, who throughout their lives insist on receiving and repaying the due meed of honour, every truly heroic action hungers after eternal glory. Myth and heroic poetry are the nation's inexhaustible treasure of great examples: from them it derives its ideals and its standards for daily life" (pp. 40–41).

Jebb, R. C. *Homer: An Introduction to the Iliad and the Odyssey*. Glasgow, 1887.

Jouse, Marcel. *Le Style Oral Rhythmique et Mnemotechnique chez les Verbo-Moteurs*. Paris, 1925.

Kagan, Donald. *The Great Dialogue: History of Greek Political Thought from Homer to Polybus*. London, 1965. According to Kagan, "Agamemnon is more royal than Achilles less because he holds the sceptre of Zeus than because he rules 'many hosts.' "

Kakridis, Johannes Th. *Homeric Researches*. London, 1949. I am indebted chiefly to the discussion of Meleagros in Book 9. Kakridis isolates the "ascending scale of affection from wife to friends" (p. 20) and points out many contrasting and comparable elements which relate the saga as Phoinix narrates it to the song itself (pp. 25 ff.). His argument that Homer added Kleopatra to the story is convincing; perhaps she *is* the model for Andromache and Penelope (p. 39). Yet Andromache stands above her model (p. 60). In some respects paralleling my own social view, Kakridis sees the *Iliad* as embodying the conflict between two scales of affection: the older, in which the progression ascends from the conjugal to the filial; and the new order, from the conjugal to the fraternal to the filial (p. 162).

———. "The Role of the Women in the *Iliad*." *Eranos* 54 (1956): 21–27.

Keller, Albert G. *Homeric Society: A Sociological Study of the Iliad and the Odyssey*. London, 1902. The nature of Helen's crime can be judged in light of Keller's analysis: "Adultery proper was only possible in the case of the chief wife, the wife of status, from whom the line of succession took its origin; only in that case were the consequences far-reaching, demanding special vengeance, and was the succession endangered" (p. 228). He explains that "the blame was one of social and economic import, for Paris violated the bond of guest-friendship and alienated his host's property" (p. 229). Keller also feels that the Homeric songs reflect a period in which "a developed blood-bond . . . opened out into a self-sacrificing and ardent patriotism" (p. 247). He adds that "family power was rapidly crumbling under adverse environment, and it is likely that the former tribal unions were amalgamating and adapting themselves into more highly developed political forms" (p. 247). It was a time "as yet in transition from a system based upon family and gens to one based upon tribe or nation" (p. 248). In my own view, the *Iliad* reflects the stage when this transition period, in which both kinds of hierarchical systems existed simultaneously and competitively, was on the brink of achieving stability precisely through the fusion of both systems into a third, synthetic, system enjoying the strengths of each. Keller notes the relatively mercenary nature of the Trojan alliance (p. 313).

Kirk, G. S. "Dark Age and Oral Poet." *Proceedings of the Cambridge Philological Society* 187 [N.S. 7] (1961): 34–48. Kirk concludes that what are usually termed "heroic" features actually belong to "the centuries *following* a heroic age" (p. 45).

———. *The Songs of Homer*. Cambridge, 1962. Here he argues that "the 'pattern of imagery' proves the unity of the epic tradition, not that there was one single originator of all the contexts in which such imagery occurs" (p. 259). Nevertheless Kirk feels that we must posit a single composer for the *Iliad* as we know it (p. 255).

———., ed. *The Language and Background of Homer*. Cambridge, 1964.

Knight, W. F. Jackson. *Many-Minded Homer*. Edited by John D. Christie. New York, 1968. Knight says Homer himself "may certainly have been able to write" (p. 46). His discussion of the combination of myth and allegory operating in Homer intrigued me, since I came across it after revising my own comments on the very passage he used as an example—Hera's seduction of Zeus in Book 14: "When Hera sleeps with Zeus it is myth; but she enlists the aid of Aphrodite and Sleep, and that is a kind of allegorical personification" (p. 128). Reconsidering the whole matter, I return to my original view—agreeing with Knight that this *is* a kind of allegory, or what would pass for allegory in an oral culture. Homer's self-awareness in the employment of images/symbols has degrees, even when we are not sure what to call the results.

Lang, Mabel L. "Homer and Oral Techniques." *Hesperia* 38, April–June 1969, pp. 159–68.

Lawton, W. C. *The Successors of Homer*. New York, 1898. I found in Lawton various details about the background of Helen and of Hephaistos (pp. 18 ff., 92 ff.).

Leaf, Walter. *A Companion to the Iliad*. London, 1892. Leaf's observation that the *Iliad* reveals no "tribal feelings as distinct from national" (p. 5) is strange in view of Achilles' sequestering of himself with the Myrmidons and limiting his loyalty to them. Similarly strange is the argument that Book 5 is probably an interpolation because here Diomedes "performs achievements which are far beyond those of Achilles himself" (p. 22). To say that wounding Ares or Aphrodite is more significant than killing Hektor is to misunderstand entirely the anthropocentrism of the poem. Leaf, too, notes the anomaly of Iris appearing in 3. 125 without being sent by anyone in particular (p. 92).

————. *Homer and History*. London, 1915. In general this work is useful for its geographical delineations of Homeric Greece. Especially important is his discussion of the fourfold variation in the use of the term "Argos" (pp. 193 ff.). Leaf also points out that "the bond of comradeship, though with an exile from a distant island, is no less strong than the bond of blood" (p. 255).

Leinieks, Valdis. "The *Iliad* and the Epic Cycle." *Classical Outlook* 52, February 1975, pp. 62–64. This is a succinct summary of Swiss-German scholars' conclusions that the epic cycles dealing with the Trojan War "were not composed after the *Iliad* to fill in the events leading up to and following those narrated in the *Iliad*. Instead, these poems were already in existence before the *Iliad* was composed and the poet of the *Iliad* was thoroughly familiar with them" (p. 63). Leinieks discusses Kakridis' distinction between chronographic and dramatic epic, concluding, rightly, that the *Iliad* is of the latter sort: "Dramatic epic and consequently character portrayal and motivation in terms of character on a large scale are in all likelihood original inventions of Homer" (p. 64). He notes that the *Little Iliad* of Lesches, "although later than the *Iliad*, does not qualify as a dramatic epic. According to Aristotle (*Poetics* 1459b), it lacks the unity of action found in the *Iliad*. The full potential of Homer's invention was not to be realized until the rise of Attic tragedy two hundred years later." The connection between the *Iliad* and Athenian tragedy is, in my opinion, an inescapable explanation of the origin of the dramatic form. Finally, Leinieks' conclusion is worth citing in full: "The *Iliad* was composed during the latter part of the eighth century . . . the time [of] the introduction of writing [based on Rhys Carpenter, 'The Antiquity of the Greek Alphabet,' *American Journal of Archaeology* 37 (1933): 8–29]. The conjunction of these two events suggests strongly that the names of Stasinus, Homer, Arctinus, and Lesches have survived because their versions of various parts of the epic cycle were the first to be written down. As long as the poems were not recorded in writing each version would normally be accepted as the singer's own creation. Once writing was introduced the versions of different singers could be recorded with their names attached. Subsequent performances by other singers could then be identified as recitations of a specific version and no longer original creations." He dates the cycle as follows, in order of narrative chronology:

Cypria (Stasinus)	11 books	730
Iliad (Homer)	24 books	720
Aethiopis (Arctinus)	5 books	730
Little Iliad (Lesches)	4 books	710
Iliou Persis (Arctinus)	2 books	730

It should be noted that this view places the *Iliad* a little earlier than has been generally accepted.

Lesky, Albin. *A History of Greek Literature*. Translated by James Willis and Cornelis de Heer. London, 1957. Lesky confirms the social role of Homeric song (p. 14) and suggests that the singing on Achilles' shield is comparable to that of the bards in the *Odyssey* (p. 15).

Lessing, Gotthold Ephraim. *Laocoon*. Translated by Ellen Frothingham. New York, 1968. Lessing notes the historical description of Agamemnon's sceptre (pp. 96 ff.), the distinction between that sceptre and the one cast down by Achilles as appropriate to the conflict of character (p. 99), the description of Pandaros' bow in terms of its origins (pp. 99–100), and the general difference between poetic and artistic representation (p. 109). His emphasis upon the fact that Homer describes the shield of Achilles in the making (pp. 116 ff.) is, of course, central to my own interpretation. He calls the shield "an epitome of all that was happening in the world" (p. 232).

Levy, Gertrude F. *The Gate of Horn*. London, 1948. Here Helen's role as a Dorian vegetation goddess is mentioned (p. 250). Levy also states: the "frequent references to quarrels between kin in the preceding generations point to a transition from the old close blood union of the clan to dependence upon a chief's personal prestige" (p. 265).

Littleton, C. Scott. "Some Possible Indo-European Themes in the *Iliad*." In *Myth and Law Among the Indo-Europeans*, edited by Jaan Puhvel. Berkeley, 1970. In a brilliant article I read too late to assimilate into this book Littleton observes that Paris' choice was really between the three "functions" identified by Lévi-Strauss (p. 233). Littleton's theory supports my alignment of Alexandros/Troy with disorder, in which the third function dominates unevenly (p. 236). Similarly, Achilles defies authority (1st function); withdraws from conflict (2nd function); and "falls victim to his sexual desires" (3rd function). Here Littleton seems carried away with the neatness of the analogy and, in so interpreting Achilles' sexual relations, detracts from his argument. It seem simplistic, too, to say that the Achaian cause is identified with the first two functions (p. 239). Achilles, in the end, will represent all three in himself. But Littleton is right in seeing the "total breakdown" of the first (juridical) function in Book 1 (p. 243).

Lloyd, William Watkiss. *On the Homeric Design of the Shield of Achilles*. London, 1854. This dated analysis of Achilles' shield nevertheless holds much interest. Lloyd notes the connection between poetry and husbandry on the shield (p. 19); the "almost undeviating use of the imperfect tense" (p. 20); the characteristics of the choreography (pp. 21–22), and the symmetry of the pictures of war and peace (p. 31). "The last circlet of the chorus contrasts with all the rest in being continuous all round . . . absolved from all references to the hopes and fears, the labours and dangers, the emulations and the contests of busy existence. Here all blend away in the delirium of social sympathy and festive art" (p. 34). Lloyd refers to Kneph, the potter who made mankind (p. 35); to the absence of history (p. 40); to the fact that here the singer "ignores heroic and personal reminiscences to gain a purely picturesque or mixed philosophical effect—philosophical in the sense in which Aristotle declared poetry to be more philosophical than history" (p. 40); to the absence of names (p. 41); to the way in which, on the shield, the world of action and simile, of war and pastoral, are united (p. 42). The parallels between the shield-events in the *Iliad* are defined (p. 43). If the essay hovers on the periphery of critical satisfaction, perhaps it is because Homer is not to be conceived quite so rigidly as Lloyd would have us believe. That is a caution applicable to my own reading as well.

Longinus. *On the Sublime*. Translated by W. Hamilton Fyfe. Cambridge, Eng., 1927.

Loomis, Julia W. "Homer, The First Psychologist." *Classical Outlook* 52. February 1975, pp. 64–67. Loomis argues, in a thoughtful and incisive essay, that Homer's psychology, like Freud's, was a struggle "to differentiate between instinct and controlling agency" and that Homer was fully conscious of instincts "such as the sex drive (eros), or the self-assertive drive (menis), or the societal instinct of right and wrong (themis). However, he never relegated them to the realm of forces in control (theoi). The ancient Greek mind could never accept the idea that instincts control human actions. They might be a motivating force, but hopefully reason was in control. And reason was a gift from outside oneself. No man on his own determination could be reasonable; nor could he fall in love. Eros might bring two persons together, but unless Aphrodite (a theos, or force in control) passed by, there would be no love" (p. 65). Her system is neat but lacks convincing textual support. That, however, doesn't mean it isn't valid, for Homeric psychology is nonetheless consistent for being implied. Loomis' conclusion coincides with mine: "When the love relationship goes wrong at either level (societal or home), civilization collapses." Her equation of *menis* with "the self-assertive drive (not 'wrath,' as it is too often translated)" (p. 65) is especially incisive: "When menis comes into conflict with hybris (overweening self-confidence and utter lack of awareness of either human feelings or the forces at work in the universe) the result is impotence . . . Only one thing can conquer impotence: huge love which draws one outside of oneself . . . In Homeric vocabulary, [Thetis] instills menos, the ability and determination to act (not 'might' as the translations give it)" (p. 65). Loomis goes on to give a psychological terminology to the "order" theme discussed in this book: "The gift of this unerring ability to act well and achieve [menos] is so important to Homer that he associates three divinities with it: Athena, Apollo, and Zeus" (p. 66). Her identification of the function of the gods is particularly interesting because it distinguishes the type of intelligence represented by Athena (more or less discursive) from that associated with Apollo ("sudden awareness of self").

Lord, Albert B. "Homer, Parry, and Huso." *Supplement to the American Journal of Archaeology* 52 (1948): 34–44.

———. *The Singer of Tales*. 1960. New York, 1965. Even though I can't agree with many of Lord's conclusions about the analogical relationship between the Homeric and the Balkan songs, his work is constantly thought-provoking and incisive. He argues that "singing, performing, composing are facets of the same act" (p. 13); that "the ideal is a true story well and truly retold" (p. 29); that "the anonymity of folk epic is a fiction, because the singer has a name" (p. 101) which is not concealed from his audience. According to Lord, the singer "is not even 'immersed' in the tradition; he *is* the tradition" (p. 147). He notes the parallelism between Achilles' refusal of the embassy and Agamemnon's refusal of Chryses' ransom (p. 189) and that "the pattern of the wrath is really a pattern of bride-stealing and rescue" (p. 190). In implying that the oral tradition operative on Homer obviates entirely the serious influence of individual talent Lord seems to contradict his own professional caution.

Lorimer, H. L. *Homer and the Monuments*. London, 1950.

Lukács, Georg. "To Narrate or Describe?" In George Steiner and Robert Fagles, eds. *Homer*, Englewood Cliffs, N.J., 1962. pp. 62–73. Very appropriate to the *Iliad* is the statement that "objects have poetic life only through their relationship to human destiny . . . The epic poet . . . speaks of the tasks objects have in the nexus of human destinies, and he does so only when the objects share in those destinies, when they partake in the deeds and sufferings of men" (p. 87).

Mackail, J. W. *Lectures on Greek Poetry*. London, 1910. Mackail calls Homer a "deus absconditus" (p. 23) and says of Helen that she is "a thing enskied. Her words over the body of Hektor are the high-water mark of the *Iliad*; and it is not of Hektor they leave us thinking, but of her" (pp. 35–36). He comments that Achilles' shield "includes the whole of ordinary human life" (p. 43), arguing that "the Homeric idealisation of life is not in any . . . golden world, above or below earth, in a conjectured future or a fabulous past, but in actual deeds of men, so predestined and so accomplished that they become a song for times to be" (p. 72). Like Greene he notes that "the somber view of life . . . is never far off anywhere," but Mackail concludes, "yet the elasticity and radiance of life are the final and lasting impression" (p. 79).

————. *Lectures on Poetry*. London, 1914. Mackail's striking statement accurately reflects the didactic nature of Homer's poem: "If the technical art of poetry consists in making patterns out of language, the substantial and vital function of poetry will be analogous; it will be to make patterns out of life" (p. 19).

MacKay, L. A. *The Wrath of Homer*. Toronto, 1948.

Mariani, Alice. "The Forged Feature: Created Identity in Homer's *Odyssey*." Ph.D. dissertation, Yale University, 1967. Many of my own formulations, especially concerning the artifacts and their significance, profited from those of Mariani whose approach to the *Odyssey* is most incisive and revealing. She argues that "anything *made*, with energy and skill and passion, is an exercise of a man's particular *arete*, and a shaping of the materials of his world to his own will and design" (p. 172). So Odysseus' marriage-bed signifies "rooted permanence . . . the unconscious effort to hold out against the precarious flux" (p. 162). It is a figure for "the living intimacy" of the marriage. Her discussion of Helen's web marks the importance of the artistic detachment I associate with Helen in her appearances in Book 3 (p. 29). Mariani also comments on the importance of the guest (p. 66); on the loom-image in its various appearances (pp. 240, 247); and on Aristotle's distinction between the "strictly true" and the "intentionally fallacious argument" (p. 314). In this last matter, Mariani identifies the distinctive character of the *Odyssey* in its departure from verisimilitude. "The twice-told tale . . . corresponds to a general feature of the Homeric style itself, the pleasurable repetition of a good story . . . rewoven on the singer's loom" (p. 315). The absence of such twice-told tales from the *Iliad* is what distinguishes its aesthetics from that of the other epic.

Martin, Roland. *Recherches sur L'Agora Grecque.* Paris, 1951. Martin agrees that the army was organized like the city, by clans, tribes, etc. Consequently the war agora may be taken as analogous to the peace agora on the shield (p. 22).

Motto, Anna L., and John R. Clark. "*Isê Dais:* The Honor of Achilles." *Arethusa* 2 (Fall 1969): 109–25. The authors see Achilles, "not as a scapegoat or a rebel, but as the avatar of society" (p. 109). They argue against the interpretation that makes Achilles' alienation total: "Just as Patroclus dies seeking to restore Menelaus' honor (17. 92) as well as Achilles' honor, so Achilles wishes to restore his own honor (before *all* the Achaeans, 16. 84) and Menelaus' honor as well. This double purpose is present in his every action. Hence, his response to Patroclus' death includes concern for the other Achaeans slain (21. 134). Achilles must revenge his own defilement (the loss of shield and friend), but he also consciously continues to avenge the dishonor suffered by Menelaus. Even at the heated moment when Hector is slain, Achilles is well aware of the glory 'we' (all the Achaeans) have won (22. 393) . . . Such mutual concern always obtains in heroic society" (p. 123). Yet by isolating Achilles from his heroic peers, the authors fail to reveal how integrally related Achilles' experience is to that of the others (for example, Nestor, Hektor, Aias).

Murray, A. S. *A History of Greek Sculpture.* Vol. 1. London, 1890. According to Murray, Homer meant "Helen's weaving to represent actual past scenes." The author also notes the emphasis on *process* in the making of Achilles' shield, the anonymity of the shield-figures (p. 45), the structural implication that Homer places the city before the countryside (p. 50), and the fact that the chorus is the "jubilant culmination" of the shield: "It stands by itself without any occasion being assigned for its existence" (p. 52).

Murray, Gilbert. *The Rise of the Greek Epic.* 3d ed., rev. and enl. Oxford, Eng., 1924. Murray has much to say about the pitiable state of the guest-stranger (pp. 84 ff.), especially in light of the "five deadly sins" of Hesiod (p. 87). He also provides background data on Helen (p. 205) and an excellent discussion of *arete* (p. 59).

Myres, John L. *Who Were the Greeks?* Berkeley, 1930. Hephaistos' craft distinguishes him from the other gods (p. 170); he is "insecurely married" to Aphrodite (p. 172). Myres calls "the Homeric poems . . . a storehouse of coherent folk-memory about a real phase in the making of the Greek world" (p. 31).

Nagler, Michael N. *Spontaneity and Tradition: A Study in the Oral Art of Homer*. Berkeley, 1974. Reopening the Homeric Question, Nagler regards the two epics "not as typical of the average performance by the average singer, but as typical of what a great singer could do with his tradition before a highly appreciative audience" (p. xviii). I agree with him completely that, "When one considers both the artistic unity of the poems and the incertitude attending ancient and modern analyses of them, to attribute the bulk of both epics to Homer seems, again, the simplest working hypothesis . . . The long tradition of discomfort with the ancient attribution of the *Iliad* and the *Odyssey* to Homer does not shift the burden of proof to those inclined to accept that ancient testimony. The poems as they exist today are so well composed and have so much to teach that even where one senses anomalies in the texts one should search long and deep for the author's purpose before resorting to theories of interpolation or—as has become fashionable now— the awkward fusion of rigid transitional entities" (p. xix). His book proceeds to offer a linguistic-anthropological reading of the Homeric poems that is brilliant in its particular insights even though its general effect is to reduce the *Iliad*, as it has been reduced too often in the past, to a linguistic structure of anthropological curiosity rather than a great artistic masterpiece. Especially important are his concept of the sphota ("preverbal template," pp. 13–21); his reformulation, "All is traditional on the generative level, all original on the level of performance"; and his analysis of the Withdrawal-Devastation-Return pattern (pp. 139 ff., 174) which corresponds to my outline of Achilles' psychological development. Even though his theory of the process of oral creativity is ingenious and more satisfactory than others I am familiar with, it doesn't convince me that the *Iliad*, as we have it, is the product of a normal oral performance; it seems much more likely that Homer recited the *Iliad*, not spontaneously, but only as deliberately and quickly as scribes could write—and may have had it read back to him. Still Nagler's book is a rare bridge between literary criticism and classical philology.

Nelson, Lowry, Jr. "The Fictive Reader and Literary Self-Reflexiveness." In *The Disciplines of Criticism*, edited by Peter Demetz, Thomas Greene, and Lowry Nelson, Jr., pp. 173–92, New Haven, 1968. This seminal essay provided me with a perspective by which to define the self-consciousness of the *Iliad*, as it is reflected in the instances of creativity within the poem's world.

Nilsson, Martin P. *The Mycenean Origins of Greek Mythology*. Berkeley, 1932. Nilsson identifies the heroic age which produced the epics with the Mycenaeans, associates the Tyndarean oath wtih Agamemnon's right to form an alliance (p. 229), notes Helen's Minoan affinities (pp. 252 ff.), marks the exemplary function of mythical tales (p. 294), and points out that only in the case of Achilles and Hephaistos does a mortal receive a gift from the gods (p. 215). He argues that the contrast of Diomedes' loyalty against Achilles' obstinance is a Homeric innovation (p. 259).

———. *Homer and Mycenae*. London, 1933.

North, Helen. *Sophrosyne: Self-Knowledge and Self-Restraint in Greek Literature*.

Ithaca, N.Y., 1966. Although *sophrosyne* is not a "heroic" virtue, according to North, "since the two greatest fighting men . . . Achilles and Ajax, are the very ones who most notoriously lack this quality" (p. 2), it does share with the Homeric *aidos* the "fear of overstepping boundaries" (p. 6). Achilles perhaps approaches such a perspective toward the end of the poem.

Notopoulos, James A. "Mnemosyne in Oral Literature." *Transactions and Proceedings of the American Philological Association* 69 (1938): 465–93. Following Joust, Notopoulos terms Homer a "mnemo-technician." He, too, assumes the didactic import of the poems: "It was the poet's task to conserve living experiences and transmit them to posterity (p. 468). . . The poet is the incarnate book of oral peoples" (p. 469). He talks about the "static" (i.e., retentive) and "creative" (thought synthesized with memory) functions of memory (p. 469).

Owen, E. T. *The Story of the Iliad*. Ann Arbor, 1946. This level-headed and frequently incisive work is a model of comprehensive exposition. Owen points out that we first see Achilles in a social role (p. 5); that the *teikoskopia* is constructed with the audience in mind (p. 34); and that the meeting between Glaukos and Diomedes provides a stark contrast with the brutality of battle (pp. 58–59). He compares Helen-on-the-wall to Andromache-on-the-wall (p. 64) and discusses the significance of Eëtion's role (pp. 66 ff.). He notes the disorderly willfulness of Achilles in Book 9 (p. 96) but insists that the hero's "urge to protect the species is still strong even when he is against" the generic (p. 106). Of Sarpedon, Owen says, "out of hopelessness he will make not hope, but glory" (p. 124). Other instructive comments include: his discussion of the way the two Aiases frame Achilles' recalcitrance (p. 155); of the relief and "release of feeling" provided by the catalogue of Nereids in Book 18 (p. 177); of the similar function performed by the great shield (p. 187); of the way in which the history of Lykaon is given to emphasize the terribleness of Achilles' present mood (p. 208); of the weird natural effects surrounding Achilles' fighting (p. 211).

Owen's description of the way in which similar images evoke similar responses is highly apt: "As the scene necessarily comes back to mind, the poem responds to the recollection; it comes back in the words. The verbal repetitions do not make the recollection; they are the memory recording itself" (p. 178). Of the meeting between Achilles and Priam, he comments: "The splendour of humanity and the sorrow of humanity here meet under the shadow of death and are reconciled in a noble and universal compassion that has no touch of resignation but is exhilarating, making the sorrow part of the splendour, plucking the splendour out of the sorrow" (p. 247). I can't agree, however, with Owen's feeling that "Hektor presents himself in far nobler light than Achilles, whose strength is helped by divine aid denied to his enemy, and whose overmastering motive is not patriotism but the gratification of a private revenge" (p. 215). Achilles' divine assistants are only the cosmic affirmation of his personal prowess.

Parry, Adam. "The Language of Achilles." *Transactions and Proceedings of the American Philological Association* 87 (1956): 1–18. This is Adam Parry's most important article in which he proves that "Achilles is . . . the one Homeric hero who does not accept the common language, and feels that it does not correspond to reality." The hero's self-expression, of course, is limited by the traditional character of Homeric speech. Therefore "Achilles can only . . . ask questions that cannot be answered and make demands that cannot be met. He uses conventional expressions where we least expect him to, as when he speaks to Patroclus in Book 16 of a hope of being offered material gifts by the Greeks, when we know that he has been offered these gifts and they are meaningless to him." Yet I don't agree that Achilles ultimately "sees no value in the glory that society can confer." Achilles comes to understand that, precisely as far as the community and its values (like glory) is concerned, present and future form a continuum.

———. "Have We Homer's *Iliad*?" *Yale Classical Studies* 20 (1966): 177–216. Here Parry defines Homer as "the poet who composed the *Iliad* at the time when it was put into writing," noting that Milman Parry originally demonstrated the antithesis "not between the oral and the lettered poet, but between the poet of a traditional and the poet of an individual style."

———, ed. Introduction to *The Making of Homeric Verse: The Collected Papers of Milman Parry*. Oxford, Eng., 1971. Adam Parry's judicious and succinct review of Homeric scholarship in this century makes another general review superfluous. His own critique of Milman Parry's work is itself a landmark, indicating that the deleterious effect of Parryism has given way to a saner perspective which combines its insights with more or less traditional critical appreciation of the poetry.

The introduction quotes Dorothea Gray's reference to Milman Parry's "proof that Homer's style is typical of oral poetry," and the editor remarks: "This is in fact what Milman Parry proved. That Homer himself, i.e., the composer or composers of the *Iliad* and the *Odyssey*, or of either of these poems, or of any substantial connected part of either of them, was an oral poet, there exists no proof whatever. Otherwise put, not the slightest proof has yet appeared that the texts of the *Iliad* and the *Odyssey* as we have them, or any substantial connected portion of these texts, were composed by oral improvisation of the kind observed and described by Parry and Lord and others in Jugoslavia" (p. xx). He calls "false" Lord's statement that "there is now no doubt that the composer of the Homeric poems was an oral poet" (p. ix). I agree with Adam Parry that it is likely that Homer made use of writing, "either directly or through a scribe," and "that the products of this composition are dependent on the oral tradition not only for their diction, but for many other distinctive features as well, such as the reticence in cross-reference . . . but that they owe to their use of writing both their large-scale coherence and their subtlety, qualities in which no known oral poem has begun to equal them" (p. xi).

Parry, Milman. *A Comparative Study of Diction as One of the Elements of Style in Early Greek Epic Poetry*. 1923. In Adam Parry, ed. *The Making of Homeric Verse*, pp. 421–36. Oxford, Eng., 1971.

———. *The Traditional Epithet in Homer*. 1928. In Adam Parry, ed. *The Making of Homeric Verse*, pp. 1–190. Oxford, Eng., 1971. Parry points out that Helen "is the only woman in Homer who clearly has distinctive epithets of her own" (p. 97). Parry sets up the problem Dimock's analysis solves: "Here is a poet who marked his works with genius not because he was able to model the words on his own thought, but because he was able to make use of traditional words and expressions" (p. 144). Dimock's argument is that the poet's *own thought* was likely to be metrical; Nagler's theory takes this a step further.

———. *Homeric Formulae and Homeric Metre*. 1928. In Adam Parry, ed. *The Making of Homeric Verse*, pp. 191–239. Oxford, Eng., 1971. The difficulty of the memorization process outlined here (p. 195) is also solved by Dimock's observation of the metrical patterns of thought. Parry's logic in this work seems peculiarly contradictory.

———. "Studies in the Epic Technique of Oral Verse-Making: I. Homer and Homeric Style," *Harvard Studies in Classical Philology* 41 (1930): 73–148. Parry here makes the outspoken assertion that "in treating of the oral nature of the Homeric style we shall see that the question of a remnant of individuality in Homeric style disappears altogether" (p. 138).

———. "Cor Huso: A Study of Southslavic Song." 1933–35. In Adam Parry, ed. *The Making of Homeric Verse*, pp. 439–64. Oxford, Eng., 1971. Parry at this late stage in his thought makes the striking statement that the *Iliad* and the *Odyssey* are each the work of a single singer: "I even figure to myself, just now, the moment when the author of the *Odyssey* sat down and dictated his song, while another, with writing materials, wrote it down verse by verse" (p. 431). The logic of his argument for the uncertainty of the song's length at a given session is obviously faulty (p. 456).

———. "On Typical Scenes in Homer." 1936. In Adam Parry, ed. *The Making of Homeric Verse*, pp. 404–7. Oxford, Eng., 1971.

Peabody, Berkeley. *The Winged Word: A Study in the Technique of Ancient Greek Oral Composition as Seen Principally in Hesiod's "Works and Days."* Albany, N.Y., 1970.

Perry, Walter Copland. *The Women of Homer*. New York, 1898. Perry reports the opinion of the scholia of Venice: "From the scenes embroidered on [Helen's] web . . . Homer took the greater part of his history of the . . . war."

Pound, Ezra. "Homer or Virgil?" In George Steiner and Robert Fagles, eds. *Homer*, pp. 17–18. Englewood Cliffs, N.J., 1962. Pound terms Homer "the imaginary spectator."

Powys, John Cowper. "Preface to *Homer and the Aether*." In George Steiner and Robert Fagles, eds. *Homer*, pp. 140–47. Englewood Cliffs, N.J., 1962. Powys calls the *Iliad* greater than the *Odyssey* because it is more "realistic and natural" (p. 140). He also observes: "The most significant and characteristic thing about his gathering, accumulating, enlarging, thickening, expanding, deepening story of human life . . . is his emphasis upon the family" (p. 147).

Prendergast, Guy L. *A Complete Corcordance to the Iliad of Homer*, edited by Benedetto Marzullo. Hildesheim, W. Ger., 1962.

Reinhardt, Karl. *Die Iliad und Ihr Dichter*. Göttingen, W. Ger., 1961. The parallelism between Hephaistos' assistance to Hera and Sleep's is noted (p. 105). Reinhardt marks the anonymity of the great shield and calls it a "timeless, nameless, glimpse of the continuity of life" (p. 405).

Robert, Fernand. *Homère*. Paris, 1950. This work is useful for discussion of the background of Hephaistos (pp. 146 ff.); of Helen (pp. 210 ff.); of the marital conflicts of the Olympians (p. 92); and for emphasizing the hierarchical concern of the poem (pp. 216, 220 ff.).

Rose, H. J., and C. M. Robertson. Articles on Hera (p. 497), Hephaistos (p. 497), and Paris (p. 781). In the *Oxford Classical Dictionary*, edited by N. G. L. Hammond and H. H. Scullard. 2d ed. Oxford, Eng., 1970. The *OCD* also includes a succinct and sensible discussion of the Homeric Question (pp. 524–25).

Rossignol, J.-P. *Les Artistes Homériques: Histoire critique de tous le artistes qui figurent dans l'Iliad et dans l'Odysée*. Paris, 1885.

Rouse, W. H. D. *Homer*. London, 1939.

Russo, Joseph A. "The Structural Formula in Homeric Verse." *Yale Classical Studies* 20 (1966): 219–40.

———. "Homer Against His Tradition." *Arion* (Summer 1968): 275–95. Russo convincingly argues that Homer was capable of appropriate improvisation. The premise: "Although Homer conspicuously carries with him many features of his tradition, there are many examples . . . of the kind of creative departure from the tradition, that point to the kind of freedom not found in the tradition-bound oral poet" (p. 278). Homer can break the "oral law," Russo argues. Four kinds of scenes are analyzed "running from most traditional to least traditional or most inventive" (p. 282). Especially useful is Russo's demonstration of the way in which the description of Agamemnon's arming characterizes the heroic king (pp. 282 ff.). He also discusses the exception in the arming pattern when Patroklos comes to the spear of Achilles (p. 286), the "originality" of the similes (p. 294), and summarizes: "The grip of the tradition seems to relax its grip, or, more accurately, the master-poet is strong enough, and original enough, to hold out against the convenience of the prefabricated thought or scene, against the pressure of the 'typical.' These are the moments . . . when the particular, the special, the unique, gain the upper hand, when we think we can see how Homer resists his tradition, when we see him refusing to take it as it comes and instead twisting it and reshaping it to his own special ends. These are the moments that give Homer the poet his existence, and bring us back to the *Iliad* and *Odyssey* again and again" (p. 294).

———, and Bennett Simon. "Homeric Psychology and the Oral Epic Tradition." *Journal of the History of Ideas* 29, October–December, 1968, pp. 483–98. This fascinating article charts the relationship between the psychology of the poet and that of his characters. It underlines the communal emphasis in Homer, "the important social role played by the bard himself. His recitations serve as a cultural repository for the history, social ideals and general world-view of his society. He reinforces his audience's sense of 'tribal' identity by continually relating the present generation of listeners to the past generations that have become the subject of epic songs; and by repeatedly relating both past and present to future generations" (p. 492). The authors note the emotional involvement of the bard and his audience (p. 492) by which the boundaries of self are dissolved.

Sandstrom, Oscar R. *A Study of the Ethical Principles of Homeric Warfare.* Philadelphia, 1924.

Schrade, Hubert. *Götter und Menschen Homers.* Stuttgart, 1952. The connection between Hephaistos, the Egyptian Ptah and Chnum, and the Babylonian Ea is speculated upon (p. 78); Hephaistos' gold robots and Pandora are related (p. 87); and Hephaistos is seen as a stranger among the Greek gods (p. 88), connected with Daidalos (p. 91).

Scott, John A. *The Unity of Homer.* Berkeley, 1921.

Sealey, Raphaël. "From Phemios to Ion." *Revue des Etudes Grecques* 70 (1957): 312–55.

Seymour, Thomas D. *Life in the Homeric Age.* New York, 1907. This book is interesting for its discussion of the adultery of Helen and of Klytaimestra (p. 149); of Hephaistos' making jewelry for Thetis (p. 171), the aegis for Zeus (p. 291), armor for Diomedes (p. 433), and a jar for Achilles' bones (p. 433). He notes that Hephaistos is presented as the only married god besides Zeus (p. 425).

Sheppard, J. T. *The Pattern of the Iliad.* London, 1922. Sheppard suggests that that shield-making process reflects the poet's rather than the blacksmith's art (p. 6), emphasizes Achilles' peacemaking role in the games (p. 201), and discusses the two kinds of strife (p. 209). He calls "the central doctrine of Homer's . . . heroic faith—a recognition of the fact of our common humanity" (p. 207).

Simon, Bennett, and Herbert Weiner. "Models of Mind and Mental Illness in Ancient Greece: I. The Homeric Model of Mind." *Journal of the History of the Behavioral Sciences* 2, October 1966, pp. 303–15. The authors detail the "therapeutic role of the bard" (p. 310), and the way in which "the audience quickly identifies itself with the characters" (p. 311). They note the importance of what I term the contexts of creativity (p. 312), especially "the poet within the poem" since "the 'mind' that is described in Homer is the 'mind' of the poets who created the Homeric poems" (p. 312). This principle has governed my own approach to the self-awareness of the poem.

Simpson, R. Hope, and J. F. Lazenby. *The Catalogue of Ships in Homer's Iliad.* Oxford, 1970. I disagree with the assertion that the epics present the heroes primarily as individuals and as equals (p. 7), as opposed to showing their hierarchical social status.

Snell, Bruno. *The Discovery of the Mind.* Translated by T. G. Rosenmeyer. New

York, 1953. Snell's monumental work is indispensable to the student of the Homeric mind. He defines the role of memory in an oral culture (p. 36), the ideal nature of the epic world (p. 40), its metaphysical structure (p. 41), and the way in which it reflects the replacement of chronic disorder with Olympian order (p. 136).

Solmsen, Friedrich. "The 'Gift' of Speech in Homer and Hesiod." *Transactions and Proceedings of the American Philological Association* 85 (1954): 1–15.

Sperduti, Alice. "The Divine Nature of Poetry in Antiquity." *Transactions and Proceedings of the American Philological Association* 81 (1950): 209–40. Sperduti sees singing on the shield as analogous to its role in Homeric society (p. 226), underlines the importance of memorialization as a social motivation (p. 226), and discusses the relationship among poetry, good government, and Zeus (p. 231).

Stawell, F. Melian. *Homer and the Iliad*. London, 1909. The author notices the impression of simultaneity in the shield-forging process (pp. 197 ff.) and says of the shield's structure: "The arrangement of the scenes in concentric rings is not only the one most naturally suggested by the words of the poem: it is far the most effective as a symbol for the imaginative content. For by this means we are shown in one sweep the varied life of man, dominated by the heavens, encompassed by the great waters, spreading out in widening circles from the concentrated interest and turmoil of the city to the calmer work of the fields and the dancing ring of the youth whose working-time has hardly yet begun" (p. 199).

Steiner, George, and Robert Fagles, eds. *Homer*. Englewood Cliffs, N.J., 1962.

———. "Homer and the Scholars." In *Homer*, edited by George Steiner and Robert Fagles, pp. 1–14. Englewood Cliffs, N.J., 1962. The authors connect heroic deeds, aesthetic beauty, and glory (p. 9), calling the similes "assurance of ultimate stability." They note that "myths . . . re-enact moments of signal truth or crisis in the human condition . . . The poet . . . is the historian of the unconscious. This gives to the great myths their haunting universality" (p. 3). One of the greatest such human disasters is the fall of the city (p. 3).

Stubbings, Frank H. "Crafts and Industries." In *A Companion to Homer*, edited by Alan J. B. Wace and Frank H. Stubbings, pp. 504–22. London, 1962.

———. "Arms and Armour." In *A Companion to Homer*, edited by Alan J. B. Wace and Frank H. Stubbings, pp. 531–38. London, 1962.

Symonds, John A. *Studies of the Greek Poets*. Vol. 1. London, 1893. Helen, according to Symonds, has "a mysterious virginity of soul. She is not touched by the passions she inspires . . . Like beauty, she belongs to all and none" (p. 109).

Tashiro, Tom T. "Three Passages in Homer, and the Homeric Legacy." *Antioch Review* 25 (Spring 1965): 63–92. Tashiro comments on the analogous relationship between Achilles' rejection of Agamemnon's offers and Agamemnon's of Chryses' (p. 66); on the connection between the marriage and judicial scenes on the shield (p. 66); on the historical significance of the necropolis (p. 75); and on the hierarchical significance of Zeus' golden chain:

"Because Homer's chain has a top and a bottom, there must be a best and a worst. Because there is a beginning and an end to the chain, Absolutes must exist. Finally, the chain is a unit; a unity holds therefore all nature, all things, together . . . What is required in the world of man, consequently, is a class society arranged according to quality (p. 79) . . . As for justice itself, it is the application of the idea of hierarchy by man to his world, as analogy to the basic order of things" (p. 80). Once again the connection is between Zeus' Olympian order and the order established among men as a result of the events in the poem.

Thomas, C. G. "The Roots of Homeric Kingship." *Historia* 15 (1966): 387–407.

Thomson, George. *Aeschylus and Athens: A Study in the Social Origins of the Drama*. London, 1941. Thomson's work is solid and evocative. He discusses endo- and exogamous relations among the various levels of social organization (p. 40), and concludes that "even after its basis in kinship had crumbled away, the tribal system still seemed the necessary foundation for any form of ordered society" (p. 40). Thomson also distinguishes between the character of the feudal-like "king-vassal" relationship and that of kinship.

Tolstoy, Leo. "Homer and Shakespeare." In *Homer*, edited by George Steiner and Robert Fagles, pp. 15–16. Englewood Cliffs, N.J., 1962.

Turolla, Enrico. *Saggio su la Poesia di Omero*. Bari, Italy, 1949.

Vico, Giambattista. *The New Science of Giambattista Vico*. Translated by Thomas Goddard Bergin and Max Harold Fisch, 1948; rev. and abridged. Ithaca, N.Y., and London, 1961. Vico's sociohistorical interpretation of the essential strife between the two cities on the shield of Achilles wanders far from the text but is nonetheless provocative for drawing attention to the shield's presentation of the creation story and of the relationship between social order and "the arts of humanity": "This picture, beautifully and truly following the order of human institutions, indicated that first of all the necessary arts were invented, such as agriculture with a view first to bread and then to wine; then the useful arts, such as herding; then the arts of comfort, such as urban architecture; and lastly those of pleasure, such as the dance" (pp. 210–11). Vico's "Search for the True Homer" (pp. 241–68) and "Discovery of the True Homer" (pp. 269–74) are seminal essays despite their obvious prejudices, which perceive the social basis of Achilles' wrath against the "sheer stupidity" of Agamemnon (p. 247), even though his reentry into the war is attributed to "a purely private grief" (p. 249); the historical evidence provided by Homer's descriptions of artifacts (pp. 251–52); the social unrest that must have characterized Homer's own time (p. 253), leading to his preoccupation with the orderly theme traced in this book; the way in which "his poetic characters, which are incomparable for the sublime appropriateness which Horace admires in them, were imaginative universals . . . to which the peoples of Greece attached all the various particulars belonging to each genus" (p. 256); the connection between memory and imagination (p. 260); that "the nations should speak in verses so that their memories might be aided by meter and rhythm to preserve more easily the histories of their families and cities" (p. 262), implying the direct connection between poetic and political action; and, finally, the equation of Homer with "the Greek peoples . . . themselves" (pp. 270–74).

Vivante, Paolo. "Homer and the Aesthetic Moment." *Arion* 4 (Autumn 1965): 415–38. Vivante's inspired article proclaims the universality of Homer's art: "What we find here is an exhaustive nomenclature, a whole system of attributes and qualifications, as if poetry had set out to explore the universe and render its outlines" (p. 417). He sees the Meleagros tale as a microcosm in the *Iliad* (p. 426), and asks whether it is "possible to discover the poet's subjectivity beneath the complex surface of the poems?" (p. 418).

———. *The Homeric Imagination: A Study of Homer's Poetic Perception of Reality*. Bloomington, Ind., 1970. Although I disagree with Vivante's assertion that the Homeric concept of glory has no connection with the future (p. 124), I have been inspired constantly by his writing.

Voegelin, Eric. *The World of the Polis. Vol. 2: Order and History*. Baton Rouge, 1957. I regret that I came upon Voegelin's incisive and stimulating work too late to assimilate it into my study, which parallels his sociopolitical conclusions in many respects. He talks about the rise of a new Greece in the ninth century B.C., starting "in the poleis of Asia Minor . . . In this border area of the emigration originated the Homeric epics, and from here they began to diffuse their influence over the islands and the mainlaind, furnishing the recovering Greeks with the consciousness of a common past. The pan-Achaean federative enterprise against Troy became the living symbol of a pan-Hellenic cultural and precariously even political bond" (p. 34). He also notes the parallel between the war among men and the war among gods (p. 35); the epics' function as a cultural cohesive force both in their language and their Olympian religion (p. 35); "the content of the Hellenic memory . . . is inseparable from the process of its growth. Whatever could be understood as a constituent factor of Hellenic society and its order in the present classic period became historically memorable" (p. 36); the emergence of the Achaians, "Greek by language, but with a syncretistic culture that becomes especially noticeable in the pantheon compound of divinities of patriarchal and matriarchal regimes" (p. 61); the feudal nature of Achaian society (p. 64); "the cultural homogeneity between Achaeans and Trojans, as well as the possession of a common pantheon, is not fictitious" (p. 65); the specific role of the Homeric epic in providing the necessary past history for a present Aegean-wide society (p. 67); that the point, with studying Homer, "is not the authorship of a work of literature, but the creation of a symbolism which expresses a new experience of human existence under the gods, of the nature of order and the causes of disorder, and of the historical decline and fall of a society" (p. 71); Homer's contribution was to break "the cosmological myth and create a non-cosmological form of social order" (p. 71); "a relationship between the poet and a divine source of revelation" in Greek epic "that resembles the relation between the Israelite prophet and the word of Yahweh" (p. 72).

He also discusses the epic poet's self-interest in survival (p. 74); the didactic quality of epic verse (p. 74); the immortality offered through memory (p. 75); the universality of disorder in the *Iliad* (p. 75); "the style of self-transcendence" (p. 76); "the authority by which the king rules over men stems from the authority of Zeus in the Olympian dispensation of the world" so that the political order partakes of the world order—and that Olympian order is not yet established fully, either on earth or among the still uneasy gods (p. 81); the connection between the blindness of the Homeric heroes and the disorderliness of their society, so that "under one aspect, therefore, the *Iliad* is a study of the pathology of heroes" (p. 83); the ordinate quality of Achilles' dilemma (p. 85) and its nihilism (p. 91); how "a lordly wrath is not a private state of emotions. A *cholos*, a wrath, is a legal institution comparable to a Roman *inimicitia* or a medieval feud" (p. 89); and the way in which Homer uses the Paris-Helen scenes "quite deliberately for the purpose of characterizing the disordered sentiments through the ranks of the constitutional hierarchy": "Paris and Helen are the gap in the Trojan order through which a dark force of destruction pours in, as Achilles was the gap in the order of the Achaeans" (p. 96).

Voegelin clearly focuses the metaphysical concerns of the *Iliad* (p. 102) and agrees that they are an impetus behind what I have called the poem's didacticism and exemplary function: "The use of the fable is part of the exhortatory style stemming from Homer. The persuasive force of the admonition is increased by suitable illustrations taken from the common stock of myth; and the argument itself is supported by the authority of the paradigmatic wisdom embodied in the mythical lore of the community. The classic example of this type of paraenesis is the exhortatory speech of Phoenix addressed to Achilles in *Iliad* IX . . . with its climax in the paradigmatic myth of the Wrath of Meleager . . . The term *ainos* . . . designates in the older language . . . the paradigmatic tale at large; the *ainos* as an illustration with a moral carries the meaning of advice" (p. 140–41). Voegelin's view of Homer's poem in the larger context of his study of mankind's political development is an example of the critical value of objective, interdisciplinary analytical perspectives.

Wace, Alan J. B. "Houses and Palaces." In *A Companion to Homer*, edited by Alan J. B. Wace and Frank H. Stubbings, pp. 521–32. London, 1962. The author notes that "Priam's house is the only realistically detailed elaboration of the structure of a house in the *Iliad*."

——— and H. P. Wace. "Dress." In *A Companion to Homer*, edited by Alan J. B. Wace and Frank H. Stubbings, pp. 498–503. London, 1962.

Wace, Alan J. B., and Frank H. Stubbings, eds. *A Companion to Homer*. London, 1962.

Wade-Gery, H. T. *The Poet of the Iliad*. Cambridge, Eng., 1952. "Homer's achievement was . . . to reduce . . . oral technique to writing" (p. 39).

Ward, Donald. "The Divine Twins: An Indo-European Myth in Germanic Tradition." *Folklore Studies* 19 (1968). This provides background for the twin Atreidae and Helen's brothers.

Webster, T. B. L. "Greek Theories of Art and Literature Down to 400 B.C." *Classical Quarterly* 33, July–October 1939, pp. 167–79. Webster, too, argues for the audience's expectations of veracity in epic poetry.

———. *From Mycenae to Homer.* 1958; 2d ed. enl. New York, 1964. Like Lorimer and Stubbings, Webster proves that while elements within the poem are historical, their contemporaneous existence with other elements indicates that the chronology of the Iliadic world is itself fictional. He indicates the eastern origin of the story of Hephaistos being hurled from Olympos (p. 126); presents the story of Meleagros as a "large-scale simile. It is a working model of the present situation and of the future course of action which the poet knows" (p. 249).

———. "Polity and Society (ii) Historical Commentary." In *A Companion to Homer,* edited by Alan J. B. Wace and Frank H. Stubbings, pp. 452–62. London, 1962.

Whitman, Cedric H. *Homer and the Heroic Tradition.* New York, 1958. In my view this is the most important contemporary critical discussion of Homeric poetry, and the extent of my indebtedness to its insights and approaches cannot be measured. I've profited from Whitman's discussion of concentric circles and hysteron proteron as mnemonic and architectonic devices (p. 98); of the sense in which "images become action; and the scene is the image dramatized" (p. 117); of the inversion of nature in the *aristeia* of Achilles (p. 137); of the sceptre's integral association with the character of its bearer (p. 161); of Achilles' sincere love for Briseis as a contrast with Agamemnon's mercenary attitude (p. 168); and of Achilles' association with singing and with Helen (p. 193). He points out the social significance of Nestor's speech to convince Patroklos that "heroism cannot be maintained in isolation, or it becomes nothing . . . Achilles alone cannot enjoy his virtue, and Patroclus is the living proof that even now he is not so indifferent as he seems" (p. 195). So the author concludes that "the fact that Achilles listens to Patroclus' appeal, the fact that he had the curiosity to send him out in the first place, shows that Achilles himself knows . . . that the heroic spirit, if it is to exist as a reality, must act in this world" (p. 196). In the scene with Priam Achilles achieves "his great communion with humanity" (p. 205).

Whitman also describes the universality of the great shield (p. 205): "The intention of the shield is wonder. It is the miracle of cosmic diversity focused into formal unity and order, as the proper adornment of the unified heroic will. When he first receives it, Achilles sees only the flash of its brightness, but before the *Iliad* is over he lives up to the fullness of its classic implications—passion, order, and the changeless inevitability of the world as it is" (p. 206). He notes that Achilles, when he meets Priam, "has attained the truly classical ideal . . . that mysterious union of detachment and immediacy, of passion and order" (p. 218).

Willcock, Malcolm M. *A Companion to the Iliad, Based on the Translation by Richmond Lattimore*. Chicago and London, 1976. The line by line commentary is a valuable aid to students reading the poem in English for the first time; and there are useful appendices on "Transmission of the Text of the *Iliad* and Commentaries on It," "Methods of Fighting in the *Iliad*," and "Mythology and the Gods."

Wilson, Pearl C. "The πάθει μάθος of Achilles," *Transactions and Proceedings of the American Philological Association* 69 (1938): 557–74. Wilson's is one of the few interpretations of Achilles' development which takes full cognizance of his changing social attitudes. "As the plot unfolds, [Achilles] shows no concern for any suffering but his own." Social commitment "has not yet been awakened by his experience. When this awakening comes, Achilles goes beyond his opponent. Hector's sympathy embraces everyone in his family and in his city. That of Achilles goes out to all humanity, and transmutes even hatred of an enemy into gentleness" (p. 560). So Achilles, in the end, honors the advice of his father that he should align himself with society and move away from egocentrism (p. 562). Wilson also comments on Achilles' deep feeling for Briseis (p. 563); his concern for the death of others caused by his recalcitrance (p. 569); and the way in which an understanding of human suffering draws Priam and Achilles together (p. 574). "The burial is made possible by Achilles, who had slain Hector . . . but had come at last to understand that the anger that parts men is born and dies, but the bond of their common humanity is everlasting."

Yoshida, A. "La Structure de l'Illustration du Bouclier d'Achille." *Revue Belge de Philologie et d'Histoire* 42 (1964): 5–15. Yoshida sees the tripartite Indo-European pattern of social structure in Mycenaean civilization. The shield, he argues, reflects this: the juridical function in the marriage and trial scenes; the military function in the city at war; and the agricultural function in the scenes from rural life. He connects Ariadne with a Minoan vegetation goddess. His conclusion is that Homer definitely intended the shield to represent his world view.

Young, Douglas. "Never Blotted a Line?: Formula and Premeditation in Homer and Hesiod." *Arion* 6 (Autumn 1967): 279–324. Young's argument against Lord's assertion that the epics were composed simultaneous with performance is commonsensical, if not proved.

Zarker, John W. "King Eetion and Thebe as Symbols in the *Iliad*." *Classical Journal* 61, December 1965, pp. 110–14. This is an incisive demonstration of the mnemonic principle behind Iliadic symbolism. Zarker concentrates on the role of Thebe in the accumulated references to it by key characters: "Homer intended for his auditors to think along certain lines and to experience certain emotions when either the king or his city were mentioned" (p. 110). He discusses, in turn, the way in which the meeting between Hektor and Andromache in Book 6 reveals the chivalric Achilles before his wrath (p. 11); the Theban connection between Chryseis, the first cause of the quarrel, and Briseis, the actual catalyst (p. 112); the significance of the grey iron from Thebes (p. 113); of Pedasos (p. 113); of Achilles' Theban lyre (p. 113) and of Andromache's Theban headdress (p. 113). The thematic effect of the allusion is that "what happened to Chryseis, Briseis, and other captive women will happen to Andromache . . . Only now Achilles' wrath is stronger, and he is no longer the man he was at Thebe. Troy, instead of the kind treatment and noble respect for the dead and captured as at Thebe, will suffer the fate of Pedasos and Lykaon. Achilles' taking of Thebe is the dramatic foreshadowing of the fall of Troy."

Line Index

Subject Index

Achaians: watching Athene descend from Olympos, 10–11; Helen's importance to, 27; social need for restoration of conjugal bed, 27, 37; watching duel of Menelaos and Paris, 30; contrasted with Trojans, 52–53; at funeral games for Patroklos, 72, 153–54

Achilles: xiii–xv, 28, 108, 112, 141, 144, 145, 155, 156, 157, 158, 161, 165, 168, 169, 183, 187, 188–245 passim, 253, 262, 272, 277, 305–10; meets with Priam, 15–16, 45–47, 49, 59, 61, 62–63, 81, 147, 151–52, 159–60, 189–93, 196–204, 216–17, 225, 227–32, 235–38, 255–57, 259, 264; quarrels with Agamemnon, 16–17, 38, 117, 118, 128, 130–33, 151–52, 189–93, 196–204, 255, 256, 259; relationship with Briseis, 29, 124, 190–92; compared to animals, 55–56, 59; duel with Aineias, 55–56, 219–22; kills Hektor, 58–59, 60, 67, 70–71, 145, 165, 203, 210–14; and Iris, 86; relationship with Thetis, 110–11, 113, 162–63, 166; as representative of the new synthesized hierarchy, 113–18, 128; relationship with Agamemnon, 113–20, 131–33, 222–25; receives nectar from Athene, 144–45, 204; uses aegis of Zeus, 146, 167–68, 308; death of Patroklos, 153, 161–66, 176, 197, 199, 200–202, 228–30, 306–7; leads funeral games for Patroklos, 153–54, 223–26, 263–64, 310; relationship with Patroklos, 158–63, 193–99, 203, 216, 222, 284; relationship with Myrmidons, 164–65, 193; and shield, 177, 183, 184, 186; relationship with Argives, 189–203, 210–11; and guest-friend relationship, 195; singing of, 198, 255, 272; bears shield into battle, 201, 211, 220; arming of, 204–8; returns to battle, 208; funeral of Patroklos, 216–17; hatred for Troy, 217–22; relationship with poet, 235; attacked by Xanthos, 238, 239; relationship with Hephaistos, 238, 239; and the tale of Niobe, 256–57; and the metaphor of Zeus' jars, 257; and Phoinix, 264–72; refuses Agamemnon's supplication, 270–

71, 275; and the sacking of Thebes, 272–76; Xanthos (horse) speaks to, 308–10. *See also* Shield of Achilles

Aegis, of Zeus: 115, 145–47, 207; used by Athene, 103–4, 145–46; used by Apollo, 125, 147, 219; used by Achilles, 146, 167–68, 308

Agamemnon: 12, 28, 96, 113–33 passim, 139, 189–90, 216, 232, 258–59, 267, 269, 278, 279; deceives army, 2; rebuffs Chryses, 8–9, 16, 17, 123–25; quarrels with Achilles, 16–17, 38, 117, 120, 128, 151–52, 189–93, 196–97, 198–200, 255, 256, 259; Helen's importance to, 27; abducts Briseis, 29, 190, 196; relationship with Chryseis, 36, 88, 123, 124, 191, 194, 196, 273, 275; compared to Priam, 52–53; as representative of heroic hierarchy, 113, 114, 116, 117, 128–29; calls assembly, 119; leads Achaians into battle, 119, 121; compared to Zeus, 121; sceptre speech of, 122, 125–26; reviled by Thersites, 126–28; reconciliation with Achilles, 131–33; supplication to Achilles, 131, 222–25, 270–71, 275; at funeral games, 224–25; relationship with Kassandra, 285; kills Iphidamas, 286–87. *See also* Sceptre

Agenor, 222

Aias, son of Oileus, 7–8

Aias, Telemonian: 144, 155–57, 176, 232; duel with Hektor, 2–3, 4, 157, 260–61; defends Achaian ships, 7–8, 280, 310–11; protects Teukros, 156; defends body of Patroklos, 156, 157, 167. *See also* Shield

Aineias, 39, 219–22, 302–4

Alexandros. *See* Paris

Alkestis, 283

Alkimedon, 308

Alkimos, 46, 47

Alkinoos, 246

Althaia, 267, 268–69

Amyntor, 264–65, 268

Andromache: 28, 29, 75–81, 269, 273, 274–75; meets with Hektor, 68–70, 75–77, 79; weaving of, 68, 76–78, 85,

347

DATE			